The Search for a Black Nationality

BLACKS IN THE NEW WORLD

AUGUST MEIER, SERIES EDITOR

Floyd J. Miller

The Search for a Black Nationality

Black Emigration and Colonization 1787-1863

UNIVERSITY OF ILLINOIS PRESS
Urbana   Chicago   London

DISCARD

Andrew S. Thomas Memorial Library
MORRIS HARVEY COLLEGE, CHARLESTON, W. VA.

91880

325.273
M613s

© 1975 by the Board of Trustees of the University of Illinois
Manufactured in the United States of America

LIBRARY OF CONGRESS CATALOGING IN PUBLICATION DATA

Miller, Floyd John, 1940–
  The search for a black nationality: black emigration and colonization, 1787–1863.

  (Blacks in the new world)
  Bibliography: p.
  Includes index.
    1. Negroes—Colonization—Africa. I. Title.
  II. Series.
  E448.M56   301.32′8′7306   75-4650
  ISBN 0-252-00263-6 lib. bdg.

FOR
Roberta

Preface

Leaving home to seek one's fortune in other parts has usually stirred up a multitude of conflicting emotions and loyalties. Partly a rejection of the emigrant's past, his native land, and even perhaps his family, emigration has also signified the hope of a future marked by economic prosperity, religious freedom, or political liberty. But for those Africans who were brought, enslaved and unwilling, across the Atlantic to a New World they never sought, emigration signified something very different.[1] For these very first Africans in the British colonies, emigration was a return to, not a flight from, their homelands and their peoples—whether in Angola or Yoruba or Mandingo. Yet for their descendants, the Afro-Americans, the return "back to Africa" was very different: they could not go *back*, for they were no longer what their fathers were.

If no longer purely African, they were still, in their own eyes and in those of the whites who castigated them, very much *black* (African, yes; but much more and much less), and it was as Afro-Americans that they shaped a relationship with the land of their birth, but not of their people. Although from the late eighteenth century until the beginning of the Civil War most free blacks in

1. "Colonization" and "emigration" are used interchangeably throughout this work, in conformity with common practice in black history. However, most students of eighteenth- and nineteenth-century black migratory activities use "colonization" to refer to those movements which are largely white-inspired—such as the American Colonization Society's efforts to found and maintain an African colony. There is a tendency to use "emigration" to describe black-initiated movements, although "colonization" has also been applied in these cases. While this usage has influenced me, I make no brief for any conceptual significance inherent in my terminology.

the North accepted the consequences of this anomaly, a significant number of articulate and forceful free blacks called upon their fellow blacks in both the United States and Canada to flee to other lands and there begin a new future intertwined by necessity and destiny with that of their black brethren. Their motives varied, as did their destinations, and their voices were heeded by only a few of the relatively small number of politically involved blacks. But during most of the seventy-five years prior to the Civil War, black emigrationists reiterated their belief that only by leaving North America to join with blacks elsewhere could they ever free themselves from further oppression and degradation.

As Part I of this study shows, blacks in Boston and in Newport and Providence, Rhode Island, all formulated emigration plans in the 1780's. Their rationale was based on two diverse but related impulses: that blacks could never achieve freedom and equality in the newly formed United States and, second, that by emigrating to Africa, American blacks would be able to carry the fruits of Western learning and religion to those they considered backward. Although these dreams of an African emigration were not fulfilled, black emigration as an idea did not die. Instead, a number of individuals with varying motives and purposes began to advocate emigration in the nineteenth century. On a voyage to Sierra Leone in 1816, a Massachusetts black sea captain, Paul Cuffe, carried a party of emigrants. Although originally interested in the Christian regeneration of Africa, Cuffe had by then become convinced that a large-scale emigration to Africa could expedite the emancipation of the American slave.

Following Cuffe's lead but acting for their own purposes, whites formed the American Colonization Society in late 1816 to encourage free blacks to move to Africa. Although throughout the 1820's most free blacks viewed the Society as a racist organization supporting forced deportation in order to protect southern slavery, some Afro-Americans saw African colonization as an opportunity to better themselves personally. Those blacks who remained suspicious of the Colonization Society did not entirely reject emigration, however. The Haitian emigration movement of the mid-1820's attracted some of the most committed black opponents of the Colonization Society, for whom the existence of an independent black republic near American shores was heartening. Moreover, leading white supporters of Haitian emigration rejected the Colonization Society's tendency to avoid established black leadership, and they thus endorsed the organization of black auxiliary societies. Nevertheless, the Haitian emigration movement failed as large numbers of dissatisfied settlers returned to the United States. By the end of the decade few blacks supported emigration of any kind.

Although there was a burst of opposition both to the Colonization Society and to emigration in general in the early 1830's, blacks rarely discussed emigration during the remainder of the decade or throughout most of the 1840's. Perhaps the emergence of a nominally biracial abolitionist movement paying at least some respect to the plight of free blacks in the North absorbed the disillusionment and anguish of even the most alienated blacks. However, in the late 1830's a relatively obscure Pittsburgh minister, Lewis Woodson, formulated an ideology which fused emigrationism and nationalism and set the intellectual basis for the development after midcentury of a cohesive movement advocating emigration for basically nationalist purposes. Part II of this study defines and traces the evolution of nationalist-emigrationism during the 1850's and early 1860's. Like Part I, it treats at length only those emigrationists who can be viewed primarily in the context of Afro-American history—not African or pan-African history. As a consequence, little attention is devoted to Alexander Crummell, who, although American-born, was primarily a Liberian educator and clergyman during the period under study. Rather, Part II focuses almost inevitably upon the activities and ideas of Martin R. Delany, once a student of Woodson and the chief organizer and ideologue of the nationalist-emigrationist movement of this period. Together with such colleagues as James Theodore Holly and, later and more tenuously, Henry Highland Garnet, Delany projected a Black Nation flourishing outside the United States and either incorporating or closely allying itself with other black peoples throughout the world. Despite this shared commitment, Delany, Holly, and many other nationalist-emigrationists differed over where Afro-Americans should create this new nationality. Eventually Holly developed an independent emigration movement which merged with the larger Haitian emigration movement of the early 1860's. Although Delany had favored emigration to a point within the Western hemisphere during the mid-1850's, he now turned to West Africa. A personal exploration of the Yoruba area in 1859 and 1860 encouraged him further, but internal war both in Africa and in the United States prevented him and his dwindling number of followers from executing their plans.

The demise of Delany's plan for establishing a Black Nationality in West Africa and the failure of the mass emigration to Haiti in the early 1860's concluded more than seven decades of agitation and activity on behalf of emigration. Almost continually, a small number of articulate and dedicated Afro-Americans had promoted the view that blacks could truly flourish as free and independent peoples only outside the confines of a nation dedicated to their suppression and degradation. Although few blacks actually emigrated, and although many blacks found any call for Afro-Americans to leave the country distasteful, emigration as a dream and as a protest never lost its attraction for those totally alienated from their oppressors.

A historian writing a book spanning several decades and bringing together a wide variety of individuals and organizations quite often is forced to roam far outside the area of his own expertise. The present author is no exception; I have drawn quite liberally upon the assistance of historians whose work suggested new directions and steered me toward valuable materials, and who themselves religiously answered my persistent queries and, in some cases, shared with me the rewards of their own labors. Librarians and archivists also conscientiously replied to my letters, politely ignored my badgering, located important sources which I had been totally unaware of, and even independently photocopied documents for my consideration. In sum, this book has literally been built upon the backs of others.

Some individuals have extraordinarily broad backs; to them I am especially grateful. August Meier read several drafts of the manuscript with incredible care and wrote lengthy and penetrating criticisms awesome in their attention to detail and their intimate knowledge of black history. Like many scholars in the field, neophytes and experienced craftsmen alike, I owe him a great deal; this book would have been a far more unwholesome creature if it had not

Preface xi

been for his efforts. Howard H. Bell and Dorothy Sterling read the dissertation which grew into this book. Both also shared with me their knowledge, their materials, and their friendship—as did Victor Ullman, like Mrs. Sterling, the author of a recent biography of Martin R. Delany. Allan H. Spear of the University of Minnesota, another friend and scholar, directed the dissertation and rendered shrewd, perceptive assistance as well as numerous personal kindnesses, all with patient good cheer. Professors Bernard Bowron, Alfred H. Jones, and Rudolph Vecoli also gave the dissertation a careful reading. Other scholars shared with me the fruits of their own labors with complete selflessness. These include David M. Dean, David M. Katzman, Edward Noyes, Joan R. Sherman, and G. Joseph Wachter. Neil Gilchrist secured materials for me in London.

Numerous librarians and archivists provided extraordinary assistance. These include James T. Abajian of San Francisco; V. Nelle Bellamy, Church Historical Society, Austin, Texas; David Blow, Archives of the Catholic Diocese of Burlington, Vermont; Kenneth Cameron, Episcopal Diocese of Connecticut Archives, Trinity College; Charles F. Cooney, Manuscript Division, Library of Congress; Clifton H. Johnson, Amistad Research Center, Dillard University; Edward H. Kass, Director, Channing Laboratory, Boston; Kermit J. Pike, Western Reserve Historical Society; Dorothy Porter, Moorland Collection, Howard University; and Richard J. Wolfe, Francis A. Countway Library of Medicine, Harvard University. The staffs of Hiram College, Oberlin College, and the University of Minnesota—my working libraries—were also extremely generous with their time and energy.

In addition, I wish to thank the personnel of the following libraries and institutions: American Antiquarian Society; American Baptist Foreign Mission Society; American Baptist Historical Society; Boston Athenaeum; Boston Public Library; Buffalo and Erie County Historical Society; Carnegie Library of Pittsburgh; Chatham-Kent Museum, Chatham, Ontario; Chatham Public Library; Cincinnati Historical Society; Connecticut State Library; Cornell University Library; Detroit Public Library; Foreign Mission Board of the Southern Baptist Convention; Free Library of Philadelphia; Friends Historical Society, London; Friends Historical Library,

Swarthmore College; General Theological Seminary; Hartford Public Library; Houghton and Widener Libraries, Harvard University; Baker Library, Harvard Business School; Historical Society of Pennsylvania; Henry E. Huntington Library and Art Gallery; Institute of Jamaica Library; Johns Hopkins University Library; Library of Congress; Maine State Library; Manchester, England, Central Library; Maryland Historical Society; Massachusetts Historical Society; Massachusetts State Archives; Michigan State Library; Middleburg College Library; Minnesota Historical Society; National Archives; National Library of Scotland; New Bedford, Massachusetts, Free Public Library; New Britain, Connecticut, Public Library; New Brunswick Theological Seminary; New Haven Free Public Library; New York Historical Society; New York Public Library; New York State Library; Newark Public Library; Newport Historical Society; North Buxton, Ontario, Museum; Ohio Historical Society; Phelps-Stokes Fund of New York; Portland, Maine, Public Library; Enoch Pratt Free Library, Baltimore; Providence, Rhode Island, Public Library; Public Archives of Canada; Public Records Office, London; Rhode Island Historical Society; Rhodes House Library, Oxford, England; Royal Geographical Society, London; Schomburg Branch, New York Public Library; Southern Baptist Convention; State Historical Society of Wisconsin; George Arents Research Library, Syracuse University; Tennessee State Library and Archives; Toronto Public Library; Bancroft Library, University of California; University of Ibadan Library; University of Illinois at Chicago Circle Library; University of Western Ontario Library; Vermont Historical Society; Western Pennsylvania Historical Society; Wilberforce University Library; Yale Divinity School Library; and Sterling and Beinecke Libraries, Yale University.

My wife, Roberta Balstad Miller, read this work in several of its mutations; in each case she has taken time from her own research to give the manuscript a close and critical scrutiny. Her willingness to assume my teaching responsibilities at a critical point in the evolution of this work enabled me to complete the manuscript. Hiram College graciously agreed to this unusual husband-wife switch. In addition, the Faculty Research Assistance Committee of Hiram College provided me with a substantial summer research grant, and fellowships from the Graduate School of the University of Minnesota helped subsidize the research for the dissertation. The hospitality of Joanna Schneider Zangrando and Robert Zangrando enabled a wandering scholar to come in from the cold one winter. Patricia Craemer, Helen Keefe, and Joyce Urbanowicz typed various drafts of this work with dispatch. Kent State University Press kindly granted me permission to incorporate into this book my article on Lewis Woodson which appeared, in a slightly different form, in *Civil War History*, December, 1971.

Contents

PART I: BEGINNINGS, 1787–1830
    CHAPTER 1 Eighteenth-Century Origins *page 3*
    CHAPTER 2 Paul Cuffe: From Missionary-Entrepreneur to Black Emigrationist *page 21*
    CHAPTER 3 The 1820's: The Rise and Fall of Emigration Sentiment *page 54*

PART II: REVIVAL AND DENOUEMENT, 1850–63
    CHAPTER 4 The Drift toward Emigration *page 93*
    CHAPTER 5 The Emergence of an Emigration Movement *page 134*
    CHAPTER 6 The Search for a Place: Africa *page 170*
    CHAPTER 7 The Search for a Place: Haiti *page 232*
    CHAPTER 8 African Dreams Deferred *page 250*

EPILOGUE *page 264*
ESSAY ON SOURCES *page 275*
INDEX *page 283*

PART I

Beginnings, 1787-1830

CHAPTER 1

Eighteenth-Century Origins

At least as early as the eighteenth century, blacks living in North America dreamed of emigrating to Africa. In Virginia and South Carolina, for example, those Africans only recently brought to the colonies—"outlandish" Africans—were particularly intent upon returning "across grandywater" to their real homes. Some New England blacks also favored emigration. In 1773 four slaves pledged to the Thompson town representative to the Massachusetts legislature their willingness "to submit to such regulations as may be made relative to us, until we leave the province which we determine to do as soon as we can from our joynt labours procure money to transport ourselves to some part of the coast of Africa, where we propose a settlement."[1] Nevertheless, enduring black organizations advocating African emigration did not exist until 1783, when black groups in Boston and Newport, Rhode Island, expressed a clear desire to emigrate to Africa; this they communicated to other black organizations in Providence and Philadelphia.

Over the next few years, these early black emigrationists developed a number of arguments which were to pervade emigrationist thought throughout the decades preceding the Civil War. First, these eighteenth-century emigrationists maintained that, since the burdens of racial oppression in the United States were unremitting, only by returning to their peoples in Africa could American blacks

1. Gerald W. Mullin, *Flight and Rebellion: Slave Resistance in Eighteenth-Century Virginia* (New York: Oxford University Press, 1972), pp. 42–44; "Petition of Peter Bestes, Sambo Freeman, Felix Holbrook, and Chester Joie, Boston, April 20th, 1773," in Dorothy Porter, comp., *Early Negro Writing, 1760–1837* (Boston: Beacon Press, 1971), pp. 254–255.

achieve happiness and prosperity. They also believed the return to Africa would help emancipate their brethren enslaved in the United States and elsewhere in the Western hemisphere. Moreover, these early Afro-American emigrationists considered themselves peculiarly suited to the task of uplifting and civilizing those Africans who had never left their native shores. But even this missionary obligation could not be assumed unless blacks in the United States united to promote the emigration cause. And in New England, with population centers relatively close to each other and continuous communication possible, the champions of emigration and black solidarity were able to mount a substantial, if ultimately unsuccessful, emigration movement.

Boston blacks were the first to act. This may have been due to the relatively advanced stage of organizational life existing among an entirely free population; slavery had been abolished in Massachusetts by the state Supreme Court in the famous *Quok Walker* case of 1783. Several years earlier, in 1776, the black tradesman and Methodist preacher Prince Hall and fourteen other free blacks formed a Masonic lodge, African Lodge No. 1, under the auspices of a British Army lodge stationed in the city. Although the black Masons did not receive a warrant until April, 1787, Hall and his Masonic followers—numbering at least thirty-four at one time—met regularly. Thus it was not uncommon in Boston for blacks to meet together. Moreover, Hall and other blacks were frequent petitioners to the Massachusetts General Court. For example, in January, 1777, Hall was among a number of blacks who asked the General Court to legislate the gradual abolition of slavery in the state because "every Principle from which America has Acted in the Cours of their unhappy Deficultes with Great Briton Pleads Stronger than A thousand arguments in favours of your petioners...." But for many Boston blacks emancipation, once realized, did not remove the burdens and shackles of caste. On January 4, 1787, more than seventy-five blacks from Boston signed a petition to the General Court, asking for assistance in removing themselves to Africa. Prince Hall was among the signatories.

The petition itself reveals two of the major themes which dominated emigrationist feeling from this time until the Civil War. The Boston blacks, some of whom had been born in Africa, believed that they would be unable to achieve happiness in the New World even as legally free individuals. Nor did they expect their children to fare better. As a result, they wished "to return to Africa, our native country, which warm climate is much more natural [and] agreable to us . . . and where we shall live among our equals and be more comfortable and happy, then we can be in our present situation. . . ." Yet if they wished to live in Africa on an equal footing with those Africans who had never left the continent, they also intended to serve their brethren "by the means of inlightening and civilizing those nations, who are not sunk in ignorance and barbarity. . . ." Christian education, of course, would eradicate heathenism. In a very real sense, the Boston blacks proposed bringing to Africa a replica of the New England religious and political arrangements they had experienced.[2]

While an advance party of blacks would negotiate for the "large tracts of uncultivated land" available in Africa, those who remained behind but who intended to emigrate later would organize themselves "into a civil society, united by a political constitution in which they shall agree." Others qualified and willing would form "a religious society, or a christian church; and have one or more blacks ordained as their pastors or Bishops." Together, then, the civil and religious societies would eventually settle on the territory acquired by the agents. Thus the new settlement would remove debased people from a land they never sought or cherished in order to spread Christianity among a heathen population. White Americans would also benefit, for developing from the new African settlement would be "a mutual intercourse and profitable commerce,

---

2. For this and the preceding paragraph: Harry E. Davis, *A History of Freemasonry among Negroes in America* (n.p.: The United Supreme Council, Ancient and Accepted Scottish Rite of Freemasonry, Northern Jurisdiction, U.S.A. [Prince Hall Affiliation], 1946), p. 21; Harold Van Buren Voorhis, *Negro Masonry in the United States* (New York: H. Emmerson, 1940), pp. 14-17; William H. Grimshaw, *Official History of Freemasonry among the Colored People in North America* (New York: Macoy Publishing and Masonic Supply Co., 1903), pp. 68-73, 78-83; Benjamin Quarles, *The Negro in the American Revolution* (Chapel Hill: University of North Carolina Press, 1961), p. 45; "Negro Petitions for Freedom," *Collections of the Massachusetts Historical Society*, 5th ser., III (1877), 436-437; House Files 2358, Massachusetts State Archives, Boston. See also Lorenzo Johnston Greene, "Prince Hall: Massachusetts Leader in Crisis," *Freedomways*, I (Fall, 1961), 238-258.

which may much more than overbalance all the expense which is now necessary in order to carry this plan into effect." Money, of course, was a serious problem. The Boston blacks, recognizing their own poverty, asked the General Court to assist them in enabling the agents to go out to procure lands for the settlement and in providing passage for the emigrants, as well as in procuring whatever clothing and other provisions would be necessary.[3]

While the Boston black emigrationists were petitioning the Massachusetts legislature, blacks in both Newport and Providence, Rhode Island, were expressing similar sentiments. Of all the New England states, Rhode Island was the most likely center for emigrationist activity. Since the beginning of the century the maritime slave trade had flourished there; it was of special importance to Newport, the center of trade in both slaves and rum and the home of twenty-two of the more than thirty rum distilleries in Rhode Island before the Revolution. Although ships leaving Newport usually sold their slaves in the West Indies or in southern ports, many Africans still entered New England by way of the bustling commercial town which served the rich Narragansett country. By 1782 one of every nine inhabitants of Newport was black; even with commerce declining in the aftermath of the Revolution, blacks still formed almost one-tenth of Newport's population in 1790. Providence's black population was somewhat less important—only one of every thirteen persons was black when the first federal census was taken in 1790. In both towns the large majority of the black population was free and thus able to meet and form community institutions. Yet with the slave trade bringing a continual influx of Africans into Rhode Island's maritime centers, at least until the state abolished the slave trade in 1788, the Africans of Rhode Island were not likely to forget their heritage or their homes.[4]

Emigration sentiment was particularly strong among both blacks and whites in Newport. Samuel Hopkins, the distinguished and longtime minister of Newport's First Congregational Church, helped

3. Massachusetts House Files 2358.
4. Lorenzo Johnston Greene, *The Negro in Colonial New England* (New York: Columbia University Press, 1942), pp. 86–87; Stanley K. Schultz, "The Making of a Reformer: The Reverend Samuel Hopkins as an Eighteenth-Century Abolitionist," *Proceedings of the American Philosophical Society*, CXV (October 15, 1971), 355; *First Census of the United States (1790)*, p. 34.

to stimulate Newport blacks to consider returning to Africa. Genuinely abhorring the slave trade and the institution of slavery, Hopkins believed that a black Christian presence in Africa would help abolish both practices. He also felt that, as inferior creatures, blacks could never achieve equality of opportunity in the United States. In fact, only his racial views distinguished his motivations from those of the Boston blacks. In 1784 he wrote to Moses Brown of Providence, a onetime slaveowner who had recently manumitted his slaves and who was becoming a prominent antislavery leader, about the advisability of blacks establishing a settlement in Africa to Christianize the heathen, help curtail the slave trade, and, finally, uplift those who would emigrate. Seven years later Hopkins again spoke in favor of a black Christian settlement. Here he explicitly advocated sending out missionaries—a plan he had formulated as early as 1773, when, together with Ezra Stiles, the minister of the Second Congregational Church of Newport and later president of Yale, he decided to prepare two of the six or seven black members of his own congregation to serve as the initial agents for the evangelization of Africa. At the time he had selected two Newport blacks born on the Guinea coast—Bristol Yamma, a slave, and John Quaumino, a free man. The Revolution interrupted Hopkins's plan. When he again favored sending out missionaries in 1791, he recommended Yamma as well as two other Newport blacks: Newport Gardner, in Hopkins's view "next to Bristol, and in some things excels him," and Salmar Nubia.[5] Fittingly, both were members of the African Union Society of Newport, a black society which advocated African emigration and black unity.

Little is known of Nubia. Brought to America from the windward coast, he could speak his native tongue as late as the early 1790's. He was a member of Stiles's Second Congregational Church of Newport and was for a time the secretary of the African Union Society. Gardner, on the other hand, cut a more impressive and memorable figure. Also African-born, he was brought to Newport as Occramer

---

5. Schultz, "The Making of a Reformer," 350–365, esp. 359–360, 362–363; Greene, *Negro in Colonial New England*, pp. 278–279; Henry Noble Sherwood, "Early Negro Deportation Projects," *Mississippi Valley Historical Review*, II (March, 1916), 497–500; Edward A. Park, "A Memoir of His Life and Character," in *The Works of Samuel Hopkins, D.D.* (Boston: Doctrinal Tract and Book Society, 1854), pp. 136–139.

Marycoo in 1760, when he was fourteen years of age. Purchased by Caleb Gardner, a prominent merchant whose wife taught the young slave to read, Newport also studied music and French and wrote original musical compositions as well as poetry. While still a slave he opened a music school which attracted some of the leading whites in the town, including his mistress. In 1791 Gardner purchased freedom for himself and most of his family with money he won in a Boston lottery. His master then freed the remainder of the family. Gardner was a member of Hopkins's church; once free, he and the minister often walked arm in arm through the streets of Newport. Years later he became the teacher of a school for blacks run by the African Benevolent Society, which absorbed the African Union Society in March, 1808. Gardner also served as the minister of the Colored Union Congregational Church, which he helped organize in 1824, and he wrote anthems for black churches. One such song ended with "Hear the words of the Lord, O ye African race; hear the words of Promise...."[6] Perhaps his most important activity was his role as an original member of the African Union Society.

Organized in November, 1780, the African Union Society was both a mutual benefit and a moral improvement society. The Constitution adopted at a subsequent meeting provided that the organization would preserve records of births, deaths, and marriages among Newport's blacks. More important to the moral tone which dominated the Society's thinking was a ban against liquor and a general statement instructing members to live morally upright lives. "We, the members of this Society, agree to avoid frolicking, and amusements that lead to expense and idleness; they beget the habits of dissipation and vice...." Elsewhere in the Constitution the Society called upon its members to be sure their marriages were performed legally and to save for their children in case they themselves

6. Park, "Memoir," pp. 136, 154–156; Charles A. Battle, *Negroes on The Island of Rhode Island* ([Newport?] R.I.: n.p., 1932), pp. 18–19, 27–29; Irving H. Bartlett, *From Slave to Citizen: The Story of the Negro in Rhode Island* (Providence: Urban League of Greater Providence, 1954), p. 12; Greene, *Negro in Colonial New England*, pp. 242, 278n, 306; Accounts of the Newport African Benevolent Society, 1809, in the back of Stephen Gould's Watch Repair Record, Newport Historical Society; Subscription Book for the African Church of Newport, 1824, Newport Historical Society.

died prematurely. The Society suggested that its members' savings "will be safest and most beneficial when laid out in lots, houses or small farms." At first the African Union Society eschewed any overt religious posture, but in 1783, at a meeting held in Newport Gardner's house, it decided to hold religious services in members' homes. More important, however, was the Society's effort to serve members in time of trial. Records testify to its concern with providing death benefits for widows and children of deceased brethren and with loaning funds to needy members.[7]

If the African Union Society's main purpose was to serve the Newport black community, it also had a larger aim: to articulate to whites and blacks in Newport and elsewhere the desire of at least some Afro-Americans (especially those more African than American) to emigrate to their homelands, where they would establish an independent black settlement—not a colony serving white interests. The African Union Society consistently maintained that African emigration was an issue to be debated and, of course, embraced by other black organizations throughout the United States —especially in the North. Whether promoted through circular letters, joint meetings, or traveling delegates, the African Union Society of Newport clearly wished African emigration to be the policy of a black community which they viewed as basically national in scope.

As early as January, 1787—at the same time Boston blacks were petitioning the Massachusetts General Court for assistance in establishing a black Christian settlement in Africa—the Newport society decided to plant its own settlement in Africa. In communication with William Thornton, a stylish and urbane Quaker from the West Indian isle of Antigua who was then visiting the United States,

---

7. Battle, *Negroes*, pp. 16–19; Robert Glenn Sherer, Jr., "Negro Churches in Rhode Island before 1860," *Rhode Island History*, XXV (January, 1966), 10; John Austin Stevens, "Churches and Public Schools of Newport," in Richard Mather Bayles, ed., *History of Newport County, Rhode Island* (New York: L. E. Preston & Co., 1888), p. 466. The chief source for the African Union Society are the manuscript records of the organization. These are in a leather book at the Newport Historical Society, where they are catalogued under "Union Congregational Church, 1790–1796." Extremely heterogeneous, the record book consists of numbered pages containing minutes of meetings, copies of incoming and outgoing correspondence, and copies of pertinent correspondence between other parties. Hereafter it will be cited as AUS Records.

the African Union Society refined its program. Thornton hoped to emancipate his own slaves and carry them to West Africa, and he believed that black Americans would make a worthy addition to his projected settlement.[8] The Newport group met with Thornton on several occasions, during which Thornton apparently listened at least as much as he spoke. The Society decided to send out an advance party of men "to see if they can obtain by gift or purchase of some of the Kings, or chief People, Lands proper & sufficient to settle upon." If the land could be acquired, they would obtain "a proper and good title to it. . . ." Then a second party would go out to prepare the settlement for the families which would follow.

Land was the essential issue for the Newport blacks. Although many of them were African-born, they, like their Boston counterparts, wished to establish a separate settlement, rather than to merge with the indigenous peoples. Consequently, they wanted to be sure no disagreements or problems developed over the right to the land they would occupy. As the Society's president, Anthony Taylor, wrote Thornton in early 1787, "We should think it not safe, and unwise for us to go and settle on lands in Africa, unless the right and [sic] of the Land is first firmly and in proper form made over to us, and to Heirs or Children."[9]

By mid-February more than seventy Newport blacks had indicated to the Society they would emigrate, and a dozen young men had expressed their willingness to serve as the advance party. The African Union Society then began to consider where in Africa they might establish their settlement. They were curious about the progress of the putative self-governing black settlement then forming at Sierra Leone. Thornton had already learned that British philanthropists, with the aid of the British treasury, had sent to Sierra Leone several shiploads of "Black Poor" from London slums, together with about seventy white prostitutes. Many of the blacks had lived in England since the American Revolution, when they had fought alongside the British. Granville Sharp, one of England's lead-

---

8. Sherwood, "Early Negro Deportation," 503–504; Gaillard Hunt, "William Thornton and Negro Colonization," *Proceedings of the American Antiquarian Society*, n.s. XXX (1920), 32–61, esp. 58–59.

9. Anthony Taylor to William Thornton, Newport, January 24, 1787, AUS Records, pp. 11–12.

ing abolitionists and a reputed guiding hand behind the experiment, was convinced that the new settlement, "Province of Freedom," would serve the noble purposes of Christianizing and civilizing the natives through the presence of missionaries and the establishment of legitimate trade between England and Africa. But the blacks of the African Union Society of Newport were suspicious. If unaware that most of the settlement's original founders, unlike Sharp, were motivated chiefly by a desire to rid England of its black Loyalists, the Newport blacks feared that "Province of Freedom" was already what it would later become—a British colony. They told Thornton that they would not become part of any colony in which they would be subservient to white interests: only if they could join or establish a free settlement where they could choose their own rulers would the Newport blacks migrate. Yet they would not categorically reject the settlement at Sierra Leone until they received further information.[10]

Members of the African Union Society were unwilling to subject themselves to the rule of a white-controlled colony, and they were equally unwilling to allow Thornton to act for them. Only blacks themselves should act for blacks. With this end in mind the Newport society suggested that the Boston group which had petitioned the Massachusetts General Court for assistance have circular letters sent to free black communities throughout the United States. Moreover, in keeping with the religious character of their society, the Newport blacks asked that the second Tuesday of July be set aside as "a Day of Humiliation, Fasting and Prayer." The Boston group agreed with both proposals. They were also wary of Thornton and were strongly opposed to his selecting a site for them. Rather, they believed "it would be better if we could charter a vessel, and send some of our own blacks."[11]

Although limited financial resources prevented both Newport

10. Thomas J. Pettigrew, ed., *Memoirs of the Life and Writings of the Late John Coakley Lettsom* (London: Longman, Hurst, Rees, Orme, and Brown, 1817), II, 507–524. For the early history of Sierra Leone, see Christopher Fyfe, *A History of Sierra Leone* (London: Oxford University Press, 1962), pp. 13–31, but see also Mary Beth Norton, "The Fate of Some Black Loyalists of the American Revolution," *Journal of Negro History*, LVIII (October, 1973), 410–413.

11. Samuel Stevens to Anthony Tiler [sic], Boston, June 1, 1787; Taylor to Stevens, Newport, October 4, 1787, AUS Records, pp. 14–17.

and Boston blacks from chartering a ship for an exploratory mission, neither group abandoned its plans. The African Union Society believed that Thornton, through his friendships with English and American philanthropists, would raise funds for an African venture; the Boston blacks, erroneously assuming that the General Court had approved their petition and would "grant us all we require of them, if we find a place to settle in," sought assistance for the advance party they wished to send out. Along with their brethren in Newport, they followed the British experiment at Sierra Leone with interest. However, Granville Sharp did little to encourage would-be black American emigrants—especially those desiring independence. Sharp was adamant that all American blacks wishing to reside in Sierra Leone "must promise to observe & maintain the present laws & regulations of the settlement which are founded on the Common Law of England."[12]

Sierra Leone, then, was an uncertain location for Afro-Americans. Moreover, without funds to enable black agents to purchase African land, African emigration was destined for failure. Yet the African Union Society continued to advocate African emigration while simultaneously asking blacks in Providence and Philadelphia to form a single organization in support of emigration. In late July, 1789, the African Union Society sent Cato Gardner and London Spear an epistle addressed "To All the Africans in Providence" and asked them to call a meeting of the Providence black community to discuss the document. The epistle itself was the Newport group's clear statement of their objectives: to flee America, where they were "outcasts in a strong land attended with many disadvantages and evils with respect to living," and to regenerate "the natives in Africa from whom we sprang, being in heathenish darkness and sunk down in barbarity...." Adding an argument omitted in the petition which the Boston blacks had presented to the Massachusetts legislature more than two years earlier, the African Union Society

12. Stevens to Tiler, Boston, June 1, 1787, AUS Records; Samuel Hopkins to William Rogers, Newport, September 22, 1788, Pennsylvania Abolition Society Manuscript Collection, I, 177, Historical Society of Pennsylvania; Pettigrew, ed., *Memoirs of Lettsom*, II, 518; Hopkins to Granville Sharp, Newport, January 15, 1789, and Sharp to John Jay, March 7, 1789, in Prince Hoare, *Memoirs of Granville Sharp* (London: Printed for Henry Colburn, & Co., 1820), pp. 340–342, 334–336.

maintained that African emigration itself was part of a larger scheme which would help to free their oppressed brethren in the West Indies and in the United States. For the Africans and Afro-Americans of the Newport organization, emigration was a banner to unite all black peoples—in Africa, the West Indies, and the United States. But black unity was obviously easier to achieve with those nearby, so the Society invited the blacks of Providence to help them "unite our brethren . . . as one Mans family" by joining in a "Union Society" meeting every three months "to consider what can be done for our good, and the good of all the Affricans. . . ." Providence blacks, as well as those from Newport, would direct the new organization.[13]

However, even among communities as close together as Newport and Providence, unity was not achieved easily. The Providence blacks did not adopt the epistle immediately. It is not clear whether opposition to the African Union Society's overture came from those Providence blacks who may have opposed African emigration in general, or from those who favored emigration but wished to maintain a separate institutional existence. When the Providence blacks finally approved the statement in early August, they retained their identity by choosing their own officers and controlling their own funds. In turn, the Newport society sent a copy of their "Rules and Regulations" to Providence; apparently the Providence group adopted these.[14] Whether further unity was accomplished is doubtful.

Although a "Union Society" bringing together blacks from the two Rhode Island towns—as well as blacks from other locales in that state and elsewhere—did not become a reality, the African Union Society was immediately presented with another such opportunity when Henry Stewart passed through Newport on his way to Boston. An emissary of the Free African Society of Philadelphia, he was to meet with Prince Hall and other black leaders.

13. African Union Society of Newport to Cato Gardner and London Spear, Newport, July 27 and July 28, 1789, AUS Records, pp. 17-18, 20-22.
14. Gardner and Spear to Taylor, Providence, August 4, 1789; Bristol Yamma and James McKenzie to African Union Society of Newport, Providence, August 5, 1789; Caesar Lyndon, Secretary, to Gardner and Spear, Newport, August 24, 1789; Lyndon to Yamma and McKenzie, Newport, August 24, 1789, AUS Records, pp. 22-26.

Like the Newport organization, the Free African Society was a mutual benefit and moral improvement society with a religious orientation. The Society was formed in May, 1787, several months before two influential black Methodists, Absalom Jones and Richard Allen, withdrew from St. George's Methodist Episcopal Church in protest against their removal to a separate section in the church's gallery. Members originally met monthly at Allen's home. Soon, however, the organization adopted practices of the Society of Friends —such as opening their meetings with a period of silence—and by 1791 they were meeting in the Friends' Free African School. Moreover, the original Constitution of the Society, in addition to prohibiting drunkenness and detailing provisions for death benefits paid to the widows of deceased members, provided that the treasurer of the Society would always be a Friend. By 1795 both Jones and Allen had abandoned the organization to establish religious societies more in keeping with their own denominational preferences (in Jones's case, Episcopal; in Allen's, African Methodist Episcopal), but the Free African Society itself retained a flickering life at least until 1799.[15] In the late summer of 1789, when Henry Stewart arrived in Newport, the Society was the sole organization in Philadelphia led by blacks for blacks.

Little is known of Stewart's visit to Newport except that he was there long enough to receive a letter from the members of the African Union Society directed to their counterparts in Philadelphia. This letter, which was in many respects identical to the communication sent to Providence, recommended African emigration as a means both of averting the "many disadvantages and evils which are likely to continue on us and our children, while we and they live in this country" and of liberating those brethren still in chains in the New World or in barbarism in Africa. However, for the Free African Society of Philadelphia emigration was unnecessary; only through

---

15. William Douglass, *Annals of the First African Church in the United States of America*... (Philadelphia: King and Baird, 1862), pp. 15-24; Winthrop D. Jordan, *White Over Black: American Attitudes Toward the Negro, 1550–1812* (Chapel Hill: University of North Carolina Press, 1968), pp. 422-423; Henry J. Cadbury, "Negro Membership in the Society of Friends," *Journal of Negro History*, XXI (April, 1936), 154-156; Carol V. R. George, *Segregated Sabbaths: Richard Allen and the Rise of Independent Black Churches, 1760–1840* (New York: Oxford University Press, 1973), pp. 51-55.

fasting and prayer, avoiding sin and transgression, could God be prevailed upon to free the oppressed.[16]

With Philadelphia's blacks indifferent and with the Providence blacks curious yet unwilling or unable to cooperate fully, overt emigration activity virtually disappeared for a few years. William Thornton maintained a correspondence with the black communities of Newport, Providence, and Boston, and the Reverend Samuel Hopkins continued to nourish his hopes of sending black missionaries to Africa. But blacks themselves did little or nothing until 1793 or early 1794. At this time the blacks of Providence, loosely tied together in an "African Society," took concrete steps to unite the black communities of the northern states behind an emigration plan which included sending three men on an exploratory expedition. Perhaps they were encouraged by the reinvigoration of the Sierra Leone experiment; in 1792 1,100 blacks from Nova Scotia arrived at Freetown, where they had migrated following service with the British Army during the Revolutionary War.[17] Then, too, the mercantile firm of Nicholas Brown, George Benson, and Thomas Ives may have stimulated the Providence society. Basically abolitionist in their attitudes, the three merchants were not ones to violate the 1788 Rhode Island prohibition against the slave trade; they also were convinced that, with England and France warring, they and other American maritime firms could capture the West African market. Perhaps the influence of Samuel Hopkins's long-time prodigy, Bristol Yamma, also motivated the Providence blacks. Yamma, who had been instrumental in the efforts to unite the Providence and Newport black communities in 1789, contemplated traveling to Sierra Leone in mid-1793. Although his death in North Carolina in January, 1794, ended these expectations, other Providence blacks—especially Yamma's friend, James McKenzie—were

16. African Union Society to Free African Society, Newport, September 1, 1789; Free African Society to African Union Society, Philadelphia, n.d. [but after October 16, 1789], AUS Records, pp. 48–50, 32–33. Both letters are also in Douglass, *Annals*, pp. 25–30.

17. Thornton to Hopkins, Philadelphia, September 29, 1790; Thornton to Taylor, Tortola, Virgin Islands, January 13, 1791, AUS Records, pp. 136–141; Park, "Memoir," pp. 136–137, 144–149. For the story of the emigration to Sierra Leone from Nova Scotia, see Fyfe, *Sierra Leone*, pp. 31–38; and Robin W. Winks, *The Blacks in Canada: A History* (New Haven: Yale University Press, 1971), pp. 61–78.

determined to send an advance party to Sierra Leone to investigate whether there was suitable land for a settlement of American blacks, and whether the British authorities would cooperate with such a scheme. But before they undertook this venture, they attempted to secure the support of blacks in other cities—in Boston, Philadelphia, and of course Newport.[18]

An obscure figure, McKenzie was one of several Providence blacks who were members of Prince Hall's Masonic lodge in Boston. In Providence he had joined Yamma in 1789 in the abortive efforts to establish a "Union Society" which would bring Rhode Island's blacks together in an organization seen as only the precursor for a larger and more ambitious effort.[19] Now, in mid-January, 1794, McKenzie was the secretary of the African Society in Providence, an empheral organization evidently led by many of those active four years earlier. The new society was almost entirely emigrationist in its orientation, and any attempts at bringing together the various black communities in the North were merely intended to ratify plans already well underway. The Providence blacks had previously decided to plant a settlement in West Africa, most probably at Sierra Leone. Now, with the encouragement of prominent Providence whites, they began to communicate with blacks in Boston, Philadelphia, and Newport. Convinced that "Now is the time if ever for us to try to Distinguish ourselves as the More remote we are situated from the white people the more we will be respected," the Providence group voted on January 15 to petition the Rhode Island General Assembly for permission to leave the state in order to settle on lands purchased from the Sierra Leone Company. They also decided to send "a man of our complexion[,] one who we may depend on" to negotiate with the British authorities in the new colony. Because of possible injury or accident, the African Society of Providence preferred that three men comprise the investigating

---

18. For background on Brown, Benson & Ives, see George E. Brooks, Jr., *Yankee Traders, Old Coasters, and African Middlemen: A History of American Legitimate Trade with West Africa in the Nineteenth Century* (Boston: Boston University Press, 1970), pp. 28–29; James B. Hedges, *The Browns of Providence Plantation*, I (Cambridge: Harvard University Press, 1952), 21; on Yamma, see Park, "Memoir," pp. 148–149. See also the following paragraph in the text.

19. Davis, *History of Freemasonry*, p. 269; Yamma and McKenzie to African Union Society, Providence, August 5, 1789, AUS Records, pp. 24–25.

expedition—one from their own group and representatives from Boston and Philadelphia. Anticipating no opposition to their plans from the African Union Society, they merely wrote to the Newport blacks informing them of their intentions and asking help in raising funds for the venture.[20]

For the African Union Society, the action of the Providence blacks represented both an endorsement of their persistent efforts on behalf of African emigration and a challenge to their interest in organizing the blacks of Rhode Island and elsewhere into a single national body capable of acting as one to establish the African settlement. Consequently, the Newport group, while supporting the Providence society's general aims of sending out agents to purchase land and petitioning the legislature, also asked to meet with delegates from the Providence society to learn more about its plans. The Newport blacks were reluctant for agents not of their choosing to act for them upon matters "unknown to us," and thus they asked the Providence society to send representatives to Newport before submitting a petition to the General Assembly.[21]

In response, the Providence Society sent William Olney to Newport with a conciliatory letter asking the African Union Society to select one of its number for the exploratory party. The communication noted that this person should be "ready to embark at a moment's notice with our Representatives"—Olney and the original agent, James McKenzie. Moreover, since the mercantile firm of Brown, Benson and Ives, the Providence society's sponsors, had asked the organization to delay sending the petition to the legislature, the letter Olney carried to Newport requested the African Union Society to secure local white abolitionists' support for the petition in the meantime. The Newport group voted to do this, after approving the contents of the petition at a meeting in late February. As their delegate to accompany Olney and McKenzie they selected Newport Gardner, the African-born music teacher and secretary of the Society who was then fifty years of age. The Society im-

20. Bonnar Brown, President, and James McKenzie, Secretary, African Society, to [African] Union Society in Newport, Providence, January 15, 1794, AUS Records, pp. 217-219.

21. Charles Chaloner, President, and Newport Gardner, Secretary, African Union Society, to African Society in Providence, Newport, February 13, 1794, AUS Records, pp. 221-223.

mediately began taking a roll of those members wishing to emigrate to the planned settlement.[22]

Neither Gardner nor Olney left for Africa, but McKenzie did. The Providence black community presumably helped finance the trip, as did Brown, Benson and Ives, then intent upon entering the trade with West Africa. In late 1794 the three merchants hired Captain Martin Benson of Newport, a man whose considerable experience in African waters had been gained principally in the slave trade, to take his sloop, the *Charlotte*, to the West African coast. They explicitly ordered him not to trade in slaves "as we desire to have nothing to do with that business." After extended inquiries about what cargoes he should take and what parts of the coast he should visit, Benson left Newport on December 5, 1795, and headed directly for Freetown, Sierra Leone, where he hoped he could compete successfully with other American ships soon to be there. His ship was laden with rum and tobacco for sale, his crew, and a man he considered "a poor miserable Creature who . . . promises to be of no service to our Voyage." This was James McKenzie, the agent of the African Society of Providence.[23]

After fifty days at sea, McKenzie and the *Charlotte* reached Freetown. The city had been recently sacked by the French, who had destroyed all the public buildings but not the houses of the black settlers. Benson hoped that, since the English authorities and the black colonists were desperately in need of supplies, he would be able to sell the rum and tobacco even though they were water-soaked because of leakage in his ship. But McKenzie interfered with Benson's chances of capitalizing upon the opportunity (at least in the captain's eyes) by informing the governor of Sierra Leone of the existence of other ships sailing toward Freetown. Whatever

---

22. Brown and McKenzie to African Union Society, Providence, February 15, 1794; Chaloner and Gardner to African Society, Newport, February 26, 1794, AUS Records, pp. 225–229.

23. B[rown], B[enson] & Ives to Martin Benson, Providence, November 29, 1794; Benson to Brown, Benson & Ives, Freetown, Africa, January 30, 1795; Journal of Martin Benson, entry for December 5, 1794, Brown Family Papers, John Carter Brown Library, Brown University; Minutes of the Sierra Leone Council, January 26, 1795, CO 270/3, Public Records Office, London. See also Benson's entry for March 17?, 1795, and compare with Benson's letter to Brown, Benson & Ives, Freetown, Africa, January 30, 1795, Brown Family Papers.

McKenzie's motives, Benson believed the black emissary hurt his chances of selling the cargo: "The Governor and Council were made acquainted with the number of vessels expected from America," Benson wrote in his journal; "this retarded our contract until I had absolutely taken leave to embark for the Gold Coast...." Moreover, Benson charged that he had to advance his crew money in order to prevent McKenzie from having them jailed after they had become, in some matter, indebted to him. In sum, the captain hoped that "for the Honor of humanity, that all Africa, cannot produce such an accomplished Villain." Yet he also admitted that McKenzie had been able to mollify whatever bad impression he might have made upon the governor, Zachary Macaulay, and the Sierra Leone Council. Indeed, Macaulay and one of the councillors, James Watt, wrote Samuel Hopkins that McKenzie's behavior, "as far as we have had the means of observing it, has been proper and becoming."[24]

Macaulay acted upon his favorable assessment of McKenzie and agreed to receive twelve families sent by the Providence society. In addition to being given ten acres of land on the nearby Bullom shore and a small town lot, each family would be "fully admitted to the Rights & Privileges of British Subjects." However, Macaulay may have harbored some doubts about McKenzie and his society, for he required the head of each family to obtain statements endorsing his moral and religious character from Hopkins, one other clergyman, and the president of the Rhode Island Abolition Society. Disturbed by what he considered "the injudicious admission of persons of doubtful character" into Sierra Leone, the governor wished to avoid any similar problems in the future. Hopkins, presumably believing McKenzie to be troublesome if not dishonest, refused to endorse the Providence group.[25]

With the failure of McKenzie's mission came the demise of the African Society of Providence and a halt to the activities of most

24. Benson's Journal, entries for January 23, 1795, and March 17?, 1795; Benson to Brown, Benson & Ives, Freetown, Africa, January 30, 1795, Brown Family Papers; Zachary Macaulay and James Watt to Hopkins, Freetown, Sierra Leone, March 19, 1795, in Park, "Memoir," pp. 150–151.

25. Park, "Memoir," pp. 150–151; Minutes of the Sierra Leone Council, February 21, 1795, CO 270/3, Public Records Office, London; Macaulay to Hopkins, Freetown, October 20, 1796, in Park, "Memoir," pp. 151–153. See also American Colonization Society, *Third Annual Report*, 1820, p. 25.

eighteenth-century black emigrationists. Emigration interest in Providence did not die entirely, however. In 1815 several families wanted to migrate to Sierra Leone with Paul Cuffe, who was then planning a voyage.[26] And Newport Gardner and Salmar Nubia still dreamed of planting a Christian black settlement in Africa—a dream they finally fulfilled momentarily in early January, 1826, when Gardner, able to speak his native tongue at the age of 80, and Nubia, then 70, left Boston for Africa, where they soon died of fever and infirmity.[27] Yet Gardner, Nubia, and the other early New England emigrationists had made their contributions long before as the first Afro-Americans to formalize an emigrationist ideology and program. Later, during the early and mid-nineteenth century, others would echo their call for blacks to organize themselves in order to leave the United States and thus flee oppression and discrimination; to further the cause of abolition; and, finally, to Christianize and civilize their black brethren in Africa and other heathen lands.

26. See William Brown to Cuffe, Providence, February 23, 1815, Paul Cuffe Papers (microfilm), New Bedford, Mass., Free Library.

27. There is some confusion about Newport Gardner's age when he left for Liberia in 1826. In *Senate Documents*, 28th cong., 2nd sess., 1844–45, IX, 166–167, his age is listed as 75, but it is generally assumed that he was born in 1746.

CHAPTER 2

Paul Cuffe: From Missionary-Entrepreneur to Black Emigrationist

The failure of James McKenzie's mission to Sierra Leone marked the end of eighteenth-century black emigration activity. Although individuals such as Newport Gardner and Salmar Nubia never abandoned the hope that they would some day return to their homelands, organized emigrationism was nonexistent. Blacks, lacking adequate resources, were unable to build the organizational structure necessary to rally large numbers of people behind emigrationism—let alone to transport these people across the Atlantic. Although some whites advocated the deportation of blacks, none of them emulated Samuel Hopkins and William Thornton, who had spoken *to* blacks about the advantages of emigration for Afro-Americans and Africans alike. Perhaps other factors were operating to dull black interest in emigration. Certainly by 1800 black emigrationism was moribund.

In the second decade of the nineteenth century, however, blacks again began to look toward Africa. Unlike their eighteenth-century forebears, few of them at first viewed Africa as a possible refuge for black Americans unable to bear the burdens of oppression. Rather, many of the early nineteenth-century emigrationists considered African emigration as a program entirely designed to benefit Africans, not black Americans. This was true of one individual who helped to stimulate a new awareness of Africa among both blacks and whites —the black ship captain Paul Cuffe. Yet in the year preceding his death in 1817, Cuffe significantly altered his course and began calling for the establishment of a colony in Africa composed of black Americans, many of them emancipated slaves. African colonization for Cuffe now became largely a means of hastening the abolition of slavery. How many of his black allies followed Cuffe on this new track is unclear. Certainly, however, the publicity Cuffe had given to Africa helped rekindle dormant interest in African colonization among many whites with purposes far different from his own.

Tall and substantial in stature, only semi-literate yet shrewdly competent, Paul Cuffe possessed a missionary spirit and a pragmatic temperament which permeated both his Christianity and his ever-increasing racial consciousness. He was the youngest son and seventh of ten children born to Ruth Moses, a Wampanoag Indian, and Cuffe Slocum, a West African who purchased his freedom from John Slocum some sixteen years after being brought to Massachusetts in 1728. Born January 17, 1759, on Cuttyhunk Island, the largest of the Elizabeth Islands halfway between Martha's Vineyard and the Massachusetts mainland, Paul Cuffe adopted his father's given name because John Slocum did not want his former slave's children to use his surname. When Paul was thirteen, his father died, leaving Paul and his brother John joint owners of the 120-acre family farm at Westport, a farming and fishing village on the colony's southern coast. Scratching out a living on the hard, rocky soil of southern Massachusetts had little appeal to the half-black, half-Indian boy. At sixteen Paul left home to sail to the Gulf of Mexico on a whaling vessel. His next voyage was to the West Indies. During the American Revolution he was captured by a British ship and confined in New York for three months. When released, Paul Cuffe rejoined his brother on the Westport farm.[1]

---

1. Information on Paul Cuffe's early life as sketched in this and the following two paragraphs is scanty. Most scholars depend upon early sketches which, in turn, often repeat the same information. Presumably Cuffe's memory was the original source for these first biographies. See, for example, *Memoir of Paul Cuffee* [sic], *a Man of Colour* (Liverpool: Egerton, Smith, 1811), a reprinting of a biography which originally appeared in *The Liverpool Mercury*; *Memoir of Captain Paul Cuffee* [sic]: *to which is Subjoined the Epistle of the Society of Sierra Leone, in Africa, Etc.* (York [England]: W. Alexander, 1812); Peter Williams, *A Discourse, Delivered on the Death of Capt. Paul Cuffe, before the New-York African Institution, in the African Methodist Episcopal Zion Church, October 21, 1817...* (New York: B. Young & Co., Printers, 1817); *The History of Prince Lee Boo, to which is added, the Life of Paul Cuffee* [sic], *a Man of Colour*

Farming was still unrewarding for the ambitious young man, so three years later Paul, with the help of his brother David, used some of the lumber located in the East River at Westport to build an open boat which the two brothers used to ply the coastal trade, stopping at fishing and farming villages on the offshore islands and on the Connecticut coast. Harassed by sea pirates who stole their cargo, the Cuffe brothers found the mercantile life difficult. David soon withdrew from the partnership, but Paul decided to continue; once the Revolution ended, he found a ready market for his goods. By the age of twenty-five he became the master of a covered ship of twelve tons, and he turned his profits into a thriving business. Later, with an eighteen-ton ship, he went to St. George's Banks off Cape Cod to fish for codfish, and he found this a valuable excursion. In 1793 Cuffe took the schooner *Sunfish* and a crew of ten men on a whaling voyage to the straits of Bell Island near Newfoundland, where they killed six whales. He then carried a load of oil and bone to Philadelphia; there he traded it for materials which he later used to build a sixty-nine-ton vessel, the *Ranger*. With a cargo worth $2,000, Cuffe sailed the *Ranger* into Chesapeake Bay and then up the Nanticoke River to Vienna, Maryland. Although the local inhabitants were surprised to see a black captain and an all-black crew, Cuffe traded without incident. He brought back to Westport a large shipment of corn, which he sold at a considerable profit. He repeated his venture.

As Cuffe's business grew, so did his ambitions. By 1806 he was able to build the *Traveller*, a 109-ton brig of which he was half owner. The same year he also became three-fourths owner of the *Alpha*, a 268-ton ship which he sailed from Wilmington, Delaware, to Savannah, Georgia, and then on to Göteborg, Sweden. By this

... (Dublin: Printed by C. Crookes, 1820). These accounts have been enriched by Ruth Cuffe to Joseph Congdon, Fall River, Mass., February 12, 1851, Paul Cuffe Papers (microfilm), New Bedford, Mass., Free Library (hereafter cited as Cuffe Papers); George A. Salvador, *Paul Cuffe, the Black Yankee, 1759–1817* (New Bedford: Reynolds-DeWalt Printing, 1969), pp. 12–15; and Sheldon H. Harris, *Paul Cuffe: Black America and the African Return* (New York: Simon & Schuster, 1972), pp. 15–23. Although a large number of items from the Cuffe Papers have been published in Harris's work—two-thirds of which consists of documents—all citations here are to the original materials. Harris's book must be used with care, since his transcriptions contain errors. However, I have followed Harris in modernizing the spelling and punctuation of quotations.

time Cuffe either owned or held an interest in several vessels, and he was the owner of a $3,500 farm and a house.

Paul Cuffe was a man of property, yet he could never forget his heritage or his black brethren. For example, Massachusetts blacks paid taxes, even though they were denied the right to vote at least until the 1783 court decision which abolished slavery in the state. Cuffe did not abide by this injustice quietly; in February, 1780, he and his brother John protested. Joined by several other blacks from the town of Dartmouth, which at the time included Westport, the Cuffe brothers petitioned the Massachusetts General Court for tax relief on the grounds that they were not represented in the legislature: "While we are not allowed the privilege of freemen of the State, having no vote or influence in the election of those that tax us, yet many of our colour (as is well known) have cheerfully entered the field of battle in the defence of the common cause, and that (as we conceive) against a similar exertion of power (in regard to taxation), too well known to need a recital in this place." The petition was not granted, and the brothers refused to pay their county property and poll taxes. Finally in December, 1780, they petitioned the Bristol Court of General Sessions for relief. This was not granted, and they were arrested for a few hours on December 19. However, the brothers paid all arrears and court costs the following June, and the case was dropped. They were equally unsuccessful in their efforts to persuade the selectmen of the town of Dartmouth to heed their requests for relief. In April, 1781, they asked the selectmen to call a town meeting "to know the mind of said town, whether all free negroes and mulattoes shall have the same privileges in this said Town of Dartmouth as the white people, respecting... choosing of officers, and the like...." The selectmen, of course, did not call the meeting, and there is no evidence that blacks received the suffrage. In fact, even as late as 1795 there was a disagreement over whether the state constitution of 1780 implicitly gave blacks the right to vote.[2]

2. The story of the Cuffe brothers' efforts to secure tax relief is a complicated one; the clearest account is in Harris, *Paul Cuffe*, pp. 33-37. See also Henry Noble Sherwood, "Paul Cuffe," *Journal of Negro History*, VIII (April, 1923), 165-166. Copies of the petitions to the General Court and to the Town of Dartmouth are in the Cuffe Papers and have been reprinted in Harris, *Paul Cuffe*, pp. 159-162. Differences of opinion over whether the Massachusetts Constitution of 1780 gave blacks

By the early nineteenth century, then, Paul Cuffe was a prosperous sea captain who, as a black man, suffered at least some of the indignities and burdens endured by his fellows. In 1808 he adopted a third dimension: he joined the Westport Monthly Meeting of the Society of Friends, having met several Friends during his business dealings in Philadelphia. Cuffe was an anomaly as a black Quaker, for although members of the Society of Friends were leading the nascent abolitionist efforts of the late eighteenth century and, in New England, had long prohibited members from owning slaves, Friends usually did not regard blacks as equals. Many Friends' Meetings would not admit blacks to membership; segregated practices were common even in those Meetings which accepted blacks. However, Cuffe joined the Westport Meeting without incident or discrimination, and Friends elsewhere, such as the Philadelphia merchant and philanthropist James Pemberton, had no hesitation in establishing a close relationship with the black mariner. Pemberton had helped organize the Pennsylvania Society for Promoting the Abolition of Slavery and had succeeded Benjamin Franklin as president of the organization in 1790.[3] With long experience in humanitarian endeavours and with numerous contacts in both America and England, Pemberton provided Cuffe with guidance and assistance in 1808, when the Westport sea captain, aware that by being "of the African race" he was bound inextricably to the land of his fathers, turned his attention to the redemption of Africa.

By this time Cuffe had come to believe that Africans, by participating in the nefarious slave trade in which they had learned to barter their brethren's flesh, had become corrupt and degraded. But if black Americans could carry Christianity, legitimate trade, and "civilized" ways to Africa, the continent and her peoples could be reborn. Afro-American emigrants could serve as midwives of a new order; Cuffe himself would assist in bringing the millennium to Africa by transporting Afro-Americans of property and morality across the Atlantic. Viewing Cuffe's intentions as consistent with

---

the right to vote can be traced in *Collections of the Massachusetts Historical Society*, 1st ser., IV (1795), 208–209, and 5th ser., III (1877), 393, 400.

3. Salvador, *Paul Cuffe*, p. 20; Harris, *Paul Cuffe*, pp. 27–28. On Pemberton, see Thomas Drake, *Quakers and Slavery in America* (New Haven: Yale University Press, 1952), pp. 93–94; *Dictionary of American Biography*, XIV, 413.

his own humanitarian impulses, Pemberton communicated those plans to the African Institution of London—a philanthropic society which had been organized in 1807 to cast a benevolent eye over the black colony at Sierra Leone, now that the Sierra Leone Company had been dissolved and the British crown had assumed control of the colony. Zachary Macaulay, former governor of Sierra Leone, was now secretary of the African Institution. He assured one of Pemberton's English correspondents that he would urge the colonial administration to do everything possible to assist Cuffe should he come to Sierra Leone. Pemberton himself forwarded to Cuffe a copy of the Institution's second annual report, but the Philadelphia abolitionist died while Cuffe and those Englishmen committed to the evangelization and commercial development of Africa were still groping toward a mutual understanding.[4]

Other Quakers were anxious to assist Cuffe in realizing his dreams of carrying emigrants, cargo, and Bibles to the benighted Africans. In 1809 and 1810 two of Cuffe's Philadelphia merchant friends, John James and Alexander Wilson, corresponded with William Dillwyn of England on Cuffe's behalf. At this time the black captain hoped to travel to Sierra Leone to learn whether he could carry black emigrants to the colony; he was also considering moving his family and business there. Although Cuffe's primary concern was still "that the inhabitants of Africa might become an enlightened people," he also hoped that any trips to Sierra Leone would be profitable ventures. He wanted to trade directly with the colony, as well as carry cargo from Africa to England. But at the time American ships could not legally trade with England or her colonies, because Congress had enacted the Nonintercourse Act of 1809 in an attempt to insure defense of neutral rights in the face of British and French encroachments. Recognizing these restrictions upon American commerce, Zachary Macaulay predicted in the late summer of 1809 that, once the American prohibition was lifted, Cuffe would be able to find a market in Sierra Leone or nearby for a wide variety of goods, including rum and tobacco.[5]

4. Pemberton to Paul Cuffe, Philadelphia, June 8, 1808; Cuffe to Pemberton, Westport, September 14, 1808; Pemberton to Cuffe, Philadelphia, September 27, 1808, Cuffe Papers.
5. John James to Cuffe, Philadelphia, June 24, 1809, with copies of Cuffe to

Macaulay's optimism was pointless in the face of the unsettled commercial climate which had resulted from the American government's erratic policies. However, by the summer of 1810 the Nonintercourse Act had expired, and Cuffe began to plan a trip to Sierra Leone. In this he was encouraged by his British friends. William Allen, an English Quaker and a member of the African Institution, was convinced that the Institution would provide assistance; he urged Cuffe to stop in England by November, when the African Institution would next meet, before continuing to Sierra Leone. The support of the Institution, however much it may have lifted Cuffe's spirits, was inadequate at this time. It was obvious to his English supporters that the black mariner would have to obtain a license from the British government before he could carry goods from Sierra Leone to England. Hopeful that the British would grant him these commercial privileges, Cuffe decided to proceed with his voyage. In the fall of 1810 he obtained permission from the Westport Meeting of Friends to leave on an extended expedition to the land of his ancestors to calculate, in a sense, the costs of carrying Christianity and civilization to the Africans. In December Cuffe traveled to Philadelphia to prepare for his journey. While there he satisfied himself that "it was not for the prospect of gain that I had undertaken this voyage" by refusing to carry John James's corn to Africa. Early the following month, on board the *Traveller*, Paul Cuffe sailed from Philadelphia toward the west coast of Africa.[6]

After fifty days at sea Cuffe first noted that "the Dust of Africa Lodged on our Riging"; a week later he could see the mountains of Sierra Leone. Finally, on the first day of March, 1811, Cuffe and his crew anchored in the harbor at Freetown, Sierra Leone. The next day Governor Edward H. Columbine permitted Cuffe to un-

---

James and Alexander Wilson, Westport, June 10, 1809, and James and Wilson to William Dillwyn, Philadelphia, June 21, 1809; James to Cuffe, Philadelphia, November 8, 1809, with copies of Dillwyn to James and Wilson, London, August 30, 1809, Zachary Macaulay to Dillwyn, Clapham, England, August 29, 1809, and Macaulay to Thomas Ludlam, London, September 1, 1809, Cuffe Papers.

6. James and Wilson to Cuffe, Philadelphia, June 30, 1810, with copy of James and Wilson to Dillwyn, Philadelphia, June 16, 1810; James to Cuffe, Philadelphia, October 29, 1810, with copies of Dillwyn to James and Wilson, Walthamstow, England, August 24 and August 30, 1810; extract of James and Wilson to Dillwyn, Philadelphia, October 29, 1810; Paul Cuffe Account Book [November 25, 1810–May 23, 1812], entries for December 4, 1810, and January 14, 1811, Cuffe Papers.

load almost his entire cargo (largely beef, bread, and flour), and Cuffe began a two-month visit in the British colony.[7] Much of his time was spent investigating the suitability of Sierra Leone for American black settlement and its potential as a commercial depot for whatever cargoes he might carry to the area. He was also very interested in assessing the religious and moral temper of the colony; to his dismay, he discovered that Christian righteousness and purposefulness were not very visible among the local residents. "Further help," Cuffe concluded, "will be requisite to establish them in the true and vital spirit of devotion." In pursuit of this ideal Cuffe attended various Christian services, distributed Bibles as widely as he could among the repatriates, and helped some of the colonists form the Society of Sierra Leone, which drew up an epistle announcing the intensity of its members' religious feelings. The Westport mariner also presented Bibles to some of the indigenous Africans living in or near Sierra Leone. At least one native chieftain, King Thomas of the Koya Temne peoples (nominally the proprietors of the Sierra Leone area), expressed a clear preference for rum, but, as Cuffe noted, "none was given." In mid-March Cuffe traveled to the Bullom shore north of the Sierra Leone River to meet with King George and other of his Bullom people. Although he believed they were "so accustomed—to wars and slavery that I apprehend it would be a difficult task to convince them of the impropriety of these pernicious practices," Cuffe nevertheless gave the King a Bible and several other works "and let him know by the interpreter the useful records contained in those books, and the great fountain they pointed unto."[8]

Bringing Christianity to Africa was, of course, not Cuffe's only mission. He was at least as preoccupied with handling his commercial matters and, as Governor Columbine observed, Cuffe was not "a mere babe in the ways of the trading world...." The black captain also investigated whether a whale fishery could be established in the waters off the coast of Sierra Leone. Most important, however,

7. Account Book, February 21, 28, March 1, 2, 1811, Cuffe Papers.
8. *Ibid.*, March 3-19, 1811; quotations from [Paul Cuffe], *A Brief Account of the Settlement and Present Situation of the Colony of Sierra Leone in Africa, as Communicated by Paul Cuffe (a man of colour) to his friend in New York...* (New York: Printed by Samuel Wood, 1812), pp. 3, 7. See also Harris, *Paul Cuffe*, pp. 83n, 84n, 85n.

he explored the possibilities of stimulating the commercial development of Sierra Leone by instituting regular trade between blacks in the colony and blacks in America, as well as between the colony and England. The trans-Atlantic trade itself would encourage a limited Afro-American emigration which would, in turn, help the economic growth of Sierra Leone; for if morally exemplary and propertied blacks were to come to the colony from the United States, a more competitive and self-motivating atmosphere would develop naturally. In his correspondence Cuffe continually spoke of his desire "of keeping open a small intercourse between America and Sierra Leone in hopes through that channel some families may find their way to Sierra Leone." At least some colonists reacted positively to his plans. With Cuffe's support eleven repatriates, including several members of the Society of Sierra Leone, petitioned Governor Columbine to support the efforts of all blacks wishing to settle in the colony and to help those "foreign brethren who may have vessels . . . establish commerce in Sierra Leone." Alluding even more directly to Cuffe's concerns, the black petitioners asked the governor to assist individuals wishing to engage in whale-fishing at the colony.[9]

Whether Columbine responded to the petition is unknown, but certainly the problems of American citizens trading with and possibly living in a British colony during a period of increasing antagonism between the two countries were too complex for the colonial authorities to resolve by themselves. This was compounded in Cuffe's case by overt jealousy on the part of at least one colonial official who wrote to England claiming that Cuffe was unprincipled and mercenary; it was three years before the African Institution was able to clear Cuffe completely of all hints of wrongdoing. Cuffe's only recourse was to take his case, as well as his plans, to England, where William Allen and other members of the Institution had long awaited his visit. Finally on May 12, 1811, Cuffe left Sierra Leone with some camwood, his crew, and Aaron Richards, an African

9. Gov. Edward Columbine's Journal, entry for March 22, 1811, Sierra Leone Colonial Government Papers, 1792–1825, University of Illinois, Chicago Circle; Cuffe to William Allen, Sierra Leone, April 22, 1811, Cuffe Papers. See also Cuffe to John Cuffe, Liverpool, August 12, 1811; Cuffe to Allen, Westport, July 15, 1812, Cuffe Papers. A copy of the petition from the inhabitants of Sierra Leone is also in the Cuffe Papers; it was printed in [Cuffe], *A Brief Account*, p. 5.

who was on board learning navigation. Richards's presence led to unanticipated difficulties; when the *Traveller* reached Liverpool on July 12, an impressment gang, considering Richards a British citizen, immediately seized him. Cuffe thus spent his first several days in England traveling between Liverpool and London and visiting such prestigious reformers as Allen, William Wilberforce, and Thomas Clarkson in what eventually was a successful effort to have Richards released from custody and restored to Cuffe's care.[10]

Cuffe's most important task was to win the support of the African Institution for his long-range plan to carry a small number of black families to Sierra Leone in order to teach Africans the religious and commercial lessons of the West. He also hoped to gain the Institution's help in convincing the British government to grant him commercial privileges—especially a license from the Privy Council to allow the *Traveller* to carry a cargo from England to Sierra Leone. Because of the labors of such friends as Allen, Clarkson, and Macaulay and because of the widespread public attention he was receiving, the government granted Cuffe permission to trade with the colony. He also spoke to the society in late August. At this meeting Cuffe presented the presiding officer, the Duke of Gloucester, with an African robe, a letter box, and a dagger—to show, Cuffe explained in his journal, "that the Africans were capable of mental endowments." Following this appearance, a committee of the Institution publicly expressed the hope that Cuffe "will continue to be influenced by the same zeal to advance the civilization of his Brethren in Africa which he has hitherto shown."[11]

Despite the African Institution's encouraging rhetoric, and the

---

10. Harris, *Paul Cuffe*, pp. 50–51; Account Book, May 12, July 12–July 23, August 21, 1811, Cuffe Papers.

11. *Ibid.*, July 25–28, August 27, 1811; copy of a resolution adopted by a Committee of the Directors of the African Institution, August 27, 1811; copy of Petition of Smiths, Martin and St. Barbe (on behalf of the African Institution) to the Privy Council, n.d., Cuffe Papers; Harris, *Paul Cuffe*, pp. 51–53; Christopher Fyfe, *A History of Sierra Leone* (London: Oxford University Press, 1962), p. 113. There is no direct evidence indicating that the license was granted, but both Cuffe's Account Book entry of July 27, 1811, and William Allen, *Life of William Allen with Selections from His Correspondence* (Philadelphia: H. Longstreth, 1847), I, p. 103, indicate that Cuffe's British friends were applying for a license for him. More crucial, Cuffe was allowed full commercial privileges upon his return to Sierra Leone.

assistance the society had provided in helping Cuffe obtain his commercial license from the government, the Institution did not decide to expend funds directly for Cuffe's limited missionary-emigration plan. Thus when the black merchant left Liverpool for Sierra Leone in mid-September, his plans were only somewhat advanced. The *Traveller* reached Sierra Leone on November 12, and Cuffe immediately turned to his commercial affairs. He also met with many of the colonists he had befriended during his earlier visit. Cuffe saw these blacks—"Westerners" yet also, by choice, Africans—as key figures in his plans to establish a commercial nexus between black Africans and black Americans. In December he organized a group of colonists who belonged to a Methodist society into the Friendly Society of Sierra Leone, an organization which would grow or buy produce to ship to England and thus break the monopoly held by the English traders. Its president was John Kizell, the son of an African chief. Born near the coast south of Sierra Leone, Kizell came as a slave to Charleston, South Carolina, before the Revolution. After fighting with the British, he migrated to Birchtown, Nova Scotia, and then to Sierra Leone in 1792.[12] Although Cuffe hoped a trading and marketing agency similar to the Friendly Society would eventually be formed by Afro-Americans, at this time he was only able to establish commercial contacts between the Society and his English merchant friends.

With the assistance of William Allen, who loaned the Society seventy pounds, the Friendly Society began a prosperous if relatively short-lived existence. Allen, with the help of Thomas Clarkson, organized a small group of Liverpool merchants to sell the produce sent by the Sierra Leone society to England. Cuffe also provided assistance by publicizing the Friendly Society's existence among black Americans sympathetic to the commercial development of Africa, and by advancing money to several members of the Society, including Kizell. The Friendly Society's secretary, James Wise, served as Cuffe's personal commercial agent, and Cuffe hoped that the So-

---

12. Account Book, November 12–December 18, 1811, Cuffe Papers; Fyfe, *Sierra Leone*, p. 113. For Kizell, see African Institution, *Report* (1812), 144–145; Archibald Alexander, *History of Colonization on the Western Coast of Africa*, 2nd ed. (Philadelphia: W. S. Martien, 1849), pp. 103–104; Robin W. Winks, *The Blacks in Canada: A History* (New Haven: Yale University Press, 1971), p. 71.

ciety itself would also represent his business interests. Moreover, he envisioned the Friendly Society assisting the black emigrants whom he would carry to the colony. Yet he was quickly disappointed by the new society. At one early meeting he observed, "more debating than business done. . . ." Typical of his commitment to Quaker precepts of individual responsibility and personal morality, Cuffe added that "if we in Sierra Leone would rouse ourselves to more industry and sobriety we certainly would get forward the better and make the better progress." Four years later, however, the Society was flourishing; Cuffe reported that Kizell and his associates held £1200 in capital. Yet they soon disbanded, preferring individual trade to collective farming.[13]

Whatever the fortunes of the Friendly Society, Cuffe realized that it was the colonial authorities, not Kizell or the other black settlers, who could directly affect the success of his plans. Before leaving Freetown, Cuffe met with Charles Maxwell, the new governor, to learn on what terms his emigrants could settle at Sierra Leone and whether land would be granted to them. Whatever Maxwell's views, Cuffe never recorded them in his journal. Several weeks later Cuffe left Freetown for the United States. However, British authorities, claiming that Cuffe did not have permission to carry three Africans then on board, seized the *Traveller* and brought the ship back into the harbor. Once Maxwell consented to Cuffe's arrangements, the *Traveller* again sailed from Freetown on the last leg of a journey that had lasted more than a year.[14] Now, having found sufficient encouragement in both Africa and England for his efforts, Cuffe's new mission was to locate a small number of Afro-American emigrants of sufficient property and learning and to find a way of

13. Allen to Cuffe, London, October 29, 1812; William Rathbone to Cuffe, Liverpool, November 30, 1812; Account Book, May 11, 1812; I.O.U. signed by John Kizell, Sierra Leone, January 24, 28, 1812; Account Book, January 23, 1812; Cuffe to Allen, Sierra Leone, February 16, 1816; Cuffe to Samuel J. Mills, n.p., August 6, 1816; Cuffe to James Wise, Westport, August 14, September 15 (with accompanying list of figures), 1816, Cuffe Papers; Fyfe, *Sierra Leone*, p. 132. Allen's group of British merchant philanthropists took the unwieldy name of A Society for the Purpose of Encouraging the Black Settlers of Sierra Leone, and the Natives of Africa generally, in the Cultivation of their Soil, by the Sale of their Produce (Harris, *Paul Cuffe*, p. 55).

14. Account Book, January 24–February 19, 1812.

circumventing commercial restrictions enforced by both England and America.

First, of course, Cuffe had to reenter the United States. Although he himself landed without incident on April 19, the customs collector at Westport confiscated the *Traveller* because, by trading with a British colony, Cuffe had violated the nonintercourse agreement put into effect solely against England under the options presented by Macon's Bill No. 2. Cuffe immediately began to gather personal recommendations with which to petition Secretary of the Treasury Albert Gallatin. Armed with letters from his attorney, Asher Robbins of Newport, to both Gallatin and President Madison, and with a general letter of recommendation signed by, among others, the two prominent Rhode Island abolitionists Moses Brown and Thomas Arnold, Cuffe left Providence for Washington on April 26. He reached the federal capital six days later, having traveled night and day in a journey eventful only for the rude behavior of a Southerner who objected, without success, to Cuffe's presence at the dining table at a coach stop between New York and Philadelphia. Shortly after arriving in Washington, Cuffe spoke with Gallatin; at a second meeting on May 4 the secretary, convinced that there was no willful violation of the law, informed Cuffe that the *Traveller* and its cargo would be returned. Gallatin also assured the black captain that the government would help him promote the welfare of Africa with whatever constitutional means were at its disposal.[15]

His mission to Washington a success, Cuffe adopted a more leisurely pace on his trip back to Westport. This enabled him to meet with groups of blacks in the large eastern cities to discuss his trips to Africa, his plans for establishing a regular commercial connection with the western coast of the continent, and, finally, his desire to transport to Sierra Leone those black Americans dedicated to the elevation of a people degraded by the slave trade and by cen-

15. *Ibid.*, April 19–May 4, 1812; copies of Asher Robbins to Albert Gallatin, Newport, April 23, 1812, and Robbins to President Madison, Newport, April 23, 1812, Cuffe Papers; statement by Gallatin, May 5, 1812, available in a true copy in the Moses Brown Papers, Rhode Island Historical Society, and in a much rougher copy in the Cuffe Papers. See also Cuffe to Moses Brown, Washington, May 2, 1812; Cuffe to Brown, Newport, May 22, 1812, Moses Brown Papers.

turies of heathenism. In Baltimore, Cuffe discussed his benevolent plans for Africa with the two black teachers of the African school, George Collins and the Reverend Daniel Coker, the latter an ordained Methodist Episcopal deacon who was preaching to a black Methodist society in Baltimore. Both men agreed to correspond with Cuffe about the best means of promoting the evangelization of Africa, and he hoped they might form a society for this purpose in Baltimore. In Philadelphia and New York he suggested to his black listeners that they form themselves into local societies to communicate with each other, with whatever group might be organized in Baltimore, and with the Friendly Society of Sierra Leone. Eventually a single society speaking for the African "nation" in America and promoting both African evangelization and African emigration might be formed. These meetings with Cuffe formed the genesis for the organization of emigration societies, called African Institutions, in both cities. The American agents in Cuffe's scheme for trans-Atlantic black trade, the African Institutions were also intended to inform sympathetic blacks about Cuffe's concerns and activities.[16]

At the time no blacks in New York and Philadelphia were willing to commit themselves as missionaries in Sierra Leone. When the Westport sea captain returned home in late May, he began to look elsewhere for potential black settlers. He decided he could not himself move there permanently because of his wife's opposition, but he hoped he could find several of the "finest characters" in Boston to accompany him back to Sierra Leone as early as September or October. A group of Boston blacks, evidently active in the African Society of Boston (a mutual benefit society organized in 1796), responded to Cuffe's overtures by inviting him to attend their July 14 commemoration of the abolition of the slave trade. Whether

16. Account Book, May 5–14, 1812; Cuffe to Allen, Westport, June 12, 1812; Cuffe to Prince Sanders, Robert Roberts, and Perry Lockes, New Bedford, June 6, 1812, New York Historical Society. On the Philadelphia African Institution, see African Institution (London), *Report* (1816), 70–71; James Forten to Cuffe, Philadelphia, January 25, 1817, Cuffe Papers. For the New York African Institution, see Cuffe to Peter Williams, Westport, n.d. [probably between August 10 and 14, 1816]; Cuffe to Williams, Westport, August 14, 1816; Cuffe to the Friendly Society, Westport, August 14, 1816; Williams to Cuffe, New York, March 22, 1817, Cuffe Papers.

Cuffe visited Boston is not known, but throughout the next few years he maintained a regular correspondence with those members of the Boston black community who, like him, favored African emigration as a means of "diffusing light, & civilization & knowledge in Africa." These included Prince Sanders, a Vermont-born teacher in the African School of Boston who later became an educational consultant to the Haitian government; Perry Lockes, a young Methodist preacher and blacksmith; and Thomas Jarvis. By mid-July, 1812, they had formed a loose organization, the African Sierra Leone Benevolent Society, which Cuffe considered as equivalent to the African Institutions then forming in Philadelphia and New York. Despite opposition within the Boston black community (which Sanders, Lockes, and Jarvis claimed was encouraged by Democratic politicians who opposed any project involving Englishmen), several black families banded together in the hope that through Cuffe's efforts they would be able to settle in Sierra Leone. But war delayed their dreams.[17]

The long-anticipated hostilities between the United States and England erupted in mid-June, when the American Congress, unaware that England had repealed the objectionable Order of Coun-

17. Account Book, May 22, 1812; Cuffe to Allen, Westport, June 12, 1812; Cuffe to Sanders, Roberts, and Lockes, New Bedford, June 6, 1812, New York Historical Society; Sanders to Cuffe, Boston, June 25, 1812, Cuffe Papers; Cuffe to Lockes, Westport, July 14, 1812, and Cuffe to Lockes, Westport, July 30, 1812, Philanthropists Collection, Historical Society of Pennsylvania, with copies at the New York Historical Society; Sanders, Thomas Jarvis, and Lockes to Cuffe, Boston, August 3, 1812, Cuffe Papers; Cuffe to Locks [sic], New Bedford, May 4, 1813, Morse Family Papers, Yale University, with another copy in the Simon Gratz Collection, Historical Society of Pennsylvania; Lockes to Cuffe, Boston, July 15, 1813, Cuffe Papers. For information on Sanders (as he spelled his name) or Saunders (as others often did), see Harry E. Davis, *A History of Freemasonry among Negroes in America* (n.p.: The United Supreme Council, Ancient and Accepted Scottish Rite of Freemasonry, Northern Jurisdiction, U.S.A. [Prince Hall Affiliation], 1946), pp. 292–293; Allen, *Life of Allen*, I, p. 223n; Earl Leslie Griggs and Clifford H. Prator, eds., *Henry Christophe and Thomas Clarkson: A Correspondence* (Berkeley and Los Angeles: University of California Press, 1952), p. 45; *Boston Recorder*, February 11, 1817, p. 27; Maxwell Whiteman, "Prince Saunders: Lecturer, Churchman and Attorney General," a single-page sketch at the beginning of a reprint edition of three works by Sanders (Philadelphia: Rhistoric Publications, 1969). Much less is known about Lockes and almost nothing about Jarvis. See, however, Cuffe to Allen, Sierra Leone, April 1, 1816, Cuffe Papers; Fyfe, *Sierra Leone*, p. 132.

cil, declared war. True to his Quaker pacifism, Cuffe considered the war "inconsistent with Christianity." It was also inconsistent with his intentions to carry Boston emigrants to Sierra Leone in the fall of 1812, and these plans were deferred indefinitely. Unaware of the American declaration of war, Cuffe's English supporters in the African Institution continued in their efforts to assist the Westport sea captain. Acting at the urging of William Allen and Thomas Clarkson, the Institution in June decided to grant Cuffe a tract of land for cultivation by his settlers, stipulating that the colonists accept British rule, be "of free Condition, and good known Character," own at least some property, and be "acquainted with some of the useful mechanical arts, or with the cultivation of tropical produce, but more particularly with the cleaning of Rice."[18]

The directors of the Institution were aware that Sierra Leone was overpopulated with craftsmen and artisans because many of the Nova Scotians who had migrated to the colony in 1792 had little, if any, agricultural experience. The hope was that black farmers from America would cultivate the soil and also teach others—the Nova Scotians, the Maroons who came in 1800, and the indigenous Africans—to raise and process rice, indigo, cotton, and tobacco. The English philanthropists had no illusions that Cuffe would be able to bring to Sierra Leone enough settlers to cultivate the entire grant, but they expected his emigrants would hire the Grummettas (a local people) or other Africans liberated from captured slave ships. Cuffe himself was encouraged to visit his settlers regularly, but the Institution did not require him to live there permanently. Only "an occasional residence" would be necessary to oversee his settlers, perhaps establish a whale fishery, and honor the "spirit of the Grant."[19]

Whatever exhilaration Cuffe may have felt upon learning of the African Institution's land grant was dampened by the declaration of war between the United States and England. For a time he hoped that, because of the obvious humanitarian nature of his plans, he would be able to circumvent the strictures which accompanied the hostilities. Perhaps, he surmised in a letter to William Allen, if

---

18. Cuffe to Lockes, Westport, July 30, 1812, Philanthropists Collection, Historical Society of Pennsylvania, with a copy in the New York Historical Society; Thomas Clarkson and Allen to Cuffe, London, July 1, 1812, Cuffe Papers.

19. *Ibid.*

the British government would grant him a license to trade in Sierra Leone, the American government would follow suit. As the months passed, however, Cuffe began to consider other ways of attacking the problem. In early February, 1813, he suggested to Perry Lockes that those Boston blacks wishing to emigrate to Africa apply "to Congress for licensing a vessell to sail from America to Africa and for the said vessell to continue to pass and repass uninterrupted with the produce of each country in order to render aid to the civilization of Africa." Shortly thereafter Cuffe took the initiative himself and attempted to apply pressure on the federal government for permission to trade with the British colony and thus further his emigration plans. At Cuffe's request Hannah Little, a friend of Dolley Madison, interposed with the President directly; Madison received Cuffe's inquiry favorably and suggested that he apply directly to Congress. In response, Cuffe quickly drew up a memorial to Congress, which he began to circulate among those of his white friends who could possibly aid him. With Congress adjourning soon after, Cuffe was forced to wait until the next session convened in December. In the meantime, his close friend William Rotch, Jr., a New Bedford merchant, and others wrote Senator Christopher Gore of Massachusetts and Laban Wheaton, Cuffe's congressman, asking for their backing. Rotch's brother-in-law, William Dean, also recommended Cuffe's proposal to another congressman, the influential Timothy Pickering.[20]

Gore and Wheaton were Cuffe's chief sponsors when his memorial was introduced in both the House and the Senate in early January, 1814. In the Senate the memorial was referred to a three-man select committee, while the House sent the petition to the Committee of Commerce and Manufactures. The memorial itself stressed Cuffe's devotion to his African brethren, victimized by the slave trade in

20. Cuffe to Allen, Westport, July 15, 1812, Cuffe Papers; Cuffe to Lockes, New Bedford, February 4, 1813, Morse Family Papers, Yale University, with a copy in the Simon Gratz Collection, Historical Society of Pennsylvania; copy of Cuffe to Hannah Little, n.p., n.d.; Elisha Tyson to Cuffe, Baltimore, May 12, 1813; Little to Cuffe, Baltimore, May 13, 1813; Tyson to Cuffe, Baltimore, July 20, 1813; Thomas Robinson to Cuffe, Newport, November 29, 1813; William Rotch to Christopher Gore, New Bedford, December 10, 1813; Rotch to Laban Wheaton, New Bedford, December 10, 1813; William Dean to Timothy Pickering, New Bedford, December 12, 1813; Dean to William Reed, New Bedford, December 12, 1813, Cuffe Papers.

which at least some of them, he believed, degraded themselves by selling other Africans. His plan, Cuffe maintained, "may ultimately prove beneficial to his [the petitioner's] brethren of the African race within their native climate." American blacks, he implied, would simply serve as the patrons of the degraded peoples of Africa and thus would not benefit directly themselves. Christianized and civilized by their experience in the New World among Europeans, they were now prepared to return to Africa "to promote habits of industry, sobriety, and frugality, among the natives of that country." Although a number of black families had indicated their desire to engage in this missionary endeavour, he was unable to transport them to Africa because of the commercial restrictions proclaimed by both England and the United States. If, however, the United States would grant him permission to carry emigrants to Sierra Leone—along with the necessary provisions and farming implements—and if England would grant a similar license, he would carry "the common advantages to those so long deprived of them." Since Cuffe maintained he would have to trade with Sierra Leone to make the venture possible, he also asked Congress to waive the existing regulations in his case.[21]

The Senate acted first. Christopher Gore, speaking for the select committee, reported a bill authorizing the president to permit Cuffe to leave the United States with a vessel and cargo for Sierra Leone and to return with a cargo. On January 27 the Senate approved the bill and sent the measure to the House, where it was referred to the Committee of Commerce and Manufactures (which was still considering Cuffe's memorial). But this committee, when reporting to the House on February 9, opposed the Senate's bill on the ground that "it would be impolitic ... to relax the prohibitions of the embargo law, on the application of an individual, for a purpose which, however benevolently conceived, cannot be considered in any other light than as speculative...." The House then dropped the matter until March 18, when the congressmen resolved themselves into a committee of the whole to consider the Senate's measure, along with the negative report of the Committee of Commerce and Manufactures. Cuffe's own congressman, Federalist Laban Wheaton, spoke in favor of the measure, as did four other New England con-

21. *Annals of Congress*, 13th cong., 2nd sess., pp. 569, 861–863.

gressmen (three of them Federalists) and two southern Democrats. Six Democrats voiced their opposition to any action on Cuffe's behalf. The debate revolved around the wisdom of allowing the departure of a vessel which would have to be licensed by England. If the British did not believe Cuffe's expedition would be beneficial to them, the opponents of the measure argued, they would not grant the black mariner a license.[22]

Larger issues, only barely disguised, were actually at stake: the nature of American relations with England, the necessity for a war so bitterly opposed by New England Federalists, and even the moral competence of the English to carry out religious and benevolent missions. Finally the House defeated the bill, 72–65. Wheaton's analysis of the vote was basically accurate: "The Democrats," he consoled Cuffe, "combined against it, and although they did not venture to defame your character, they endeavoured to thro' the object into ridicule and contempt, and were too powerful." Voting for the measure was an almost solid bloc of Federalists, most of them from New England and New York, supported by a few Democrats. For the Federalists, championing Cuffe's bill was an opportunity to express again their hostility to the war with England. In defeat Cuffe still believed Congress would pass the necessary legislation if the British government first granted him a trading license.[23]

Unfortunately for Cuffe and the other backers of his missionary-emigration scheme, the British were no more inclined to waive their commercial restrictions during wartime than had been the House of Representatives. Even after the peace treaty between the two countries was signed at the end of 1814, England would not guarantee protection for Cuffe should he sail for Sierra Leone. Cuffe's English friends acquiesced in the government's negative decision. "On the whole, it appeared to us," William Allen concluded in September, 1815, "that we could not ask P. Cuffe to run the risk, nor could we advise the African Institution to do it." Regardless of the risk involved, however, Cuffe was determined to go; although the English

22. *Ibid.*, pp. 570, 572, 599, 601, 602, 1150, 1195–96, 1265, 1880–81.
23. *Ibid.*; Wheaton to Cuffe, Washington City, March 19, 1814, Cuffe Papers; Cuffe to Jedediah Morse, Westport, May 2, 1814, Dreer Collection, Historical Society of Pennsylvania. Party identification of the legislators was drawn from the *Biographical Directory of the American Congress, 1774–1961* (Washington, D.C.: Government Printing Office, 1961).

government still refused to issue Cuffe a trading license, in late December Lord Bathurst asked Sierra Leone's governor Charles McCarthy to afford the Westport ship captain every possible assistance should he arrive in Freetown. Ironically, McCarthy, a staunch defender of the British monarchy who held a personal abhorrence for republicanism, had been strongly enforcing the commercial regulations against American traders; new restrictions on foreign commerce, passed in August, gave the governor complete control over the entry of foreign traders into the colony.[24] Neither these more stringent regulations nor McCarthy's attitudes dissuaded Cuffe, still committed to his dream of regenerating Africa through the infusion of American blacks, propertied and respectable.

From mid-August, 1815, if not before, Cuffe had been working to round up would-be emigrants. He spent five weeks away from Westport on this mission, and by late September he reported that six to eight families were ready to depart with him at the end of October. In mid-November, after unexpected delays, Cuffe approached the Westport Meeting of Friends for permission to leave for Africa. On December 10, with eighteen adults and twenty children aboard the *Traveller*, he guided his brig out of the harbor at Westport. Of the thirty-eight blacks, four were from Philadelphia, two from New York, and the rest—including Perry Lockes, Thomas Jarvis, and their families—from Boston. At least two of the emigrants were African-born, and all were common laborers. Most of the emigrants undoubtedly hoped to help "redeem" Africa as well as to improve their own condition, for few, if any, satisfied the African Institution's requirements—property owners with extensive experience in tropical agriculture. Nevertheless, Cuffe believed they would be "serviceable" to the colony at Sierra Leone.[25] Whether Charles McCarthy would agree remained to be seen.

24. African Institution, *Report* (1814), 18; Allen, *Life of Allen*, I, 180–181; George E. Brooks, Jr., *Yankee Traders, Old Coasters, and African Middlemen: A History of American Legitimate Trade with West Africa in the Nineteenth Century* (Boston: Boston University Press, 1970), p. 168n. On McCarthy's monarchical and protectionist views, see p. 167 of Brooks's volume.

25. Cuffe to Thomas Thompson, New York, September 26, 1815, Gibson Manuscripts, Friends House Library, London; copy of a resolution signed by Ebenezer Baker, Clerk, Monthly Meeting of the Religious Society of Friends, Westport,

The *Traveller* anchored at Freetown in early February after fifty-six days, twenty of which Cuffe described as "the most tremendous weather" he had ever experienced at sea. Unfortunately for him, Lord Bathurst's instructions evidently had not yet reached Sierra Leone, for Governor McCarthy prohibited Cuffe from unloading his cargo; McCarthy did allow the emigrants to disembark with their baggage. A few days later, when Cuffe was considering leaving the colony, McCarthy agreed to discharge all of his goods except for the tobacco and naval stores. The Westport sea captain then unloaded and sold his cargo or traded it for camwood, which he hoped to dispose of upon his return to the United States. Despite McCarthy's restrictions, Cuffe sold his tobacco on the coast near Freetown to the Friendly Society of Sierra Leone, the mercantile collective he had helped organize during his previous visit. The organization was now establishing a trading post among the Africans at Port Loko.[26]

Besides trading goods, Cuffe conferred with the British governor about the conditions under which his Afro-American emigrants would be accepted at the colony. He was gratified to learn that McCarthy would grant them plots of land equivalent in size to those given the original settlers. Of Cuffe's nine families, five from Boston —including those of Lockes and Jarvis—immediately banded together to cultivate ten acres of land, while sixty-year-old William Guin, also from Boston, began to work McCarthy's plantation. Samuel Wilson of Philadelphia supported his family by hiring himself out to a local resident, and the two Africans, Antony Survance of Philadelphia and Charles Calumbine of New York, planned to return to their homes in the Congo and Senegal. The emigrants who remained at Sierra Leone soon disappointed McCarthy, who had expected them to have more experience with tropical agriculture.[27]

November 16, 1815; Cuffe to Allen, Westport, December 4, 1815; Catalogue of the Families on board the brig Traveller going from America for Sierra Leone ... sailed 12 month 10 1815 from Westport; Cuffe to Allen, Sierra Leone, April 1, 1816.

26. Cuffe to William Rotch, Jr., Sierra Leone, February ?, 1816; Cuffe to Allen, Sierra Leone, February 6, 1816, and April 1, 1816, Cuffe Papers.

27. Cuffe to Allen, Sierra Leone, April 1, 1816, Cuffe Papers; African Institution, *Report* (1817), 40–41.

They also must have disappointed Cuffe, who had hoped that, if their crops were successful, they would be able to repay him for the provisions he had advanced them.

Cuffe remained in Sierra Leone for two months to oversee the adjustment of his settlers, handle his own commercial affairs, and confer with both the governor and the Friendly Society. In mid-April he left Freetown, having transplanted his small group of Christian "civilizers" to Africa, yet already aware that benevolence would prove costly. Besides the large sums he had advanced to the emigrants, the Sierra Leone prices for his goods had been poor. Unlike the situation five years earlier, an excess of American goods had been accumulating in Freetown during the war. This, combined with the ability of British administrators to control the entry of goods more or less at whim, had driven prices down. Finally, Cuffe discovered when he arrived in New York on May 28 that the sixty-one tons of African camwood he had carried across the Atlantic were not in demand; he sold it several months later at a loss.[28]

By June Cuffe had returned to his family in Westport to contemplate the future of the Afro-American beachhead he had established on the West African coast. Although he received several inquiries from blacks in Boston and Providence who wished to follow the original thirty-eight settlers to Sierra Leone, Cuffe had no intentions of returning to Africa for another year. His motivations were several. Sincerely concerned with the welfare of the first group of settlers, he wanted to see how they adjusted to Africa and how the British treated them before carrying over additional settlers. He was also worried about his own financial stake in the emigration scheme. If the first group of emigrants could not repay their debts to him, he feared that future settlers would fare no better. Of course, assistance from his London friends could help diminish the magnitude of his problem. A profitable trading relationship with both Africa and England could also do so. But he was acutely aware of the commercial disadvantages of trading in the African colony without a license, and the African Institution of London had been

---

28. African Institution, *Report* (1817), 40–41; Brooks, *Yankee Traders*, pp. 167–168; Cuffe to Samuel R. Fisher, New York, May 28, 1816; Cuffe to ?, n.p., June ?, 1816, Cuffe Papers; Sherwood, "Paul Cuffe," 203.

unable to secure one for him.[29] With an immediate voyage to Africa out of the question, he increasingly turned his attention to domestic concerns.

During the more than four years since he had helped to establish black emigration societies—the African Institutions—in both Philadelphia and New York, Cuffe had watched the somewhat faltering efforts of the groups with interest. Upon returning from Africa in the spring of 1816, he wrote brief accounts of his voyage to the leaders of the Institutions. Unfortunately, in the months that followed, Cuffe could discover little energy or interest on the part of the societies. "The Institutions that hath been formed in America among the african race," he wrote to William Allen in December, "are not so... lively as I could wish, either for the want of spirit or property."[30] Cuffe nevertheless hoped that the two groups (especially Peter Williams, Jr.'s New York organization) would be able to encourage large numbers of able and respectable blacks to emigrate. He also believed that the black societies could be one point in a "triangular trade" with the Friendly Society of Sierra Leone and such English commercial men as Allen and William Rathbone of Liverpool; ideally, the result would be a legitimate commerce profitable to all three parties.

To this end Cuffe encouraged a correspondence between John Kizell's Friendly Society and Williams's African Institution of New York. The son of a Methodist sexton and himself the religious leader of a group of black Episcopalians belonging to, yet worshipping apart from, the largely white Trinity Church, Williams was not without secular concerns. Already known for an aggressive if wordy tract against the slave trade, he now advocated what Cuffe had previously proposed—the development of a black mercantile line to carry cargo between the United States and Africa. Ostensibly, the Friendly Society would handle the African side of the trade.[31]

29. Cuffe to Peter Williams, Jr., Westport, June 14, 1816; Cuffe to Jedediah Morse, Westport, August 10, 1816; Cuffe to William Harris, Westport, August 10, 1816; Cuffe to Fisher, Westport, August 14, 1816; Cuffe to Lockes, Westport, August 14, 1816; Cuffe to Thomas Fay, Westport, September 7, 1816, Cuffe Papers.

30. Cuffe to James Forten, New York, May 29, 1816; Cuffe to Williams, Westport, June 14, 1816; Cuffe to Allen, Westport, December 19, 1816, Cuffe Papers.

31. Cuffe to Williams, Westport, August 14, 1816; Cuffe to the Friendly Society,

Cuffe, of course, supported Williams's scheme. Yet, while in no way abandoning his commitment to the spiritual and economic development of Africa, Cuffe also began a subtle yet significant alteration of his views. Where he had previously encouraged the emigration of qualified individuals to an existing polity such as Sierra Leone, he now advocated the establishment of a separate settlement capable of absorbing large numbers of black Americans. His plans, once directed almost entirely to the religious and material welfare of Africans, became a vehicle to aid Afro-Americans as well.

Over the last six months of 1816 Cuffe focused his attention more and more upon blacks in the United States—especially those held in bondage in the South. He had previously been an outspoken foe of the foreign slave trade, and he had hoped that his emigrationist plans would in some small way hamper that trade. But now Cuffe was concerned about the evils of slavery itself, and he was convinced that should the bondsmen rebel, white Southerners would ruthlessly put them down. "There never [was] a time," he argued in mid-August, "when it calls louder for something to be done for the African Nation besides violence to suppress an insurrection." Emigration alone was not the answer, but the establishment of federally supported colonies would perhaps induce southern slaveholders to deport their slaves and thus avert a tragic bloodbath. Although he believed that two colonies—one in an unsettled part of the United States and one in Africa—would be needed, his first thought was to locate a place on the African coast. Suspecting that the British would have little inclination to absorb large numbers of emancipated American slaves into Sierra Leone, Cuffe wrote Kizell asking whether there were other coastal sites suitable for settlement by black Americans.[32] Almost simultaneously he received inquiries from whites

---

Westport, August 14, 1816; Cuffe to James Wise, Westport, August 14, 1816; Cuffe to Williams, Westport, n.d. [but probably between August 10 and 14, 1816]; Cuffe to Williams, Westport, August 30, 1816, Cuffe Papers. See also Forten to Cuffe, Philadelphia, February 15, 1815, *ibid*. On Williams, see Carol V. R. George, *Segregated Sabbaths: Richard Allen and the Rise of Independent Black Churches, 1760–1840* (New York: Oxford University Press, 1973), pp. 143–144; Peter Williams, *An Oration on the Abolition of the Slave Trade; Delivered in the African Church, in the City of New York, January 1, 1808* (New York: Printed by Samuel Wood, 1808).

32. Cuffe's new emphasis can be pieced together from his letters to: Samuel

equally captivated by the idea of planting a distinct Afro-American colony in Africa.

The Reverend Robert Finley, a New Jersey Presbyterian minister, contacted Cuffe in early December seeking information about Sierra Leone as well as possible locations for an American black colony. Finley had already decided that, by colonizing in Africa free blacks and those slaves emancipated by their owners, he would be serving the needs of Africa as well as enabling whites to rid themselves of an alien and discordant people. "The great desire of those whose minds are impressed with this subject," he wrote Cuffe, "is to give an opportunity to the free people of color to rise to their proper level and at the same time to provide a powerful means of putting an end to the slave trade, and sending civilization and Christianity to Africa...."[33]

Like Cuffe, Finley was aware that large-scale colonization would be impossible without federal financing. During December he diligently sought to rally influential Washington figures behind his African colonization plans. He soon succeeded in bringing Henry Clay, John Randolph of Roanoke, and several other politicians behind that part of his proposal limited to the removal of free blacks; Clay especially opposed any hint that colonization might help hasten the abolition of slavery. By the end of the month Finley had helped organize the American Colonization Society, chiefly as a means of securing governmental assistance. Convinced that they would receive this support, the colonizationists started to consider where in Africa they could locate their proposed settlement for free blacks. Even before the Colonization Society was formally organized, the Reverend Samuel J. Mills, the traveling agent for the Presbyterian-sponsored African Education Society which had already agreed to train blacks for missionary and administrative duties in Finley's projected colony, turned to Cuffe for advice. It would not be sur-

---

J. Mills, n.p., August 6, 1816, published in the American Colonization Society, *Report* (1818; D. Rapine edition), 27; Samuel C. Aiken, Westport, August 7, 1816; Fisher, Westport, August 14, 1816; John Kizell, Westport, August 14, 1816; Stephen Gould (postscript), Westport, September 20, 1816, Cuffe Papers. The quotation is from Cuffe to Fisher.

33. Robert Finley to Cuffe, Washington, December 5, 1816, Cuffe Papers. On Finley, see Philip J. Staudenraus, *The African Colonization Movement, 1816-1865* (New York: Columbia University Press, 1961), pp. 15-22.

prising, Mills told Cuffe, "if the General Government during their present session were to direct a vessel to be dispatched with the proper persons to the coast of Africa for the purpose of making discoveries." He asked whether Cuffe would be willing to go out as the government's agent if granted the proper support.[34]

For Cuffe, the establishment of a national society which would further both his own long-standing missionary-emigration plan and his more recent design for independent Afro-American colonies was gratifying. Perhaps he never understood how thoroughly most white colonizationists had rejected Finley's marriage of colonization and emancipation. In letters to both Finley and Mills, Cuffe encouraged their efforts, providing detailed information on the physical and commercial characteristics of Sierra Leone and suggesting possible locations for a settlement elsewhere.[35] He mentioned Sherbro Island, where John Kizell had been living off and on since 1810, when Sierra Leone Governor Edward Columbine commissioned him to construct a model town, free from direct European interference, on this island south of the British colony. Kizell, who had been born inland not far from Sherbro, was enthusiastic when he learned from Cuffe of the new American interest in establishing a black colony; the former South Carolina slave was convinced that African land "would cost a small trifle." He recommended Sherbro "or any parts where there is plenty of camwood[,] palmoil and a little Ivory." Cuffe spoke approvingly of Kizell, but he felt that while Sherbro "may do for a small settlement or small beginning ... were there a willingness for a pretty general removal of this people ... the south part of Africa (viz.) the Cape of Good Hope if it could be obtained ... looks most favorable...."[36]

---

34. Staudenraus, *African Colonization*, pp. 23–30; Mills to Cuffe, Washington, December 26, 1816. For Mills and the African Education Society, see Staudenraus, p. 18.

35. Cuffe to Mills, n.p., January 6, 1817; Cuffe to Finley, Westport, January 8, 1817, Cuffe Papers. Although Cuffe's letter to Mills was reprinted in the American Colonization Society, *Report* (1818; D. Rapine edition), 26–27, the part in which Cuffe suggested that the African Institutions in New York and Philadelphia "be brought as much into action as would be best" was expurgated. Cuffe's letter to Finley was also published in an abridged form. See Isaac V. Brown, *Biography of the Rev. Robert Finley ...*, 2nd ed. (Philadelphia: John W. Moore, 1857), p. 126; *Boston Recorder*, April 8, 1817, p. 54.

36. Alexander, *History of Colonization*, pp. 103–104; Kizell to Cuffe, Freetown,

Cuffe, then, had come to support the efforts of the white colonizationists, even though his own purposes were strikingly opposed to those supporters who rejected tying emancipation to colonization. His own colonization plans, moreover, pointed to two colonies, not one. "[If] there was a spot fixed on the coast of Africa, and another in the United States of America," he wrote Finley in early 1817, "would it not answer the best purpose to draw off the colored citizens." Cuffe, like the Massachusetts blacks who in 1774 petitioned Governor Thomas Gage for some "unimproved land, belonging to the province, for a settlement," believed that blacks could separate themselves from whites while remaining in the country. For those blacks, free as well as slave, who preferred not to leave North America, a colony in the unsettled western regions of the United States would be a convenient and palatable alternative to the west coast of Africa. His dual colonization scheme would also provide undefined opportunities for those free blacks bound inexorably by race and humanity to their enslaved brethren in the South. "If the free people of color could exert themselves, more & more in industry and honesty," he wrote the black Philadelphia sailmaker and abolitionist James Forten after explaining his new scheme, "it would be a great help towards liberating those who still remain in bondage."[37] Most likely, Cuffe thought independent black colonies would demonstrate to white Americans the capabilities of blacks. Perhaps he also held nascent free labor views—that free labor produce and goods could, if patronized, challenge the economic underpinnings of the slave South.

While aware that blacks themselves, limited by insufficient resources, would not be able to provide much of a spur for colonization, Cuffe also recognized what the white colonizationists would never acknowledge: that only black leaders and organizations could

---

Sierra Leone, February 19, 1817, Cuffe Papers. For Cuffe's comments, see his letters to Mills and Finley cited in note 35.

37. Cuffe to Finley, Westport, January 8, 1817; Cuffe to William Gibbons, Westport, January 16, 1817; Cuffe to James Brine, Westport, January 16, 1817; Cuffe to Forten, Westport, March 1, 1817, Cuffe Papers. See also the citations in note 32. For the 1774 petition, see "Negro Petitions for Freedom," *Collections of the Massachusetts Historical Society*, 5th ser., III (1877), 435. On Forten, see Ray Allen Billington, "James Forten: Forgotten Abolitionist," *Negro History Bulletin*, XIII (November, 1949), 31-36, 45.

reach large masses of black people. He suggested to Mills that the colonizationists draw upon the black societies he had helped form in New York and Philadelphia: "I wish these institutions to be brought as much into action as would be best, by that means the Coloured Population of these large cities would be more awakened, than from an individual & a stranger, and thereby prevailed on to act for their own good, &c."[38] The black African Institutions, however, were forced to confront many blacks who saw African colonization as a deportation scheme directed by whites and designed to oppress further a rejected and abused people. As early as June, 1816, when Cuffe returned from carrying his thirty-eight emigrants to Sierra Leone, many Philadelphia blacks expressed hostility to that colony. Soon after the American Colonization Society was organized in Washington, black people in Philadelphia and elsewhere voiced their outrage, believing compulsory deportation was the ultimate aim of the Society. Yet even while opposing the Colonization Society, some blacks agreed with the colonizationists' premise that free blacks and whites could not live together harmoniously. In Georgetown, District of Columbia, in early January, 1817, free blacks condemned the Colonization Society and simultaneously asked Congress to grant them "a territory within the limits of our beloved Union." Both the Georgetown group and those free blacks attending a similar anti-Colonization Society meeting a few weeks later in Richmond, Virginia, suggested that land adjacent to the Missouri River be set aside for black Americans.[39]

A more direct attack upon the American Colonization Society came from a reported 3,000 blacks meeting at Richard Allen's Bethel Church in Philadelphia in early January. Both eschewing any call for a separate black settlement within the United States and avoiding a denunciation of African emigration in general, the meeting unanimously adopted resolutions which were directed solely at the objectives of the Colonization Society. The white colonizationists, the resolutions charged, planned to strengthen the institution of slavery by ridding the nation of free blacks whom the coloniza-

38. Cuffe to Mills, n.p., January 6, 1817, Cuffe Papers.
39. Cuffe to Williams, Westport, June 14, 1816, Cuffe Papers. On the Georgetown meeting, see *Poulson's American Daily Advertiser*, January 10, 1817, p. 3; on the Richmond meeting, see the *Boston Recorder*, February 18, 1817, p. 32.

tionists regarded both as inferior beings and as antislavery agitators. In an apparent anomaly, the leaders of the Cuffe-inspired African Institution of Philadelphia—Allen, James Forten, and Russell Parrott —participated actively at the meeting. Forten served as chairman, Parrott as secretary, and both Forten and Allen were appointed to a committee of eleven charged with communicating the temper of the gathering to Joseph Hopkinson, a distinguished lawyer and Federalist congressman from Philadelphia.[40]

For historians who have long emphasized Forten and Allen's opposition to the Colonization Society, their leadership in the African Institution of Philadelphia and not their presence at the Bethel Church rally is the anomaly. Given their steadfast advocacy of Christian humanism and racial awareness, however, it is not surprising that they should have initially endorsed Cuffe's early view that industrious and morally upright black Christians should bring the Gospel and western commercial practices to Africa.[41] Nevertheless, Allen, Forten, and other members of the African Institution were still able to lead a sharp and popular attack upon the Colonization Society. By rejecting what the white colonizationists were proposing, the members of the African Institution were not necessarily turning their backs on Cuffe, for the black mariner's new design did not involve what many blacks were finding so abhorrent in the program of the Colonization Society: the idea that by leaving the United States, free blacks would be abandoning their enslaved brethren. Soon after the protest meeting Forten and Allen demonstrated their willingness to entertain plans far more grandiose than

40. Forten to Cuffe, Philadelphia, January 25, 1817, Cuffe Papers; William Lloyd Garrison, *Thoughts on African Colonization* (Boston: Garrison and Knapp, 1832), part II, pp. 9–10. Forten and Parrott are listed as officers of the Philadelphia African Institution in a letter to the Directors of the African Institution of London, printed in the London Society's *Report* (1816), 70–71. The evidence for Richard Allen's participation is less direct, but see Forten to Cuffe, Philadelphia, January 25, 1817; Kizell to Cuffe, Freetown, Sierra Leone, February 19, 1817, Cuffe Papers. The figure of 3,000 may well be an exaggeration, for by 1820 Philadelphia's black population numbered only 7,582, with another 4,309 blacks residing within Philadelphia County but outside the city itself. W. E. Burghardt Du Bois, *The Philadelphia Negro: A Social Study* (Philadelphia: Pub. for the University [of Pennsylvania], 1899), p. 47.

41. The only expression of the collective views of the African Institution of Philadelphia can be found in the letter to the African Institution of London cited in note 40.

those Cuffe had originally proposed. As members of the committee selected at the Bethel rally, they met in Philadelphia with Robert Finley, then troubled by black opposition to the Colonization Society. After two hours of discussion, so Finley recounted, the New Jersey clergyman had persuaded the blacks in attendance that the colonization scheme was purely benevolent. But apparently Finley had extended his interpretation of colonization well beyond that recently accepted by the Society, for only eight of the eleven blacks present favored Africa as the best site for a colony; the rest preferred territory in the United States. According to Finley's account, Forten and Allen led the supporters of African colonization. Allen announced that he would emigrate if he were younger; he also spoke favorably of Cuffe, as well as of the British colony of Sierra Leone. Forten was even more outspoken. He feared that, for blacks to settle in a separate colony within the United States, "our condition must become before many years as bad as it now is, since the white population is continually rolling back, and ere long we must be encompassed again with whites."[42]

If Finley's recounting of his meeting with the Philadelphia blacks is accurate, then Forten and Allen had moved beyond merely advocating a limited missionary-emigration to Africa to the point of viewing African emigration as the solution for the problems of black Americans. Forten repeated these sentiments in late January when, in describing the Bethel protest meeting to Cuffe, he asserted that American blacks "will never become a people until they come out from amongst the white people, but as the majority is decidedly against me I am determined to remain silent, except as to my opinion which I freely give when asked." Given Forten's standing within Philadelphia's black community, however, it is difficult to imagine that he would have been as passive at the Bethel gathering as he indicated to Cuffe. Certainly his chairmanship of the meeting and his appearance on the committee of eleven suggests that he had not deviated from the anti-Colonization Society resolutions which the gathering adopted unanimously. Perhaps he was less than candid in

---

42. On Finley's meeting with the Philadelphia blacks, see the *Boston Recorder*, March 25, 1817, p. 51; and, more completely, Brown, *Biography of Finley*, pp. 122–124. Forten's comment (*ibid.*, p. 123) has been transcribed from third to first person. See also Forten to Cuffe, Philadelphia, January 25, 1817, Cuffe Papers.

both situations—in describing his own participation to Cuffe, and in dealing with the Philadelphia blacks who were so hostile to the Society. Or perhaps in January, 1817, Forten and Allen hoped to mount a large-scale African emigration scheme free from the coercion and degradation implicit in the Colonization Society's program. But Forten, for one, soon completely abandoned emigration. In August he chaired a meeting which not only attacked the Colonization Society by name, but also maintained that African colonization itself "must insure . . . MISERY, *sufferings and perpetual slavery*" to multitudes of blacks.[43]

Free from any doubts about the validity of his views and totally open in his pronouncements, Paul Cuffe was disappointed yet undaunted by the black opposition to colonization developing in early 1817. He urged Forten not to be alarmed, "but be quiet and trust in God who hath done all things well." Refusing to abandon his colonization proposals, he remained convinced that by establishing a colony in the United States as well as one in Africa, blacks would be helping, not fleeing from, their brethren in chains.

But by the winter of 1817 Cuffe's attention began to shift from the regeneration of Africa and the emancipation of the American slave to his own failing health. From February on, he was generally sick and was often wracked by intense pain. Increasingly his thoughts turned to his Maker: "I know that my works are gone to judgement before me, but it is all well, it is all well." Although he recovered briefly in July, he relapsed into fever and continual coughing. In early September he called in his neighbors to share with them his final thoughts. Fittingly, his last audience was the blacks from Westport and environs; with piety, he advised them to follow the teaching of Christianity and to lead morally righteous lives. On September 7, at the age of fifty-eight, Paul Cuffe passed away.[44]

43. *Ibid.*; Garrison, *Thoughts on Colonization*, part II, pp. 10–13.
44. Cuffe to Forten, Westport, March 1, 1817, Cuffe Papers. Cuffe's illness can be traced in Cuffe to Brine, Westport, February 28, 1817; David Cuffe to Freelove Cuffe, Westport, July 8, 1817; Rhoda Cuffe to ?, Westport, September 10, 1817, Cuffe Papers. For the description of Cuffe's last day, see Stephen Gould to Thomas Thompson, Newport, R.I., May 20, 1822, Portfolio 29/38, Friends House Library, London. Cuffe's remarks on divine judgment are quoted in Salvador, *Paul Cuffe*, p. 68.

During the last nine years of his life Cuffe was steadfast in his commitment to his two new enthusiasms—the Society of Friends and emigrationism. As an emigrationist, Cuffe, like Newport Gardner and other New England black emigrationists in the late 1780's and early 1790's, generally was more concerned with redeeming Africa than with emancipating American slaves. Yet there is considerable evidence that for more than a year before his death, Cuffe, long an opponent of the slave trade, focused more and more attention on the plight of those blacks still enslaved in the southern states; he now maintained that colonies in Africa and the United States might expedite the abolition of slavery. Exactly why he changed his orientation is not clear. Still, he was the first black of stature to connect colonization with emancipation. Unlike the white colonizationists, Cuffe was primarily concerned with the future of his black brethren, whether in the United States or in Africa. Although he supported some of the goals of the Colonization Society, he never agreed with those colonizationists who held that blacks were inherently inferior to whites.[45] Rather, Cuffe saw the black man as capable of material and spiritual achievement. His own life had been a model of Christian virtue and incessant industriousness—two traits he thought inseparable and at the very core of man's ability to serve his God.

Cuffe's values, then, were clearly Western, and it was these values

---

45. There is no evidence to suggest that Cuffe criticized the Colonization Society, although this view has persisted. Both Edwin S. Redkey, *Black Exodus: Black Nationalist and Back-to-Africa Movements, 1890–1910* (New Haven: Yale University Press, 1969), p. 19; and Hollis R. Lynch, "Pan-Negro Nationalism in the New World, before 1862," *Boston University Papers on Africa*, II (1966), 155, draw upon Henry Noble Sherwood, "Paul Cuffe and His Contribution to the American Colonization Society," *Proceedings of the Mississippi Valley Historical Association*, VI (1912–13), 370–402, and/or Sherwood, "Paul Cuffe," to support this position. Sherwood's only pertinent comment in this: "When the measure [deportation] took on its most colossal program in 1817, Cuffe cautioned his brethren to watch its operation for a year or two before taking sides for or against it" ("Paul Cuffe," 227). There is no citation for this passage, but evidently Sherwood had misread Cuffe's comments following the latter's return to the United States in 1816. "I recommend to the people of colour in Boston," Cuffe wrote Jedediah Morse from Westport on August 10, 1816, "not to flatter themselves with too great prospect of the first appearance of new things, but after one or two years progress of the new settlers they then will be able to form a more correct idea...." See also Cuffe to William Harris, Westport, August 10, 1816, Cuffe Papers.

which he wished to carry to Africa. In the long run, he argued, Christianity and commerce would turn Africa into a black replica of Western society. Yet, like Martin R. Delany and other emigrationists in the 1850's, Cuffe believed that blacks themselves must come together to control this benevolent if imperialistic venture. And while he never fully developed his views, Cuffe demonstrated nationalistic tendencies which prefigured the full-blown nationalism of the 1850's. He acknowledged the unity of black people in Africa and America, and he hoped that, by encouraging the formation of local black societies in the United States, he would be able to construct a proto-nationalistic organization which would free blacks from their total dependence upon whites and white institutions.

CHAPTER 3

The 1820's: The Rise and Fall of Emigration Sentiment

The death of Paul Cuffe and the formation of the American Colonization Society presented a dilemma for those blacks who had previously embraced emigration. In addition to losing their most effective and best-known advocate, they were confronted with a new symbol of repression. Whatever the exact mixture of benevolence and racism which characterized the Colonization Society at this time, most Afro-Americans viewed the organization as a deportation society whose members believed both in black inferiority and in the necessity of ridding the country of its free black population in order to preserve the institution of slavery. Nevertheless, some blacks worked with or endorsed the Society. There were those who decided that, regardless of the motives of the Colonization Society's members, planting an Afro-American colony in West Africa would free blacks from the degradation they experienced in the United States and present them with new social and economic opportunities. For others, the Colonization Society provided a means of transportation to Africa, enabling them to fulfill missionary ambitions. As a result, in the early 1820's several hundred black Americans with varying purposes emigrated to the colony of Liberia.

Moreover, not all blacks who rejected African colonization were opposed to emigration as such. For a number of these individuals emigration to a nearby black nation such as Haiti provided an alternative to suffering continued oppression at home. Indeed, encouraged by the Haitian government, several thousand blacks reportedly migrated to the Caribbean republic in 1824 and 1825.

However, a large proportion of the emigrants quickly became dissatisfied with their new homes and returned to the United States.

Opposition to African colonization also revived following the collapse of the Haitian emigration movement; by the end of the decade it had broadened into a general attack upon all forms of emigration. In 1831 William Lloyd Garrison orchestrated numerous black protest meetings announcing that blacks would not leave the United States, and after 1833 the national black conventions (which met consecutively from 1830 through 1835) registered opposition to "all plans of colonization any where," while also denouncing the American Colonization Society.[1]

THE FOUNDING OF LIBERIA

When the Colonization Society announced in the fall of 1819 that it would be sending a party of blacks to Africa with the assistance of the federal government, several hundred would-be emigrants applied to the Society.[2] Among those who eventually sailed from New York on the Society's maiden voyage in February, 1820, was the Reverend Daniel Coker, a Baltimore minister and formerly a supporter of Paul Cuffe's initial plan for a limited missionary-emigration to Africa. Not materially equipped to found their colony unassisted, the black settlers were compelled to depend upon both the Society and the federal government to a much greater extent than they had desired. Coker, caught between his friendship with the white agents who led the expedition and the increasingly independent black settlers, was at or near the center of the difficulties and tensions which dominated the two years between the departure of the first emigrants and the actual planting of the colony of Li-

1. *Minutes and Proceedings of the Third Annual Convention, for the Improvement of the Free People of Colour in these United States...1833* (1833). Reprinted in Howard H. Bell, ed., *Minutes of the Proceedings of the National Negro Conventions, 1830–1864* (New York: Arno Press, 1969), pp. 23, 26–28.

2. G. Joseph Wachter, "Early Negro Colonization and America's West African Settlers of 1820–1822" (M.A. thesis, Morgan State College, 1972), pp. 92–93, 95. Wachter's work is an intensive treatment of the two years between the departure of the first Colonization Society vessel in early 1820 and the eventual founding of a black colony on Cape Mesurado in the summer of 1822. It is the first thorough analysis of the role of blacks in this early colonization venture and the only study adequately treating the African side of colonization.

beria at Cape Mesurado on the west coast of Africa. However, after the arrival in March, 1821, of a second emigrant vessel, Coker's pivotal role in the search for a colony was increasingly assumed by the Reverend Lott Cary, a Baptist missionary from Richmond, Virginia. Although Cary was initially an antagonist of the agents, his leadership was eventually recognized by both whites and blacks. Basically committed to preaching the Gospel to indigenous Africans, Cary also recognized what neither Coker nor the American Colonization Society ever understood: that the black American emigrants regarded the Society as a means of transporting them to a land where they hoped to live free from the intrusions of white domination.

Well before the Colonization Society's first group of emigrants departed from New York, its leaders had started to look for territory for the projected colony. In 1817 and 1818 Samuel J. Mills and Ebenezer Burgess, agents of the Society, had undertaken a "mission of inquiry" to England and Africa. Although Mills died before returning to the United States, Burgess arrived in the summer of 1818 ecstatic about Sherbro Island, the home of John Kizell, president of the Friendly Society and a man Mills had regarded as "a second Paul Cuffe." The island, Burgess reported, was "a land stored with the choicest minerals, bearing the richest fruits and covered with a profuse and luxuriant vegetation...." With misleading optimism, he assured the Colonization Society that "the kings in Sherbro promised tracts of land... whenever any of the free people of colour might move thither." Letters Burgess brought back from members of the Friendly Society and from some of the emigrants Cuffe had carried to Sierra Leone also extolled the virtues of the Sherbro region. One of the early emigrants, Perry Lockes, argued that because "there is no man of colour that can say he is not ashamed in America," blacks should come to Africa and work for the conversion of the heathen Africans. Combining providential and materialistic tones, Lockes claimed that "it is the will of GOD for you to come into the possessions of your ancestors." Another emigrant who accompanied Cuffe, Samuel Wilson, heralded the economic advantages of Africa and maintained that his own personal fortune had grown from almost nothing when he arrived in Africa to a hundred pounds. Wilson also criticized the A.M.E. Church

Bishop Richard Allen, who was now an unequivocal foe of African colonization. "When will you become a nation," Wilson finally queried, "if you refuse to come?"[3]

Whatever impact the publication of these letters in the United States may have had, blacks from various parts of the country began to respond to the Colonization Society's attempts to enlist emigrants for a projected expedition. From the Illinois Territory, one Abraham Camp wrote that a large number of free blacks living on the Wabash River were ready to go to Africa, for "... our freedom is partial, and we have no hope that it ever will be otherwise here; therefore, we had rather be gone, though we should suffer hunger and nakedness for years." By the spring of 1819 free blacks from the Wabash area had sold their lands and were waiting to leave for Africa. Significant numbers of blacks from most major cities in the North and South also wrote to the Colonization Society expressing their desire to migrate to Africa. At the same time, President Monroe bowed to the pressure of zealous colonizationists and decided that provisions of the Slave Trade Act of 1819 requiring the government to relocate recaptured Africans would allow cooperation with the Colonization Society. Financial aid would be provided to send to Africa black colonists who could also serve as government laborers constructing camps for the victims of the slave trade.[4]

With federal funds now available and with applications from potential black colonists pouring into the Colonization Society's Washington office, there was no longer any reason to postpone the beginning of the colonization venture. In the fall of 1819 an agent for the Society chartered a 300-ton British-built vessel, the *Elizabeth*, for the trip to Africa, and the charter was quickly transferred to the government. As prospective emigrants began arriving in New

---

3. Philip J. Staudenraus, *The African Colonization Movement, 1816–1865* (New York: Columbia University Press, 1961), pp. 46–50; Wachter, "Early Negro Colonization," pp. 76–79 (quotations from pp. 77, 78); *The Latter Day Luminary*, I (February, 1819), 297–300. A full account of the Mills-Burgess mission can be found in Staudenraus, pp. 41–46; Wachter, pp. 66–76. For Mills's reference to Kizell as "a second Paul Cuffe," see Gardiner Spring, *Memoir of the Rev. Samuel J. Mills* (New York: New York Evangelical Missionary Society, 1820), p. 182.

4. American Colonization Society, *Report*, 3rd (1820), 123–127; Staudenraus, *African Colonization*, pp. 50–56; *Niles' Weekly Register*, XVII (November 27, 1819), 201.

York, the three whites scheduled to lead the expedition—Samuel Bacon and John Bankson, the government agents, and Samuel Crozer, acting for the Colonization Society—selected eighty-eight blacks. The agents never explained what criteria they used in choosing the emigrant party.[5]

Undoubtedly impressed with Coker's superior qualifications, Bacon designated him to help supervise the loading operations. Coker shepherded the other colonists onto the *Elizabeth* and into their cabins on January 31 and was soon invited to live in Bacon's cabin.[6] The willingness of Bacon and the other agents to give Coker special treatment gradually pulled the clergyman away from the other black colonists, who, perhaps swayed by his clerical and educational achievements, were initially very willing to recognize his leadership. At first Coker was the perfect go-between, capable of conversing with both blacks and whites and of mediating whatever disputes might arise.

Dignified in manner, almost regal in appearance, near-white in color, Daniel Coker was a man who had lived much of his life in a netherland between white and black. Called Isaac Wright when he was born in Maryland around 1785 from a union between Susan Coker, an English indentured servant, and an African slave owned by the same master, he assumed his half-brother's name—Daniel Coker—only after leaving Maryland for New York. Coker received his religious education in New York in the Methodist Episcopal Church, and in 1808 Bishop Francis Asbury ordained him a deacon. Soon after his ordination Coker answered a call from several blacks to return to Baltimore to establish a school for black children. More important than his contribution as a teacher, however, was his role in the creation of the African Methodist Episcopal Church. Working with those blacks who had seceded from the white-dominated Methodist congregations, Coker became the first minister of the African Methodist Episcopal Bethel Society, incorporated in 1816. Later in the same year he and the Bethel Church joined with similar black Methodist congregations in Philadelphia, Wilmington, Attleborough, Pennsylvania, and Salem, New Jersey, to create the Af-

---

5. Wachter, "Early Negro Colonization," pp. 92, 96–97; Staudenraus, *African Colonization*, pp. 56–57.

6. Wachter, "Early Negro Colonization," p. 105.

rican Methodist Episcopal Church. Originally elected to serve as the first bishop of the new church, Coker, for reasons which remain unclear, almost immediately resigned this office in favor of Richard Allen. He continued to play an active role in the church, however, until April, 1818. Then, on the basis of charges whose nature has never been disclosed, he was expelled from the A.M.E. Church. Although the expulsion was brief, Coker never regained his former position. Restless, he turned his sights toward African colonization, a subject which had interested him at least as early as 1812, when Paul Cuffe had discussed his plans with Coker and other Baltimore blacks. Although he was not an emissary of the A.M.E. Church, Coker's major purpose in traveling to Africa was to convert the native heathens to Christianity.[7]

As a man accepted at first by both the white agents and his fellow colonists, Coker serves as a prism through which the attitudes of many of the black emigrants can be seen. First of all, Coker was a mediator dealing with individuals with sharply opposing views of Colonization Society and government roles in the settlement venture, as well as of the legitimacy of the authority the white agents were exercising. Moreover, neither the Colonization Society nor Crozer, its agent, had clearly outlined the settlers' relationship with either the Society or the government. Nor did the blacks, when they left New York, have any idea of how the proposed African colony

---

7. There is no adequate biography of Coker. Consequently, my sketch has attempted to sort out the information presented in the often confusing and misleading sources. The following proved the most helpful: Daniel A. Payne, *History of the African Methodist Episcopal Church* (Nashville: Publishing House of the A.M.E. Sunday School Union, 1891), pp. 13, 15, 28, 88–89; James M. Wright, *The Free Negro in Maryland, 1634–1860* (New York: Columbia University Press, 1921), pp. 212–219; David Smith, *Biography of Rev. David Smith, of the A.M.E. Church ...* (1881; reprint ed., Freeport, N.Y.: Books for Libraries Press, 1971), pp. 29–31, 34–37; Francis Asbury, *Journal and Letters of Francis Asbury* (Nashville: Abingdon, 1958), II, pp. 65, 497, 568; Charles H. Wesley, *Richard Allen, Apostle of Freedom* (Washington, D.C.: Associated Publishers, 1935), pp. 130–131, 140–142, 150–154, 166–167, 169; Paul Cuffe's Account Book, entry for May 6, 1812, Paul Cuffe Papers (microfilm), New Bedford, Mass., Free Library. On Allen's attitude toward Coker's mission, compare Wesley, p. 216, and Carol V. R. George, *Segregated Sabbaths: Richard Allen and the Rise of Independent Black Churches, 1760–1840* (New York: Oxford University Press, 1973), pp. 119–120. There is no evidence to support George's claim that Allen endorsed Coker's missionary undertaking in Africa and that Coker "was a representative of the A.M.E. Church...."

would be established or governed. Many simply assumed they would be sovereign in all territorial and political matters. Then, too, government and Colonization Society agents disagreed as to the role of the blacks on board the *Elizabeth*. The former ostensibly saw the blacks as government employees hired to build a station for recaptured Africans, while Crozer held that the blacks were basically colonists who were also prepared to fulfill certain obligations for the government. No one really knew where the government's responsibility ended and where the Society's started, or where the white agents' authority stopped and where the blacks' right to make decisions for themselves began.[8]

Aware that the settlers' uncertainty was giving way to resentment, the agents attempted while en route to Africa to assert their authority and clarify the blacks' obligations. Samuel Crozer decided to produce the skeletal instructions the Society had given him, and Samuel Bacon read this 150-word document to an assembled group of colonists on the first of March. Varying amounts of land were to be granted to the colonists, depending upon marital status and number of children; laborers and mechanics were granted additional acreage. The colonists were to reside on the land and cultivate it; otherwise they would forfeit their holdings. According to the Colonization Society's instructions, they could also lose their land for "misconduct." Finally, Bacon told the blacks that only the white agents could negotiate with the Africans for land. Despite the grants, then, the white agents were still in authority, and it was this thrust of the document which most angered Bacon's listeners. After he was through, Coker moderated a heated debate in which the colonists argued about the terms of the agreement and whether to accept them. Some of the blacks openly opposed the authority of the whites. Following the debate, Coker concluded that some of the more militant blacks were threatening the uneasy truce which had existed since the beginning of the voyage, and he called all the black males to the deck. Defending his own role as confidant and cabinmate of the white agents to those blacks who may have questioned his behavior, Coker argued that "it was determined by the Almighty, that I shall be in the Cabin with the white Agents that I might see and hear for you what was going on." Coker then asked what

---

8. Wachter, "Early Negro Colonization," pp. 110–111.

colonists were "willing to put their confidence in the white Agents, or who had rather have colour'd Agents to go forth to get the land. . . ." All but two of the emigrants followed Coker in supporting the whites.[9]

Despite Coker's success in winning a declaration of loyalty to the white agents, the agents remained afraid of what Samuel Bacon considered "a mutinous spirit" underlying the entire controversy. They tried to assuage the blacks by appointing a few of the colonists to civil and judicial boards. The agents chose three justices or "Members of Council": Coker, first justice; Thomas Camaraw, a 45-year-old New York potter, second justice; and Zerah Hall, 55, a Philadelphia hatter, third justice. The agents also appointed Frederick James, 29, a Philadelphia carpenter, and Nathaniel Peck, 22, of Maryland, to a committee of trade, and they selected a 21-year-old Virginian, Nathaniel Brander, as colonial secretary, and Edward T. Wigfall, a New York tailor, as register of public acts.[10]

With the situation somewhat under control, the *Elizabeth* arrived at Sierra Leone in early March, and the agents began to prepare for the acquisition of land for an Afro-American settlement. Unfortunately for the settlers, Charles McCarthy, the British governor, did not offer the American agents any assistance. Although Bacon, Bankson, and Crozer assured McCarthy that land in West Africa would be purchased by a private organization, the American Colonization Society, and not by the United States government, the Brit-

9. Jehudi Ashmun, *Memoir of the Life and Character of the Rev. Samuel Bacon, A.M.*... (Washington: Jacob Gideon, 1822), pp. 249–250, 287; Wachter, "Early Negro Colonization," p. 247n; Elijah Johnson, Esq's Journal, pp. 301–302, as copied by Christian Wiltberger, Jr., in the rear of the Wiltberger Diary, February 2, 1821–December 31, 1831, Manuscript Division, Library of Congress; Daniel Coker, *Journal of Daniel Coker, a Descendant of Africa...in the ship Elizabeth, on a Voyage for Sherbro in Africa* (Baltimore: Press of Edward J. Coale, 1820), pp. 18–19.

10. Coker, *Journal*, p. 19; Ashmun, *Memoir of Bacon*, pp. 249–251; [Edward T. Wigfall], *The First and Accurate Account of One of the American Colonists, Who Has Returned to the United States of America* (New York: Printed for the Author, 1821), p. 2. The *Elizabeth*'s colonists are listed and identified in "Roll of Emigrants That Have Been Sent To The Colony of Liberia, Western Africa, By the American Colonization Society and Its Auxiliaries, To September, 1843, &c.," *Senate Documents*, 28th cong., 2nd sess., 1844, IX, pp. 152–154. Wigfall, however, is incorrectly identified. See *Longworth's American Almanac, New York Register and City Directory, 1819*.

ish governor was not satisfied. He refused to waive the existing trade regulations, and he made no overtures of temporary aid for the landless blacks. The agents immediately decided to investigate whether John Kizell would help, and Bankson quickly departed for Sherbro Island to confer with Kizell.[11]

When the government agent arrived at Sherbro, he found Kizell more than willing to provide the black settlers with temporary accommodations at his own site, Campelar. The Sherbro trader had previously constructed huts for the blacks whom Mills and Burgess had indicated would be coming shortly, but as the months had passed Kizell had lost all hope. Now he was overjoyed to learn that the first settlers would soon arrive at Sherbro. The *Elizabeth*'s colonists actually descended upon Campelar only a few days after Bankson had departed the island, for Bacon and Crozer decided to leave Freetown before Bankson's party had returned. Fortunately, the *Elizabeth* met Bankson heading back toward Sierra Leone. Once united, the entire party sailed toward Kizell's encampment on Sherbro. Their first glimpse of the island must have been unnerving. "[W]e can see the little towns on the shore," Coker observed, "eight and ten houses together, built round and thatched with grass. The natives sit naked on the shore, looking on us with surprise as we sail."[12]

Soon after the colonists arrived, Kizell stepped into the middle of a dispute which on the surface merely reflected many of the colonists' personal hostilities toward Coker but which at root was an outgrowth of the deeply felt suspicions of many of the blacks toward the white agents and anyone acting in their stead. The trouble erupted when Crozer, the Colonization Society agent, charged one of the settlers, Francis Creecy, with stealing provisions. When Coker presided over the trial, Creecy objected vigorously, proclaiming that he would not permit a mulatto to judge him. Kizell then intervened on Coker's side, arguing that the strikingly fair

11. Coker, *Journal*, p. 21; Ashmun, *Memoir of Bacon*, pp. 255–256; Wachter, "Early Negro Colonization," pp. 121–123, 126–128; George E. Brooks, Jr., *Yankee Traders, Old Coasters, and African Middlemen: A History of American Legitimate Trade with West Africa in the Nineteenth Century* (Boston: Boston University Press, 1970), p. 167; [Wigfall], *First and Accurate Account*, p. 3.

12. [Wigfall], *First and Accurate Account*, pp. 3–5; Ashmun, *Memoir of Bacon*, pp. 257–258; Coker, *Journal*, pp. 32–33.

minister was still "a descendant of Africa," and that no further distinctions should be made. If the colonists would not support Coker, Kizell and his supporters would. The Sherbro trader concluded by arguing that although some men refused to accept any rule—black, white, or mulatto—at Campelar, "the civil authority must and shall be obeyed." Found guilty, an enraged Creecy assaulted Crozer.[13]

Aside from Creecy's trial, the first few days at Campelar were idyllic. The weather was cool and pleasant, and the emigrants spent their free moments throwing out nets for the plentiful fish in the river nearby. Soon, however, previously unnoted fatal flaws in Kizell's paradisiacal retreat became painfully apparent. The site was poorly located; this itself could threaten the health of the party. Situated midway on the eastern side of Sherbro, Campelar was a flat, muddy area of little vegetation. Mangrove trees sheltered the area from the normal wind currents, and the air hung heavy. The water was so foul that, unknown to the colonists at first, Kizell himself imported fresh water. In early April fever began to strike down the colonists with unmerciful regularity. By April 6 twenty-one of them were sick; in the following days the number of ill colonists mounted, while the white agents also succumbed. By April 10 Bacon was the only agent able to function at even a minimal level, and he was depressed by mounting complaints and the widespread pilfering of supplies.[14] More serious, the blacks again openly challenged his authority. Coker, whose influence among the emigrants was waning, sided with Bacon while still trying to give some of the blacks the impression that in reality his loyalty was theirs. Sick, hungry, and disillusioned by what was transpiring at Campelar, few of the blacks were receptive to either his claims or Bacon's.

Many of the blacks simply wanted to leave Campelar for higher—and healthier—ground. After a month in Africa they were no closer to founding their colony than they had been when they arrived. A rumor that the sick agents and Coker were about to return to Sierra Leone deepened the emigrants' long-standing distrust of the white

13. Ashmun, *Memoir of Bacon*, p. 258; Coker, *Journal*, pp. 36–37; Wachter, "Early Negro Colonization," pp. 143–144.

14. Coker, *Journal*, p. 35; Charles H. Huberich, *The Political and Legislative History of Liberia* (New York: Central Book Co., 1947), I, pp. 125, 127–128; [Wigfall], *First and Accurate Account*, p. 5; Ashmun, *Memoir of Bacon*, pp. 260, 264–268. See also the following four paragraphs.

authorities and those who identified closely with them. Fearful of being abandoned and aware of how little influence they had upon the daily operations of the expedition, the blacks sent Samuel Bacon a petition which asserted that they had rights which the agents must respect, and which demanded that they be given advance knowledge of what actions the agents were planning to take. They poignantly reminded Bacon of the extent of their suffering: "We have now arrived to the trying point[;] we are sick, almost naked and really do suffer of such things as was said to be in store for us. . . ." Not surprisingly, Coker's name was not among those appended to the petition.[15]

Bacon immediately called a meeting to be held in Kizell's church. But suddenly the racial animosity, which was never far from the surface, emerged. Jonathan Adams, a Philadelphia tanner, rose and claimed that "Mr K[izell], the King & the head men, are waiting for our Agents, and they will not let a *white* man have the land, but the head man whom they give the land to must be a *black* man." Adams then brought Kizell even more directly into the confrontation by claiming that Kizell would not negotiate with the native chieftains unless he was given a free hand. When Kizell interjected that Adams had misunderstood him, Bacon would not accept the Sherbro trader's explanation and accused Kizell of rallying the emigrants against him.[16]

Both Bacon and John Bankson died within a few weeks of the protest, and Coker became the acting agent for both the government and the Colonization Society. In addition to assuming responsibility for the colonists remaining at Sherbro, he also became the only individual who could legitimately negotiate with the local chieftains. Unfortunately, Coker was unable to arrest the steady decline in the expedition's fortunes; by mid-June twenty blacks had died.[17] Not surprisingly Coker, the white agents' surrogate, also replaced them as the target of the settlers' enmity. Almost anyone assuming charge of the party would have received the censure of the colonists, still

---

15. Ashmun, *Memoir of Bacon*, p. 271; Wachter, "Early Negro Colonization," pp. 144-145; Johnson Journal, p. 307.

16. Johnson Journal, pp. 307-308.

17. Ashmun, *Memoir of Bacon*, pp. 277-278, 288; Johnson Journal, p. 310; Huberich, *Liberia*, I, 134-136.

acutely aware of the yawning gap between their dreams of happiness and prosperity in Africa and the reality of bare sustenance in the marshy lowlands of Kizell's Campelar. Coker, however, brought special liabilities to his new position. Despite his previous efforts to occupy a middle ground, many of the settlers had come to think of him as more interested in maintaining his influence among the white agents than in protecting the blacks' own interests. In addition, Coker's alliance with Kizell proved only temporary. Undoubtedly resentful that Coker, not himself, had replaced the whites, the Sherbro trader quickly sided with the emigrants in the ongoing strife at Campelar. Once the defender of Coker against the charges of a black who refused to accept the judgment of a mulatto, now Kizell was able to use Coker's complexion to fan the smoldering resentment of the settlers. Later, in defending his own behavior, Kizell made clear his own racial views: "White blood is good, and black blood is good, but they [the natives] know that mulattos are bastards, and will have no dealings with them."[18]

For the settlers at Campelar, Coker's actions upon assuming the Colonization Society and government agencies were the immediate cause for dissatisfaction. Claiming that he was responsible for providing for the recaptured Africans who would eventually come under his care, Coker refused to give the colonists all of the provisions they requested. Some of the blacks would not accept Coker's explanation. Wigfall, the register of public accounts, later recounted that Coker "took great care to secrete [sic] a great deal for himself, and let his fellow creatures suffer for want, many of whom died...." Yet the emigrants were ever mindful of the precarious nature of their own health and of the necessity of leaving Kizell's ill-fated settlement. Accordingly, when Coker arranged to move the group temporarily to higher ground, a place called Yonie, the settlers rejected Kizell's last-minute attempts to induce them to remain at Campelar and voted to follow Coker.[19]

On the surface, conditions improved at Yonie. Many of the settlers regained their health. Yet the ill feeling between Coker and

---

18. [Wigfall], *First and Accurate Account*, pp. 6, 8; Huberich, *Liberia*, I, 129–130.

19. Johnson Journal, pp. 313–315; [Wigfall], *First and Accurate Account*, pp. 6, 8.

the emigrants only festered. No progress was made in the negotiations for land; the Sherbro headmen maintained that they would not cede land to the emigrants as long as Coker presided over the expedition. Angry because they were still without land, convinced that Coker was denying them provisions rightfully theirs, and generally dissatisfied with the leadership of a man who had only occasionally identified himself with their interests, the settlers began to threaten Coker's hegemony. Although the blacks began to demand pay for whatever labor they performed and even for attending religious services, more serious was a direct challenge to Coker's authority in August. Wigfall, Zerah Hall (the third justice and thus also a member of the skeletal civil authority which had been established), and several others moved to form a seven-man committee which, while ostensibly committed to helping the sick, would essentially act to secure a more equitable share of the provisions for the colonists. Coker's response was immediate. Charging that Wigfall was "mutinizing the people," Coker refused to consider the emigrants' demands.[20]

Coker finally decided his position at Yonie was so tenuous that it would be wise for him to leave the settlement. It is not clear whether he abandoned the colonists, as many of them later charged, or left because a loose alliance of emigrants and native chieftains threatened his continued hegemony—if not his life. He was no doubt exhausted by the dissension which swirled around him, and he was also aware he would not be able to continue much longer as agent for both the Colonization Society and the government. Threats of violence against his person undoubtedly played a part in his decision, for in September an African said that Coker "ought to be cut into pound pieces," and he suggested that the minister leave Sherbro. Coker and twelve other settlers immediately left the island for Freetown, waiting there for reinforcements and additional provisions from America.[21]

Coker had been at the British colony only a few days when an American naval ship arrived with instructions from the Colonization

20. Johnson Journal, p. 313; Huberich, *Liberia*, I, 122, 125, 129; [Wigfall], *First and Accurate Account*, pp. 7–9.
21. [Wigfall], *First and Accurate Account*, pp. 9–10.

Society. For Coker, the arrival of the American vessel presented an opportunity to give his own version of what had transpired at Sherbro. Coker charged that Kizell had prevented the colonists from successfully negotiating with the native chieftains, and that he had encouraged discord among the settlers themselves. Coker also pointed his finger at rebellious blacks, and, acting upon the advice of Navy Captain Alexander Wadsworth, discharged several from the party. Wadsworth insisted that Coker keep the settlement at Yonie together until another emigrant party arrived. He gave Coker fresh supplies for the remnant of the *Elizabeth*'s colonists at Yonie, as well as additional presents to expedite negotiations.[22]

Coker's return to Yonie was far from a triumphant homecoming, for the blacks who had remained on Sherbro had not forgotten what they considered to be his treacherous behavior. Nor did the sight of Coker coming ashore accompanied by two white naval officers mollify their anger, because the emigrants immediately understood that the acting agent was returning in an attempt to regain his personal authority as well as that of the Colonization Society and the American government. However, before Coker and the colonists could begin the inevitable hostilities, Kizell arrived, claiming that Coker was responsible for the dissension which had all but destroyed the colonization venture. In Kizell's recounting, Coker had continued the practices of the deceased agents by refusing to give the Sherbro chieftains the amount of rum obviously necessary to conclude successful negotiations. Offended also when Coker called them "nothing but imposters and blood-suckers," the Africans would not grant the emigrants land as long as Coker represented the party. The chieftains, Kizell further explained with the colonists nodding in approval, also spurned Coker because of his fair complexion. In fact, Coker's skin color reminded the emigrants of the America they had fled: "[We] have seen enough of slavery, that we are now in a free country where we mean to enjoy liberty, ease and comfort, and will not be under the government of whites, and particularly under that of Mr. Coker, a mulatto." Overwhelmed by this hostility, Coker left the island again in late October to re-

22. American Colonization Society, *Report*, 4th (1821), 20–21; [Wigfall], *First and Accurate Account*, p. 10; Huberich, *Liberia*, I, 116–132.

turn to Sierra Leone and await instructions from the agents on the next colonization ship.[23]

Finally the second emigrant vessel, the *Nautilus*, reached Freetown on March 8—almost a year after the *Elizabeth* had arrived in Africa. Two agents representing the government (Jonathan Winn and Samuel Bacon's brother Ephraim) and two Colonization Society agents (the Reverend Joseph R. Andrus and his assistant, Christian Wiltberger) headed the expedition. The thirty-two new black emigrants included Coker's wife and two children and two black missionaries from Richmond, Lott Cary and Colin Teague.[24] Cary was born a slave around 1780 in Charles City County, Virginia. Sent to Richmond in 1804, he was hired out as a common laborer at the largest tobacco warehouse in the city. After teaching himself to read and write, the Virginia slave was promoted to superintend the warehouse and oversee the work of other laborers. In 1813 Cary was able to purchase freedom for himself and his two children—his wife having previously died. Teague, a skilled saddle and harness maker, had also purchased his freedom.

Both Cary and Teague were members of Richmond's First Baptist Church, a congregation that until 1842 was interracial, though largely black in membership. The devout Cary became deeply interested in Christianizing his African brethren, and in 1815—at the very time that Cuffe was maturing his plans to establish a Christian mission in Africa—he and William Crane, a white member of the First Baptist Church, organized the Richmond African Baptist Missionary Society. Two years later the Society convinced the Triennial Baptist Convention to go on record as favoring an African mission, but it was not until the American Colonization Society decided to establish a settlement that Cary personally committed himself to missionary work in Africa. In January, 1821, Cary and Teague, his colleague in the Richmond African Baptist Society, left for Africa with funds provided by the Society and the Baptist Board of Foreign Missions.[25]

23. [Wigfall], *First and Accurate Account*, pp. 11-12; Huberich, *Liberia*, I, 130.
24. Wachter, "Early Negro Colonization," pp. 170-173.
25. On Lott Cary, see Ralph R. Gurley's sketch in the appendix to Gurley, *Life of Jehudi Ashmun, Late Colonial Agent in Liberia*... (Washington, D.C.: J. C. Dunn, 1835), pp. 147-148; *The Latter Day Luminary*, VI (December, 1825), 353-354; Solomon Peck, "History of the Missions of the Baptist General Con-

Although friction on board the *Nautilus* was minimal during the trip across the Atlantic, the problems that arose once the new colonists arrived in Sierra Leone were a virtual replication of those encountered by the emigrants on the *Elizabeth*. Conditions at the new colonists' temporary site, a plantation at Fourah Bay near Freetown, in no way approached those which the first expedition had endured at Sherbro. But even at Fourah Bay sickness and internal dissension soon tempered the once heady mood of agents and settlers alike. Fever struck several of the new emigrants—including Coker's two sons—and later was responsible for the deaths of two of the agents. More important, lack of a clear understanding as to the relationship between the settlers and the agents again led to bickering and strife. Almost from the moment the *Nautilus* arrived in Africa, Cary and Teague were unhappy with their ambiguous status, uncertain about their responsibilities to the government and to the Colonization Society, and, finally, disturbed by demands from the agents which they feared would hinder their work as missionaries. Cary quickly became so dissatisfied that he wrote to the Baptist Board of Foreign Missions to complain about the agents for both the Colonization Society and the government. "If you intend doing anything for Africa," he concluded, "you must not wait for the Colonization Society, nor for the government, for neither of these are in search of missionary grounds." Moreover, when a dispute broke out between the colonists and the agents at Fourah Bay, Teague and Cary announced that they would not be bound by the Colonization Society's

---

vention," in *History of American Missions to the Heathen, from their Commencement to the Present Time* (Worcester: Spooner & Howland, 1840), p. 443; Lucius E. Smith, ed., *Heroes and Martyrs of the Modern Missionary Enterprise: A Record of their Lives and Labors* ... (Providence, R.I.: O. W. Potter, 1860), pp. 355-356; *The Missionary Jubilee: An Account of the Fiftieth Anniversary of the American Baptist Missionary Union, at Philadelphia, May 24, 25, and 26, 1864...*, rev. ed. (New York: Sheldon and Co., 1871), pp. 18-19; *Maryland Colonization Journal*, n.s. IV (April, 1848), 167. For Teague, see "Roll of Emigrants," p. 155; *The Latter Day Luminary*, I (May, 1819), 401; *Maryland Colonization Journal*, n.s. III (August, 1846), 220-221. On their efforts to become African missionaries, see *Proceedings of the General Convention of the Baptist Denomination...1817*, p. 134; *The Latter Day Luminary*, I (May, 1819), 384; and II (May, 1821), 399; *Missionary Jubilee...*, pp. 215, 242, 267; Peck, "History of Missions," p. 439; *Genius of Universal Emancipation*, I (April, 1822), 161. See also Luther P. Jackson, "Religious Development of the Negro in Virginia from 1760 to 1860," *Journal of Negro History*, XVI (April, 1931), 221, 224.

agents. Almost two months later the two missionaries accused Andrus, the Society's chief agent, of hoarding provisions for the agents; the following week they again opposed the Colonization Society's authority by refusing to sign the Society's Constitution when Andrus and Wiltberger circulated it among the colonists.[26]

Daniel Coker recognized that the problems between the *Nautilus*'s colonists and the agents were reminiscent of what had transpired on board the *Elizabeth* and at Sherbro. However, his role as an onlooker to the disputes of others quickly ended when some of the blacks from Yonie drifted into Fourah Bay with tales of Coker's behavior which were far different from what the black minister had recounted to the white agents. By mid-May the charges against Coker had grown to such proportions that the chief government agent, Jonathan Winn, arranged for Coker and the Sherbro settlers to confront one another. Here the emigrants accused Coker of exaggerating the extent of the rebelliousness at Sherbro, and they implied that he had abandoned them at Yonie. Finally, John Kizell descended upon Fourah Bay, repeating his earlier charges to the naval officers. Although neither Andrus nor Bacon believed Kizell, both Winn and Christian Wiltberger found the accumulation of criticisms against Coker more and more persuasive.[27] Coker even alienated some of the new black colonists; in September a few of them challenged the propriety of having him perform a wedding ceremony, and Teague feared that if the Baltimore clergyman presided over the occasion, the result would be "the Splitting of the Colony."[28]

With Coker clearly isolated from any position of influence, Cary and Teague sought to organize the settlers for united action in their relationships with the white agents. Under their leadership, blacks from both emigrant groups formed the American African Union Society in December to mediate disputes among the colonists and to

---

26. Wachter, "Early Negro Colonization," pp. 180–181, 190–194, 202; *The Latter Day Luminary*, II (May, 1821), 398–399; Wiltberger Diary, pp. 43–44. Lott Cary is in error when he says Samuel Coker died on the *Nautilus* while the ship was crossing the Atlantic. See *The Latter Day Luminary*, II (May, 1821), 397, 399.

27. Wachter, "Early Negro Colonization," pp. 195–200; Wiltberger Diary, pp. 68, 80, 89–90, 103, 109–110; Daniel Coker Diary, April 12, 1821–September 12, 1821, Manuscript Division, Library of Congress, esp. pp. 11, 12, 16–17, 21.

28. Wiltberger Diary, p. 230.

represent them in controversies with the agents. Cary served as president and Teague as vice-president; even Coker, perhaps hoping to bridge the gap between himself and the settlers, agreed to become corresponding secretary. But when a committee from the new society sought to confer with Dr. Eli Ayres, who had been the principal agent for both the American Colonization Society and the United States government since late October, they were flatly rebuffed. Ayres simply told Cary that he would not deal with the black organization, and this embryonic attempt to secure representation and influence was quashed.[29]

Although still subordinate to Ayres's authority, most of the blacks moved in early April to Cape Mesurado, some two hundred and fifty miles to the south. By raising the spectre of American naval intervention, Ayres and Navy Lieutenant Robert Field Stockton had forced several native chieftains there to deed land to the Colonization Society for less than $300 worth of trinkets, food, guns, and rum. Coker and several other blacks elected to remain in Sierra Leone, the Baltimore minister accepting Governor McCarthy's offer to administer an African resettlement village at Hastings in the British colony.[30] Cary and Teague somewhat reluctantly joined those who journeyed to Cape Mesurado. Although confronted by hostile Africans, an advance party had cleared ground and constructed huts on Perservance Island, across the Mesurado River from the mainland. The island was far less healthy than the Cape itself, but the settlers were afraid to cross the river. In mid-May, when provisions and arms were running short and several of the colonists had taken ill, Ayres advocated abandoning the settlement. Cary and several other settlers led a majority who refused to leave. As Ayres later recounted the event, the blacks "were afraid if they left the place, there might some circumstance occur by which they might lose the situation, and they had rather risk their lives in the place, than run the least hazard of losing a place possessing so many advantages." When both Ayres and Wiltberger left the area, Cary and

29. *Ibid.*, p. 267; Wachter, "Early Negro Colonization," p. 208.
30. Wachter, "Early Negro Colonization," pp. 214–215, 218–219, 268n; Christopher Fyfe, *A History of Sierra Leone* (London: Oxford University Press, 1962), pp. 133, 181; "Report from the Select Committee on the Present State of the Settlements of Sierra Leone and Fernando Po," *Parliamentary Papers*, X (1830), appendix, 134.

Elijah Johnson, a 35-year-old New Yorker, assumed leadership of the small band of blacks. Together, they supervised the defense of the settlement after the colonists defied the Africans by moving to the mainland in July.[31]

The settlement was far from secure when a new Colonization Society agent, Jehudi Ashmun, arrived in August. Ashmun organized the colony into a military and civil force, appointing Johnson as commissary of stores; R. H. Sampson, a 50-year-old Virginia black who had purchased his freedom, as commissary of ordnance; and Cary as health officer and government inspector. Cary quickly learned enough basic medicine to care for the ill. He also helped rally the settlers in warding off an estimated 800 Africans who attacked in early November, and another 1,500 a month later. Far from discouraged by the hostilities, the Richmond missionary compared the colonists' efforts to those of the Jews and declared that "there has never been an hour or a minute, no not even when the balls were flying around my head, when I could wish myself back in America." Cary's leadership did not go unnoticed, for an American captain sailing along the African coast during this period later recalled that the missionary "was at times left as the sole agent of the colony, and it would have been broken up and abandoned were it not for his indominable firmness, and persevereing [sic] energy."[32]

Despite Cary's efforts on behalf of the colony, he and many of his followers retained their skepticism about the legitimacy and wisdom of the white agents. In their own eyes the blacks were independent settlers, and eventually, after a succession of crises, they were able to compel the Colonization Society to effect a reorganization that took their demands into account. First Ayres, returning

---

31. Wachter, "Early Negro Colonization," pp. 214–219, 226; Huberich, *Liberia*, I, 199–213; J[ehudi] Ashmun, *History of the American Colony in Liberia from December 1821 to 1823* (Washington, D.C.: Way and Gideon, 1826), pp. 8–14, 16; American Colonization Society, *Report*, 6th (1823), 9–11. On Johnson, see Huberich, *Liberia*, I, 225.

32. Staudenraus, *African Colonization*, pp. 87–89, 269n; Archibald Alexander, *History of Colonization on the Western Coast of Africa*, 2nd ed. (Philadelphia: W. S. Martien, 1849), p. 181; Ashmun, *History of the American Colony*, pp. 27–29; Gurley, *Life of Ashmun*, appendix, pp. 149, 151; *The Latter Day Luminary*, VI (December, 1825), 355; Norman R. Bennett and George E. Brooks, Jr., eds., *New England Merchants in Africa: A History through Documents, 1802 to 1865* (Boston: Boston University Press, 1965), p. 113.

briefly to the colony late in 1823, aroused many of the settlers by what they deemed his arbitrary reassignment of land sites. Those who had arrived earliest in the colony had already constructed homes on some of the sites which he was reassigning in accordance with his policy of giving all settlers equal amounts of land. Outraged when Ayres announced that he would stop all food rations after June 1, 1824, unless the dissension ended, the protesters drew up a remonstrance to the Colonization Society charging that the lots were unfairly and improperly distributed, that a regulation to build on the lots within two years was impracticable, and that the agents the Society was sending out were incompetent. After Ayres returned to the United States in December, 1823, the protesters challenged Ashmun by refusing to engage in the required two days a week of public labor. Moreover, a large group would not work on the land survey. When Ashmun threatened to refuse rations to those who would not work, Cary led a party of colonists into the storehouse, where they seized food and arms. After Cary and his followers took arms for a second time, Ashmun, realizing he could no longer govern, fled Monrovia.[33]

The issue was really not the distribution of the land sites, but the question of how much authority and control Cary and his followers would accept. Recognizing the seriousness of the missionary's challenge, a representative of the Colonization Society, Ralph R. Gurley, concluded that the colonists would have to be granted more responsibility. While investigating the colony in the summer of 1824, Gurley drafted a new plan of civil government which, although retaining power in the hands of the Society's board of managers, nevertheless provided for the creation of a colony advisory council to be composed of black settlers. The Colonization Society, then, had retained hegemony over the colony while at the same time recognizing the settlers' right to petition and to control their own affairs to a limited degree. Cary himself profited by the new arrangement, for in September, 1826—two and a half years after his rebellion—he was appointed vice-agent of Liberia.[34] Cary and his

33. Staudenraus, *African Colonization*, pp. 90–93; Gurley, *Life of Ashmun*, pp. 182–183, 186–187, 189–195; Huberich, *Liberia*, I, 296, 310–313.

34. Staudenraus, *African Colonization*, pp. 94–96; Gurley, *Life of Ashmun*, appendix, pp. 150, 153.

followers had finally made the point that the Sherbro settlers had earlier tried to make: that they expected to have some impact upon the administration of the colonization venture, and that they would not abide by the needless suffering and poor management which black emigrants had endured ever since the *Elizabeth* left New York in February, 1820. For many of these early black colonists, the white presence in Liberia was a necessary yet unwelcome intrusion.

Toward Nearer Shores: Haiti

Despite the fact that some three to four hundred blacks emigrated to Liberia during the early 1820's, opposition to African colonization still ran deep. Former Cuffe supporters James Forten and Richard Allen continued to oppose African colonization, partly because they were dubious of the motives of the scheme's white sponsors, and partly because they feared Liberia's treacherous climate and hostile neighbors. However, such men did not necessarily reject all emigration proposals. Like many of their fellow blacks in the North during the early part of the nineteenth century, they often moved back and forth between competing—and sometimes contradictory—ideological positions. Although almost all of the alternatives proposed by black leaders of this period rested upon a common belief in racial solidarity and the necessity for independent black action, the pressures of the moment and of their constituencies usually pushed them in one particular direction or another. Consequently, it is not surprising that, when white organizers of an emigration movement to Haiti shrewdly encouraged blacks to form separate emigration societies in the mid-1820's, many black leaders outspoken in their opposition to African colonization seriously considered the claims of the nearby black nation.

A significant episode in the evolution of Afro-American emigration, the Haitian emigration movement of the 1820's must also be seen as a development rooted in Haitian history. In trying to attract thousands of black Americans to Haiti, the country's leaders were engaged in only the latest of several such attempts undertaken in the twenty years after Haiti became independent. In 1804 the governor-general of Haiti, hoping to enlarge his army and augment the depleted male population, offered American ship captains financial incentives to transport blacks to the island. More than a decade later Joseph Balthazar Inginac, the secretary-general, wrote on behalf of King Henri Christophe to urge blacks in New York City to emigrate to his country. Assuring American blacks that they "will find but little difference in our manner of living from that of the place they shall leave," Inginac spoke enthusiastically of the commercial and agricultural possibilities awaiting blacks upon their arrival in Haiti. The government itself, which would protect them, also pledged to pay the passages of penurious emigrants and to grant "bounties of land" to the new arrivals.[35]

Few if any blacks accepted Inginac's offer. Then in 1820 the British abolitionist Thomas Clarkson and Cuffe's former supporter, Prince Sanders, developed a plan whereby Haiti would serve as an asylum for emancipated slaves from the United States. Christophe displayed a keen interest in the project and was willing to supply a vessel and an initial donation of $25,000 to help defray the expenses of the venture. He and Sanders were about to sign a formal agreement when the king committed suicide in October, 1820. Yet Sanders, aware that Haiti was short of skilled labor and needed emigrants, did not give up his hopes for a large-scale emigration of American blacks to Haiti. Undoubtedly his motivation was in part pecuniary; he wanted to establish a commercial bridge between Haiti and the United States, and he probably believed that a sizeable emigration to Haiti would be highly beneficial to his own interests. By the spring of 1823 Sanders was convinced that there were thousands of free blacks in various parts of the United States who were anxious to move to Haiti. "These same persons," he emphasized, *"are waiting, anxiously waiting....* If there could be an interval of tranquillity and good government of sufficient duration for them to remove and get a little established, they would soon be so numerous —they would have a favourable influence in producing a salutary change upon the whole state of things there."[36]

35. *American Missionary Register*, VI (October, 1825), 293; *Niles' Weekly Register*, XV (October 17, 1818), 117–118. See also John Edward Baur, "Mulatto Machiavelli, Jean Pierre Boyer, and the Haiti of His Day," *Journal of Negro History*, XXXII (July, 1947), 324.
36. Earl Leslie Griggs, *Thomas Clarkson: The Friend of Slaves* (London: George Allen & Unwin, 1936), pp. 133-134; Earl Leslie Griggs and Clifford H. Prator, eds., *Henry Christophe and Thomas Clarkson: A Correspondence* (Berkeley and Los

By early 1824 some black Americans were beginning to contemplate emigration to the Caribbean nation, and the Haitian government again assured friends in the United States of its continued interest in recruiting black emigrants. "Make known, sir, to the unfortunate descendants of Africans, in the United States," a close aid to President Jean Pierre Boyer of Haiti wrote to a Massachusetts correspondent in January, "that when they may be at liberty to come hither, they will find in us brothers, ever ready to receive them." By spring a few blacks had accepted Haiti's invitation. The Reverend Thomas Paul, the organizer of the black Baptist church in both New York and Boston and a former missionary in Haiti, helped send five Boston Afro-Americans to Inginac; the secretary-general paid their passages and put them to work on one of his coffee plantations. Nevertheless, the likelihood of this trickle becoming a steady stream of emigration was slight unless an organization was formed in the United States to capitalize upon the already favorable attitude which now existed in the minds of many blacks.[37]

Ironically, the catalyst was a young white agent of the American

---

Angeles: University of California Press, 1952), pp. 226–227, 249; Prince Sanders to Robert[s] Vaux, Philadelphia, December 31, 1822, Vaux Papers, Historical Society of Pennsylvania. On Sanders's earlier attempts to promote the attractions of Haiti to black Americans, see *Poulson's American Daily Advertiser*, January 30, 1817, p. 3; Griggs and Prator, eds., *Christophe and Clarkson*, pp. 226, 248. Although Sanders frequently criticized the Haitian government in his letters to Clarkson, he still retained faith in the future of the country. See his letter to Vaux cited above. Moreover, Sanders returned to Haiti in 1823 or 1824 and later became attorney general. *Société Philanthropique d'Haiti*, no. 2 (September, 1824), 10; Maxwell Whiteman, "Prince Saunders: Lecturer, Churchman and Attorney General," note preceding the republication of three works by Sanders—*Haytian Papers, 1818; An Address Delivered at Bethel Church, Philadelphia: 1818;* and *A Memoir Presented to the American Convention for Promoting the Abolition of Slavery, 1819* [i.e., 1818] (Philadelphia: Rhistoric Publications, 1969). See also Betty Fladeland, *Men and Brothers: Anglo-American Antislavery Cooperation* (Urbana: University of Illinois Press, 1972), pp. 97–103.

37. *Genius of Universal Emancipation*, III (June, 1824), 177–178; Gen. B. Inginac to Jacob Peabody, Port-au-Prince, June 25, 1824, with an English translation and a copy of a guarantee of passage money for the emigrants signed by five citizens of Boston, Houghton Library, Harvard University; *Boston Recorder*, August 7, 1824, pp. 125–126. On Paul, see John Dowling, "Rev. Thos. Paul and the Colored Baptist Churches," *The Baptist Memorial and Monthly Record*, VIII (September, 1849), 295–297; *The Latter Day Luminary*, V (April, 1824), 110–112; George, *Segregated Sabbaths*, pp. 145–147.

Colonization Society, the Reverend Loring D. Dewey, who at the time was working in New York. Finding it difficult to stimulate support for African colonization, Dewey turned to Haitian emigration and in early 1824 was corresponding with President Boyer. Believing Dewey was acting as a representative for the Colonization Society, Boyer pledged that his government would transport Afro-Americans to Haiti and grant the emigrants land for homesteads. He then dispatched a black man, Jonathan Granville, to the United States to act as the agent of the Haitian government. Meanwhile in New York, Dewey, disregarding the opposition of the American Colonization Society and its New York auxiliary, organized white colonizationists into the Society for Promoting the Emigration of Free Persons of Colour to Hayti. A few weeks later Episcopal Bishop James Kemp and other whites formed the Baltimore Emigration Society as an auxiliary to the New York group.[38]

While Dewey was moving among New York City's white colonizationists, blacks in the city were becoming intrigued by the Boyer government's overtures. In mid-June a group of them held a meeting to initiate an organization which would assist in the selection of emigrants and help those chosen. Yet they were suspicious of the whites active in the new movement. Speaking for those attending the organizational meeting, the Presbyterian minister Samuel Cornish and Peter Williams, the Episcopal clergyman who had earlier led the Cuffe-allied African Institution of New York, castigated white participants in the Haitian movement for describing free blacks as degraded and vicious inhabitants of the lowest strata of society. Despite this denunciation, the white society soon approved the establishment of the black auxiliary, the Haytian Emigration Society of Coloured People. Shortly thereafter Granville assured the new black organization that emigrants would find little difficulty in adjusting to Haiti. "Your religious belief differs, in some points, from ours," he admitted, "but we all worship the same

38. Staudenraus, *African Colonization*, pp. 79–84; *Genius of Universal Emancipation*, III, Supplement (1824), 193–197; New York *Commercial Advertiser*, June 24, 1824, p. 2; *New York Statesman*, June 24, 1824, p. 2; Loring D. Dewey, ed., *Correspondence relative to the Emigration to Hayti of the Free People of Colour in the United States together with Instructions to the Agent sent out by President Boyer* (New York: Mahlon Day, 1824), pp. 29–31; Baltimore *American and Commercial Advertiser*, July 21, 1824, p. 2.

God." Yet, fearful of the impact of servitude and oppression upon American blacks, he cautioned the indolent against coming to Haiti.[39]

Granville's admonition dissuaded neither the members of the Haytian Emigration Society of Coloured People nor those blacks who formed similar auxiliaries in Philadelphia and Baltimore. Among the leaders of the Haytien Emigration Society of Philadelphia, formed in the summer of 1824, were Richard Allen and James Forten. The latter, like Allen, was a former associate of Cuffe who had become a leading foe of African colonization. Convinced that a society of black men could best help other blacks "leave a country, where it is but too certain the coloured man can never enjoy his rights," those present at the initial meeting at Allen's Bethel Church resolved "that we do approve of the ... proposals of President Boyer; also heartily agree with him in the belief that the emigration to the Island of Hayti will be more advantageous to us than the Colony in Africa." Perhaps already envisioning Haiti as a missionary field for his African Methodist Episcopal Church, Allen accepted the presidency of the new group. His son served as secretary, and Forten was a member of the board of managers. Although an emigration society was not formed in Baltimore, Granville discussed the subject with a large audience in Bethel Church when he visited the city in September, and the blacks present voted to "use all honourable means to procure a speedy and effectual emigration of the free people of colour." They also appointed a large committee to stimulate emigration.[40]

Throughout the late summer and fall of 1824, black emigrationists in the three cities promoted Haitian emigration to a population which grew increasingly receptive to the viewpoint that moving to a nearby, independent black nation was a viable alternative to laboring under continued oppression in the United States. Emigration operations were soon underway. The sixty emigrants who departed

39. Dewey, *Correspondence*, p. 31; New York *Commercial Advertiser*, June 26, 1824, p. 2; July 30, 1824, p. 2; *Genius of Universal Emancipation*, III, Supplement (1824), 196; *Boston Recorder*, July 17, 1824, p. 115; *Niles' Weekly Register*, XXVI (August 7, 1824), 373-374.

40. *Poulson's American Daily Advertiser*, July 5, 1824, p. 2; July 13, 1824, p. 2; [Haytien Emigration Society], *Information for the Free People of Colour Who Are Inclined to Emigrate to Hayti* (Philadelphia: J. H. Cunningham, 1825), pp. 2, 4; *Genius of Universal Emancipation*, IV (November, 1824), 27-28.

from Philadelphia on August 23 on the *Charlotte Corday* were the first to sail; ten days later the *DeWitt Clinton* left New York with 120 blacks. Prior to the sailing the Reverend Peter Williams, addressing the emigrants on behalf of the Haytian Emigration Society of Coloured People, exhorted them to "Go to that *highly favoured, and as yet only land*, where the sons of Africa appear as a civilized, well-ordered, and flourishing nation. Go, remembering that the happiness of millions of the present and future generations, depends upon your prosperity, and that your prosperity depends much upon yourselves."[41]

The *Charlotte Corday* and the *DeWitt Clinton* were only the first of a number of ships which carried blacks to Haiti from eastern seaboard ports that autumn. A week after the New York emigrants departed, a ship sailed from Baltimore with twenty-one blacks, most of whom were reputed to be mechanics, and a full cargo of goods. In mid-October the *Concordia* left New York with 160 blacks, and another ten ships in various ports were reported on the verge of embarking for Haiti. In mid-November 280 emigrants sailed from Baltimore, and the Baltimore Emigration Society claimed that another forty to fifty applicants were rejected because of limited space on the vessel. Although undoubtedly exaggerating, Dewey announced that 2,000 blacks from Philadelphia had sailed or were about to sail for Haiti. Blacks from as far east as Providence, Rhode Island, were arriving in New York seeking berths on ships headed for the black Caribbean nation; as far west as Cincinnati, well outside the orbit of Haitian emigration activity, blacks formed the Cincinnati Haytien Union to raise money for an agent to visit the island and report on the feasibility of emigrating there.[42]

For many of the emigrants, Haiti was the very paradise they had anticipated. The Société Philanthropique d'Haiti, a quasi-official

---

41. New York *Commercial Advertiser*, August 24, 1824, p. 2; *Poulson's American Daily Advertiser*, August 13, 1824, p. 2; September 4, 1824, p. 3; September 6, 1824, p. 3; *Address of the Board of Managers of the Haytian Emigration Society of Coloured People, to the Emigrants Intending to Sail to the Island of Hayti in the Brig De Witt Clinton* (New York: Mahlon Day, 1824), pp. 3–8, quotation on p. 7.

42. *Poulson's American Daily Advertiser*, September 11, 1824, p. 3; October 15, 1824, p. 2; November 17, 1824, p. 3; November 20, 1824, p. 2; *Genius of Universal Emancipation*, IV (November, 1824), 22–23; IV (December, 1824), 34–35; *Boston Recorder*, November 13, 1824, p. 183.

agency charged with helping the emigrants adjust to their new country, welcomed the settlers. Secretary-General Inginac, the organization's president, told one shipload of new arrivals that "because the common blood of GREAT AFRICA makes unbreakable ties, all blacks are brothers regardless of language and religious distinctions." Many of the emigrants initially responded in kind. For example, one settler enthusiastically reported that he had found the country "much better... than I expected to find it.... Trees are breaking down with coffe & all kinds of fruits."[43]

Despite this initial enthusiasm, it soon became apparent that not every migrant was satisfied with conditions in Haiti. For some people the climate was uncomfortable, and the linguistic, religious, and legal barriers were far more burdensome than had been anticipated. They further discovered that both the Haitian upper class and the peasants considered them outcasts and treated them accordingly. In mid-February a contented settler, Charles Fisher, admitted that there were disgruntled emigrants. But he added, "Every one that will patiently bear a little privation at first, can live here, and do well." Two months later his tone was more defensive: "I do not believe the evil reports of the emigrants who have left this glorious Haytien nation." Despite Fisher's claim, emigrants began to return to the United States in the spring of 1825. For example, fifty-six emigrants sailed back to the United States with Peter Williams, who had surveyed conditions first-hand for the Haytian Emigration Society of Coloured People.[44]

At first both black and white American supporters of the Haitian emigration movement attempted to minimize the impact of the colonists' despondency and bitterness. In Philadelphia, Richard Allen's Haytien Emigration Society disputed what it considered unfounded criticisms: "We would assure our brethren... that our information from the emigrants is generally of a favourable kind. ... We regret that reports of a different character are flying about,

43. *Société Philanthropique d'Haiti*, no. 1 (August, 1824), 5–8; no. 2 (September, 1824), 15–19; *Genius of Universal Emancipation*, IV (January, 1825), 58.

44. Ludwell Lee Montague, *Haiti and the United States, 1714–1938* (Durham: Duke University Press, 1940), pp. 71–72; Baur, "Boyer and Haiti," 326–327; *Genius of Universal Emancipation*, IV (July, 1825), 152; IV (August, 1825), 173–174. On Williams's visit, see also Williams to Gerrit Smith, New York, November 11, 1834, Gerrit Smith Papers, Syracuse University.

as we ... believe them all false." White emigrationists were more direct in their attacks upon disgruntled emigrants. Campaigning to keep the movement alive in Baltimore, Benjamin Lundy, the noted Quaker abolitionist editor who also supported a number of diverse colonization schemes during the 1820's and 1830's, explained to blacks that those complaining about conditions in Haiti were "effeminate" and unaccustomed to hard work. Although the indolent would retard the movement, Lundy felt that the industrious emigrants would ultimately tell the true story. Loring Dewey, the mainstay behind the movement, journeyed from New York to Haiti on his own inspection tour; he sent word back to the United States that most of the emigrants were quite happy in Haiti and that they were doing better economically than they would have been if they had remained in their native country. Back in the United States, Dewey assured a meeting of blacks in Baltimore that the emigration to Haiti was successful. Shortly thereafter the young minister wrote two lengthy letters to the *United States Gazette* in Philadelphia in an attempt to belittle the significance of the emigrants returning.[45]

Despite Dewey's confident words, Haitian authorities were finding the situation disquieting. In April, 1825, President Boyer, troubled by the emigrants' complaints and claiming that an agent had absconded with his country's money, discontinued the travel stipends and land grants he had originally provided. The mass movement of 1824–25 came to an abrupt end as a result. With it died the hopes of those Afro-Americans who believed what a Philadelphia black had expressed upon his arrival in Port-au-Prince in October, 1824—that the coming of American blacks to Haiti was "the precursor of African liberty in the United States." Some emancipated slaves came to Haiti after April, 1825, but larger by far was the number of emigrants leaving the Caribbean country to return to the United States. By April, 1826, Inginac estimated that one-third of the official number of 6,000 government-sponsored settlers had fled Haiti. Others simply left their rural homesteads and flocked to the Haitian cities. Twelve years after the initial migration, one traveler

---

45. [Haytien Emigration Society], *Information for the Free People of Colour*, pp. 5, 12; *Genius of Universal Emancipation*, IV (March, 1825), 81; IV (April, 1825), 100; IV (March, 1825), 88–91; IV (May, 1825), 121; *United States Gazette*, May 31, 1825, p. 2; June 1, 1825, p. 2.

reported that he did not find any blacks still living on land originally granted to them by the government.[46]

REACTION AND APOSTASY: CORNISH AND RUSSWURM

With the failure of what was, after all, an emigration movement sponsored by an independent black nation, many black emigrationists expressed their profound disappointment and frustration by reasserting their opposition to the activities of the American Colonization Society. Moreover, individuals such as Allen, Forten, and Samuel E. Cornish demonstrated the ideological instability and ambivalence so typical of black leaders of the period by now completely rejecting all forms of emigration. Allen and other Philadelphians, protesting against the Colonization Society at two public meetings in early 1827, maintained both that there was no evidence that emigration would help liberate the slaves and that blacks should seek their fortunes in the United States, where opportunities were expanding and conditions improving.[47] In New York, too, former Haitian emigrationists stepped up the tempo of their attacks on African colonization.

Cornish was a pivotal figure in the fight against African colonization during the late 1820's. Born free around 1796, Cornish grew up in Delaware and spent his first twenty years in rural areas. Moving to Philadelphia, he received an education from John Gloucester, a black Presbyterian minister, and later taught at Gloucester's African School. Cornish became licensed to preach in 1819; he exhorted Maryland slaves until moving to New York, where in 1821 he was ordained and became the pastor of the First Colored Presbyterian Church (later the Shiloh Presbyterian Church). Cornish also worked among the city's blacks as a missionary for the New York Evangel-

---

46. Baur, "Boyer and Haiti," 326–327; *Société Philanthropique d'Haiti*, no. 3 (October, 1824), 10–12; *Genius of Universal Emancipation and Baltimore Courier*, June 3, 1826, pp. 313–317; Benjamin S. Hunt, *Remarks on Hayti as a Place of Settlement for Afric-Americans* (Philadelphia: T. B. Pugh, 1860), pp. 11–12. For the estimate of 6,000 emigrants which the Haitian government financed, see *Genius of Universal Emancipation*, IV (August, 1825), 173–174; *Missionary Herald*, XXV (October, 1829), 333. Lundy reported in 1829 that 8,000 black Americans had moved to Haiti during the decade. *African Repository*, V (August, 1829), 185.

47. *African Repository*, II (December, 1826), 295–298; *Genius of Universal Emancipation*, February 24, 1827, p. 111.

ical Missionary Society. Although certainly aware of the indignities blacks continually endured, he decided after the abortive Haitian emigration movement that flight was an inadequate alternative. Early in 1827 Cornish became senior editor of *Freedom's Journal*, the first black paper in the United States.[48]

Two months after its appearance on March 16, 1827, *Freedom's Journal* opened its anti-colonization campaign by running a letter by James Forten. Writing under the pseudonym "A Man of Colour," Forten castigated Congressman Henry Clay for supporting colonization and also charged that a pro-colonization memorial issued by blacks in Baltimore the previous December "was not the unanimous sentiment of the coloured people, for I am credibly informed that at least two-thirds of the meeting dissented from it." In reply, white colonizationists denounced both "A Man of Colour" and *Freedom's Journal* for publishing Forten's letter. Defending the right of his paper to discuss the colonization issue, Cornish then repeated the familiar arguments against colonization itself: he doubted whether colonization was aiding the fight against the slave trade; he disputed the notion that blacks were better suited than whites to the African climate; and he struck hard at colonizationists' assertions that blacks would never achieve full equality in the United States. "We are unwavering in our opinion," he argued, "that the time is coming (though it may be distant,) in which our posterity will enjoy equal rights." Christian missions, however, were worthy of support and encouragement: "Let a single [African] nation be converted through the instrumentality of a Mission family, and they will become far better pioneers in effecting the work of civilization,

---

48. For biographical information on Cornish, see Jane H. Pease and William H. Pease, *Bound with Them in Chains: A Biographical History of the Antislavery Movement* (Westport, Conn.: Greenwood Press, 1972), p. 141; Andrew E. Murray, *Presbyterians and the Negro—A History* (Philadelphia: Presbyterian Historical Society, 1966), p. 42; Bella Gross, "Freedom's Journal and the Rights of All," *Journal of Negro History*, XVII (July, 1932), 286; *The Rights of All*, May 29, 1829, p. 3; Raymond A. Mohl, *Poverty in New York, 1783–1825* (New York: Oxford University Press, 1971), p. 205. See also Alice Dana Adams, *The Neglected Period of Anti-Slavery in America (1808–1831)* (1908; reprint ed., Gloucester, Mass.: Peter Smith, 1964), p. 92; W. B. Davidson to R. R. Gurley, Philadelphia February 6, 1827, Domestic Letters, American Colonization Society Papers, Manuscript Division, Library of Congress (hereafter cited as ACS Papers). For Gloucester, see George, *Segregated Sabbaths*, pp. 150–151.

and salvation throughout... Africa, than any colonists that are likely to emigrate to that country."[49]

Other blacks also employed the pages of *Freedom's Journal* to express disapproval of African colonization in general and the American Colonization Society in particular. William Watkins, whose articulate opposition to colonization helped convert Garrison to an anti-colonization position, employed the pseudonym of "A Colored Baltimorean" to denounce those members of the Colonization Society who owned slaves and who propagated "the anti-christian doctrine that justice cannot be done to us while we remain in this land of civilization and gospel light." *Freedom's Journal* also reprinted a letter by the late Russell Parrott, who had concluded shortly before his death in 1824 that America, "with all her imperfections, still ... is my country, the home of my affections, in which is centered my most ardent hopes." In addition, the junior editor of *Freedom's Journal*, John Brown Russwurm, launched his own bombardment against African colonization in July, 1827. Reacting to what he called the Colonization Society's success "in imposing upon the public, the foolish *idea*, that we are longing to emigrate to their land of *'milk and honey*,'" Russwurm declared it imperative to announce "that we are all, to a man, opposed, in every shape, to the Colonization Society."[50]

A month later, Russwurm became the sole editor of *Freedom's Journal* when Cornish resigned for reasons that are not clear.[51] Born in Jamaica to a black mother and a white Virginia planter, Russwurm was sent to school in Quebec before moving to Maine, where his father married. After the elder Russwurm died in 1815, John Brown Russwurm remained with his father's widow and the rest of her family and received an education in Maine. He then insisted

49. *Freedom's Journal*, May 18, 1827, p. 38; June 8, 1827, pp. 50–51. Forten is identified as "A Man of Colour" in *The Colored American*, May 13, 1837, p. 2.

50. *Freedom's Journal*, July 6, 1827, p. 66; July 27, 1827, pp. 77–78; August 17, 1827, p. 91. On Watkins's identification as "A Colored Baltimorean," see Wendell Phillips Garrison and Francis Jackson Garrison, *William Lloyd Garrison, 1805–1879: The Story of His Life as Told by his Children* (Boston: Houghton, Mifflin, 1894), I, pp. 145n, 147–148. On Parrott, see also William Douglass, *Annals of the First African Church in the United States of America...* (Philadelphia: King and Baird, 1862), pp. 124–125.

51. *Freedom's Journal*, September 14, 1827, p. 107; Gross, "Freedom's Journal." 248.

upon returning to Jamaica, but he was unhappy in the Caribbean. Back in the United States, he taught at African schools in Philadelphia, New York, and Boston. His foster mother advised him to emigrate to Liberia, but he decided to earn a college degree first. In the fall of 1824 Russwurm entered Maine's Bowdoin College; by his last year at Bowdoin, however, Russwurm had turned his thoughts to Haiti. "If not particularly invited by the Haytian Govt," he wrote his cousin, "then, I shall study Medicine in Boston previous to an emigration to Hayti." One of the first two black college graduates in America, Russwurm spoke at his commencement in early September, 1826; he lauded the Haitian Revolution and the subsequent establishment of a republican form of government in Haiti. Evidently he received no offers from the Haitian government, for in the fall of 1826 he attended anatomy lectures at the Bowdoin College Medical School while simultaneously informing the American Colonization Society of his interest in a lucrative post in Liberia as a teacher or as an assistant to the colony's agent. However, when the Colonization Society presented Russwurm with an offer, he consulted with friends for several weeks before declining in late February, 1827.[52]

Russwurm's ambivalence toward Liberia and colonization was reflected in his behavior after he assumed complete responsibility for *Freedom's Journal*. Although he did not modify the paper's editorial position on African colonization for more than a year, a curious

52. This sketch has been drawn from *General Catalogue of Bowdoin College and the Medical School of Maine, 1794–1912* (Brunswick, Me.: Bowdoin College, 1912), p. 76; Nehemiah Cleaveland and Alpheus Spring Packard, *History of Bowdoin College*... (Boston: James Ripley Osgood & Company, 1882), pp. 352–353; undated newspaper clipping, John Brown Russwurm files, Bowdoin College Library; *Maryland Colonization Journal*, n.s. VI (March, 1853), 350–351; Philip S. Foner, ed., "John Brown Russwurm, A Document," *Journal of Negro History*, LIV (October, 1969), 393–397; Horatio Bridge, *Personal Recollections of Nathaniel Hawthorne* (New York: Harper & Brothers, 1893), p. 30; John B. Russwurm to John S. Russwurm, Brunswick, Maine, January 9, 1826, John S. Russwurm Papers, Tennessee State Library and Archives; Calvin Stockbridge to R. R. Gurley, North Yarmouth, Maine, October 23, 1826; John B. Russwurm to Gurley, New York, February 26, 1827, Domestic Letters, ACS Papers; Gross, "Freedom's Journal," 242. Although it has been quite widely believed that Russwurm was the first black to be graduated from an American college, Edward Jones was graduated from Amherst a few weeks before Russwurm's commencement at Bowdoin. Foner, "Russwurm, A Document," 393n.

tolerance to pro-colonization material began to appear almost immediately. In Russwurm's inaugural issue he simultaneously condemned the Colonization Society and published the first of what proved to be a series of letters advocating colonization by John H. Kennedy, assistant to Ralph R. Gurley, the Society's corresponding secretary since mid-1825. While Russwurm maintained his opposition to colonization, *Freedom's Journal* published Kennedy's long, ponderous letters well into the fall of 1827.[53] Early the following year Russwurm again demonstrated confusion regarding colonization when he questioned the glowing reports from black colonists in Liberia published in the Colonization Society's *African Repository*, while at the same time acknowledging his ties with those blacks still in bondage in a strikingly ambivalent statement, "[N]ever shall we consent to emigrate ... until their [slaves] prior removal from this land of their degradation and suffering," he announced. "And even then, we would not ask the aid of the American Colonization Society to carry us to their land 'flowing with milk and honey.'"[54]

Not until late January, 1829, did Russwurm decide to end his association with *Freedom's Journal* and emigrate to Liberia. He then privately informed the Colonization Society that when his present arrangement with the paper terminated around the first of April, he would be free to leave for Liberia under the Society's auspices. "I am willing to be employed in the colony," Russwurm further explained, "in any business, for the performance of which you may deem me qualified." Gurley, certain that winning Russwurm to the colonization camp would help the Society in its often frustrating campaign to gain black support, suggested that the young editor emigrate under the Society's sponsorship to superintend the colony's school system and run a printing establishment. Russwurm indicated his willingness to leave for Liberia in May.[55]

Only a few weeks after deciding to emigrate to Liberia, Russwurm tore down the veil shielding his attitudes and declared in

---

53. Kennedy's letters were published in the issues of September 14, 21, 28, October 5, 19, 26, November 16, 1827.
54. *Freedom's Journal*, January 25, 1828, p. 175.
55. Russwurm to Gurley, New York, January 26, 1829; Russwurm to Gurley, New York, February 24, 1829, Domestic Letters, ACS Papers.

Freedom's Journal that African colonization was the most suitable choice for black Americans. In preferring Liberia over Haiti, he explained that although he still thought highly of the leadership of the Caribbean black republic, he had lost confidence in Haitian emigration after hearing the reports of returned emigrants. Russwurm's readers immediately denounced the editor for his sudden reversal. For his part, Russwurm began to develop arguments in support of the movement that he now fervently embraced. Central to his position was his belief that blacks would never be free from oppression while living in the United States. Go to Liberia, Russwurm urged, for only in the black colony on the west coast of Africa—where the soil was rich and the land productive—could blacks ever achieve freedom and dignity; there "the Man of Colour... may walk forth in all the majesty of his creation—a new born creature—a *Free Man!*" Moreover, Russwurm claimed that emancipation would never become a reality without colonization. Employing the same arguments used by white colonizationists in the late eighteenth century, the young editor maintained that unless there was a place to receive the emancipated slave, neither Northerners nor Southerners would ever consent to emancipation.[56]

Subject after the final issue of *Freedom's Journal* in March, 1829, to what he described as "a violent persecution... raging against me... on account of my change," Russwurm turned to the Colonization Society for help. Gurley had not yet secured approval for his plan from the American Colonization Society's board of managers, and by late spring, still without an appointment, Russwurm visited Baltimore. There he met with Hezekiah Grice, a twenty-year-old black ice carrier and butcher who was a friend of Benjamin Lundy. Grice was already engaged in developing a black trading company to create commercial ties between black Americans and black Liberians and to transport blacks from the United States to Liberia. Totally without resources himself and more interested in securing an official position in Liberia than in committing himself to Grice's venture, Russwurm could only encourage Grice in what proved to be an unsuccessful effort. In the summer of 1829 the board

---

56. Russwurm's argument can be found in *Freedom's Journal*, February 14, 1829, p. 362; February 21, 1829, p. 370; March 7, 1829, p. 386; March 14, 1829, p. 394; March 28, 1829, p. 410. The quotation is from the March 7 issue.

of managers of the Colonization Society finally agreed to support Russwurm's emigration to Liberia. A few months later Russwurm left the United States for Africa where, except for one brief visit to the United States, he lived out the rest of his days.[57]

Well before Russwurm left for Liberia—in fact, only two months after the demise of *Freedom's Journal*—Samuel E. Cornish began publishing another anti-colonization newspaper, *The Rights of All*. Attempting to combat whatever influence Russwurm's apostasy may have had among blacks, Cornish declared that Russwurm's conversion simply was one of the "novelties of the day," but that he himself knew that "the views of the intelligent of my brethren generally, are the same as ever in respect to colonisation." In sum, Cornish believed that although a few who emigrate might benefit, and certainly missionaries in Africa could contribute toward the coming of "the glorious period, when civilisation and religion shall have spread over the vast and important continent of Africa," African colonization in general could in no way help the condition of the millions of blacks living in the United States.[58]

Cornish reiterated his opposition to colonization in various ways. African colonization was not, he argued, a solution for the problems of American blacks, and the American Colonization Society should regard Liberia as "what it should have been considered from its first establishment—A Missionary Colony and a home for recaptured and emancipated slaves." Occasionally Cornish's hostility to African colonization moved him to support halfheartedly emigration to Canada West and Haiti, but only for those blacks who felt it absolutely necessary to leave the United States. Commenting on the blacks fleeing from Cincinnati to Canada after the riot of 1829, Cornish urged those forced to leave the country at least to

57. Russwurm to Gurley, Philadelphia, May 7, 1829; Russwurm to Gurley, New York, April 8, 1829; Russwurm to Gurley, New York, June 16, 1829; Russwurm to Gurley, New York, July 3, 1829; C. C. Andrews to Gurley, New York, June 25, 1829, and July 1, 1829; Russwurm to Gurley, New York, July 24, 1829; Russwurm to Gurley, Boston, August 15, 1829, Domestic Letters, ACS Papers. On Grice, see *The Anglo-African Magazine*, I (October, 1859), 305–310; George F. Bragg, *Men of Maryland* (Baltimore: Church Advocate Press, 1914), p. 71; Robin W. Winks, *The Blacks in Canada: A History* (New Haven: Yale University Press, 1971), p. 163; Grice to Gurley, Baltimore, March 15, 1829; C. C. Harper to Gurley, Baltimore, April 9, 1829, Domestic Letters, ACS Papers.
58. *The Rights of All*, May 29, 1829, pp. 2, 3.

remain in North America. "We do not," he said, "ask the Colonization Society to provide a home for us, we can do it for ourselves, when necessary, and a far better one than they have to offer." Cornish's animosity toward colonization carried him to the point that in August, 1829, he rejected the view that blacks have separate interests. "The ridiculous doctrine of a *separate people, separate interest, extraneous mass, dangerous evil*, &c.," he declared, "is fraught with 10,000 evil consequences of the kind."[59]

Although Cornish's *The Rights of All* ceased publication in the fall of 1829, the anti-colonization position which the paper and its editor had articulated represented the dominant view among black Americans at this time. In the early 1830's the longstanding hostility of many blacks to the American Colonization Society—stimulated further by Garrison—broadened into a general condemnation of all forms of emigration. Even the black national convention movement of the 1830's, inaugurated originally to consider the plight of the blacks of Cincinnati, approved only temporarily a plan providing for the displaced Ohio blacks to move to Canada.[60] Admittedly, some blacks continued to migrate to Liberia under the Colonization Society's auspices, but certainly no black of the stature of either Daniel Coker or John B. Russwurm left the United States for Africa. Haitian emigration was even more moribund.

The disappearance of black interest in colonization at this time was undoubtedly due to a combination of factors. Very likely, the frustrations and disillusionment engendered by the failure of the Haitian movement awakened an intense opposition to colonization in all forms and to all locales. If an emigration movement directed to a nearby black nation and sponsored, in part, by local black leaders should bring with it widespread misery and despair, what could blacks expect from the exclusively white Colonization Society's scheme to remove free blacks to the shores of distant Africa? Moreover, the change from gradualism to immediatism among antislavery advocates in the early 1830's could only have reinforced the already

---

59. *Ibid.*, September 18, 1829, p. 34; August 14, 1829 (front page misdated August 7), pp. 26, 28; October 19, 1829, p. 46.

60. *Minutes of the 1833 Convention*, pp. 22–23. See also Howard Holman Bell, *A Survey of the Negro Convention Movement, 1830–1861* (New York: Arno Press, 1969), pp. 29–32.

existing anti-colonization tendencies within the black community. A number of abolitionists—Lundy, Garrison, Arthur and Lewis Tappan, James Birney, and Gerrit Smith among them—had supported colonization during the 1820's largely because they believed the emigration of large numbers of blacks would diminish the possibility of racial conflict following emancipation. After 1830 the call for an immediate rather than a gradual end to slavery was accompanied by the belief that racial prejudice was a moral evil to be extirpated through personal conversion; thus most antislavery proponents rejected colonization as thoroughly as they did gradualism.[61] Finally, the widespread appearance of antislavery societies and newspapers during the early 1830's coincided with the onset of the black convention movement, and together these developments opened up new avenues of protest for many blacks. The growth of this more visible and more militant antislavery crusade may well have dampened any lingering emigration tendencies, leaving few blacks willing to challenge the prevailing anti-emigration sentiment until after midcentury.

61. On the relationship between antislavery and colonization—especially during the 1820's—see Merton L. Dillon, *Benjamin Lundy and the Struggle for Negro Freedom* (Urbana: University of Illinois Press, 1966), pp. 65, 91; Adams, *Neglected Period of Anti-Slavery*, pp. 199–202; David Brion Davis, "The Emergence of Immediatism in British and American Antislavery Thought," *Mississippi Valley Historical Review*, XLIX (September, 1962), 225; Bertram Wyatt-Brown, *Lewis Tappan and the Evangelical War Against Slavery* (Cleveland: Press of Case Western Reserve University, 1969), pp. 85–87; Leon F. Litwack, *North of Slavery: The Negro in the Free States, 1790–1860* (Chicago: University of Chicago Press, 1961), p. 27.

PART II

Revival and Denouement, 1850-63

CHAPTER 4

The Drift toward Emigration

The marked decline of interest in emigration during the late 1820's and the subsequent two decades was followed by a resurgence of support for emigration after 1850. Led by Martin R. Delany, nationalist-emigrationism flowered in the 1850's both as an ideology replete with calls for racial solidarity and "national" unity and as an identifiable movement based upon this ideology. Yet, as Part I of this study has shown, Delany's movement had several ideological forerunners. As early as the 1780's free blacks who had organized themselves in support of emigration believed that emigration would help them escape the persecutions they confronted daily, hasten the emancipation of their brethren still in bondage, and enable them to carry Western civilization to Africa. In diverse ways —and acting upon diverse motives—Newport Gardner, Paul Cuffe, Richard Allen, and others contributed to the continuation of an emigrationist tradition within the black community. Even those blacks whose support for emigration proved ephemeral—Allen and Samuel Cornish, for example—advocated the establishment of separate black institutions and thus acknowledged the fact that blacks were a separate caste within the larger American society. If the nationalism espoused by these individuals tended to exist largely independent of their occasional emigrationism, the ethnocentric tendencies they promoted still provided a supporting intellectual tradition for the nationalist-emigrationists of the 1850's.

Even during the 1830's and 1840's interest in emigration with and without accompanying nationalist tendencies never completely disappeared. Several individuals during this period contributed to the emergence of a more substantial nationalist-emigrationist ideology and suggested schemes similar to those Delany would propose. Of these, the most significant—because his influence was the most direct—was Delany's teacher, the Reverend Lewis Woodson of Pittsburgh. By the late 1830's Woodson had formulated the basic tenets of a nationalist-emigrationist ideology. Subsequently three other individuals—Henry Bibb, James Theodore Holly, and Mary Ann Shadd—also sharpened and promoted nationalist-emigrationist positions. All three migrated first to Canada; when prejudice and discrimination there destroyed the heady optimism they had carried with them, they turned their sights elsewhere and advocated emigration to various points in the Caribbean and Latin America. All three were also alike in visualizing emigration as a corollary of larger nationalistic plans. In the early 1850's Bibb and Holly formulated a concrete nationalist-emigrationist position along the lines Woodson and others had proposed earlier. Thus they contributed to the impulse which coalesced in the development of Delany's nationalist-emigrationist movement in 1853 and 1854.

IDEOLOGICAL FOREBEAR: LEWIS WOODSON

Although well known in the Pittsburgh black community, the Reverend Lewis Woodson was in no way a national leader. He led no mass movement, nor did he establish a newspaper or spark the formation of a national convention or society. His significance derives from the fact that, moving well beyond the episodic and disjointed efforts of Gardner, Cuffe, and others, Woodson was the first to articulate a genuine nationalist-emigrationist creed and place it in a coherent ideological framework. Between 1837 and 1841 he outlined the basic beliefs underpinning the rhetoric and actions that were to characterize his student, Martin R. Delany, the leading advocate of nationalist-emigrationism during the 1850's and early 1860's.

Born into slavery in Virginia in January, 1806, Lewis Woodson remained in bondage until his father purchased his freedom when he was nineteen. After living in Ohio for several years, he moved to Pittsburgh in 1830 or 1831. For at least the next three decades he resided in Pittsburgh, teaching school, barbering, and ministering to an African Methodist Episcopal congregation. In September, 1831, he served as secretary of the Ohio annual conference of the

A.M.E. Church, then meeting in Pittsburgh. However, his most significant activities at this time were his efforts to provide moral and religious educational opportunities for black children—a role he had also played in Chillicothe, Ohio, where, in 1827, he had spearheaded the organization of an African Education and Benevolent Society.[1] At a meeting at the African Church in Pittsburgh in January, 1832, Woodson and John B. Vashon, a bathhouse proprietor who had supported Garrison in the latter's efforts to found *The Liberator*, led in the formation of the Pittsburgh African Educational Society. Designed to combat the "ignorance [which] is the sole cause of the present degradation and bondage of the people of colour in these United States," the society also aimed to demonstrate "that the intellectual capacity of the black man is equal to that of the white, and that he is equally susceptible to improvement...." Shortly thereafter, the Society bought a white Methodist church on Front Street for a school and employed Woodson as the teacher at an annual salary of $150.[2]

Woodson also served as the secretary of the Pittsburgh auxiliary of William Whipper's American Moral Reform Society. That organization was created in 1835 at the last of the early black national conventions, when those defining the tasks of reform in broad, general strokes triumphed over those advocating specific programs to combat the distinct problems of blacks. In this capacity he was plagued by the contradiction between his desire to organize the local black community around the basic principles of moral reform —the belief in Christian rectitude, industry, thrift, and temperance —and the parent society's steadfast opposition to racial separatism and to blacks acting along purely racial lines. Woodson himself alluded to his dilemma shortly after the Pittsburgh group was organized in December, 1836: "And may we not indulge the hope

---

1. Manuscript Schedules, Seventh Census of the United States: 1850—City of Pittsburgh; *Colored American*, August 31, 1839, p. 2; James Pyle Wickersham, *A History of Education in Pennsylvania*... (Lancaster, Pa.: Inquirer Publishing Company, 1886), p. 254; *The Pittsburgh Gazette*, September 30, 1831, p. 3; *Genius of Universal Emancipation*, March 31, 1827, p. 172. Genealogical information can be found in Minnie Shumate Woodson, comp., *The Woodson Source Book* (Washington, D.C., 1975), pp. 3, 7-10, 138.

2. *Hazard's Register of Pennsylvania*, IX (February, 1832), 115-116; Wickersham, *Education in Pennsylvania*, p. 254. On Vashon, see Benjamin Quarles, *Black Abolitionists* (New York: Oxford University Press, 1969), p. 20.

that the *American Moral Reform Soc.* will soon become the centre of union for the whole colored population of our land?" Moreover, the Pittsburgh auxiliary, despite its adherence to the abstract principles of the national society, was clearly a race-oriented organization. Its major leaders were deeply involved in the fight against disfranchisement and equally devoted to improving economic and social conditions in the Pittsburgh black community. For example, in the summer of 1837 Woodson and Vashon served on a five-man committee which investigated "the moral, social, and political condition" of Pittsburgh's black population and reported that while blacks "are endeavoring to sustain themselves honorably, and respectably ... [w]hatever of ignorance or degradation there is among us, owes its existence chiefly to ... Slavery, that unrighteous, and unnatural state in which so many of us were raised...."[3]

Caught between his own belief in the necessity for racial solidarity on the one hand, and his nominal attachment to Whipper's American Moral Reform Society on the other, Woodson chose anonymity to express his separatist position. He wrote a series of letters which appeared in *The Colored American* under the nom de plume "Augustine." Unifying all of Woodson's "Augustine" letters was the assumption—occasionally made explicit—that Afro-Americans constituted a separate caste within the Republic, that they suffered from "prejudice of caste," and that their position and problems were distinct from those of white Americans. Referring undoubtedly to Whipper and others within the Moral Reform Society, Woodson admitted that there were blacks "who think it impolitic and improper for us to acknowledge and speak of ourselves as a distinct class...." However, this was sheer fatuity: "The condition in which we have for generations been living in this land, constitutes us a distinct class. We have been held as slaves, while those around us have been free. They have been our holders, and we the held. Every power and privilege have been invested with them, while we have been divested of every right." Only through the creation of a "national feeling," Woodson argued in his letters, would blacks, as a

---

3. *National Enquirer and Constitutional Advocate of Universal Liberty*, January 17, 1837, p. 71; August 3, 1837, p. 82. For the American Moral Reform Society, see Howard H. Bell, "The American Moral Reform Society, 1836–1841," *Journal of Negro Education*, XXVII (Winter, 1958), 34–40.

class with a "general character," lift themselves from degradation —and then perhaps only through the development of separate institutions.⁴

Specifically, Woodson maintained that the black church, in which he served, should retain its independent existence. Contrary to Whipper's urging, it should not work for inclusion in the white religious structure: ". . . the [white] church will never relinquish her prejudices against color, until she has abolished her slavery—until she has cleansed her skirts of the blood and souls of men. . . . And until it is accomplished, it will be positively necessary for the colored people, wherever they exist in sufficient numbers, to have separate places of worship for themselves." To Woodson, in fact, the greatest sin of the white church was not that it excluded blacks, but that it prevented them from building their own houses of worship. Moreover, black churches must be staffed by competent black clergy, for only "men identified with ourselves" could properly fulfill the

---

4. *Colored American*, December 2, 1837, p. 2; December 9, 1837, p. 2. It is doubtful that the "Augustine" pseudonym was very effective, since the letters contain abundant clues pointing to Woodson as the author. First, there is the marked similarity between Woodson's public positions and those of "Augustine" on two issues: the importance of training competent black clergymen and the necessity that a state convention meet to protest the disfranchisement statute enacted by the Pennsylvania legislature. Compare *Colored American*, July 1, 1837, p. 3 (A) and July 8, 1837, p. 2 (LW); and March 6, 1841, pp. 1–2 (A) with the reports of Woodson's activities in the *Proceedings of the State Convention of the Colored Freemen of Pennsylvania held in Pittsburgh on the 23rd, 24th and 25th of August, 1841* . . . (Pittsburgh: Matthew M. Grant, 1841), pp. 4–5. More significant is the internal evidence in the "Augustine" letters themselves. They indicate that the author was born in the South (Woodson was born in Virginia), lived in Ohio for a number of years (other evidence indicates Woodson lived in Ohio as early as 1827), resided in Columbus, Ohio, in 1830 (as did Woodson), had a father in Jackson County, Ohio, in 1830 (Thomas C. Woodson, Lewis's father, lived in Jackson County in 1830), and traveled to Philadelphia and New York in 1836 (as Woodson did with Delany). See *Colored American*, July 28, 1838, p. 90; August 4, 1838, p. 94; February 9, 1839, p. 2; August 31, 1839, p. 2; and compare with Seventh Census of the United States: 1850; Quarles, *Black Abolitionists*, p. 101; Carter G. Woodson, *Free Negro Heads of Families in the United States in 1830* (Washington: Association for the Study of Negro Life and History, 1925), pp. 125, 127; Wickersham, *Education in Pennsylvania*, p. 254; and Frank A. Rollin, pseud. [Frances E. Rollin Whipper], *Life and Public Services of Martin R. Delany, Sub-Assistant Commissioner, Bureau Relief of Refugees, Freedmen and of Abandoned Lands, and Late Major 104th U.S. Colored Troops* (Boston: Lee and Shepard, 1868), p. 45.

ministerial functions necessary for the moral elevation of the race.[5]

Woodson's stress on the importance of black clergy was predicated upon his attitudes toward the moral functions of ministers and the moral responsibilities of the laity. Charging elements in the black community with irresponsible conduct—drinking and wantonness—Woodson argued that only by adhering to Christian virtues of moral purity could blacks uplift themselves from a wretched condition which, he added, could not be entirely blamed upon their white oppressors. He further maintained that "CONDITION and not *color*, is the chief cause of the prejudice, under which we suffer"—a position clearly at variance with his view that blacks suffered from "prejudice of caste." He also claimed that, once young blacks undertook personal responsibility for changing their condition,

> they would then find that elegant language and polished manners would give them greater currency in society, than a smooth beaver, or a golden headed rattan; and that a cultivated mind is of higher consideration than dollars and cents. They would cease to haunt our church doors and the corners of our streets, offending the moral sense of all who go in and out, or that pass by, and [instead] crowd into the lecture room or library; and instead of drinking grog or smoking tobacco, they would read the newspaper.

Moreover, he called upon blacks to learn trades, work extra hours, and save money—principally by investing in banking institutions. Fittingly, during a period when white Americans were celebrating agrarian virtues and the inherent dignity of the individual producer, Woodson exalted farmers and mechanics as the ideal social models.[6]

Considering farming a *"trade,"* Woodson exhorted his urban readers—especially those without trades—to leave the city for the countryside because "a more powerful means of changing our present dependent and precarious condition, into one of comfort and independence, could not be devised, than of our settling in the

---

5. *Colored American*, July 1, 1837, p. 3; October 27, 1838, p. 142; July 1, 1837, p. 3.

6. *Ibid.*, February 16, 1839, p. 2; February 17, 1838, p. 23; February 9, 1839, p. 2. Critical as he was at this time, Woodson was willing later to recognize improvement in behavior and conduct; this he did in 1860, when he looked back on the period since the A.M.E. Church was formed in 1816. *The Weekly Anglo-African*, March 24, 1860, p. 1.

country and becoming the cultivators of the soil." Yet Woodson's position went beyond merely urging the unemployed to migrate westward to smaller towns and rural areas—an attitude both Delany and militant abolitionist Henry Highland Garnet also enunciated a decade later. Rather, Woodson advocated the establishment of separate settlements, as he had urged in 1828 while living in Chillicothe. At that time he had responded favorably to an offer from Colonel Joseph Watson to establish an all-black farming community, "Africania," on a hundred-acre plot Watson owned in Guernsey County, Ohio. Woodson approved of the general idea, while warning that at least 3,000 acres would be necessary for a separate settlement where "we should be all on perfect equality... free from the looks of scorn and contempt... free from all the evils attendant on partial and unequal laws." Watson countered with an offer for 1,000 acres, but this was apparently inadequate.[7]

Despite his long residence in Pittsburgh, Woodson's rural inclinations were still strong when he commented on another plan for an all-black settlement in 1838. Perhaps this was because his father had been living in a separate settlement in Jackson County, Ohio, for the preceding eight years. Thomas Woodson's settlement in Milton Township was economically prosperous and socially independent, with a separate church, day and Sunday schools.[8] His son, believing that ample land was available in the Midwest and that restrictive legislation existing in such a state as Ohio would not hinder prospective settlers, propounded a lengthy rationale for such communities in several of his "Augustine" letters. Citing the Bible and the Declaration of Independence in support of his position, he again argued that in separate settlements blacks would be able to establish an egalitarian society and thus free themselves from their traditional dependence upon whites. Most important, Woodson observed, the

---

7. *Colored American*, February 17, 1838, p. 23; *Freedom's Journal*, December 5, 1828, p. 283; January 31, 1829, pp. 344–345.

8. *Colored American*, February 17, 1838, p. 23; July 28, 1838, p. 90; Woodson, *Free Negro Heads of Families*, p. 125. Like his son, Thomas Woodson was active in racial affairs. In September, 1844, he attended a state convention of blacks which approved a resolution recommending that blacks in Ohio towns and cities buy land in the country. The elder Woodson was also an agent in Jackson County for the *Palladium of Liberty*, a black newspaper published in Columbus. *Palladium of Liberty*, September 25, 1844, p. 3; October 2, 1844, pp. 3, 4.

eventual emergence of black farmers, tradesmen, and mechanics in these settlements (all elevated by the presence of indigenous religious and educational institutions) would demonstrate to whites their true abilities. The condition of blacks would, as a result, improve throughout the United States. His father's community served as evidence: when the residents leave the settlement, "no colored people . . . are more respected, or treated with greater deference than they are."[9]

Rural settlements, despite their advantages, might still give insufficient opportunity and security to black Americans. Woodson recognized this in his "Augustine" communications when he merged the ideas of separation and emigration. Moving cautiously at first, he suggested that blacks had overreacted to emigration, with many considering the subject *"criminal"* because of their inability to distinguish between emigration and the colonization scheme (or, in his words, "exile") adopted by the American Colonization Society: "Emigration, to be legitimate, must be voluntary and free. The benefit of the emigrants and their posterity must be its sole object. The mode, time, and place, of emigration must be left wholly to their choice. The emigrants must be men of intelligence and judgment; capable of devising, and executing whatever is necessary to their own and their posterity's welfare." Woodson found the Colonization Society's program to be quite the opposite because it attempted to capitalize upon the weaknesses of a downtrodden people by expelling them, without their consent and without consultation, to a distant land. This degraded them "by discouraging the hope of moral elevation and preferment; and by heaping upon them every species of contempt and scorn."[10]

To those who continued to reject any form of emigration and to insist upon the necessity of staying in the United States, at least partly on the grounds that free blacks must remain to aid those in bondage, Woodson replied that he would not conform to a policy he considered to be sheer folly:

> I can do more good by living than by dying; and especially in our case. Suppose all the free people of color of the United States were

9. *Colored American*, August 31, 1839, p. 2; February 17, 1838, p. 23; July 28, 1838, p. 90.
10. *Ibid.*, May 3, 1838, p. 54.

exterminated, what, to all human appearance, would become the hope of the slave?—Too many of my brethren are just beginning to live happily in the West Indies, and in Canada, for me to think of dying just now. I had rather be a *living freeman*, even in one of these places, than a "dead nigger" in the United States.

Woodson's specific mention of Canada and the British West Indies was central to his conception of emigration. The relative proximity of these locales (especially the former) would serve as an easily accessible "safety valve" for what he estimated to be thousands of idle, unemployed blacks concentrated in the nation's urban centers. Answering Cornish and others who generally opposed any form of emigration, Woodson explained that free blacks who moved to Canada and the British West Indies would not be abandoning their brethren in chains. On the contrary, "*a colony of our choice*" in either or both of these places would preserve a people otherwise destined to extinction. It would also serve as an agent of liberation through the use of economic power, not military force. Foreshadowing the rhetoric of Delany by more than a decade, Woodson declared, "The landing . . . of a single vessel from such a state, laden with its rich products, would do more to unrivet the fetters of the slave, than the death of a hundred thousand freemen."[11]

But emigration, as Woodson conceived of it, involved more than merely the voluntary removal of a few individuals from the United States. Rather, for Woodson, emigration was to be a "*national*" decision. Instead of scattering themselves in a variety of locales, blacks should all move "on one *plan*, or to one place." To accomplish this, he exhorted, in a reiteration of a theme he continually returned to in his "Augustine" correspondence, "We need a *national* organization . . . to which all subjects of this nature can be referred." Woodson's suggestion was more than simply the latest of many similar proposals—beginning in 1789 with the attempt by the African Union Society of Newport to form one central body for all the blacks in Rhode Island. He envisioned a national or general convention which would establish a permanent governing board to provide continuity and stability between the meetings of the convention. In addition, "Auxiliaries of the National Institution would of course exist wher-

11. *Ibid.*, September 22, 1838, p. 122; November 10, 1838, p. 150; October 27, 1838, p. 142.

ever our people are found; and would supercede particular institutions... on account of their being united in one Great National Head." A permanent organization would also "create *national feeling*... and inspire *confidence, energy*, and *self-respect*," and consequently would provide cohesion to a widely scattered people and substitute collective strength for weak and ineffective individual action.[12]

Woodson's wide-ranging program exposed him to criticism from blacks holding diametrically opposed views. For example, Samuel E. Cornish, although like Woodson a champion of racial solidarity and racial unity, chastized the Pittsburgh minister for espousing the establishment of separate black settlements and for advocating emigration: "Alas! alas! has the expatriating spirit got hold of our good brother? If it have, would to Heaven he had gone to his rest, before his seduction and the promulgation of views so monstrous." On the other hand, the American Moral Reform Society struck hard at Woodson's exhortations for "moral works for colored men"—preferring "moral works for all men." Whipper's organization also issued a steadfast refusal to abide by racial distinctions of any kind: "we are opposed to the principle on which every existing institution is based... that makes complexion a qualification for membership. ... And we call on our brethren throughout the country, if they desire to make a successful appeal for the abolition of complexional distinctions, to first throw up their African Characters."[13]

Whatever the impact of these attacks, Woodson's influence within the Pittsburgh black community was secure. There he discarded his pseudonym to labor for the calling of a national convention. In June, 1840, he was active at two Pittsburgh meetings which approved holding such a conference but which opposed what was regarded as a premature attempt by David Ruggles to have a convention in New Haven in September. The convention was never

12. *Ibid.*, January 19, 1839, p. 2; December 23, 1837, p. 2; July 4, 1840, p. 1; December 30, 1837, pp. 2–3; February 10, 1838, p. 18. Earlier calls for the establishment of a national organization can be traced in the Records of the African Union Society of Newport, Newport, R.I., Historical Society, pp. 20–22 (see also pp. 217–223); *Poulson's American Daily Advertiser*, January 10, 1817, p. 3; *The Rights of All*, September 18, 1829, p. 34.

13. *Colored American*, July 28, 1838, p. 90; October 27, 1838, p. 142; November 10, 1838, p. 150; *The National Reformer*, I (January, 1839), 71.

held, and Woodson, once again as "Augustine," turned to the less grandiose and more localized activity of attacking the anti-black suffrage legislation recently adopted by the Pennsylvania legislature. Here he characteristically favored the Pittsburgh-supported plan for a state convention over the more legalistic petition efforts advocated by Philadelphia blacks. The convention proposal eventually prevailed, and the State Convention of the Colored Freemen of Pennsylvania met in Pittsburgh in August, 1841, with Woodson in attendance.[14]

Lewis Woodson's thoughts and deeds during the remainder of the 1840's were, for the most part, unrecorded. Along with Samuel E. Cornish, Henry Highland Garnet, and others, he served on the board of managers of the Union Missionary Society. This organization was formed in 1841 by black ministers from various denominations to aid the *Amistad* captives—the Mendi Africans who had been imprisoned in New Haven after having commandeered a Cuban slave ship—and to promote antislavery missions in the United States and elsewhere. Whites quickly took over the society, which, at the instigation of the American and Foreign Anti-Slavery Society, joined with two other missionary organizations to form the American Missionary Association in 1846. Woodson also participated in local Liberty party affairs and, with Delany among others, attempted to form a "Citizens' Union" to secure full legal and political rights for blacks.[15]

Evidence from the early 1850's, however, indicates that for unknown reasons Woodson had come to renounce emigration while retaining his commitment to the establishment of separate racial organizations. He explicitly rejected emigration in late 1853 while using language reminiscent of his "Augustine" writings more than a decade earlier to urge blacks to avoid discord and to unite among

14. *Colored American*, July 18, 1840, p. 2; August 15, 1840, p. 2; March 6, 1841, pp. 1–2; March 13, 1841, p. 2; *Proceedings of the Pennsylvania Colored Convention, 1841*, pp. 5, 16.

15. *Union Missionary*, October, 1844, p. 28; Bertram Wyatt-Brown, *Lewis Tappan and the Evangelical War against Slavery* (Cleveland: Press of Case Western Reserve University, 1969), pp. 292–293, 306n; *Saturday Visiter*, April 29, 1848, p. 2; *The Mystery*, December 16, 1846, p. 2. For the story of the formation of the A.M.A., see Clifton Herman Johnson, "The American Missionary Association, 1846–1861: A Study of Christian Abolitionism" (Ph.D. dissertation, University of North Carolina, 1958), pp. 52–92.

themselves—principally to pursue wealth for the improvement of the race. Woodson was not an innovator in thus divorcing his call for distinct racial institutions from emigrationism; as early as 1817, the Georgetown blacks who had condemned the American Colonization Society had suggested the creation of a black "universal association" for the purpose of achieving racial solidarity. Moreover, in 1849 Frederick Douglass, certainly no friend of emigration, had drawn up a tentative constitution for a National League—one permanent body, with local auxiliaries, to unify Afro-Americans and to work for the emancipation of the slave and for the economic and political liberation of free blacks. Douglass was undoubtedly convinced of the importance of racial solidarity and independent racial action because of his own experience in abolitionist ranks—especially his establishment, with Delany's help, of a black antislavery newspaper over Garrison's objections. He also may have been seeking a black constituency for the fledgling paper. However, after the proposed National League proved abortive, Douglass joined Woodson and several others in May, 1850, to propose the formation of an American League of Colored Laborers to stimulate employment opportunities by encouraging black industrial enterprise. Based on the assumption that "the attainment of Learning and Riches" was necessary for racial progress, the League's plan called for the creation of locally administered funds to send money to prospective black businessmen, and for the training of young blacks in the mechanical arts.[16]

Although the American League of Colored Laborers seems never to have functioned, it is evident that as late as the mid-1850's Woodson still espoused many of the nationalistic ideas he had formulated earlier. If he, like Douglass, was demonstrating that emigrationism need not be intertwined with nationalism, others—including Woodson's onetime student, Martin R. Delany—retained the total philosophy. In the years following the Fugitive Slave Act of 1850 they

16. For Woodson's views in the 1850's, see *Frederick Douglass' Paper*, September 23, 1853, p. 3; October 28, 1853, p. 2; December 23, 1853, p. 1. (A later criticism of emigration by Woodson is in *The Weekly Anglo-African*, September 3, 1859, p. 3.) For the Georgetown blacks, see *Poulson's American Daily Advertiser*, January 10, 1817, p. 3. The National League proposal is in *The North Star*, August 10, 1849, p. 2; the plan for the American League of Colored Laborers can be found in *The North Star*, June 13, 1850, p. 2.

began to ask themselves whether unity and racial solidarity *within* the United States would enable Afro-Americans to achieve full dignity and equality.

"Fugitives" in Canada: Shadd, Bibb, and Holly

Several years after Lewis Woodson created a full-fledged nationalist-emigrationist philosophy, three blacks—two free and one a fugitive slave—emigrated to Canada West, where they fused a concrete program onto Woodson's basic ideas. For Henry Bibb, James Theodore Holly, and Mary Ann Shadd, the move to Canada was only the latest of several attempts to find a home free from oppression for themselves and for other black Americans who might follow. Of the three, Mary Ann Shadd's intellectual journey was the most circuitous; not until the convening of Delany's emigration convention in 1854 did she accept the nationalist-emigrationist position. Nevertheless, her presence in Canada West in the early 1850's was a factor in sharpening the emerging debate over nationalism-emigrationism.

Born on October 9, 1823, she was the eldest of the thirteen children of Abraham D. Shadd, a shoemaker who was a prominent abolitionist and a leading participant in the conventions of the early 1830's. Although he participated in a protest against African colonization at Wilmington, Delaware, in 1831, Abraham Shadd had favored emigration in the early 1830's. He also aided fugitive slaves in Delaware and Pennsylvania until the early 1850's, when he moved to Canada West and there became the only black to achieve elective office prior to the Civil War. At the age of ten Mary Ann Shadd left Wilmington for West Chester, Pennsylvania, where she attended a Friends school for six years. Returning to Wilmington to open a school for black children, she subsequently taught in West Chester, New York City, and Norristown, Pennsylvania. During the late 1840's Shadd argued that blacks must avoid any appearance of frivolity and should act for themselves without "waiting for the whites of the country...." In 1849 she published a twelve-page pamphlet, *Hints to the Colored People of the North*, which criticized blacks for attempting to imitate the consumption patterns of whites: "We forget that we are, as a people, [too] deficient in the 'needful' to support such things.... What profits a display of ourselves? Is it to be seen by one another? How does that better our condition?"[17]

After the passage of the Fugitive Slave Act in September, 1850, Shadd turned her didacticism to other purposes and moved to Canada West, where she taught school—apparently first at Sandwich to the children of black refugees and then, sponsored by the American Missionary Association, in Windsor. There she met with some eighteen to twenty students until 1853, when the A.M.A. suspended her because she was not evangelical. Meanwhile she was also working to aid fugitives; in the process she came to the position that it was folly for blacks to remain in the United States. In 1852 she published another pamphlet, *Notes of Canada West*. Although she included brief descriptions of the British West Indies, Central America, Mexico, and Vancouver's Island, Shadd's essential purposes were to provide information on the social and political conditions of Canada West for fugitives in need of guidance and to tout Canada to prospective emigrants. Her conclusions were forthright: "... no settled country in America offers stronger inducements to colored people."[18]

One of Shadd's countrymen who agreed in general with her en-

17. "Life Sketch of Mary Ann Shadd Cary, June 29, 1960," and "Re: other members of family of Mary Ann Shadd, January 17, 1961"—original typescripts by D[avid] Shadd, Mary Ann Shadd Cary Papers, Public Archives of Canada, Ottawa; Hallie Q. Brown, comp., *Homespun Heroines and Other Women of Distinction* (Xenia, Ohio: Aldine, 1926), pp. 92–96; Martin Robison Delany, *The Condition, Elevation, Emigration, and Destiny of the Colored People of the United States, Politically Considered* (Philadelphia: By the Author, 1852), p. 24; *The North Star*, March 23, 1849, p. 3; June 8, 1849, p. 3. See also Harold B. Hancock, "Mary Ann Shadd: Negro Editor, Educator, and Lawyer," *Delaware History*, XV (April, 1973), 187–194; Elsie M. Lewis, "Mary Ann Shadd Cary," in Edward T. James, ed., *Notable American Women, 1607–1950: A Biographical Dictionary*, I (Cambridge: Harvard University Press, 1971), 300–301. On Abraham D. Shadd, see Harold B. Hancock, "Not Quite Men: The Free Negroes of Delaware in the 1830's," *Civil War History*, XVII (December, 1971), 329–330; *The Anglo-African Magazine*, I (February, 1859), 64; Robin W. Winks, *The Blacks in Canada: A History* (New Haven: Yale University Press, 1971), p. 215.

18. "Cary Life Sketch," Cary Papers; *Voice of the Fugitive*, January 29, 1852; Winks, *Blacks in Canada*, pp. 225, 226; Mary A. Shadd, *A Plea for Emigration; or Notes of Canada West, in Its Moral, Social and Political Aspects*... (Detroit: George W. Pattison, 1852), esp. pp. 37, 44. The book was reviewed in *The Pennsylvania Freeman*, July 3, 1852, p. 106.

thusiastic evaluation of their adopted land was Henry Bibb. Born a slave in Kentucky in 1815, Bibb had escaped and been recaptured five times before his final flight in 1842. From then until the passage of the Fugitive Slave Act he lived in Detroit. Although Bibb's education was limited to two weeks at a school taught by the Reverend William C. Monroe, a leader in the Detroit black community, he was an able speaker and competent writer who gave antislavery lectures along the Canadian border and in New York and Ohio, as well as in Michigan, where he campaigned for the Liberty party in 1844. He was also involved in illegal operations helping former slaves escape to the British provinces. Concerned too with the lot of free blacks in the North, Bibb served as the agent for the Raisin Institute, a manual labor school for black youth in southeastern Michigan, and spoke for black suffrage and equal rights before the state's constitutional convention in 1850. In 1849 he published the story of his own flight, *Narrative of the Life and Adventures of Henry Bibb, an American Slave*. When the Fugitive Slave Act went into effect, he crossed the Detroit River into Canada West, where he lived until his death in the summer of 1854 at the age of 39.[19]

An emigrant radicalized by his forced departure from the United States (a departure motivated in large part by his pessimism about the future prospects of Afro-Americans), Bibb joined emigrationism to a quasi-nationalist position not long after his arrival in Canada. In June, 1851, *The Voice of the Fugitive*—Bibb's own newspaper and Canada's first black paper—published a "Call for a Great North American Anti-Slavery Convention" which agreed that there was a need for a convention which transcended national boundaries, and that American blacks should consider the virtues of Canada. Several well-known black abolitionists and convention figures such as Martin R. Delany of Pennsylvania, H. O. Wagoner and John Jones of Illinois, and Amos G. Beman of Connecticut endorsed the call, as did two obscure Burlington, Vermont, blacks—James L. Taylor, a forty-two-year-old barber of relatively ample means, and James Theodore Holly, a bootmaker. Over the next few years Holly

---

19. Winks, *Blacks in Canada*, pp. 395–397; David M. Katzman, *Before the Ghetto: Black Detroit in the Nineteenth Century* (Urbana: University of Illinois Press, 1973), pp. 15–16, 39, 41; *Frederick Douglass' Paper*, August 11, 1854, p. 3.

would turn some of the major tenets of Woodson's nationalist-emigrationist ideology into a concrete program.[20]

Perhaps the emigrationism Holly advocated rested partly upon his own mobile past. By June, 1851, when he was only twenty-one, Holly was already something of a wanderer. Born in Washington, D.C. (where his father, a shoemaker by trade, had made the shoes James Madison wore at his inauguration in 1809), Holly attended a school for blacks run by Dr. John H. Fleet, a prominent black doctor. In 1844 Holly's family moved to Brooklyn to avoid what he later described as "*some* of the disabilities free Colored men labor under in the South." His elder brother Joseph, also a shoemaker, evidently was able to make a living in Brooklyn, for William C. Nell, the black Garrisonian writer and lecturer, claimed that Joseph Holly's "customers are no less satisfied with his work on account of a complexion unlike their own." Encouraged by a Spanish priest, James Theodore Holly studied mathematics and classics before obtaining a clerkship in Lewis Tappan's American Missionary Association office in the late 1840's. After the family moved in early 1850 to a French Canadian and Irish working-class neighborhood in Burlington, both brothers established themselves as bootmakers, with assistance from Tappan. Whatever the attractions of Vermont, James Theodore Holly was uncomfortable in his new surroundings; in June he wrote the American Colonization Society expressing a desire to emigrate to Liberia "provided I could make myself useful to the community in a manner agreeable to my predilections...." Holly's predilections were quite specific: while he indicated his willingness to teach school in Liberia, he wished to practice hydropathy and homeopathy there, and he asked the Society to support his training—preferably in hydropathy.[21]

---

20. Katzman, *Before the Ghetto*, p. 42; *The Voice of the Fugitive*, June 18, 1851, p. 3; August 13, 1851, p. 4; August 27, 1851, p. 1; Manuscript Schedules, Seventh Census of the United States: 1850—Burlington, Vermont. For Taylor's property (listed as $300 in real estate on the census) and land dealings, see the Burlington Grand List, 1850, p. 51, and the Burlington Land Records, 19, 151; 21, 538; and 23, 185. I am indebted to David Blow, Burlington, for the above property and census information.

21. David McEwen Dean, "James Theodore Holly, 1829–1911, Black Nationalist and Bishop" (Ph.D. dissertation, University of Texas, 1972), pp. 4, 7, 9; J. Theodore

The Colonization Society would not support Holly's medical education. However, the Society also advised Holly that "No class of men are more needed in Liberia, than *teachers* of a high order," and encouraged him to acquire more education. William McLain of the Society's Washington office was so intrigued by the young shoemaker who could write "a really *first-class* letter" that he asked the Reverend Joseph Tracy, corresponding secretary of the Society's Massachusetts auxiliary, to "inquire about *Holly*—& in your Yankee way, make up an opinion about him." Tracy's investigation evidently was brief, and for unknown reasons McLain did not answer Holly's final letter to the Society in early September.[22]

Despite the termination of his correspondence with the Colonization Society, Holly continued to advocate some form of colonization or emigration. During the summer of 1850 he had publicly supported colonization when debating with his brother the question, "Can the colored people of the U.S. best elevate their condition by remaining in this country or by emigrating to Liberia?" Joseph Holly, who had sharply attacked the American Colonization Society in a lengthy letter to Henry Clay from Brooklyn in January, did not spare his younger brother—if one can judge from the skill with which he ridiculed colonizationists only two years later. At that time, with a poet's skill for hyperbole (he published a volume of poetry, *Freedom's Offering*, in 1853), he raged that any black supporter of the Colonization Society was "a traitor, compared with whom Benedict Arnold was a pure patriot and Judas Iscariot an exemplary Christian."[23] The intensity of his brother's views evidently affected

---

Holly to William McLain, Burlington, June 25, 1850, August 8, 1850, Domestic Letters, American Colonization Society Papers, Manuscript Division, Library of Congress (hereafter cited as ACS Papers). Nell's observation is in *The North Star*, July 6, 1849, p. 3. For Holly and the A.M.A., see J. T. Holly to Joshua Kimber, January 7, 1884; Holly to George Flichtner, March 8, 1882, Domestic and Foreign Missionary Society Papers: Haiti Papers, Church Historical Society, Austin, Texas.

22. McLain to Holly, Washington, July 31, 1850; McLain to Rev. Joseph Tracy, Washington, August 14, 1850, ACS Letterbooks; Holly to McLain, Burlington, September 3, 1850, Domestic Letters, ACS Papers.

23. Holly to McLain, Burlington, August 8, 1850, Domestic Letters, ACS Papers; *The North Star*, February 1, 1850, pp. 2–3; *Frederick Douglass' Paper*, August 27, 1852, p. 3. Joseph Holly's poetry—which he had been writing since at

James Theodore Holly, for when he emerged as a forceful advocate of North American black solidarity and Canadian emigration in a series of four letters published in Bibb's *Voice of the Fugitive* in June and July, 1851, he was careful to distinguish voluntary emigration to Canada from the white-controlled Liberian colonization scheme which he, like Joseph, now opposed.

To Holly, Canadian emigration represented "an alternative we can spontaneously adopt ourselves, without having it marked out for us by doubtful philanthropists"—such as those controlling the American Colonization Society. The proximity of Canada was a more important argument in its favor. Holly maintained that blacks fleeing to Canada would not be abandoning their brethren in chains as they would be if they emigrated to Africa, or even to Haiti or the British West Indies. Rather, large-scale free black emigration to Canada would hasten emancipation by providing "greater hope to the slave because we can offer him a more secure asylum, and . . . greater terror to the oppressor, because we will thereby transfer our already alienated hearts to the attitude and allegiance of aliens."[24]

Holly's emigrationism was also closely related to his call for the establishment in Canada of a single organization to serve blacks living throughout North America. He visualized a "centre of Unity" —a central organization which would first unite and then "mould the destiny of the whole Afro American race." Such an organization would alleviate the present fragmentation of effort and would serve functions analogous to those envisioned for the "One Great National Head" which Lewis Woodson had seen uniting local auxiliaries. Holly believed that a central or national agency must be located in Canada, because there it would transcend the local rivalries and jealousies which had marked black organizational efforts in the United States; it would also provide "a point, of sufficient commanding influence to establish a central authority and to harmonize the isolated tendencies of each individual locality." Consequently, when J. T. Fisher of Toronto suggested the convening of the provincial convention of Canadian blacks, Holly countered by asking

---

least 1847—was published in *The Voice of the Fugitive*, September 23, 1852, p. 1; October 21, 1852, p. 1. His *Freedom's Offering* (Rochester: Charles H. McDonnell, 1853) was reviewed in *Frederick Douglass' Paper*, July 22, 1853, p. 3.

24. *The Voice of the Fugitive*, June 4, 1851, p. 2; July 2, 1851, p. 1.

The Drift toward Emigration

the convention's promoters to invite delegates from the United States as well.²⁵ Almost simultaneously Bibb promulgated his call for a North American convention.

When the convention opened in Toronto on September 11, neither Holly nor his Burlington ally, James L. Taylor, was in attendance, although a dozen American delegates (including Delany) were present. Lack of money must have kept Holly and Taylor in Vermont. However, in addition to designating Fisher as their proxy, they sent the delegates a fraternal statement which was read at the convention. Eschewing another exhortation for Canadian emigration, the letter called upon the convention to adopt a constitution for a North American League—Holly's "central authority" for Canadian and American blacks—as a permanent organization headquartered in Toronto with auxiliaries scattered throughout the United States and the provinces. As outlined in the Holly-Taylor statement, the League would serve three major functions: aiding fugitive slaves upon their arrival in Canada; encouraging the emigration to Canada of free blacks from the United States; and, finally, helping the new black settlers establish themselves upon the soil. However, "after agriculture becomes well developed," Holly and Taylor further explained, the emigrants would be encouraged "to erect mills and manufactories—after the erection of mills and manufactories to proceed to commercial exportation."²⁶

Not surprisingly, the Toronto Convention urged slaves and free blacks from the United States to flee to Canada because of the continued oppression which the Fugitive Slave Act symbolized. The convention also moved well beyond the Holly-Taylor plan for unifying Canadian and American blacks into a "national" organization. The delegates decided that the proposed black union should include the British West Indies, as well as Canada and the United States. This plan incorporated the suggestion of William Wemyss Anderson, a white Jamaican appointed by his country's House of Assembly to visit Canada and the United States to determine the feasibility of encouraging blacks to migrate to Jamaica to establish small farms. Moreover, the convention agreed on the agricultural league's specific economic functions, which Holly and Taylor had

25. *Ibid.*, July 2, 1851, p. 1; July 30, 1851, p. 2.
26. *Ibid.*, September 24, 1851, pp. 2, 3.

described only in the most general terms, and linked these directly to the plan for continental union. Basically, the proposed league would raise capital by selling shares in the organization for fifty dollars each—to be paid in ten annual installments, the money being deposited in the Bank of Upper Canada. The league's assets would then be used to purchase land and agricultural implements in Canada and the British West Indies, and the land would be sold to emigrants.[27]

During the months following the convention, writers to *The Voice of the Fugitive* developed an elaborate ideological rationale for the proposed agricultural league. They argued not only that the league would insure the development of a prosperous black farming community in Canada and the British West Indies, but that it would also encourage the growth of free-labor produce. Employing the same arguments used by the Philadelphia-based Colored Free Produce Society in the early 1830's and, more recently, by black abolitionist Henry Highland Garnet while lecturing in England in 1850 and 1851, these correspondents held that the products of black agriculturists would undercut the South's economy and eventually bring destruction to the slave power and emancipation of those in bondage. One anonymous writer envisioned Canadian blacks raising corn, beef, flour, and pork to trade with Jamaican blacks growing cotton, sugar, and rice. *The Voice of the Fugitive* developed another argument for the league which was consistent with the anti-Liberian views of many convention delegates: by fostering the "national development [of blacks] on the continent of America," the league would "supersede the necessity of migrating to Africa."[28]

During the summer of 1852 Bibb claimed that the constitution

27. *Ibid.*, September 24, 1851, p. 2; October 22, 1851, p. 1; *New York Daily Tribune*, September 24, 1851, p. 6. Anderson wrote the fact sheet on Jamaica included in the appendix to *Arguments, Pro and Con, on the Call for a National Emigration Convention, to be Held at Cleveland, Ohio, August, 1854* (Detroit: M. T. Newsom, [1854?]). An endorsement for Jamaica by Henry Bibb followed Anderson's account; see pp. 31–32. For biographical information, see "William Wemyss Anderson," *Journal of the Institute of Jamaica*, II (July, 1896), 218–219.

28. See, for example, December 3, 1851, p. 2; July 1, 1852, p. 2. For black contributions to free produce activity, see *Genius of Universal Emancipation*, XII (May, 1831), 6; *The Non-Slaveholder*, V (November, 1850), 241–242; *The Anti-Slavery Reporter*, n.s. VI (June 2, 1851), 87.

for the "American Continental and West India League" had been promulgated, and that a provisional organization had been formed with an auxiliary already operating in the Windsor area. Holly was the secretary—evidently for both the Windsor body and the parent provisional organization. By this time, however, it was apparent that there had been no success in implementing the Toronto convention's plan for continental unity; what remained was largely a paper organization created by Bibb and Holly to lend an abstract justification for their two less lofty efforts—*The Voice of the Fugitive* and the Refugee Home Society, a cooperative land-jobbing scheme then under heavy attack from other Canadian blacks. Holly himself, now a full-time aid to Bibb, during the spring of 1852 spent six weeks in New England and the Middle States as the corresponding editor and traveling agent for *The Voice of the Fugitive*. In early June he settled in Windsor with his wife. He became co-editor of the paper, as well as Bibb's leading supporter in the controversy surrounding the Refugee Home Society.[29]

Organized in January, 1852, with Bibb, his wife Mary, and Josiah Henson among the leaders, the Refugee Home Society was one of a number of black land-settlement experiments in Canada formed with the assistance of white philanthropy in the 1840's and 1850's. Like some of the other settlements, the Refugee Home Society divided the black community in Canada West. Samuel R. Ward was a fugitive slave prominent as a Garrisonian lecturer and editor before fleeing to Canada after the passage of the Fugitive Slave Act of 1850; he and Mary Ann Shadd led a persistent attack upon the Society. Objecting to the organization on a number of grounds, Shadd remained true to the militant self-help views she had voiced before migrating to Canada by opposing black organizations such as the Refugee Home Society, which depended upon white support. At the same time, both Ward and Shadd charged that the Society was fostering segregation. In answering such denunciations, Holly was particularly careful to explain why the Refugee Home Society urged blacks to live together cooperatively. Although "it is desirable that *color* should be eradicated as a basis for the social distinctions of *rank*," Holly explained, "... this will be done by the

29. *The Voice of the Fugitive*, July 1, 1852, p. 2.

colored man himself, when in a state of freedom, after he becomes *thoroughly* educated, and the personal sense of slavery shall be lost in free-born generations of descendants...."[30]

In their preoccupation with defending the Refugee Home Society, Bibb and Holly did not lose sight of the larger cause of continental black unity. Perhaps this was because they were becoming aware of their ambiguous position in Canada, where they were second-class citizens socially and economically, although not legally. They were active at the General Convention for the Improvement of the Colored Inhabitants of Canada, held in June, 1853, at Amhestburg, Canada West. This gathering was an undisguised attempt to resurrect the triad of concerns which the two men had been propounding for the previous couple of years: North American and British West Indian black cooperation, the encouragement of commercial enterprises, and emigration. Holly was especially influential in pushing these principles. As leader of a three-man committee on emigration which reported back to the convention, he argued that free blacks in the United States, destined to live under continual oppression, must choose between emigration and revolution. Concluding that Afro-Americans lacked the resources necessary to engineer a successful revolution, Holly's committee maintained that only through emigration could free blacks alleviate their own condition and simultaneously work for the emancipation of the slaves. The report continued with an extensive analysis of the advantages presented to prospective emigrants by various localities. While stating a clear preference for Canada because of its proximity to the United States, the committee also discussed the virtues of the British West Indies, Haiti ("the first nationality established by our race"), and Central America. The report closed by urging the convention as a body to follow the actions of the 1851 Toronto convention and formulate plans for a continental league, because "a systematic combination should go hand in hand with every band of emigrants wheresoever they may go on the continent, uniting them

---

30. William H. Pease and Jane H. Pease, *Black Utopia: Negro Communal Experiments in America* (Madison: State Historical Society of Wisconsin, 1963), pp. 109–122; Winks, *Blacks in Canada*, pp. 204–208; *The Liberator*, March 4, 1853, p. 36. On Ward, see his *Autobiography of a Fugitive Negro: His Anti-Slavery Labours in the United States, Canada, & England* (London: John Snow, 1855).

in cooperative efforts with those they leave behind, or who may be scattered throughout its different parts."[31]

Thus, although neither Holly's committee on emigration nor the Amherstburg convention as a body referred specifically to a Black Nationality, both the report on emigration and the resolutions of the convention merged proposals for continental black unity with emigrationism. Fittingly, this effort was pushed by Bibb and Holly—both relatively recent emigrants whose alienation from the United States had led them to blend proposals for racial solidarity transcending political boundaries with the more expected exhortations for American blacks to emigrate to Canada. If other blacks in Canada who had also abandoned the United States did not accept all of Bibb and Holly's positions, still several of them—most prominently Mary Ann Shadd—would eventually adopt a nationalist-emigrationist orientation. Yet even before this occurred, Martin R. Delany, one of the American delegates to the 1851 Toronto convention, emerged as the most influential and tireless North American proselytizer of a nationalist-emigrationist ideology.

Martin R. Delany: The Alienation of an Abolitionist

By the summer of 1851, when he first arrived in Canada to lecture on physiology in the weeks before the Toronto convention, Martin R. Delany no longer adhered to the traditional abolitionist shibboleths which he had espoused so frequently and effectively as an editor and orator during the 1840's. At that time he had combined militant abolitionism with less fiery activities on behalf of political antislavery, black suffrage, and the more amorphous principles of moral reform and the "elevation" of the race. After 1850, however, Delany emerged as a leading advocate of nationalist-emigrationist positions and thus departed sharply from the attitudes he had held during the previous decade. From Delany's perspective, however, this development must have appeared inevitable. Not only had he been nurtured on the whole range of similar ideas which Lewis

---

31. *Minutes and Proceedings of the General Convention, for the Improvement of the Colored Inhabitants of Canada, Held by Adjournments in Amherstburgh* [sic], *C.W. June 16th and 17th, 1853* (Windsor, C.W.: Bibb & Holly, 1853), pp. 2-3, 11-16.

Woodson had developed in the late 1830's and early 1840's, but he also claimed to be a descendant of a Golah village chieftain on his father's side and a Mandingo prince on his mother's side.³²

When Martin Delany was born in Charlestown, Virginia (now West Virginia), on May 6, 1812, his father Samuel was still a slave, although Pati, his mother, was free. He received a scanty education in Charlestown before his mother took her family to Chambersburg, Pennsylvania, in 1822; later Delany's father joined them there. In 1831 the nineteen-year-old Delany traveled over the mountains to Pittsburgh. There he spent the next twenty-five years working first as a barber, then as a "cupper and leecher," and, finally as a physician. He also served the causes of moral reform and abolition; his decision to resume his education by attending Woodson's school proved especially fortuitous for these endeavors.³³

Delany's relationship with Woodson extended far beyond the classroom. In 1836 the two men traveled to Philadelphia and New York, looking for the meeting of a national convention which was never held. After the American Moral Reform Society was organized, Woodson and Delany participated in moral reform activities in Pittsburgh. Like Woodson, Delany attended the meeting at which the Pittsburgh auxiliary was formed; Woodson was elected corresponding secretary and Delany became one of the seven managers. They also served as officers of the Temperance Society of the People of Color of the City of Pittsburgh. In March, 1838, teacher and student were active at a series of three Pittsburgh meetings which urged the calling of a statewide convention to protest the disfranchisement of blacks, first by the Supreme Court of Pennsylvania and then by the state constitutional convention. When the State Convention of the Colored Freeman of Pennsylvania was held in August, 1841, at Pittsburgh, Delany and Woodson served on a committee to prepare the agenda for the three-day affair.³⁴

32. *The Impartial Citizen*, August 23, 1851, p. 3; Rollin, *Life of Delany*, pp. 15–17.

33. *Ibid.*, pp. 14, 25–26, 33–38, 43–47, 68–69; Dorothy Sterling, *The Making of an Afro-American: Martin Robison Delany, 1812–1885* (Garden City, N.Y.: Doubleday, 1971), pp. 48–55.

34. Rollin, *Life of Delany*, p. 45; *National Enquirer and Constitutional Advocate of Universal Liberty*, August 24, 1836, p. 1; January 7, 1837, p. 71; *Colored*

By the mid-1840's Delany was essentially a political activist who supported the Liberty party and championed abolition and the rights and privileges of the disfranchised and oppressed Afro-American living in what he considered the "nominally free States" of the North. A powerful speaker who once held the attention of a Zanesville, Ohio, audience for nearly three hours, he impressed the more widely known William Lloyd Garrison and Frederick Douglass when he accompanied them briefly during their antislavery tour in western Pennsylvania in August, 1847. Garrison described Delany as "a fine fellow of great energy and spirit," who spoke "on the subject of prejudice against color in a very witty and energetic manner"; in Douglass's eyes, he was "one of the most open, free, generous, and zealous laborers in the cause of our enslaved brethren, which I have met ... in a long time."[35]

Although an orator and an organization man active in conventions and petition campaigns, Delany was foremost a newspaper editor at this time. From August 30, 1843, through late 1847, he edited *The Mystery*, then the only black paper published in Pennsylvania and one of the very few black papers in the country. Through the pages of *The Mystery* the Pittsburgh physician and editor lambasted the institution of slavery and proudly championed antislavery activities. Publishing the paper was a financial strain, however, and on at least one occasion, unable to handle the burdens, he temporarily resigned as editor. Even after Delany transferred the ownership to a committee in the middle of 1844, he was forced to contribute to the paper from his other income. He also lectured widely in Ohio and eastern Pennsylvania in search of subscriptions. While his financial situation hardly distinguished him from other black editors of the period, he may have had added difficulties because he was more than willing to criticize his brethren if he believed they were

---

American, April 12, 1838, p. 47; *Proceedings of the Pennsylvania Colored Convention, 1841*, pp. 3-4.

35. *Pittsburgh Daily Dispatch*, September 9, 1847, p. 3; *Anti-Slavery Bugle*, October 1, 1847, p. 3; *Palladium of Liberty*, May 15, 1844, p. 2; Wendell Phillips Garrison and Francis Jackson Garrison, *William Lloyd Garrison, 1805-1879: The Story of His Life as Told by his Children* (Boston: Houghton, Mifflin, 1894), III, 193-194; *Pennsylvania Freeman*, September 2, 1847, p. 3. Delany referred to the "nominally free States" in *The North Star*, July 28, 1848, p. 2.

shirking their responsibilities. As he confessed when he terminated his relationship with *The Mystery*, "we had frequently to touch subjects that once affected the pride and interests of our brethren, who often in consequence looked upon us more as an injurer than as a friend." In fact, one black man—"Fiddler" Johnson—sued Delany for libel in the spring of 1847 after *The Mystery* had called Johnson "a slave-catcher." Convicted, Delany was fined $150, but this was remitted by the governor.[36]

In late 1847, having abandoned *The Mystery*, Delany joined with Frederick Douglass in publishing *The North Star* from Rochester, New York. Douglass's first editorial venture soon became a widely known antislavery newspaper. Although partners, the two editors saw each other only occasionally, for Douglass remained in Rochester to handle the editorial work of the paper while throughout 1848 Delany pleaded for subscriptions before antislavery audiences in Ohio and Pennsylvania. His success was limited, and for a while Douglass blamed his traveling partner for the struggles *The North Star* was enduring. Nevertheless, the two editors spoke together at public meetings in western New York in early August, and in September they were both active participants at the Colored National Convention in Cleveland—the first black "national" convention in the West, and one which Delany had been calling for as early as December, 1846, while still editing *The Mystery*. In mid-December the Pittsburgh abolitionist closed his tour of eastern Pennsylvania and Delaware on behalf of *The North Star* with an appearance at the State Convention of Colored Citizens of Pennsylvania at Harrisburg. Although Delany continued to write for *The North Star* well into 1849, he was spending less time lecturing and raising subscriptions for the paper. In fact, at the end of June, 1849, he resigned his position with the newspaper, and Douglass assumed sole re-

---

36. *The North Star*, January 21, 1848, p. 2; August 18, 1848, p. 2; *Palladium of Liberty*, May 15, 1844, p. 2; June 19, 1844, p. 3; *Pennsylvania Freeman*, July 9, 1846, p. 3; August 20, 1846, p. 3; *Pittsburgh Morning Chronicle*, April 12, 1847, p. 2. For a relatively detailed recollection of the publishing history of *The Mystery*, see *The Elevator*, April 19, 1867, p. 2. Unfortunately, only two issues of Delany's paper —April 16, 1845, and December 16, 1846—are extant; both are available at the Carnegie Library of Pittsburgh. Fortunately, the *Palladium of Liberty*, *The Liberator*, *Pennsylvania Freeman*, and even the *Maryland Colonization Journal* reprinted items from *The Mystery*.

sponsibility for *The North Star*'s editorial and financial condition.[37]

In terminating his relationship with *The North Star*, Delany was simultaneously closing more than a decade of activity as a propagandist for antislavery and moral reform. Articulating his views at local, state, and national conventions and abolitionist forums and through the antislavery press, Delany had been in the mainstream of contemporary black thought. Yet implicit in the attitudes he articulated so fervently and so effectively were certain tendencies and assumptions which, when brought to the surface after 1850, would exacerbate his alienation and drive him thoroughly into the nationalist-emigrationist position he argued after 1852.

Prior to midcentury, however, Delany rarely commented on emigration at all. Occasionally he made ephemeral remarks which touched upon the African colonization movement, but which were directed toward ends other than those of approving the activities and orientation of the American Colonization Society. For example, in late 1846, shortly after he had denounced the American Colonization Society in *The Mystery*, Delany saluted the efforts of the Chesapeake and Liberia Trading Company. This shipping company was formed in 1845 under the auspices of Dr. James Hall and the Maryland State Colonization Society, with the expectation that as more and more blacks in the United States and Liberia became stockholders, they would eventually assume control of the company. By that time, it was hoped, the firm would be sending ships manned by black officers and all-black crews to Liberia laden with both cargo and emigrants, thus fulfilling the fondest hopes of Paul Cuffe, Hezekiah Grice, and others who had envisioned the formation of a black trading company. However, the Chesapeake and Liberia Trading Company never achieved its purpose. In 1852, when it was

37. Frederick Douglass to Martin R. Delany, Rochester, January 12, 1848; Douglass to Julia Griffiths, Rochester, April 28, 1848, Frederick Douglass Papers (microfilm), Manuscript Division, Library of Congress; *The North Star*, August 25, 1848, p. 2; *Report of the Proceedings of the Colored National Convention, Held at Cleveland, Ohio, On Wednesday, September 6, 1848* (Rochester: John Dick, 1848); *The Mystery*, December 16, 1846, p. 2; *Minutes of the State Convention of the Colored Citizens of Pennsylvania, Convened at Harrisburg, December 13th and 14th, 1848* (Philadelphia: Merrihew and Thompson, 1849), pp. 4–6; *The North Star*, June 29, 1849, p. 2. Delany's travels are recorded almost weekly in *The North Star*.

disbanded, blacks owned less than 15 percent of the stock; of this amount, almost all was in the hands of Liberians. Yet during the company's early years, Delany applauded the development: "We want trading expeditions to Africa, we must have them, and that well manned by colored seamen, properly built, and fully equipped for fast sailing, and the emergencies of the enterprise." As he said on another occasion, among the "hundreds of avenues to industry and enterprise opened to our young men and capitalists," the West Indian and African trade provided special opportunities. At the same time, he was also following developments in Liberia, where independence had been achieved in 1847. He at first complimented the new black republic for freeing itself from white influence and thus having thwarted the objects of its founders. Yet he soon changed his view and castigated the country's president, Joseph J. Roberts, for acting as a servant to white interests.[38]

Delany's shifting attitudes toward Liberia were filtered through his major emphasis in the 1840's—a self-help philosophy consistent with the moral reform tradition he had participated in while still a young man. Implicit in Delany's self-help frame of reference was the assumption that American society was so fluid that blacks who worked diligently, learned trades, followed moral precepts, and practiced personal thrift could overcome the burdens of caste. Delany appeared to be arguing that there was room at the top for the industrious. In his mind, many blacks were indolent and wanton, and he expended much of his energy during the 1840's castigating the shiftless and unproductive whose material failures he blamed entirely upon their moral laxity. For those still capable of reformation, Delany urged hard work, thrift, education, the acquisition of a trade, the formation of a "Self-Elevation Tract-Society," and the like. In January, 1848, he exhorted: "Colored People! we want more business men among us; farmers, mechanics and tradesmen. We must, in order to be respected and gain our lost rights and privileges. ... Let our people put their children—first to school, next to trades."

38. *Maryland Colonization Journal*, n.s. III (June, 1846), 197–198; (January, 1847), 299; *The North Star*, December 15, 1848, p. 3; February 4, 1848, p. 2; March 2, 1849, p. 2. On the Chesapeake and Liberia Trading Company, see *Maryland Colonization Journal*, n.s. III (April, 1846), 147–148; n.s. IV (October, 1847), 72; (November, 1847), 73–76; n.s. VI (November, 1852), 274–277.

The Drift toward Emigration

A year and a half later, he could see marked progress—at least in Pittsburgh and adjacent Allegheny City, where blacks were acquiring real estate; in Pittsburgh, moreover, several blacks "have put their property to the best of uses and built tenements which are now let out yielding them a handsome percentage of their investments...."[39]

In Delany's opinion, then, occupational status was an index of interior moral and intellectual development; it could also provide an entree into the larger society. Thus defending himself from charges that he had criticized black women for working as domestics, Delany maintained that "it is no disgrace, to live out...[but] when you can do better, it is your duty to do so, if you cannot, it is no shame to do the best you can." While writing to *The North Star* from the various Ohio cities and towns he was visiting, Delany devoted lengthy passages to detailing the occupational categories of the black communities he visited. In Cincinnati, for example, he commended the many blacks working as tradesmen and thus "amply demonstrating our capacity to take care of ourselves." He followed this with a similar list of blacks running their own small businesses. "This is what I desire to see," he exulted, "—our people coming out of old employments of domestic servitude and menial occupations. This must be done if we expect ever to be elevated to an equality with the dominant class." Delany's commitment to this point of view was so strong that at the Colored National Convention in Cleveland in September, 1848, he criticized those blacks who were forced to accept menial employment; for this he was roundly chastized.[40]

For Delany, "equality with the dominant class" was more than simply material equality; it brought with it certain rights and privileges. In Columbus, for instance, he found "invariably... that the farmers and mechanics among colored brethren, command the same civil respect of their neighbors that others do." Yet even if whites

39. This composite view can be drawn from, among other items, *The North Star*, April 28, 1848, p. 2; May 12, 1848, p. 2; May 26, 1848, p. 2; June 9, 1848, p. 2; June 16, 1848, p. 2; November 17, 1848, p. 2; December 1, 1848, p. 2; February 16, 1849, p. 2; April 27, 1849, p. 2; June 15, 1849, p. 3. Quotations are *ibid.*, February 11, 1848, p. 2; July 6, 1849, p. 3. See also *The Mystery*, December 16, 1846, p. 2.

40. *Palladium of Liberty*, February 21, 1844, p. 2; *The North Star*, June 9, 1848, p. 2; *Report of the Colored National Convention, 1848*, pp. 5, 13.

were willing to respond cordially to those blacks who had "elevated" themselves, self-help had far greater implications in Delany's conception: it was a prerequisite for the psychological as well as the political emancipation of all black people. By "demonstrating our capacity to take care of ourselves" individually—as were the Cincinnati tradesmen and, presumably, the Pittsburgh landlords—blacks would free themselves from undue dependence upon whites. "I am satisfied, from experience and otherwise," Delany noted in November, 1848, "that we must act and do for ourselves—we must, in order to accomplish so desirable an end as our elevation, morally, religiously and socially, become our own representatives." Although Frederick Douglass was similarly blending self-help and racial solidarity, few blacks were as attached as Delany was to the belief that "None can properly represent us but ourselves."[41] In sum, personal self-help led inexorably to racial self-sufficiency and, by implication, racial solidarity.

Self-help also pointed the black editor toward another issue: the nefarious influence of religion which, in Delany's view, encouraged resignation and dependence by focusing upon the spiritual rather than the temporal. Religion was, first of all, too influential among blacks: "[A]mong our people generally, the church is the Alpha and Omega of all things. It is their only source of information—their only acknowledged public body—their State Legislature . . . their only acknowledged adviser. . . ." But the real evils of the church moved well beyond its domination of black intellectual and moral concerns. Rather, the church—and Christianity itself—taught doctrines which reinforced debasement and degradation because the doctrines themselves were passed along to blacks by slaveholders and pro-slavery apologists: "All that you know, in morals or religion, you have learned from your oppressors. . . ." Christian otherworldliness, in fact, fostered servility by teaching blacks the erroneous view that "Prayer . . . is all-sufficient for *all* things." But the spiritual and temporal realms were separate—each with its own

---

41. *The North Star*, April 28, 1848, p. 2; November 17, 1848, p. 2; August Meier, "Frederick Douglass' Vision for America: A Case Study in Nineteenth-Century Negro Protest," in Harold M. Hyman and Leonard W. Levy, eds., *Freedom and Reform: Essays in Honor of Henry Steele Commager* (New York: Harper & Row, 1967), pp. 135-136.

The Drift toward Emigration

rules, each with its own ends. "Prayer is a spiritual means," Delany held, "used in conformity to the spiritual law, and can only be instrumental in attaining a spiritual end.... [Neither] physical wants, nor temporal demands of man can be supplied by it." Blacks must free themselves from docility and oppression by casting off the shackles of a religion designed to enervate and stultify; "Prayer and praises only fill one's soul with emotion, but can never fill his mouth with bread, nor his pocket with money." The answer, then, was a self-help philosophy which depicted energetic, self-motivated blacks in "respectable occupations"—business and the trades. "Give us wealth," Delany had decided, "and we can obtain all the rest."[42]

Thus Delany had developed a world view which held, in part, that energetic and morally responsible blacks could acquire material prosperity and social acceptability in the United States. He contended that blacks suffered from discrimination because of their condition, not their color. When they improved their condition, they would be accorded full social and political equality. Yet it is questionable whether Delany himself fully accepted this position. As a black man who had established a newspaper to fight not only slavery in the South, but also discrimination in the North, Delany could not have been oblivious to the fact that color itself led to oppression. He well recognized, for example, that in most northern states blacks were disfranchised regardless of their economic or social standing; in fact, he had campaigned for black suffrage in Pennsylvania, and in the pages of *The Mystery* he had lauded similar efforts in Michigan.[43] Like Lewis Woodson before him, Delany was caught in the grip of a contradiction. The peculiarly critical nature of his self-help ideology compelled him to view as laggards those blacks who failed to rise in the social order. On the other hand, his perceptions of the existing reality led Delany to acknowledge that the restrictions placed upon blacks made no allowance for ability or respectability. Far from being merely a rhetorical problem, Delany's dilemma was crucial. If he finally concluded that blacks suf-

---

42. *The North Star*, February 16, 1849, p. 2; April 13, 1849, p. 2; March 23, 1849, p. 2; April 20, 1849, p. 2.

43. *Colored American*, April 12, 1838, p. 47; *Proceedings of the Pennsylvania Colored Convention, 1841*, pp. 7, 8, 12–13; *Minutes of the Pennsylvania Colored Convention, 1848*, pp. 4–6; *Palladium of Liberty*, February 21, 1844, p. 2.

fered from what Woodson once called "a prejudice of caste," then he would be forced to admit that for blacks in the United States the self-help philosophy was an abortive concept. If blacks—respectable and wanton, rich and poor, learned and illiterate—were all treated alike, then it would be impossible to urge them to believe in an open society in which industriousness and respectability actually paid.

Between 1849 and 1852 Martin R. Delany resolved this dilemma by deciding—with what must have been the bitterness reserved for only disabused true-believers—that all blacks were, after all, treated as debased pariahs and subject to "a prejudice of caste." Having parted ways with the American Dream, it was almost inevitable that Delany would wish to cut himself off from America itself. Emigration, then, became an alternative ideology. The passage of the Fugitive Slave Act of 1850 and the direct impact of the law upon the Pittsburgh black community were undoubtedly factors in Delany's loss of faith. More significantly, he himself was learning that his very real abilities and accomplishments did not protect him from the consequences of American racism. Before midcentury, of course, he had experienced personal abuse: he was ordered from a stage in Columbus in 1844 after he had purchased a ticket, insulted and temporarily refused a stagecoach passage in Buffalo three years later, and attacked by an angry anti-abolitionist mob in Marseilles, Ohio, the following year. But now there occurred the event that was probably most directly responsible for intensifying Delany's alienation—his experience at Harvard Medical School in the fall of 1850 and the winter of 1851. After a group of medical students had petitioned the school's faculty asking for the removal of three black students—Delany as well as Daniel Laing and Isaac Snowden, both training for medical careers in Liberia with the support of the Massachusetts Colonization Society—he withdrew at the end of the semester as requested.[44] Disillusioned and bitter, Delany must have

44. *Pittsburgh Morning Chronicle*, November 28, 1844, p. 2; *Saturday Visiter*, December 25, 1847, p. 3. The incident at Marseilles, Ohio, is described in Rollin, *Life of Delany*, pp. 56–58, and by Delany himself in *The North Star*, July 14, 1848, pp. 2–3. A general report of the Harvard Medical School incident is in *The Boston Medical and Surgical Journal*, XLIII (December 18, 1850), 406. Petitions in opposition to the attendance of the black students (as well as one supporting the students) can be found in the Harvard Medical School, Dean's Office File, c1839–1900; this file includes the Minutes of the Medical Faculty for a critical meeting

appeared a likely convert to the plans for emigration and continental black unity which Henry Bibb, J. T. Fisher, and James Theodore Holly were developing in the fall of 1851 in anticipation of the North American Convention at Toronto.

Oddly enough, Delany refused to support the Toronto Convention's exhortation for blacks to leave the free states, although his presence at the convention suggests that he had forsaken his earlier belief in an "open America." Acting upon motives not entirely clear, he led a four-man "American" delegation which registered their disapproval at the convention's emigration resolution. Ostensibly they believed that open recruitment of northern free blacks by black residents of Canada or elsewhere marked an invitation for Afro-Americans to abandon their brethren still in bondage. More likely, however, Delany's action was prompted by a personal desire to maintain an independent and dominant role in any nationalist-emigrationist movement which might develop. In addition, he may have believed that in Canada a relatively scattered black population existing in the midst of a white majority could provide few recruits for any new nation-state congealing around the concept of a black nationality; he later referred to the "sixty-one and a fraction, whites, to one black! . . . so that colored people might never hope for anything more than . . . occupying a secondary position to the whites of the Canadas."[45]

While Delany's role at the Toronto convention was undoubtedly marginal and his position unclear, he soon emerged as the major exponent of a nationalist-emigrationist ideology with the publication in April, 1852, of *The Condition, Elevation, Emigration and Destiny of the Colored People of the United States, Politically Considered*. This pro-emigration work included a strong denunciation of the activities of the American Colonization Society. In developing

---

on December 13, 1850. A more revealing meeting was held on December 26, 1850; a report of this is in the Records of the Medical Faculty at Harvard University. All Harvard Medical School records are housed at the Francis A. Countway Library of Medicine, Harvard University. See also the *Boston Daily Journal*, December 17, 1850, p. 2; December 19, 1850, p. 1.

45. *The Voice of the Fugitive*, September 24, 1851, p. 2; *Proceedings of the National Emigration Convention of Colored People; Held at Cleveland, Ohio, on Thursday, Friday and Saturday, the 24th, 25th and 26th of August, 1854* (Pittsburgh: A. A. Anderson, 1854), p. 38.

a defense for emigrationism, Delany presented the view—directly at odds with what had been implicit in his earlier writings—that blacks would never achieve full equality in the United States. Nonetheless, his "hastily-written work"[46]—as he himself later described it—reflected many of the positions he had forged into a coherent ideology by mid-century. For example, he appeared still to believe that American whites found the lowly condition of blacks offensive, and not their color. "What is necessary to be done," he explained in terms reminiscent of his writings of the 1840's, "is to change the condition, and the person is at once changed." Blacks, then, must imitate whites by learning trades, entering professions, and establishing businesses. Obviously they must also eschew employment as servants, for as long as blacks "do the drudgery and menial offices of other men's wives and daughters; it is useless ... to talk about equality and elevation in society." Above all, blacks must lift themselves from degradation. "Our elevation," Delany stressed, "must be the result of *self-efforts*, and the work of our *own hands*."[47]

If his book reiterated themes he had previously articulated, his basic thrust had altered significantly. Continued residence in the United States was intolerable in Delany's mind. Although unwilling to renounce a claim to the natural rights he believed all Americans possessed, he recognized that blacks were essentially without political rights and were thus "aliens to the laws and political privileges of the country." Emigration represented the only possible remedy. Yet in adopting an emigration policy, blacks were not surrendering their freedom of action to whites, for blacks would resist being "driven" from the United States "by any policy that may be schemed against us."[48] Opposition to Liberia was therefore axiomatic, and he used his book to develop his criticisms.

Expressing disappointment that the young republic had not achieved real independence from its white creators, Delany concluded that Liberian colonization was a sham, and that Liberia herself was, in a sense, a captive nation "unworthy of any responsible consideration from us"—"*it is not* an independent nation at all; but

46. *The Liberator*, May 21, 1852, p. 83.
47. Delany, *Condition*, pp. 43–45.
48. *Ibid.*, pp. 48–49, 157–158.

a poor *miserable mockery*—a *burlesque* on government—a pitiful dependency on the American Colonizationists...."[49] Afro-Americans, then, must look elsewhere if they would establish an independent, commercially viable and diplomatically powerful black nation.

Yet they need not look far, Delany advised. "We must not leave this continent; America is our destination and our home." Providence had willed the American continent outside of the United States "as an asylum for all nations of the earth"; there blacks, too, would find a promised land. Yet the entire continent was certainly not equally blessed, for blacks must not only leave the United States—they must also avoid settling in Canada. Although Delany admitted that Canada might well be the most accessible if not the only refuge from oppression for the fugitive from southern slavery, he still feared that the British provinces would soon be swallowed up by American expansion. In fact, he observed that among Canadians there was already "a manifest tendency ... to Americanism." For blacks, then, the future in Canada was bleak because with annexation, "the fate of the colored man, however free before, is doomed, doomed, forever doomed."[50]

Go South—to Central America, South America, and the British West Indies, Delany exhorted. He offered several arguments in support of this position. Not only could the slave reach Mexico as easily as he could Canada, but in addition, the threat of annexation was virtually nil: with its huge slave population, the United States would not attempt to incorporate other large black populations. Third, Delany maintained that the Caribbean and Latin American countries, with a population only one-seventh white, would never consent to annexation or subjugation by the United States. Such an attitude would be strengthened with the infusion of North American blacks committed to "defend and protect the country that embraces us." Finally, he asserted that Providence itself would protect the blacks of the Americas. God had decided to assign Central and South America to blacks, and the judgment day had arrived when blacks could not only claim their homes, but also "go forward and take their position, and do battle in the struggle now

49. *Ibid.*, pp. 169–170.
50. *Ibid.*, pp. 171, 174–175, 177.

being made for the redemption of the world." Black people in Central and South America would then form their own nation, "a glorious union," to redeem mankind.

As grandiose as Delany's plan was, it was rooted in practical concerns. He stressed that Central and South America were rich in natural resources and that blacks should contribute to the commercial potentiality of the area by "cultivating the soil, entering into the mechanical operations, keeping of shops, carrying on merchandise, trading on land and water, improving property—in a word ... become the producers of the country, instead of the consumers." If black people uplifted themselves by becoming prosperous and economically productive, they would not be abandoning the slaves still in the South, but rather would be working most efficaciously for their freedom.[51]

Whether blacks emigrated or not, Delany maintained that they definitely could no longer depend on white abolitionists to liberate them either from servitude or from mere discrimination and oppression. All but calling white abolitionists hypocrites, Delany—like Samuel Cornish before him—called attention to their paternalism if not outright prejudice. He cited in particular their unwillingness to employ blacks in their own establishments, especially on abolitionist newspapers and in abolitionist offices. Blacks had assumed that abolitionists would at the very least have shown preference to black applicants. This was a tragic illusion:

> Instead of realizing what we had hoped for, we find ourselves occupying the very same position in relation to our Anti-Slavery friends, as we do in relation to the pro-slavery part of the community—a mere secondary, underling position, in all our relations to them, and anything more than this, is not a matter of course affair—it comes not by established antislavery custom or right, but like that which emanates from the proslavery portion of the community by mere sufferance.

Blacks, Delany continued, had a legitimate claim to all antislavery positions. In fact, he later expatiated upon the implications of his antagonism: blacks must assume full responsibility for their own condition and must not accede to white leadership. Nor should

51. *Ibid.*, pp. 178–188, 205.

they allow religion and its emphasis upon the spiritual to dissuade them from acting for themselves.[52]

In sum, Delany in his book had openly called for blacks to emigrate to Central and South America, where they would unite with other black peoples to establish their own nation, and he had castigated white abolitionists with unprecedented candor. Thus he had separated himself personally and ideologically from many of his past activities, attitudes, and acquaintances. Certainly, the book's strident emigrationism raised to the surface what for the past decade had remained at best latent sentiment among American black leaders. Even Delany himself felt more comfortable advocating emigration on paper than on the public platform. While the book was being printed in mid-April in Philadelphia, he chaired a meeting in the same city which, in addition to approving the usual condemnations of the American Colonization Society, endorsed two resolutions opposing emigration in general. The first announced that "in common with other American citizens we are attached to this our native land, and we will never forsake it"; the second, that "Believing that our destiny is to be fulfilled in this, the land of our birth, we therefore recommend to our brethren to stand firm, and contend for 'Life, Liberty and Happiness' in the United States." If Delany registered any opposition to this, he omitted his response from the report of the meeting which he, as chairman, prepared.[53]

The publication of his book eradicated any doubts as to Delany's attitudes on emigration as well as on other issues, and reaction was predictable. The colonization press, for example, bridled at Delany's castigation of Liberia. *The Colonization Herald* ridiculed the author by quoting from his book's appendix, which had outlined a plan

---

52. *Ibid.*, pp. 25–29, 37–40. Compare Delany's remarks here with those of Martin H. Freeman, Delany's friend and ally from Pittsburgh, who many years later recalled the "patronizing sympathy which so often characterized the bearing of the old abolitionists toward the Negro...." Gardner W. Allen, *The Trustees of Donations for Education in Liberia: A Story of Philanthropic Endeavour, 1850–1923* (Boston: [Thomas Todd Company, Printers], 1923), p. 30. See also Jane H. Pease and William H. Pease, "Ends, Means, and Attitudes: Black-White Conflict in the Antislavery Movement," *Civil War History*, XVIII (June, 1972), 117–128, but esp. 124–125 for a substantiation of Delany's charges.

53. *Frederick Douglass' Paper*, April 29, 1852, p. 1.

for an exploring expedition of East Africa to establish first a colony, then a black nation, and finally a transcontinental railroad to foster trade between the area and the Americas. Liberians, too, responded to Delany's hostility to their country; in fact, Edward Blyden—the West Indian expatriate then a lay preacher in Monrovia, later a Liberian educator and diplomat and prominent Pan-African theorist —replied angrily to Delany's dismissal of Liberia as a "dependency" of the American Colonization Society. Proclaiming Liberia's independence and national integrity, Blyden also disputed Delany's charge that the American Colonization Society was the creation of slave owners, for he credited Paul Cuffe with fathering the colonization movement. But even more offensive to Blyden than the attack on his country was Delany's call to blacks to emigrate to Central and South America: "Why? Have the colored people in the United States any right to it? It is not their fatherland. . . ." Moreover, the large Indian populations would not acquiesce peaceably to black domination; as a result, North American blacks would first have to civilize the South American "aborigines" before establishing a viable nation.[54]

Delany never replied to Blyden, perhaps because he did not feel directly challenged by the harsh words of the Liberian patriot. More troublesome, however, was the adverse reaction to his book by most of the white and black abolitionist press. Although Bibb's *Voice of the Fugitive* lauded Delany for his relatively favorable treatment of Canadian emigration (while simultaneously disregarding Delany's clear preference for Central and South American emigration), other abolitionist editors were less generous. Douglass simply ignored the work. Garrison and Oliver Johnson were naturally annoyed by Delany's treatment of white abolitionists and struck back. Johnson, a staunch Garrisonian, used the pages of his *Pennsylvania Freeman* to issue a brief but harsh attack which claimed that Delany had presented "many facts which are in themselves interesting and valuable, which, if they were less bunglingly and

---

54. *The Colonization Herald*, June, 1852, p. 94; *Liberia Herald* (Monrovia), October 6, 1852, pp. 1–2. Blyden's career can be followed in Hollis R. Lynch, *Edward Wilmot Blyden, Pan-Negro Patriot, 1832–1912* (London: Oxford University Press, 1967).

egotistically presented and not mixed up with much that is of questionable propriety and utility, might be . . . [beneficial] to the reader. . . ." Johnson's verdict was blunt: "We could wish that, for his own credit, and that of the colored people, it had never been published." Garrison's *Liberator* was slightly more judicious and admitted that Delany was "a vigorous writer, an eloquent speaker, and full of energy and enterprise." Yet the Boston abolitionist found the contents of Delany's book disturbing. While replying ambiguously to Delany's condemnation of the efforts of white abolitionists, Garrison contended that Delany's "tone of despondency" was regrettable and hardly warranted the separatist position Delany had adopted. For Garrison, Delany's emigration plan was indistinguishable from that of the colonizationists, save for the substitution of the Americas for Africa.[55]

Not surprisingly, the criticisms of Johnson and Garrison angered Delany. In *The Freeman*'s condemnation Delany saw proof of his own charges, because in attempting "to disparage me, and endeavor to injure the sale of the book, especially among the colored people—upon whose ignorance you presume, and take advantage of your position . . . [, the article] but furnishes a striking proof of *your* negro-hate, in common with many of your less pretending fellows." Delany's final words to Johnson were blunt: "I therefore despise your sneers and defy your influence." Delany adopted a less antagonistic if still militant stance when answering Garrison. In an impassioned letter he maintained that he did not favor caste or separation as a principle, but as a realistic response to the conditions confronting blacks: "I would as willingly live among white men as black, if I had an equal possession and enjoyment of privileges; but shall never be reconciled to live among them, subservient to their will—existing by mere sufferance, as we, the colored people, do, in this country." Nor should black abolitionists respect Garrison's pacificist views. Rather, Delany echoed the militant abolitionism that he himself, Henry Highland Garnet, and others had advocated in the 1840's:

55. *Frederick Douglass' Paper*, July 23, 1852, p. 3; *The Voice of the Fugitive*, June 3, 1852, p. 2; *The Pennsylvania Freeman*, April 29, 1852, p. 70; *The Liberator*, May 7, 1852, p. 74.

> 'Were I a slave, I would be free,
> I would not live to live a slave;
> But boldly *strike* for LIBERTY—
> For FREEDOM or a *Martyr's* grave.'[56]

Delany's stirring call for slave resistance did not dissuade Garrison from attempting to calm the black activist's anger. The Boston editor maintained that Delany should try to profit from *The Freeman*'s criticisms, for they were not written "in the spirit of unkindness, but rather from a sense of duty and with an honest fidelity, though hard to bear." Delany was far from assuaged, for he strongly believed that blacks must free themselves of the pernicious nature of white influence. He communicated this to Douglass a little more than two months after Garrison's second reprimand. Complaining of the "cold and deathly silence" Douglass had "heaped" upon his book, Delany also implicitly reiterated his support for emigration by sending along a statistical summary of five Central American countries. But Delany's major concerns were elsewhere. He repeated the scorn he had leveled at *The Pennsylvania Freeman* and now expanded the scope of his antagonism to include almost all whites: "I care but little what white men think of what I say, write, or do; my sole desire is to benefit the colored people; this being done, I am satisfied—the opinion of every white person in the country or the world to the contrary notwithstanding." Moreover, blacks must plan their own strategies free from the interference of whites. "We have always adopted the policies that white men established for themselves," Delany contended, "without considering their applicability or adaptedness to us. No people can rise in this way. We must have a position, independently of anything pertaining to white men as nations."[57]

Douglass and others who abhorred any murmur of emigration sentiment agreed with Delany's final thoughts. In fact, it was this very agreement on such an implicitly nationalistic position that allowed blacks who differed on the emigration issue to unite briefly in 1853. Yet as more and more black leaders agreed that they should create nationalistic institutions to serve and protect all black Amer-

---

56. *The Pennsylvania Freeman*, May 6, 1852, p. 74; *The Liberator*, May 21, 1852, p. 83.

57. *Ibid.*, May 28, 1852, p. 86; *Frederick Douglass' Paper*, July 23, 1852, p. 3.

icans, Delany and others who were most committed to the assumptions underlying such a separatist orientation again questioned the ultimate value of developing such institutions in a land plagued with virulent and persistent racism. For these individuals, a nationalistic viewpoint required the acceptance of emigrationism as well. Consequently, the process of organizational fragmentation which occurred during the last five months of 1853 and during 1854 both widened and deepened the gap between preexisting ideological positions.

CHAPTER 5

The Emergence of an Emigration Movement

As Lewis Woodson had developed a nationalist-emigrationist philosophy which built from some of the separatist assumptions of the anti-emigrationist editor Samuel E. Cornish, Martin R. Delany's emigration movement likewise rested upon precepts which Delany's opponents held to faithfully. Such black leaders as Frederick Douglass argued that blacks should remain in the United States to labor for the emancipation of the southern slave and the elevation of the northern free black. But they also recognized that, as an oppressed people held in a subordinate position within the larger society, blacks had distinct interests which could only be served if they united to form distinct "national" institutions. The National Council, established by the Colored National Convention at Rochester in 1853, was clearly regarded by Douglass and many others as such an institution. However, for Delany and those blacks who supported his emigration plans, racial solidarity and the creation of separate organizations to serve the needs of black people would not be effective unless they led to the founding of a Black Nationality flourishing outside the confines of the United States. By August, 1854, with the convening of a National Emigration Convention, Delany and the nationalist-emigrationists had developed a well-articulated ideology; while holding to the traditional opposition to African colonization, they argued that blacks should emigrate to some point within the Western hemisphere and establish the new nationality. Never a mass movement, emigrationism did at this time attract several of the most articulate and lettered blacks living in the North and in Canada West. But this limited success brought with it the seeds of discord, for by the end of 1857 Delany's movement had broadened to the point of schism. Although Delany retained leadership over a group of secular nationalists who expressed little, if any, interest in the religious redemption of those areas blacks might populate, James Theodore Holly and his followers dreamed of a regeneration both black and Christian.

Delany and the Emigrationists

A genuine emigration movement did not develop immediately following either the publication of Delany's *Condition, Elevation, Emigration, and Destiny of the Colored People of the United States, Politically Considered* or the controversy which the book generated in the spring of 1852. Perhaps the few who seriously entertained the view that emigration was a viable option were not yet prepared to separate themselves entirely from other elements within the black community. Consequently, the 1853 Colored National Convention and its institutional offspring, the National Council, were of special importance to the emergence of an emigration movement. They provided a platform for a large number of black leaders—regardless of their differences on the emigration issue—to voice their agreement on certain matters: that blacks were a distinct group within the United States with distinct "national" interests that required them to act in unity through separate racial institutions. On the basis of this broad consensus, those who questioned whether even such united racial action within the United States would adequately serve the needs of Afro-Americans could join together around a common commitment to emigration and the establishment of a black nation outside the United States.

For reasons probably more personal than ideological, Delany was not among the 140 delegates who met in the spacious Corinthian Hall in Rochester in early July, 1853. Although remaining in Pittsburgh, Delany still applauded the convening of what was the first general gathering of blacks since the 1848 Cleveland convention. Thoroughly alienated from white America, Delany welcomed the apparent desire among blacks to unify themselves on a national basis free from the intrusions of whites. He hailed the "Call for a National Convention" when it was first published with his name appended in *Frederick Douglass' Paper*. "This is the thing *precisely*; this and this alone, is what we now want," he maintained. Later, when the convention actually began, it included men such as James M. Whitfield, the Reverend William C. Monroe, and the Reverend Augustus R. Green, all of whom would soon be active associates of Delany in the emigration movement. But the gathering was dominated by individuals who were committed "to plant our trees on American soil, and repose beneath their shade." Consequently, the delegates condemned the American Colonization Society and failed to discuss the question of emigration to other parts of the Americas which Delany, Bibb, and Holly had been advocating for the past two years. Yet the delegates also recognized that blacks were a separate caste within the larger society, united by the oppression which they faced in common, and they sought to capitalize on this sense of group identity by forging a network of separate institutions—under the aegis of a National Council—for the advancement of the race.[1]

The National Council was not a new idea; as we have seen, emigrationists and non-emigrationists alike had proposed similar institutions, all reflecting the increasingly common view that blacks must unite for racial advancement. As promulgated at the 1853 Rochester meeting, in accordance with the plan of organization which Dr. James McCune Smith proposed and which Woodson introduced, the National Council would consist of two members from each of the ten states represented at the convention. Additional members would be chosen later by the individual state councils, which were to be elected by all resident blacks paying a ten-cent poll tax. The Council would select four committees which would operate independently of, although responsible to, the larger governing body. Developed to by-pass exclusive dependence upon the white economic and political structures and upon white abolitionists, the committees on publication, the manual labor school, protective union, and business relations were designed to provide parallel services to

---

1. *Frederick Douglass' Paper*, July 15, 1853, p. 2; May 20, 1853, p. 3; June 17, 1853, p. 3; *Proceedings of the Colored National Convention, Held in Rochester, July 6th, 7th and 8th, 1853* (Rochester: Office of Frederick Douglass' Paper, 1853), pp. 6–7, 18–19, 26, 39–40.

The Emergence of an Emigration Movement 137

blacks by drawing upon the collective strength of the "national" community. Even more significant for the nationalistic thrust of the plan was an attempt by the Rochester convention to circumvent the legal apparatus of the dominant white society. Administered by the committee on business relations, local arbitration units—one for each 3,000 blacks—would handle disputes among blacks and thus avoid the American judicial system.[2]

While the committees never became anything other than paper organizations, the National Council convened several times during its two-year existence before meeting a quiet death at another national convention in 1855.[3] Yet even before the Council succumbed to internal discord, another group with obviously different aims threatened the equilibrium achieved at Rochester. The nationalist tendencies of the Rochester Convention were clearly inadequate for men such as Delany and Holly, both of whom had already committed themselves to emigration in repudiation of the National Council's basic premise that blacks could, through unity, operate outside the structure of white society while remaining within the United States. In August, 1853, only six weeks after the Rochester convention had disbanded, Delany issued the "Call for a National Emigration Convention" to be held a year later for the purpose of considering plans of emigration to other countries in the Western hemisphere. Among the twenty-six signers were eighteen associates of Delany from Pittsburgh and Allegheny County, Pennsylvania; Molliston M. Clark of Philadelphia, a boyhood friend; and James M. Whitfield. Additional supporters signed the call over the next few months, as the debate over emigration and the advisability of holding an emigration convention grew heated.[4]

2. *Proceedings of the Colored National Convention, Rochester, 1853*, pp. 18–19, 30; *National Anti-Slavery Standard*, July 30, 1853, p. 38. Inexplicably, the arbitration plan was omitted from the final draft for the organization of the National Council as printed in the proceedings of the Rochester convention.

3. *Frederick Douglass' Paper*, December 2, 1853, p. 2; July 28, 1854, p. 2; September 1, 1854, p. 2. See also *Proceedings of the Colored National Convention, Held in Franklin Hall, Sixth Street, Below Arch, Philadelphia, October 16, 17th and 18th, 1855* (Salem, N.J.: National Standard Office, 1856), pp. 33–34.

4. *Frederick Douglass' Paper*, August 26, 1853, p. 3; [M.T. Newsom, comp.], *Arguments, Pro and Con, on the Call for a National Convention, to be Held in Cleveland, Ohio, August 24, 1854...* (Detroit: George E. Pomeroy & Co., 1854), p. 7.

Whitfield became the major protagonist for the emigrationists and thus freed the movement from the possible obloquy that Delany's imprint might have generated. He was a newcomer to neither emigration nor nationalism. In 1838 and 1839, when barely sixteen years old, Whitfield had been the major spokesman for the Young Men's Union Society of Cleveland when the group had urged blacks to form separate settlements either within the United States or on its borders—primarily in California. Despite his silence on these matters in the 1840's, his bitterness toward the United States had not subsided. By 1841 he had moved to Buffalo, where he combined writing poetry and the barbering trade—to the mortification of such contemporaries as Douglass, who lamented the fact "That talents so commanding, gifts so rare, poetic powers so distinguished, should be tied to the handle of a razor and buried in the precincts of a barber's shop ... by the malignant arrangements of society. ..." Douglass urged Whitfield to abandon the barber shop in favor of employment "more favorable to the development of his genius, and the display of his talents...." Apparently this was impossible, for he continued to practice his trade. His book of poetry, *America and Other Poems*, published in 1853 and dedicated to Delany, was a bittersweet testimonial to Whitfield's rejection of America—"Thou land of blood, and crime, and wrong ... / From whence has issued many a band/ To tear the black man from his soil...." Nevertheless, the black poet attended the Rochester convention and signed its Address to the People of the United States, which called for white Americans to allow blacks full access into what Whitfield still considered his "native land."[5] However, Whitfield must have been at best ambivalent toward the statement, for by late September he was espousing an overtly emigrationist position.

With a lengthy letter to *Frederick Douglass's Paper* written from Buffalo in the fall of 1853, Whitfield opened what proved to be an extended debate over the merits of Delany's call for a National Emigration Convention. Replying to Douglass's charges that the emi-

---

5. *Ibid.*, pp. 16–17, 24; *The Colored American*, March 2, 1839, pp. 1–3; March 9, 1839, p. 3; May 18, 1839, p. 2; March 13, 1841, p. 2; *Anti-Slavery Bugle*, August 24, 1850, p. 1; *Pennsylvania Freeman*, September 29, 1853, p. 154; James M. Whitfield, *America and Other Poems* (Buffalo: J. S. Leavitt, 1853), p. 9; *Proceedings of the Colored National Convention, Rochester, 1853*, pp. 7–18.

gration movement, by giving the impression of being "opposed in spirit and purpose to the Rochester Convention" (as it was), would comfort the race's enemies by demonstrating a lack of unanimity among Afro-Americans on essential issues. Whitfield argued that those committed to the subjugation of blacks would have more to fear from the Cleveland than the Rochester convention. He used a carefully selected analogy to make his point:

> [Just] as a master would have the greater reason for fearing the loss of the slave, who arms himself, and leaves his premises with the determination to be free or die, than he would the one who, after a few vain supplications, submits to the lash, and devotes the energies which should be employed in improving himself and his children, to be building up the fortune of a tyrant, whose constant endeavor is to crush him lower in degradation, and entail the same hopeless condition upon his posterity.

In a more conciliatory tone, Whitfield proceeded to depict the projected emigration convention as the natural and welcome outcome of the recent Rochester meeting, whose purpose "was to endeavor to create a union of sentiment and action among the colored people, and to give it efficiency, by forming a kind of national organization here, under the overshadowing influence of our oppressors." But the forthcoming convention would, in fact, go "a step further in the same direction, and ... walk in the path which the Rochester Convention has pointed out," for blacks must emigrate and then form a black nationality. Only then would they have access to the power necessary to elevate all blacks everywhere and free the slave.[6]

Douglass himself did not reply to the Buffalo poet; rather, his associate editor, William J. Watkins, assumed the task. As strident in his opposition to emigration now as he had been in the late 1820's, Watkins argued that white colonizationists would rejoice if blacks

6. [Newsom], *Arguments, Pro and Con*, pp. 7–10. Whitfield's first letter was printed in *Frederick Douglass' Paper* in either the October 6, 13, or 20 issue of 1853—none of which is extant. His second letter was printed in the issue of November 25, 1853, p. 3, while his final communication was never printed in the newspaper—probably because it ran more than 3,500 words, and William J. Watkins, the associate editor of the paper, had continually chided Whitfield for his verbosity. All of Whitfield's letters and Watkins's replies were printed in *Arguments, Pro and Con*, cited in note 4 above.

left the country. Emigration, in fact, represented a capitulation to white racists—North and South—and an acceptance of their definition of Afro-Americans as aliens or outsiders who could never be accepted into American society. Abandon your plans, Watkins told the emigrationists, "put [your] ... shoulders to the wheel of the first national car of the colored people ever set in motion in these United States." Presumably the "national car" was the National Council; although Watkins did not make this explicit, his message was clear. He, Douglass, and their followers would remain in the United States. In fact, his adamant rejection of the views of the nationalist-emigrationists carried him almost to the point of implicitly rejecting the National Council and the efforts he and Douglass had been making on behalf of internal unity and racial solidarity. "We will not *willingly* segregate ourselves from the rest of mankind," Watkins wrote in his last reply to Whitfield. "We are part and parcel of the *American Nation*."[7] But by helping to establish the separatist National Council he and Douglass had already admitted they were not yet fully "part and parcel" of the American *nationality*.

As Whitfield and Watkins wrote their replies, answers, rejoinders and sub-rejoinders, both sides of the debate also worked to marshal broader support. Douglass's position as the most influential black newspaper editor of the period was vital to the development and proliferation of anti-emigration sentiment, and his paper recorded letters, reports of meetings, and resolutions approved—almost all condemning Delany's call and the upcoming National Emigration Convention. For example, a Pittsburgh correspondent doubted whether "any considerable number of our Pittsburgh people will subscribe to this movement."[8] David Jenkins, although an admirer of Delany in 1844 while editing the *Palladium of Liberty* in Columbus and an advocate of mass emigration as late as 1849, now led a group of Columbus blacks in opposing the emigration meeting. Jenkins and his followers also urged Cleveland blacks to prevent the convention from being held in their city as planned: "Let us, if possible, keep our State from this great curse and pollution." A statewide convention of Illinois blacks, meeting in Chicago, also

7. [Newsom], *Arguments, Pro and Con*, pp. 12, 18–19, 22.
8. *Frederick Douglass' Paper*, September 16, 1853, p. 2.

denounced the planning of an emigration convention and discovered in the call "a spirit of disunion which, if encouraged, will prove fatal to our hopes and aspirations as a people in this country." Other anti-emigration meetings were held in Boston and New Bedford, Massachusetts.[9]

Not surprisingly, Delany had his defenders. At two public meetings in San Francisco they successfully opposed a resolution condemning the emigration movement.[10] Delany also received oblique support from William Howard Day's *Aliened American*, although Day was obviously more interested in attacking Douglass and Watkins for their treatment of Delany and the emigration movement than he was in defending emigration itself. An 1847 Oberlin College graduate who five years later had married Lucy Stanton, the first black to graduate from the college's Ladies' Courses, the twenty-seven-year-old Day was a man of great oratorical powers; an observer at the Rochester Convention commented that his "voice mingled persuasion with authority, and in music and power was hardly inferior to Douglass. . . ." Day had previously put his speaking abilities to good use at several Ohio state conventions where he had steered an erratic course. He had opposed emigration at the 1849 Ohio state convention, but moderated his stand at the January, 1852, gathering, where he combined opposition to general emigration with a statement indicating that he "would not discourage individuals who proposed to emigrate to the coast of Africa, the West Indies or elsewhere." He registered his disapproval of white-inspired African colonization at another state convention the following January; yet in April, 1853—in the first issue of *Aliened American*—Day printed two letters from African missionaries; a review of a book containing both "evil" and "valuable" material on African colonization by an Ohio agent of the American Colonization Society; and a favorable commentary on Delany's *Condition, Elevation, Emigration, and Destiny of the Colored People of the United States, Politically Considered*. Still, this review closed with a state-

9. *Ibid.*, October 23, 1853, pp. 1, 4; March 31, 1854, p. 2; September 30, 1853, p. 3. On Jenkins, see the *Palladium of Liberty*, February 21, 1844, p. 3; June 19, 1844, p. 3; November 13, 1844, p. 2; *Minutes and Address of the State Convention of the Colored Citizens of Ohio, Convened at Columbus, January 10th, 11th, 12th & 13th, 1849* (Oberlin: J. M. Fitch's Power Press, 1849), p. 7.

10. *Frederick Douglass' Paper*, July 6, 1854, p. 4.

ment opposing "an emigration *en masse*." But after the Ohio Senate in early 1854 had voted 17 to 10 to deny Day access to the Senate chambers as a reporter, the editor became more sympathetic to the emigrationist argument that blacks would never receive equal rights in the United States. Nevertheless, remaining as paradoxical as ever, Day never openly declared for emigration during this period, but simply expressed his sympathy by harassing Douglass and Watkins.[11]

Within the black community in Canada West, as in the United States, there were varying opinions concerning the wisdom of Delany's call. Those blacks previously most active in advocating continental black solidarity and emigration were true to form and supported the Afro-American emigrationists. James Theodore Holly eventually signed the call, and in January, 1854, he wrote an introduction for *Arguments, Pro and Con, on the Call for a National Emigration Convention*, a compendium of the Whitfield-Douglass-Watkins correspondence. In his introduction, Holly (like Whitfield earlier) considered the projected emigration convention as the natural outgrowth of the Rochester Convention and the establishment of the National Council. Holly, however, was critical of the National Council which he and his Canadian followers had joined only months earlier. Now the Council was "... an informal national organization of a denationalized people, whereby an organic though premature and sickly birth was given to the idea of national independence...." If the National Council had floundered, the emigrationists had developed "a new conception... in embryo with evident signs of hopeful delivery." Acting upon this belief, Henry Bibb also signed the convention call.[12]

---

11. *Ibid.*, January 13, 1854, p. 2; February 17, 1854, p. 2; *Aliened American*, April 9, 1853, pp. 1–3. On Day, see Robert Samuel Fletcher, *A History of Oberlin College* (Oberlin, Ohio: Oberlin College, 1943), II, 533; *New York Daily Tribune*, July 15, 1853, p. 6; *Minutes of the Ohio State Colored Convention, 1849*, p. 13; *The Anti-Slavery Reporter*, n.s. III (March 1, 1852), 39; 3rd ser., II (April, 1854), 83; *Proceedings of the Ohio State Convention of Colored Freeman, Held in Columbus, January 19–21st, 1853* (Cleveland: Aliened American Office, 1853), pp. 6–7; *New York Daily Times*, January 30, 1854, p. 3. As often as Delany and his allies were charged with advocating mass emigration, they denied it. See Whitfield's comments in [Newsom], *Arguments, Pro and Con*, p. 11.

12. *Ibid.*, pp. 3–4, 7, 32–33. The Reverend Matthew T. Newsom of Cass County, Michigan, an emigrationist and a signer of the call, compiled the pamphlet. After the Civil War, Newsom was active in the Mississippi Constitutional Convention

Yet Holly's and Bibb's support was becoming less valuable. By late 1853, with *The Voice of the Fugitive* in serious straits and the Refugee Home Society under increasing attack, public leadership among Canadian blacks was passing to those opposed to Bibb and Holly and to emigration anywhere other than to Canada West. By then Samuel R. Ward, Mary Ann Shadd, and several other blacks had organized their own publishing venture, the *Provincial Freeman*, which first appeared in March, 1853, in Windsor and then on a more sustained basis a year later from Toronto. Committed to the belief that Canadian blacks should regard themselves as British subjects and not as transient refugees from the United States, the *Freeman* reacted cautiously to Delany's plan for an emigration convention. Aware that Delany was primarily interested in emigration to Central and South America and thus dubious that the convention would take any decisive action to assist Canadian blacks, the *Provincial Freeman* questioned the motives and intentions of the nationalist-emigrationists while still refraining from overtly opposing the convention. In its search for a black nirvana, Delany's group, the *Freeman* argued, was overlooking the real advantages Canada provided. In addition, the newspaper maintained that the structure of the convention provided for representation for each American state but not for Canada—a criticism which Delany answered by inviting delegates "from British America, Russian America, (has it any *colored* inhabitants), Mexico and the West Indies."[13]

More important, however, in raising the hackles of the Ward-Shadd group was the nationality issue which Delany and Whitfield had propounded. The *Freeman* maintained that Canadian blacks were part of British America—and a British *nation*—and thus should not support a black nationality which transcended or negated their present allegiance. Doubting whether blacks could form their own separate nation in the Western Hemisphere, the *Provincial Freeman* urged blacks to come to Canada, where they would be "part of the Colored British nation"—a nation which "knows no one color above another, but being composed of all colors ... is evidently a *colored*

---

of 1868; he subsequently served in the Mississippi House of Representatives. Vernon Lane Wharton, *The Negro in Mississippi, 1865–1890* (Chapel Hill: University of North Carolina Press, 1947), pp. 147–148, 150, 173.

13. *Provincial Freeman*, March 25, 1854, p. 2; April 15, 1854, p. 3.

nation." Touting Canada's attractions, the *Freeman*'s editors asked those intent upon establishing a black nation in a tropical climate: "What will you do ... when, surrounded by big spiders, lizards, snakes, centipedes, scorpions and all manner of creeping and biting things? Do you want to be sun-struck? Do you court yellow fever and laziness, haughty employers, and contemptible black prejudice? If you do, go in peace."[14] The journal's opposition to a separate black nationality influenced the paper's positions on other issues as well. Ward and Shadd denounced the Rochester Convention, and they applauded William Howard Day's successful attempts at disrupting the Council. In order to bolster their position within the Canadian black community, they formed an organization known as the Provincial Union just three weeks prior to the opening of Delany's National Emigration Convention. Obviously referring to both the Refugee Home Society and the more elaborate nationalistic plans of Delany and his followers, the preamble to the Provincial Union's constitution attacked the advocates of separate settlements.[15]

Despite the qualified opposition of major Canadian black spokesmen and the more virulent criticisms of Douglass, Watkins, and other anti-emigrationists, Delany's National Emigration Convention met at the Congregational Church on Prospect Street in Cleveland for three days of sessions beginning on August 24, 1854. The event was of singular importance for Delany personally. As Holly, watching the acknowledged leader of the movement from one of the secretaries' tables, observed years later, "All other events in his life, before then, culminated in the part he took in that movement. All events of his life, after that convention, took their point of departure from the principles which he sustained and promulgated there."[16] However, for most of the other emigrationists present, the convention was of less long-range significance. For many it was their first— and probably last—participation in racial politics.

Some 101 "executive delegates" from eleven states and Canada

14. *Ibid.*, April 15, 1854, p. 3; May 20, 1854, p. 2.
15. *Ibid.*, August 5, 1854, p. 1; *Constitution of the Provincial Union, Organized at Toronto, August 9th, 1854* (Toronto: Provincial Freeman Office, [1854?]); Robin W. Winks, *The Blacks in Canada: A History* (New Haven: Yale University Press, 1971), p. 226.
16. James T. Holly, "In Memoriam," *A.M.E. Church Review*, III (October, 1886), 120.

were in attendance; as representatives of the convention proudly pointed out, they included six delegates from four slave states. Yet, like other pre–Civil War black conventions, the affair was really quite localized. Almost half of the delegates were from Pittsburgh and its environs.[17] This prompted one of the convention's critics to quip that the gathering should have been held in Pittsburgh "and thus... have secured the six or seven hundred dollars which, undoubtedly, found their way into the coffers of the Cleveland and Pittsburg [sic] Railroad Company...." Moreover, the convention was clearly "western." In fact, the issue of eastern hegemony within the "national" black community was strong enough to attract to the convention some delegates only moderately sympathetic to emigration. Only three of the delegates resided east of Pittsburgh; two of these were from Buffalo, almost a western city in the geography of the day. One of these was Holly, who had been hired as the first black principal of Buffalo's Vine Street Colored School in response to the demands of the city's black population. Whitfield, although forced to return to Buffalo early, also attended the convention.[18]

Geographical concentration aside, the composition of the convention was unusual. Unlike the other pre–Civil War black conventions where women appeared infrequently, if at all, the feminine presence at Cleveland was significant. One-third of the entire body and slightly more than half of Delany's Allegheny County contingent (which included Delany's wife, Catherine) were women. This was not surprising in view of Delany's advocacy of female participation at the 1848 National Convention.[19] Of the women delegates, only Henry Bibb's widow, Mary, was widely known. Of the men present, relatively few were well known as emigration-

---

17. *Proceedings of the National Emigration Convention of Colored People; Held at Cleveland, Ohio, on Thursday, Friday and Saturday, the 24th, 25th and 26th of August, 1854* (Pittsburgh: A. A. Anderson, 1854), pp. 16–18. Asterisks next to the names of delegates indicated that they were not present at the convention. See p. 78.

18. *Frederick Douglass' Paper*, November 17, 1854, p. 3; Buffalo, N.Y., Department of Education, *Eighteenth Annual Report, Year 1854*, p. 23; *Proceedings of the National Emigration Convention*, p. 31.

19. *Report of the Proceedings of the Colored National Convention, Held at Cleveland, Ohio, on Wednesday, September 6, 1848* (Rochester: North Star Office, 1848), p. 10. Note that Delany introduced resolution 3, not 33, as the report indicates. See *The North Star*, September 29, 1848, pp. 1–2.

ists. Besides Delany, Holly, and Whitfield, the only delegates of repute were the Reverends William C. Monroe of Detroit and Augustus R. Green, who was then living in Cincinnati, both signers of the call and both long-time friends of Delany.

A former agent for Delany's *Mystery* in Authursville and Scottsfield, Pennsylvania, Green had served as an elder in the A.M.E. Church in Pittsburgh in the mid-1840's before moving temporarily to Ohio. There, as a member of the committee of the Ohio circuit of the church, he attempted to establish a manual labor school near Columbus. By the summer of 1848 he had returned to Pittsburgh, where he served as superintendent of the A.M.E. Book Concern and the editor of the Church's newspaper, *The Christian Herald*, Pittsburgh's only black paper following the demise of *The Mystery*. As early as 1851 Green had emerged as an advocate of emigration to Canada, a country which he favored since he believed it would not be absorbed by the United States. England, he maintained, was "too proud to let a foot of her territory be annexed to any government, unless it is some great advantage to herself." Like Holly and Bibb, he emphasized the proximity of Canada to the slaves still in bondage, touted the commercial viability of Canadian agriculture by claiming that fertile land could be purchased cheaply, and suggested that blacks searching for a warmer climate should emigrate to the West Indies, where they could raise enough sugar, cotton, and rice to divert English ships from southern ports.[20]

Tropical regions did, in fact, attract the fifty-five-year-old Monroe. As a young man he had attempted to enter Bowdoin, Amherst, and Dartmouth Colleges—at least one of which accepted him on what Monroe considered as "only . . . such degrading terms, as no one who had any sense of the rights of man would accept." Thwarted in his efforts to attend college, Monroe was able to secure an education for the Presbyterian ministry, but after graduation he changed

20. *Palladium of Liberty*, October 16, 1844, p. 3; *The Mystery*, April 16, 1845, p. 1; December 16, 1846, p. 1; *Pennsylvania Freeman*, November 11, 1847, p. 3; *The North Star*, July 3, 1848, p. 3; August 18, 1848, p. 2; *The Voice of the Fugitive*, April 19, 1851, p. 3; August 27, 1851, p. 1; A. R. Green, *A Discourse for the Times, on Our Condition as It is and Might Be; or Duty Rewarded* (Philadelphia: Hughes & Company, Printers, 1853), pp. 15, 19. See also George H. Singleton, *The Romance of African Methodism: A Study of the African Methodist Episcopal Church* (New York: Exposition Press, 1952), p. 128.

his theological orientation and became a Baptist minister. His first post was in Portland, Maine, where he served the city's small black population. In April, 1835, Monroe was appointed a missionary to Haiti by the board of managers of the Baptist General Convention of the United States. The Board had decided that the Baptists among the American black population in Haiti—most of whom were the remnants of the 1824–25 migration—would benefit from the presence of a black missionary. At Port-au-Prince in May he "preached the first Sabbath ... within the sound of the Marshal Drum, and lectured at Night within the sound of the Congo dance...." Except for one visit to the United States, Monroe remained in Haiti for almost three years. Although he established a small Baptist Church at Port-au-Prince and also weathered an attack by several detractors who claimed he was not adhering to the Baptist faith, he found laboring in the Caribbean republic discouraging. Shortly after his wife died in January, 1838, Monroe returned to the United States.[21]

By 1840 Monroe had established himself in Buffalo, where he became president of the local Union Moral and Mental Improvement Society and was active in statewide protest activity. He moved to Detroit in late 1840 or early 1841. There he participated in the Michigan Anti-Slavery Society and the state Liberty party, and he presided over the 1843 Michigan State Colored Convention that challenged the white-only suffrage provisions of the state constitution. During his years in Detroit, Monroe also taught at both private and public black schools. In addition, he served as a leader in the Amherstburg Association, a group composed of black Baptists from Canada West and the Detroit area. In September, 1846, he was ordained a deacon in the Protestant Episcopal Church; the following month he helped establish St. Matthew's Episcopal Church, soon the dominant black church in Detroit. There he became a priest in March, 1854. Although he attended the Rochester Convention

---

21. Carleton Mabee, *Black Freedom: The Nonviolent Abolitionists from 1830 Through the Civil War* (New York: Macmillan, 1970), pp. 145–146; Henry S. Burrage, *History of the Baptists in Maine* (Portland, Me.: Marks Printing House, Printers, 1904), p. 387; W. Munroe [sic] File, American Baptist Foreign Missionary Society Papers, American Baptist Foreign Missionary Society, Valley Forge, Pa. Monroe's name was also spelled Monro, Munro, and, quite frequently, Munroe. For the sake of consistency, "Monroe" will be used throughout this study.

and was selected one of Michigan's two delegates to the National Council, by January, 1854, Monroe was committed to Delany's emigration movement, for he both signed the call and contributed a brief statement touting the advantages of Central America as an appendix to the *Arguments, Pro and Con, on the Call for a National Emigration Convention.* By emigrating to Central America, Monroe asserted, Afro-Americans could "prepare to inaugurate a new era in the world, by developing the colored races on the southern portions of the continent to a higher degree of christianity and civilization than the world had ever yet introduced." Monroe's age and manner helped to make him a perennial convention officer. Considerably older than Delany, Holly, or Whitfield—in fact, the only one of the group to be born in the eighteenth century and to die before the Civil War—he was kindly and dignified, if perhaps pious but ineffective in the eyes of some. Not surprisingly, the emigrationists selected Monroe as the presiding officer when the convention began.[22]

The first day's activities were generally routine yet not unimportant. A challenge to the convention's decision to listen only to friendly voices was swiftly put down when Delany, serving as temporary presiding officer, denied permission to speak against emigration to John Malvin, the Cleveland abolitionist who carried fugitive slaves through Ohio on his canal boat. Delany was shrewd

---

22. *The Colored American*, July 4, 1840, p. 1; September 19, 1840, p. 2; *Signal of Liberty*, April 28, 1841, p. 1; October 27, 1841, p. 2; February 20, 1843, p. 1; *Minutes of the State Convention of the Colored Citizens of the State of Michigan, Held in the City of Detroit, on the 26th, and 27th of October, 1843*... (Detroit: William Harsha, 1843), p. 7; *Narrative of the Life and Adventures of Henry Bibb, an American Slave*, reprinted in Gilbert Osofsky, ed., *Puttin' On Ole Massa* (New York: Harper & Row, 1969), p. 154; David M. Katzman, *Before the Ghetto: Black Detroit in the Nineteenth Century* (Urbana: University of Illinois Press, 1973), pp. 16, 21, 23–24; Winks, *Blacks in Canada*, p. 342; "A Brief History of St. Matthew's Protestant Episcopal Church," brochure without title page (n.p.: Episcopal Diocese of Michigan, n.d.); George D. Gillespie, *A Manual for the Use of Rectors, Wardens and Vestrymen in the Diocese of Michigan, with Annals of the Diocese* (Ann Arbor: Dr. Chase's Steam Printing House, 1868), p. 116; *Proceedings of the Colored National Convention, Rochester, 1853*, pp. 6, 46; [Newsom], *Arguments, Pro and Con*, pp. 7, 33; *The Weekly Anglo-African*, March 17, 1860, p. 3; H. P. Baldwin to S. D. Denison, Detroit, November 13, 1858; C. C. Trowbridge to Denison, Detroit, November 15, 1858, Domestic and Foreign Missionary Society Papers: Haiti Papers, Church Historical Society, Austin, Texas.

enough not to alienate neutrals, however, for he invited Day, covering the convention for *The Daily Cleveland Herald*, to sit at an official table. When permanent officers were chosen, Monroe became the president, Holly one of the three secretaries, and Delany chairman of the all-important twelve-member business committee which also included Holly and Green. In the afternoon Delany delivered a brief eulogy on the life of Henry Bibb which so touched a reporter for *The Cleveland Morning Leader* that he described it as "superior in sentiment and language to a majority of similar productions by Members of Congress, pronounced over deceased members."[23]

After this, Delany presented a Platform or Declaration of Sentiments of the Convention, and for seven hours the next day he read a Report on the Political Destiny of the Race on this Continent which, while bearing the signatures of the entire business committee, was really his own work. Taken together, the two documents embodied the convention's general attitudes and underlying assumptions as well as the gathering's specific positions on emigration and nationalism. First, Delany expressed his concern with the practical exercise of political power when he added to his protest against the disfranchisement of the black man the following: "the elective franchise necessarily implies *eligibility to every position* attainable; the indisputable right of being chosen or elected as the representative of another...." Delany expatiated upon this principle in the course of the platform, asserting that blacks would never be satisfied until "acknowledged a necessary *constituent* in the *ruling element* of the country in which we live."[24]

Yet Delany was convinced that blacks would never obtain po-

23. *Proceedings of the National Emigration Convention*, pp. 6–10; *The Daily Cleveland Herald*, August 25, 1854, p. 3; *Cleveland Morning Leader*, August 25, 1854, p. 3. On Malvin, see Benjamin Quarles, *Black Abolitionists* (New York: Oxford University Press, 1969), pp. 60, 108–109, 147.

24. *Proceedings of the National Emigration Convention*, pp. 23–27, 33–70. The report was later reprinted in *Report of the Select Committee on Emancipation and Colonization*, House Report No. 148, 37th cong., 2nd sess., IV (Washington: Government Printing Office, 1862), pp. 37–59; and in Frank A. Rollin, pseud. [Frances E. Rollin Whipper], *Life and Public Services of Martin R. Delany, Sub-Assistant Commissioner, Bureau Relief of Refugees, Freedmen and of Abandoned Lands, and Late Major 104th U.S. Colored Troops* (Boston: Lee and Shepard, 1868), pp. 327–367. Quotations are from *Proceedings*, pp. 24, 26. See also pp. 33–35.

litical power in the United States; emigration, then, was the only viable strategy. Initially dismissing Canada on the grounds that the United States would annex British America and absorb with it the relatively small number of black residents—the same argument he had presented two years earlier—he maintained that "our attention must be turned in a direction towards those places where the black and colored man comprise, by population, and constitute by necessity of numbers, the *ruling element* of the body." Central and South America were "those places"; in support of his claim Delany presented a detailed demographic survey of the area, followed by a documented narrative of the settling of the Americas—both items designed to substantiate his argument that blacks had a rightful claim to the hemisphere. More important, the people of the West Indies, Central and South America would be willing to merge with North American blacks to establish a civilized and economically viable black nation; in fact, "They now desire all the improvements of North America, but . . . have no confidence in the whites of the United States. . . ." However, if Central and South American emigration proved unworkable, Canada would be the next-best locale, and thus he suggested that blacks buy the cheap land readily available there.[25]

Following Delany's presentation of the report, Green spoke on behalf of the document, as did H. Ford Douglass of New Orleans. A young Virginia-born barber, Douglass had been active in the black communities of Cleveland and Columbus before moving to New Orleans. While in Cleveland in 1850 he had served as the local agent for Bibb's *Voice of the Fugitive* and had organized and spoken at mass meetings and celebrations of blacks; in addition, he had argued the case for full political and civil rights for blacks in one of the city's white newspapers. Two years later Douglass was less sanguine about achieving his rights as an American citizen, for he championed emigration at the 1852 Ohio State Convention in Cincinnati. At the time of the Cleveland convention Douglass was clearly in accord with most of Delany's sentiments. He was not, however, in agreement with Delany's preference for Central or South America; according to Day's report, Douglass's "first choice" was Canada.

25. *Ibid.*, pp. 37–38, 43, 57, 65–66.

The Emergence of an Emigration Movement

In fact, conditions in the United States had so alienated Douglass that he vowed that "rather than stay here I would go to Africa." Although other delegates did not utter this heresy, at least one—Joseph H. Foster, a thirty-four-year-old mason from Lenawee County, Michigan—also advocated Canadian emigration and thus belied the uniformity of opinion which Delany's "State Paper" had attempted to convey.[26] More disruptive—at least in an immediate sense—were the remarks by John Mercer Langston. Although not a delegate, he was considered sympathetic to the convention's purposes when asked to speak during an informal session on the evening of the second day.

A young black from Oberlin, Ohio, then studying law in the nearby offices of an Elyria attorney, Langston had been born in 1829 in Louisa County, Virginia, to a slaveholder and his mistress, a former slave. Sent to Ohio at the age of five, he later attended Oberlin College, graduating in 1849. With his older brother Charles, he had been active in black community affairs in Ohio since the state convention of 1849. At that time Langston had unsuccessfully opposed the adoption of an anti-emigration resolution, plaintively informing the convention that "the very fact of our remaining in this country, is humiliating, virtually acknowledging our inferiority to the white man...." Anticipating Delany by a few years, Langston added that "we must have a nationality, before we can become anybody." At the next state convention in Cincinnati, in January, 1852, Langston still favored emigration, for he spoke for nearly two hours in support of hemispheric emigration. Contending that "there is a natural repellency between the two races," he announced that he would "never consent [to] ... the absorption and extinction" of blacks. Undoubtedly Langston's previous stand prompted the 1854 emigration convention to call him to the podium. If so, he was to

26. *The Daily Cleveland Herald*, August 26, 1854, p. 3. For Douglass, see copy of marriage certificate for H. Ford Douglass and Satira Steele, Racine, Wis., October 26, 1857, in Douglass's veteran's pension records, National Archives; *The Voice of the Fugitive*, January 1, 1851, p. 2; *Anti-Slavery Bugle*, August 24, 1850, p. 1; *Daily True Democrat* (Cleveland), March 27, 1850, p. 3; *Proceedings of the Convention of Colored Freemen of Ohio Held in Cincinnati, January 14, 15, 16, 17, and 19 [1852]* (Cincinnati: Dumas and Lawyer, 1852), pp. 5, 9. Foster is listed in the manuscript schedules, Seventh Census of the United States: 1850—Woodstock Township, Lenawee County, Michigan.

disappoint Delany and surprise many of his listeners by declaring that he intended "to work out my destiny in Lorain County, Ohio." Speaking only two weeks before being admitted to the Ohio bar as one of the nation's first black lawyers, Langston proclaimed that "success was certain for the colored man in common with the white man in the United States."[27]

Langston's apostasy did not go unanswered. H. Ford Douglass bitterly attacked his inconsistency—"for wiring in and wiring out" —and charged that when he had last heard him speak, Langston had favored both emigration and black nationality. Douglass then argued the classic position of the nationalist-emigrationists—"that the surest way of affecting slavery and hastening its downfall in this nation is to establish, if possible, a 'COLORED NATIONALITY,' on this Continent...." But Douglass moved beyond the arguments that Delany, Holly, and others had made so familiar, and he repeated the traditional Garrisonian position which he had adopted in a debate with Day three years earlier in Columbus: the Constitution was a proslavery document, and slavery itself would not be abolished until the Union was dissolved. To Douglass, however, this appeared a long time coming: "I am willing to forget the endearing name of home and country, and ... seek on other shores that freedom which has been denied me in the land of my birth."[28]

To assist those wishing to leave the United States, the convention

27. *The Daily Cleveland Herald*, August 26, 1854, p. 3; William J. Simmons, *Men of Mark: Eminent, Progressive and Rising* (Cleveland: Geo. M. Rewell & Co., 1887), pp. 510–513; John Mercer Langston, *From the Virginia Plantation to the National Capital or the First and Only Negro Representative in Congress from the Old Dominion* (Hartford, Conn.: American Publishing Company, 1894), pp. 31, 123; William F. Cheek, III, "Forgotten Prophet: The Life of John Mercer Langston" (Ph.D. dissertation, University of Virginia, 1961), pp. 37–38; *Minutes of the Ohio State Colored Convention, 1849*, p. 8; *Daily Cincinnati Gazette*, January 15, 1852, p. 2. For an overview of Langston's activities in the 1850's, see Cheek's "John Mercer Langston: Black Protest Leader and Abolitionist," *Civil War History*, XVI (June, 1970), 101–120.

28. *The Daily Cleveland Herald*, August 26, 1854, p. 3; *Speech of H. Ford Douglass, In Reply to Mr. J. M. Langston Before the Emigration Convention, at Cleveland, Ohio...* (Chicago: Wm. H. Worrell, 1854), pp. 7, 16. For the Day-Douglass exchange on the nature of the constitution (and Day's retort that he was "wrapping myself in the flag of the nation..."), see *Minutes of the State Convention of the Colored Citizens of Ohio, Convened at Columbus, Jan. 15th, 16th, 17th, and 18th, 1851* (n.p.: E. Glover, Printer, 1851), pp. 9–10.

established a permanent organization—a National Board of Commissioners. Finally, three committees were created, with the committee on foreign relations the most important.[29] Although Delany was a member, major responsibility for the committee's functions would be borne by the special foreign secretary, Professor Martin H. Freeman, a twenty-eight-year-old Middlebury College graduate then teaching at the Avery Institute for blacks in Pittsburgh. The committee itself was charged with opening "correspondence with all Foreign Countries . . . [to] enquire into and obtain such information as may be obtainable, pertaining to the political and domestic relations, climate, soil and productions of such countries." Equally suggestive in terms of the future role of the National Board of Commissioners was the committee's other major task: to "hold correspondence with the Foreign Mission which shall be sent out by the Board and do everything else pertaining to a Foreign Office. . . ." Somewhat more mundane were the operations of the other two committees. The committee on financial relations was assigned the onerous task of raising money to support the National Board, while the primary responsibility of the committee on domestic relations was to investigate real estate prices and recommend to both the Board and the black community in general the most attractive investments.[30]

With the National Board of Commissioners organized, the delegates dispersed to their homes to await reaction to their efforts. The reaction, when it came, was predictable. In Pittsburgh the Democratic *Daily Morning Post* ran a long commentary upon the convention with special attention to Delany's report. Although complimentary to Delany personally, the *Post* debunked the report as "a vast conception of impossible birth" and claimed that many European nations as well as the United States "would oppose the Africanization of more than half of the Western Hemisphere . . . [and] that Uncle Sam, Johnny Bull, Johnny Crappeau, Queen Christina and the Dutch, will all interpose most formidable obstacles to the success of this splendid project." In sum, the *Post*

29. *Proceedings of the National Emigration Convention*, pp. 71–77.
30. Manuscript schedules, Seventh Census of the United States: 1850—City of Pittsburgh; *Frederick Douglass' Paper*, July 22, 1853, p. 3; *Proceedings of the National Emigration Convention*, pp. 71–72.

suggested that blacks shun "such impracticable theories" and turn to Liberia, where they could "enjoy the dignity of manhood, the rights of citizenship" and "become an agent in carrying civilization to a benighted continent."[31] The white colonization press also urged the black emigrationists to consider the attractions of Liberia, although it was generally pleased with the new interest blacks were showing in leaving the country.[32]

Frederick Douglass was less approbatory, although apparently unperturbed. Douglass first wrote a short sarcasm designed to deflate the emigrationists without appearing to take them too seriously; a week later he frankly admitted his intention of ignoring Delany and his allies. "When we can be induced to believe that Mr. Delany, or any who are not advocating this wholesale measure of Emigration scheme, seriously mean to emigrate, we may, perhaps, reopen a discussion with them...." In the meantime, Douglass allowed George B. Vashon to assume the burden of criticizing the emigrationists. The son of John B. Vashon of Pittsburgh and Langston's first teacher in Chillicothe, Ohio, Vashon was the first black man to graduate from Oberlin College when he received his degree in 1844. After studying law, he was admitted to the New York bar in 1847 and then spent thirty months in Haiti (an experience he would later remember quite fondly) before returning to the United States.[33] Vashon's Haitian visit did not mollify his opposition to what transpired at the Cleveland Convention, for he used the pages of *Frederick Douglass's Paper* to ridicule the emigrationists.

Vashon's remarks were directed largely toward the personal failings of his opponents. Attempting to cast the emigrationists as political neophytes, he attacked the convention for consisting largely of "new men, who apparently rushed upon the arena of public life, solely for the purpose of giving *eclat* to the grand exodus which

---

31. *Ibid.*, p. 15; *Daily Morning Post*, October 18, 1854, p. 4.

32. *New York Colonization Journal*, November, 1854, p. 2. See also *Maryland Colonization Journal*, November, 1854, pp. 283–286; *African Repository*, XXXI (January, 1855), 21–24.

33. *Frederick Douglass' Paper*, September 8, 1854, p. 2; September 15, 1854, p. 2; William Wells Brown, *The Rising Son; or, the Advancement of the Colored Race* (Boston: A. G. Brown & Co., Publishers, 1874), pp. 476–477; Langston, *From the Virginia Plantation*, p. 74; Fletcher, *History of Oberlin*, II, 533; *The Imperial Citizen*, February 8, 1851, p. 3; *Douglass' Monthly*, October, 1862, pp. 727–728.

they were planning." In addition, the emigrationists had neglected to follow the wisdom of their fathers—those blacks in Pittsburgh who in 1831 had rejected African colonization and declared that they would not leave the United States. (Vashon himself was certainly not guilty of filial neglect, for the 1831 statement he had quoted without citation was written by his father.) Finally, he argued that the constitution of the National Board of Commissioners was nothing but "a part of the Constitution of the National Council —with the *impracticable* idea of emigration added...."[34]

With Delany, like Douglass, choosing not to involve himself directly in the debate, Special Foreign Secretary Martin H. Freeman took up the cudgels for the emigrationists. Freeman chose to meet Vashon's arguments head on. The plans propounded at the Cleveland Convention, he asserted, were no more impractical than those for a national council or an industrial school—all of which assumed a union of sentiment within the black community. Moreover, Freeman attempted to deny the pertinence of Vashon's use of the 1831 Pittsburgh anti-colonization statement by suggesting that "it is *barely* possible that a people like us, in a transition state from slavery to freedom, may outgrow a platform in twenty-three years." He added to this refutation a few lines which Delany found so striking he could quote them almost verbatim five years later: "If not [able to outgrow a platform], we may as well go back a few decades further and adopt the creed of our grandfathers... like the following: Here (on Massa's plantation) we were born—here will we live, if Massa don't sell us—and here we will die, and let our bones lie with the rest of Massa's niggers."[35]

Aside from the Vashon-Freeman exchange, there was little overt reaction to the National Emigration Convention within the black community. Some opponents of emigration (such as Douglass) ob-

---

34. *Frederick Douglass' Paper*, November 11, 1854, p. 3. The elder Vashon's statement was in the form of a series of resolutions passed at an anti-emigration meeting he chaired in 1831 in Pittsburgh. William Lloyd Garrison, *Thoughts on African Colonization* (Boston: Garrison and Knapp, 1832), part II, pp. 34-35.

35. *Frederick Douglass' Paper*, December 15, 1854, p. 3; December 22, 1854, p. 3; January 4, 1855, p. 1. Freeman's replies bore only an "F" for identification; however, Delany, when in Liberia, referred to the Vashon-Freeman exchange and quoted the passage mentioned above. *The Weekly Anglo-African*, October 1, 1859, p. 1.

viously believed indifference would be the best strategy to follow. Others, more ambivalent on the issue, were perhaps exhausted by the entire controversy and by the grandiose plans which both Delany and his followers on the one hand, and Douglass and his supporters on the other, had been projecting. Only in Cincinnati, where emigration had been salient ever since the riots of 1829, did the black community divide publicly on the merits of the Cleveland Convention. With African colonization winning new adherents among whites throughout Ohio as well as within the city itself, all elements within the Cincinnati black community registered opposition to the American Colonization Society. In early October, 1854, Augustus R. Green, Philip Toliver (also a delegate to the Cleveland gathering), and nine other emigrationists submitted a "Memorial" to the Cincinnati district of the white Methodist Episcopal Church. While protesting the church's support of "negro hating, slave supporting American Colonization," the memorial carefully distinguished the plans of the Emigration Convention (which they openly supported) from those of the Colonization Society. However, the next day a meeting of other Cincinnati blacks condemned both African colonization and the emigration plans developed in Cleveland. Reportedly there was no dissent from this broad condemnation. Green and Joseph Fowler, another signer of the memorial to the Methodist Episcopal Church, were both present, and they either refrained from opposing the majority or were simply ignored when the vote was taken.[36]

Divided as Cincinnati blacks were on the merits of emigration, the conflict even there was muted. This was also true of the larger "national" black community, even though the consensus reached at Rochester in 1853 had definitely evaporated. Yet despite the opposition of Frederick Douglass and his allies, the emigrationists had emerged as an identifiable group which adopted the public position that they, and not the Douglass-inspired National Council, represented the true interests of the race, and that emigration was the inevitable corollary of all attempts to unite oppressed and degraded black Americans.

36. Memorial from A. R. Green *et al.*, Cincinnati, October 3, 1854, Samuel Williams Collection, M.E. Church Papers, Cincinnati Historical Society; *Frederick Douglass' Paper*, October 20, 1854, p. 1.

The Emergence of an Emigration Movement   157

A MOVEMENT BROADENING—AND DIVIDING

In truth, the National Emigration Convention proved to be a mixed blessing for Delany. Although he had marshaled many prominent and articulate blacks in support of his program, differences of opinion within the emigration movement had already surfaced. During the two years between Delany's first emigration convention and a second gathering in 1856, these divisions would have a pronounced effect in restricting Delany's role in the movement. An autonomous base of power within the emigration movement developed around the person and beliefs of James Theodore Holly. For Holly, nationalist-emigrationism took on an overtly missionary cast which contrasted sharply with Delany's own secular views. However, if this troubled Delany, he could only have viewed another development far more favorably. For while the movement was fragmenting, it was also broadening in scope.

Mary Ann Shadd, the dominant figure behind the *Provincial Freeman* ever since it began to be published regularly in March, 1854, abandoned her earlier hostility toward the emigration movement and brought both the paper and its supporters into Delany's camp. Exactly what motivated the *Provincial Freeman* group to alter its position is unclear. Shadd's initial hostility to any form of black separatism and her conviction that black Canadians should consider themselves essentially British led her to use the *Freeman* to register disapproval of Delany's call for the 1854 National Emigration Convention. However, with the dissolution of the Refugee Home Society following Henry Bibb's death and Holly's departure from Canada, the paper slowly shifted to an open endorsement of the emigration movement.

For Shadd, the change to the nationalist-emigrationist position was probably not a conscious one at first. Rather, the sweeping criticisms of the anti-emigrationists helped push her toward Delany's camp. As an ardent supporter of Canadian emigration, she was subject to the attacks of those blacks who refused to distinguish between her desire for blacks to come to Canada, where they would integrate themselves into a British nationality, and Delany's blending of emigrationism with exhortations to establish a Black Nationality. For example, in December, 1854, in Cincinnati, Shadd made common cause with one of Delany's chief allies to ward off successfully the attacks of the anti-emigrationists. Speaking at a series of meetings which were part of a fund-raising tour for the *Provincial Freeman*, she claimed that blacks would never receive equal treatment in the United States and thus should emigrate to Canada—which would not, she stressed, be annexed to the United States. The Reverend Augustus R. Green, a follower of Delany but also an advocate of Canadian emigration, secured a resolution praising Shadd and endorsing the *Provincial Freeman*. In the process he was forced to overcome the opposition of a close ally of Frederick Douglass—John I. Gaines, a wealthy Cincinnati boat manufacturer who had been an agent for Delany's *Mystery* in the mid-1840's. The debate subsequently continued in the pages of the *Freeman*, where Gaines and Peter H. Clark (another Cincinnati anti-emigrationist and, after the Civil War, a pioneer socialist, principal of the black high school, and prominent black Democrat) continued to press their positions.[37]

The completion of Shadd's shift to nationalist-emigrationism coincided with a parallel change on Delany's part. Reporting to the emigration movement's National Board of Commissioners in late August, 1855, Delany modified his previous cautiousness toward Afro-American emigration to Canada. The *Freeman*, naturally pleased, devoted the entire front page of its October 13 issue to printing the report, commending the address as one "like every production of the Doctor's, good, and will well pay to read it." For his part, Delany was clearly ecstatic as he looked northward. Proudly pointing to the relatively sizeable real estate holdings among black Canadians, Delany now considered Canada an approved refuge for the black man who desired to flee oppression in the United States. He soon demonstrated that his revised attitude represented

---

37. *Frederick Douglass' Paper*, January 4, 1855, p. 1; *Provincial Freeman*, January 13, 1855, p. 2; January 20, 1855, p. 2; February 17, 1855, p. 3; March 17, 1855, p. 10; March 24, 1855, pp. 14-15; *The Mystery*, April 16, 1845, p. 1. On Clark, see John B. Shotwell, *A History of the Schools of Cincinnati* (Cincinnati: School Life Company, 1902), pp. 458-459; August Meier, *Negro Thought in America, 1880-1915: Racial Ideology in the Age of Booker T. Washington* (Ann Arbor: University of Michigan Press, 1963), pp. 28, 48; Herbert G. Gutman, "Peter H. Clark: Pioneer Negro Socialist, 1877," *Journal of Negro Education*, XXXIV (September, 1965), 413-418.

The Emergence of an Emigration Movement

more than mere rhetoric, for in February, 1856, he moved to Chatham, where he was welcomed by the *Provincial Freeman*. Delany immediately established himself as a physician specializing in the diseases of women and children, with an office in the private front parlor of Bell's Hotel. Shortly after his arrival he delivered two lectures at a local church, and in May he testified to his new allegiance by speaking at the Chatham Town Hall at a celebration honoring the Queen's birthday.[38]

Although he had removed himself from his Pittsburgh base, Delany still wished to retain control over his emigration movement. This could be accomplished partially by capitalizing upon his physical proximity to the *Freeman* group. For example, in midsummer of 1856, he used the pages of the *Freeman* to lash out at Frederick Douglass for the latter's editorial, "Canada—Liberia—H. Ford Douglass—Mary A. Shadd." Although Douglass had commented favorably on the activities of both Shadd and H. Ford Douglass, who was also residing in Canada by then, Delany castigated the Rochester editor for having failed to notice Shadd's talents earlier, and he ridiculed Douglass for his kind references to Liberia, charging that he was "actually lauding Colonization to the skies by eulogising Liberia...."[39] Delany also directly attempted to maintain his position in the emigration movement he had spawned. In late May, 1856, he responded to Monroe, who, as the president of the 1854 Emigration Convention, had previously announced that a second convention would convene in Cleveland in August. Asking all members of the movement to attend the scheduled meeting, Monroe had closed his proclamation with the reminder that "the Kansas issue in this country, the state of affairs in the West India islands, the movements in Central America, and the future policy of European nations in regard to their interests in the Western Hemisphere, are all conspiring to precipitate a momentous crisis in the Afric-American destiny on this continent." In reply to this call of alarm, Delany revealed a plan which he claimed he had "held in mature contemplation" since the 1854 convention—"the suggestion of holding a great Continental Convention of colored men, to meet

38. *Provincial Freeman*, October 13, 1855, pp. 97–98; February 23, 1856, pp. 162–163; March 1, 1856, p. 166; March 22, 1856, p. 178; May 31, 1856, p. 26.
39. *Ibid.*, July 12, 1856, p. 50.

at some great convenient central point, *out* of the United States." Although suggesting that the conference be held in Kingston, Jamaica, Delany agreed to hold in reserve a full report of his plan until the upcoming meeting in Cleveland. In fact, he turned his attention to the August gathering only a few days later when, as president of the National Board of Commissioners, he officially informed the Board of the upcoming meeting.[40]

Shadd and the *Freeman* cooperated fully with Delany's plans, for the paper printed both Monroe's Proclamation and Delany's two statements. The *Freeman* also endorsed the call for the 1856 convention and announced that it would print additional copies of the call at a reduced rate for those interested in circulating the announcement. Mary Ann Shadd advised anti-emigrationists to consider the claims of "those who have long since out-grown the policy that has guided the colored people of the States for many years." Arguing that the anti-emigrationists had refused to listen to opinions other than their own, she urged them to "Go to the Cleveland Convention and determine to remove to a country or to countries, where you may have equal political rights, and thus be *elevated* at once." Although Mary Ann Shadd's words fell on deaf ears, they symbolized the depth of support which Delany had won from the entire *Provincial Freeman* circle—a group which included Shadd, her brother Isaac D. Shadd (who was the publisher of the *Freeman* and later speaker of the Mississippi House of Representatives during Reconstruction), Louis Patterson, and H. Ford Douglass.[41] Given the intensity of the *Freeman*'s earlier opposition to Delany's movement and the strategic importance of Shadd and her allies as blacks who had already emigrated, the addition of this group to Delany's camp was significant.

Yet as Delany's movement was broadening in the two years after the 1854 Cleveland convention, internally it was losing its cohesiveness. This reflected long-held disagreements over where blacks should emigrate, differences already evident during the 1854 convention. For example, not all the delegates had followed Delany in

---

40. *Ibid.*, May 31, 1856, p. 26; May 10, 1856, p. 14; June 7, 1856, p. 30.
41. *Ibid.*, May 10, 1856, p. 14; May 31, 1856, p. 26; June 7, 1856, p. 30; June 28, 1856, p. 42; July 5, 1856, p. 46. On Isaac D. Shadd, see Wharton, *Negro in Mississippi*, p. 176.

downgrading Canadian emigration, since H. Ford Douglass, Joseph H. Foster, and, very likely, the Reverend Augustus R. Green had spoken in favor of emigration to the British provinces.[42] More important in terms of the long-run evolution of the emigration movement were those who had advocated that the convention support an exodus to an established black nation—specifically Haiti—where Afro-Americans could unite to bolster and strengthen the existing nationality. James Theodore Holly had been the leader of this group; he was joined by William Lambert, a Detroit tailor and lay leader in St. Matthew's Church, and H. Ford Douglass, evidently a supporter of several possible locations other than Delany's choice of Central America.[43] Of these individuals, Holly proved to be the most active during the two years following the 1854 convention. Capitalizing upon the institutional ties presented by the Episcopal faith which he had recently embraced, Holly was able to organize other black Episcopalians into a distinct group of missionary-nationalists within Delany's larger emigration movement.

A man of energy and initiative, Holly was committed to both the creation of a Black Nationality and the propagation of the Episcopal faith. A relatively unusual phenomenon among blacks of the period, Holly's attachment to the Protestant Episcopal Church was crucial in defining the nature of his emigrationism and his nationalism. Baptized in the Roman Catholic Church as a youth in Georgetown, he was attracted to the Episcopal Church while a resident of Burlington, Vermont, in 1850. When living in Canada in 1852, Holly first took Episcopal communion from the Reverend William C. Monroe at the Detroit minister's St. Matthew's Episcopal Church. In 1853 he was admitted as a candidate for holy orders by Bishop Samuel A. McCrosky of the episcopal Diocese of Michigan, and on June 17, 1855, in Monroe's church, the Bishop ordained Holly a deacon.[44]

42. *The Daily Cleveland Herald*, August 26, 1854, p. 3.
43. *The Chatham Tri-Weekly Planet*, February 15, 1861, p. 3. For an undated obituary of Lambert, see the "William Lambert Folder," Burton Historical Collection, Detroit Public Library.
44. George F. Bragg, *Men of Maryland* (Baltimore: Church Advocate Press, 1914), p. 79; J. Theodore Holly to the Rt. Rev. J. H. Hopkins, Port-au-Prince, Haiti, March 5, 1868, John Henry Hopkins Papers, General Theological Seminary, New York; "A Brief History of St. Matthew's"; Holly to "My Dear Chrysa,"

Meanwhile Holly was becoming more outspoken in his championing of Haitian emigration, which he had first advocated at the Amherstburg Convention in June, 1853. By 1855 his position was well known, and when he expressed his desire to inspect the Caribbean island, the National Board of Commissioners approved his appointment as an "official commissioner" to visit Haiti and, at his discretion, Jamaica, St. Thomas, Nassau, Martinique, Guadalupe, and Central America. Both Holly and the National Board agreed that he would survey Haiti and report back as to the advisability of encouraging North American blacks to emigrate there. However, Holly was not content to travel solely for the benefit of Delany's emigration movement. Convinced of the need for an Episcopal mission in Haiti, in May, 1855, he prevailed upon a white layman to ask the Protestant Episcopal Board of Foreign Missions to send him to the island to determine whether the Board should establish a mission there. Monroe also expressed an interest in returning to Haiti, where, it will be recalled, he had served as a Baptist missionary during the 1830's.[45]

The Board of Foreign Missions delayed action upon Holly's request. Nevertheless, Holly drew upon his own resources, some money from the emigrationists, and whatever he could borrow; he left New York for Haiti on July 10—only three weeks after his ordination. Upon arriving at Port-au-Prince, Holly candidly explained to Haitian authorities that he planned to investigate both the advisability of encouraging black emigration to Haiti and the possibility of establishing an Episcopal mission. He met with the ministers of the interior and exterior, the emperor's chamberlain, and the British consul; he also attempted to open negotiations with the government concerning the conditions under which black emigrants from North America would be incorporated into the Haitian nation.

Perhaps mindful of the difficulties encountered by black Americans who had emigrated to Haiti in the mid-1820's, Holly suggested

---

Port-au-Prince, August 17, 1903, James Theodore Holly Papers, Archives of the Episcopal Diocese of Connecticut, Hartford.

45. *Chatham Tri-Weekly Planet*, February 15, 1861, p. 3; *Provincial Freeman*, October 13, 1855, p. 97; Horace Hille, Jr., to S. D. Denison, Detroit, May 5, 1855, Domestic and Foreign Missionary Society Papers: Haiti Papers.

terms which he considered highly attractive to potential emigrants. Not only would the Haitian government follow its earlier practice of granting private homesteads to the settlers, but it would also ensure that the new element, unlike the 1824–25 emigrants, would receive equal civil and religious rights. Holly's proposals relieved all immigrants from military duty for seven years, allowed immigrants to import duty free "all materials, tools, furniture, &c. brought... for the purpose of carrying on their labors," and provided for citizenship to be granted after a year's residence. In return, the National Board of Commissioners would guarantee the emigration of at least two hundred families annually for five years.[46] How much consideration Holly received for these proposals is unknown, for he had ample time to pursue his other interests. He apparently spent most of his time visiting the various Protestant missions already functioning on the island, as well as conversing with Judge Emil de Ballette, who had previously communicated with Monroe about the advisability of establishing an Episcopal mission in Haiti. From Holly's investigations of the activities of the three Protestant groups in Port-au-Prince—the English Wesleyans, American Methodists, and American Baptists—he concluded that the Episcopalians could establish a viable mission. Part of his enthusiasm was based upon what he, like Prince Sanders years earlier, inferred to be a hostile attitude on the part of the Haitian government toward the existing Roman Catholic establishment.[47]

Returning to New York from Port-au-Prince in early September, Holly immediately approached the Foreign Board in search of

46. For this and the preceding paragraph, see *Provincial Freeman*, October 13, 1855, p. 97; *New York Daily Tribune*, September 5, 1855, p. 6; James Theodore Holly to Frank P. Blair, Jr., New Haven, January 30, 1858, in Blair, *The Destiny of the Races of this Continent*... (Washington, D.C.: Buell & Blanchard, Printers, 1859), pp. 36–37.

47. This account is based on an undated letter written by Holly to the Foreign Board from Port-au-Prince, probably in August, and on three manuscripts—"Considérations générales sur la fondation et le soutien d'une Eglise épiscopale au Port au prince par Emile de Ballette" (Document A), "Remarks on the preceding general considerations" by Holly, and "Confidential considerations favorable to the establishments [*sic*] of Episcopal Mission in Haiti" (Document B), also written by Holly. Holly explains Documents A and B in his letter to the Foreign Board, New York, September 10, 1855. All the above material is in the Domestic and Foreign Missionary Society Papers: Haiti Papers. On Sanders, see Chapter 3 above and *Boston Recorder*, February 11, 1817, p. 27.

support for a Haitian missionary station which, as he envisioned it, would consist of at least two and preferably three families. The Board took no immediate action until after Monroe had visited New York in October to reiterate his and Holly's desire to establish the Haitian mission. Informed at that time that Holly had prepared a series of lectures on his observations concerning Haiti, the Board arranged for him to deliver them in churches in New York City and Brooklyn. In appearances before lay audiences of both white and black Episcopalians in late October and early November, Holly spoke of the opportunities Haiti provided for the spread of Christianity and civilization to a beleaguered black people whose Roman Catholicism was worse than pure paganism. Moreover, as Holly explained in a lecture at St. Luke's Chapel in Brooklyn, the pagan African rituals of the former slaves—"the religious superstitions and practices of that ancient land of darkness"—had understandably not yet been fully eradicated. Despite these difficulties, the existing Protestant missionaries, aided by the government's sympathetic attitude toward their activities, were extremely successful. These efforts, however, were insufficient, for only through the participation of black Episcopal missionaries could Christians bring civilization and light to a benighted people. Of course. the results of Episcopal missions would extend far beyond Haiti, Holly informed his listeners. After Christianity and civilization had converted and elevated the Haitian people, "posterity may witness, at some future and not distant day, national emissaries issuing from that people—descendants of Africa—bearing in their hands... Religion, Education, and Industry... to their ancient fatherland and rekindle the beams of her ancient civilization and Christianity...." Although Holly's eloquence may have impressed his audience, it had little effect upon the Foreign Board. Dubious about the ability of black clergymen to labor free from white supervision and also $10,000 in debt, the Board informed Holly in late November that for the present and for the foreseeable future its "financial condition shuts them out from efforts in any new field."[48]

48. Holly to Foreign Board, New York, September 10, 1855; Foreign Committee Minutes: entries for September 25, October 23, 1855, Domestic and Foreign Missionary Society Papers. Holly's lecture at St. Luke's Chapel was reported in *The Churchman*, XXV (November 1, 1815), 288. For his other lectures, see *The Church*

By late 1855, then, Holly was still rootless—a man with a spiritual mission, but without a physical church. However, in January of the new year, the Diocese of Connecticut, acting upon letters from Monroe, the Reverend Samuel V. Berry (a black Brooklyn Episcopal clergyman who had recently attempted to secure a missionary position in Liberia), and two black New Haven Episcopal laymen, elevated Holly to the priesthood and appointed him rector of St. Luke's Episcopal Church of New Haven. Formed by the diocese in 1844 in response to a petition from the black members of New Haven's predominantly white Trinity Church, St. Luke's was first served by the Reverend Eli Worthington Stokes, a black rector who was later a missionary in Monrovia. St. Luke's evidently appealed to the more stable, middle-class element within New Haven's black population.[49] Although a small church, it was to serve over the next few years as James Theodore Holly's base for the propagation of both the Episcopal faith and Haitian emigration. It would also serve as the center of emigration activity within Delany's emigration movement, although largely independent of his direct influence. This became evident both during and after the second National Emigration Convention in 1856.

Unlike the 1854 meeting, attendance was small when Monroe opened the convention at the A.M.E. Church in Cleveland on Au-

---

Journal, October 25, 1855, p. 309; November 1, 1855, p. 314; November 8, 1855, p. 322. Holly gave almost the identical lecture at Trinity Church in New Haven on July 13, 1856 (*The Church Journal*, July 31, 1856, p. 210). For the Board's decision, see S. Denison to Rev. J. T. Holly, New York, November 22, 1855, S. Denison Letterbooks, Domestic and Foreign Missionary Papers; David McEwen Dean, "James Theodore Holly, 1829-1911, Black Nationalist and Bishop" (Ph.D. dissertation, University of Texas, 1972), p. 47.

49. Supporting letters for Holly from Monroe, Detroit, December 22, 1855; Berry, Brooklyn, December 21, 1855; and four members of St. Luke's Church, New Haven, December 24, 1855 (based upon evidence given them by Berry) are located in the Standing Committee Papers of the Diocese of Connecticut, Archives of the Episcopal Diocese of Connecticut. The basic history of St. Luke's Church can be followed in Robert A. Warner, *New Haven Negroes: A Social History* (New Haven: Yale University Press, 1940), pp. 86-88; *New Haven Register*, May 18, 1969, pp. 26, 35. For Stokes, see George F. Bragg, *History of the Afro-American Group of the Episcopal Church* (Baltimore: Church Advocate Press, 1922), pp. 104, 106, 189. On Berry, see *Spirit of Missions*, XVIII (May, 1853), 171; Alexander Crummell to Foreign Secretary, Monrovia, January[?] 28, 1854, Domestic and Foreign Missionary Society Papers: Liberia Papers.

gust 27. In fact, Delany himself was absent due to illness, and of his Chatham allies, only Isaac Shadd was in Cleveland. Nevertheless, several of the most prominent emigrationists were in attendance, including Holly, Shadd, James M. Whitfield, John P. Anthony (a lay leader in Holly's St. Luke's Church), and E. P. Walker (a Toledo barber who had attended the first National Emigration Convention and had once supported an effort by white colonizationists to establish an "Ohio in Africa"). Little business was probably transacted during the two days of regular sessions. All that is definitely known—other than that Holly reported on his Haitian trip—is that the emigration movement enlarged its organizational apparatus. This involved many emigrationists who were not at the convention but who evidently agreed to participate in the various ancillary bodies that were created. Two new groups—a Board of Trade and a Board of Publications—were formed. Not surprisingly, the central headquarters for the movement were shifted to Chatham. Delany retained the presidency of the National Board with Monroe serving as vice-president, Lambert as treasurer, and Holly as foreign corresponding secretary. Seven Chatham blacks—including Isaac D. Shadd and H. Ford Douglass—were added to the National Board; the convention selected the *Provincial Freeman* as the official emigrationist organ and Douglass as "Travelling Agent and Lecturer."[50]

The purposes and composition of the two new boards illuminated the diverse directions which Delany's emigration movement was now taking. The Board of Publications was assigned the responsibility of producing the *Afric-American Quarterly Repository* as a periodical "of the Literature, Art and Science of our race." Whitfield was appointed senior editor, and eight corresponding editors were added: Delany, Holly, Monroe, Mary Ann Shadd, Mary E. Bibb, the Pittsburgh school teacher Martin H. Freeman, the Reverend Augustus R. Green, and John N. Still of New Jersey. The Board of Trade, created to operate a North American and West India Trading Association, was, of course, only the latest of

50. *Provincial Freeman*, February 2, 1856, p. 150; November 25, 1856, p. 62; M. R. Delany, *Official Report of the Niger Valley Exploring Party* (New York: Thomas Hamilton, 1861), p. 10; Blair, *The Destiny of the Races on this Continent*, p. 36. For Walker, see *Toledo, Ohio, City Directory*, 1858, p. 179; 1860, p. 148; *African Repository*, XXVI (July, 1850), 219. On Anthony, see the following paragraph in the text and note 51.

such proposed ventures put forth at least as early as the second decade of the nineteenth century by Paul Cuffe and Peter Williams. A joint stock venture like the American Continental and West India League drawn up after the 1851 Toronto convention, the new Association was to be composed of shareholders—each of whom would buy shares at $50 apiece, to be paid for in five annual installments. The Board itself was composed of six members, all of whom were from Connecticut, and four of whom belonged to Holly's St. Luke's Church. These four were Holly himself; Anthony, the President of the Board of Trade and the proprietor of a clothing store in New Haven; Henry S. Merriman, a coachman; and Thomas Prime, a clothes cleaner. The other members of the Board were William W. Quonn, a New Haven hairdresser, and Henry Nott, a Hartford porter.[51]

Apparently neither of the two boards functioned; in fact, the *Afric-American Quarterly Repository* was never published. Nevertheless, the Board of Trade's formation and membership reflected the personal influence of Holly as an independent force within a clearly diversified emigration movement having quasi-autonomous centers at Chatham and New Haven. Furthermore, unlike the militantly secular Delany, Holly's priestly role strengthened his leadership position among the emigrationists. Sometime in 1856, for example, he spearheaded the formation of the Protestant Episcopal Society for Promoting the Extension of the Church among Colored People. Although primarily devoted to the propagation of the Episcopal faith among blacks, it was also agitating for the establishment of an Episcopal mission in Haiti and, implicitly, for black emigration to the island. Monroe, Lambert, Anthony, and Berry joined Holly in leading the new organization.[52] Tied together by

51. *Provincial Freeman*, November 25, 1856, p. 62. Information on the occupations and church participation of the members of Holly's church can be found in the *New Haven City Directories*, 1848–49 through 1864. Merriman appears to have been the most active member of St. Luke's, serving as clerk, vestryman, chorister, and sexton. Warner, *New Haven Negroes*, p. 87. Nott is listed in the *Hartford City Directories*, 1846–63. With the exception of Prime, all of these men were active in black conventions in Connecticut. See *Proceedings of the Connecticut State Convention of Colored Men, Held at New Haven on September 12th and 13th, 1849* (New Haven: William H. Stanley, Printer, 1849); *Frederick Douglass' Paper*, May 4, 1854, p. 1; May 19, 1854, p. 3.

52. Reports of the second and fourth annual conventions of the Society can be

the bonds of a common faith as well as by a strong interest in Masonry, these men represented a distinct element within the nationalist-emigrationist movement. Yet they were able to use the apparatus of the parent organization to support their advocacy of Haitian emigration. Anthony, for example, acted as the agent for the Afric-American Printing Company (theoretically a subsidiary of the Board of Publication created at the 1856 convention) in overseeing the publication of Holly's *Vindication of the Capacity of Negro Race, for Self-Government, and Civilized Progress, As Demonstrated by Historical Events of the Haytian Revolution*—a call for blacks to combine with the Haitian people and bolster the already extant black nationality.[53]

Dedicated to Monroe, Holly's essay was a striking reaffirmation of his faith in both Christianity and the Haitian people. First, it presented a lengthy recital of the major events of the Haitian Revolution which Holly saw as "one of the strongest proofs that can be adduced to substantiate the capabilities of the negro race for self-government." Holly also defended Haiti's monarchical form of government for providing greater liberty than the republican despotism of the United States. Finally, Holly sharpened the vision of the future that he had first unveiled at St. Luke's Chapel in Brooklyn in the fall of 1855, following his trip to Haiti. Afro-Americans, he again maintained, should dedicate themselves to strengthening "this negro nationality of the New World until its glory and renown shall . . . redeem and regenerate by its influence in the future the benighted Fatherland of the race in Africa . . . for Civilization and Christianity is passing from East to West. . . ."[54]

By glorifying a Black Nationality, Holly's rhetoric coincided with the philosophy Delany had been formulating during most of the decade. Yet because Holly's Christian commitment completely permeated his ties to the nationalist-emigrationist movement, De-

---

found in *The Calendar*, XIII (August 22, 1857), p. 269; and *The Weekly Anglo-African*, October 22, 1859, p. 2.

53. James Theodore Holly, *A Vindication of the Capacity of the Negro Race for Self-Government and Civilized Progress, As Demonstrated by Historical Events of the Haytian Revolution* (New Haven: Afric-American Printing Company, 1857), title page, pp. 47–48. On the Masonic ties, see *The Ancient Landmark*, III (February, 1854), 107.

54. Holly, *Vindication*, pp. 10, 40–43, 45.

lany could not join with his former ally. Whether Delany fully realized the extent to which Holly and his Episcopal following had moved outside the scope of his own leadership is not known. What is apparent, however, is that by the spring of 1858, even though he had recently expressed interest in the Central American designs of Frank P. Blair, Jr., a Missouri congressman,[55] Martin R. Delany began to develop a nationalist-emigrationist program which broke sharply with his own plans of creating a Black Nationality in Central and South America, as well as with Holly's long-range hopes for regenerating Africa through the bolstering of a Black Christian Nationality in Haiti. Now a new Black Nationality would be planted directly on the west coast of Africa. Delany's plans were neither totally new for himself, nor were they unique.

55. M. R. Delany to Frank P. Blair, Jr., Chatham, C.W., February 24, 1858, in Blair, *The Destiny of the Races on this Continent*, p. 34. For background on Blair's advocacy of Central American colonization, see Willis Boyd, "Negro Colonization in the National Crisis, 1860–1870" (Ph.D. dissertation, University of California at Los Angeles, 1954), pp. 123–125; Eric Foner, *Free Soil, Free Labor, Free Men: The Ideology of the Republican Party before the Civil War* (New York: Oxford University Press, 1970), pp. 272–274.

CHAPTER 6

The Search for a Place: Africa

From the spring of 1858 into early 1862, a significant segment of the black intelligentsia in the northern United States and Canada West looked tolerantly upon emigration to West Africa—especially to the Yoruba region inland from Lagos. Only a small number actively advocated African emigration, but even among those who did not, there was a willingness to listen to those proposing emigration plans. Significantly, too, there was a modest revival of a practice often followed before 1830—the acknowledgment of their identities as partly African. In New York City, for example, *The Anglo-African Magazine* and *The Weekly Anglo-African*, both founded in 1859, championed racial pride aggressively and effectively. While neither the magazine nor the newspaper formally endorsed emigration, both opened their columns to arguments and news which favored emigration in general and the development of a black colony in Yoruba in particular.

Delany was the most active promoter of nationalist-emigrationist sentiments, but of almost equal influence was the militant abolitionist Henry Highland Garnet. Although not involved in the emigration battles of the mid-1850's, Garnet emerged in 1858 as one of the leaders of the white-backed African Civilization Society, an organization which infused large amounts of missionary zeal into the complex of ideas which Delany had been articulating for some time.

Origins of the Niger Valley Exploring Party

In light of Martin R. Delany's earlier denunciations of the American Colonization Society and his devotion to New World emigration, his decision early in 1858 to locate a colony in the Niger Valley region of West Africa could only have been startling. In fact, as recently as June, 1855, Delany had castigated African colonization as the "*most* pernicious and impudent of all schemes for the perpetuity of the degradation of our race."[1] Nevertheless, beginning in the spring of 1858, Delany spent an entire year attempting to organize a preliminary Niger Valley exploring party that would first investigate what was, after all, a geographical area almost totally unknown to Westerners who were still searching for the mouth of the Niger River, and second, if possible, secure land for an actual settlement. Recruiting members for the expedition was extremely difficult. Funds for the projected trip were scarce, compelling Delany to turn to such dissimilar sources as Jonathan J. Myers, a successful Wisconsin black businessman, and the American Missionary Association. Finally, in a search for public support for his expedition, Delany attempted to rally to his side the vestiges of the emigration movement he had helped found several years earlier.

Delany's motives in embracing African colonization must have been mixed. By 1858 his emigration movement had long lost its cohesiveness, as we have seen, with Holly and his fellow Episcopalians urging a missionary-emigration to Haiti. Delany, who believed that excessive religiosity weakened the capacity of blacks to labor for their own interests, could not agree with Holly's emphasis upon Christian regeneration. It is also doubtful whether Delany wished to share his leadership with the New Haven minister. In addition, Delany probably realized that Haiti's national existence precluded Afro-Americans from ever achieving a predominant

---

1. Martin R. Delany, "Introduction," in William Nesbit, *Four Months in Liberia; or African Colonization Exposed* (Pittsburgh: J. T. Shyrock, 1855), pp. 3–8. Nesbit, a Hollidaysburg, Pennsylvania, agent for Delany's *The Mystery* in the 1840's, had sailed for Liberia in the fall of 1853 as one of a group of emigrants sent out by the American Colonization Society on the *Isla de Cuba*. Nesbit was a member of a large Pennsylvania contingent headed by the Reverend Samuel Williams of Johnstown, also a former agent for Delany's paper. After a short and unhappy stay in Liberia, Nesbit returned to the United States and wrote the "exposé" which Delany introduced. Two years later, Williams replied—including some special remarks for Delany. See Samuel Williams, *Four Years in Liberia; A Sketch of the Life of the Rev. Samuel Williams; With Remarks on the Missions, Manners and Customs of the Natives of Western Africa; Together with an Answer to Nesbit's Book* (Philadelphia: King & Baird, Printers, 1857), esp. pp. 27, 65.

role in forging the country's destiny, and thus negated any possibility of establishing a *new* Black Nationality.

However, Delany's longstanding emotional attachment to Africa was probably more important in motivating him to change his position. As early as his Pittsburgh school days, Delany and his boyhood friend, Molliston M. Clark, later an A.M.E. minister, had promised each other to visit Africa. Each would eventually fulfill this vow—Delany first and then Clark, who traveled to Liberia in 1860 and 1861. But long before Delany left for Liberia in May, 1859, he had started planning an African exploration. At the age of twenty-four—only a few years after he had made his compact with Clark—Delany developed the elaborate design for an *East African* exploration to locate a site for a colony; the plan was eventually revised and published in the appendix of Delany's *Condition, Elevation, Emigration, and Destiny of the Colored People of the United States, Politically Considered* in 1852. Delany also followed developments in Liberia with a concern unusual among those blacks strenuously opposing the Colonization Society. Particularly interested in the possibility that Liberia might serve as one terminal of a trans-Atlantic black trading connection, he was also intrigued by the implications of Liberian independence when the black republic legally cast off its ties to the Colonization Society. At one time Delany believed that "Liberia in its present state . . . [has] thwarted the design of the original schemers, the slaveholding founders. . . ." Even though he soon modified this position, Delany never entirely rejected the idea of settlement in Africa as a possible alternative to colonization in the New World.[2]

Delany, moreover, believed he might be able to rebuild his movement around the idea of African emigration. By 1858 Delany, still residing in Canada, was far from his Pittsburgh base of support and thus isolated geographically. Although he had incorporated a number of Chatham blacks into the emigration movement, their numbers

2. M. R. Delany, *Official Report of the Niger Valley Exploring Party* (New York: Thomas Hamilton, 1861), p. 8; *The Colonization Herald*, September, 1860, p. 484; *The Weekly Anglo-African*, October 15, 1861, p. 3; Martin Robison Delany, *The Condition, Elevation, Emigration, and Destiny of the Colored People of the United States, Politically Considered* (Philadelphia: By the Author, 1852), pp. 9, 209–214. On Delany's early attitudes toward Liberia, see Chapter 4 above; the quotation is from *The North Star*, March 2, 1849, p. 2.

were small and the depth of their commitment uncertain. An African exploration could help him win new support for a divided and flagging movement.

In the spring of 1858 he began to consider implementing, with major modifications, the plan he had published in 1852. At that time he had proposed that a small number of men—"embody[ing] among them, the qualifications of physician, botanist, chemist, geologist, geographer, and surveyor"—would explore eastern Africa in search of a location for a colony of black men from North America. One or two special "Representatives of a Broken Nation" would travel to England and France to raise funds to maintain the exploring party in Africa for three years. For the European powers, advantage would accrue from the future commercial gains achieved from trading with a powerful and economically productive black nation situated on Africa's eastern coast. When Delany turned again toward Africa in 1858, East Africa was absent from his plans. He now focused upon West Africa—recently the subject of the writings and exploration of both the Reverend Thomas J. Bowen, a Southern Baptist missionary to the Yoruba country, and David Livingstone, the English traveler. Stimulated by Bowen's *Central Africa: Adventures and Missionary Labors* and Livingstone's *Missionary Travels and Researches in South Africa*, Delany found an alternative to both Liberia and East Africa in the Niger Valley.[3]

In the spring Delany began recruiting members for his exploring expedition. Although not everyone he approached would accept, at least a few blacks had become convinced that African emigration was the only solution to the problem of continued oppression and degradation in the United States. Martin H. Freeman, then principal of the Avery Institute for black youth in Pittsburgh, certainly was one, and Delany very likely asked his former supporter in the emigration movement to join his party. Freeman wrote Delany in April, regretting that he had not emigrated to Africa earlier when he was still free from family ties. He, too, had read Bowen and was about to read Livingstone. Through his work with young blacks, Freeman was extremely conscious of the tendency of all blacks, but especially children, to judge themselves against Anglo-Saxon standards and thus belittle themselves and their own efforts.

3. Delany, *Official Report*, p. 10; Delany, *Condition*, pp. 209–214.

Blacks must "develop ... self-respect, self-reliance, and hatred of oppression." Yet clearly there was little possibility that this could be achieved in the United States. "I am more and more convinced," he informed Delany, "that Africa is the country to which all colored men who wish to attain the full stature of manhood, and bring up their children to be men and not creeping things, should turn their steps...." But Freeman's family responsibilities were too burdensome for him to accompany Delany at this time, although several years later he emigrated to Liberia.[4]

With Freeman unable to join the exploring expedition, Delany was still casting around for companions when, in late May, he wrote two old Philadelphia friends: Dr. James H. Wilson, a physician, and Robert Douglass, Jr., son of the prominent Philadelphia black leader. Douglass, a former sign painter who had gained something of a reputation as a portrait painter, was well traveled, for he had visited Haiti in the 1830's, Jamaica in 1848, and had studied in Europe on several occasions. Delany asked Douglass to serve as the party's artist and Wilson as surgeon and naturalist. Although favorably disposed to the enterprise and flattered by Delany's invitation, Wilson declined. Douglass gave his tentative acceptance—conditional upon whether he would receive what he considered "a proper outfit and salary." Douglass also informed Delany that Robert Campbell, a teacher in Philadelphia, had agreed to "accompany the Expedition, if proper support for his family in his absence were assured."[5]

Money, then, was obviously Delany's major problem. In fact, lack of resources would plague him constantly during the entire year prior to his departure for Africa. Even before writing to

---

4. Delany, *Official Report*, p. 13; M. H. Freeman, "The Educational Wants of the Free Colored People," *The Anglo-African Magazine*, I (April, 1859), 115–119. Middlebury College, *General Catalogue: Sesquicentennial Edition* (Middlebury, Vt: Middlebury College, 1950), p. 130.

5. Delany, *Official Report*, pp. 11–13. For Douglass, see Henry J. Cadbury, "Negro Membership in the Society of Friends," *Journal of Negro History*, XXI (April, 1936), 192–193; *Genius of Universal Emancipation*, XIII (February, 1833), 59; *Colored American*, June 16, 1838, pp. 65–66; *The North Star*, June 2, 1848, p. 1; *Pennsylvania Freeman*, December 26, 1850, p. 2; Benjamin Quarles, *Black Abolitionists* (New York: Oxford University Press, 1969), pp. 22, 134.

Douglass and Wilson, Delany had attempted to overcome this handicap by conferring with a black grocer in Madison, Wisconsin, named Jonathan J. Myers. A man of energy and initiative, the forty-one-year-old Myers had migrated from Pennsylvania, where he was born, to Indiana and Illinois before finally settling in Milwaukee in 1849. By the next year he had acquired some $300, and was established as a grocer. In the mid-1850's Myers moved to Madison, where he operated an ice cream parlor and, later, a fruit store and confectionery. Active in Madison's small black community, Myers was concerned about the fate of a black suffrage bill which the legislature put before the state's voters in the fall of 1857; the overwhelming defeat of the bill may have contributed directly to his decision to turn his thoughts to Africa in late 1857 or early 1858. Not surprisingly, Delany began to look toward Myers.[6]

According to Delany's testimony, the two black emigrationists held "several councils," most probably in early 1858, with Myers supposedly representing a group of Wisconsin blacks contemplating resettlement in Africa. It is doubtful, however, whether any Wisconsin association ever existed, although Myers did meet or correspond with Ambrose Dudley, 38, a Milwaukee cook and waiter and Wisconsin's sole delegate to the first National Emigration Convention in 1854. Possibly with the tacit backing of other Wisconsin blacks, Myers and Dudley contacted Delany. For the Chatham physician, Myers's wealth—which would amount to over $5,000 in real estate in 1860—must have served as a strong inducement to establish a working relationship.[7] For Myers, Delany's prominence

---

6. Delany, *Official Report*, p. 10. On Myers, see manuscript schedule, Seventh Census of the United States: 1850—Milwaukee County, First Ward, and Town of Franklin; *Milwaukee Sentinel*, March 24, 1852; *Madison City Directory and Business Advertiser for 1858*, p. 83; *Madison City Directory, 1858–1859*, p. 7; William J. Vollmar, "The Negro in a Midwest Frontier City: Milwaukee, 1835–1870" (Master's thesis, Marquette University, 1968), pp. 72, 111; Edward Noyes, "A Negro [William H. Noland] in Mid-Nineteenth Century Wisconsin Life and Politics," *Wisconsin Academy Review*, XV (Fall, 1968), 3; *Wisconsin Daily State Journal*, April 23, 1857. I am grateful to Professor Noyes of Wisconsin State University at Oshkosh for sharing with me his notes on Myers.

7. On Dudley, see the 1850 manuscript census for Milwaukee County; *Milwaukee City Directory, 1851–1852*, p. 41, and *1858*, p. 69; Vollmar, "Negro in Milwaukee," p. 2; *Proceedings of the National Emigration Convention of Colored*

as a black leader and his commitment to both the establishment of an African colony and the development of commercial ventures suited to an Afro-American intrusion into Africa were sufficient attractions.

Although the exact contours of this partnership are obscure, it is clear that in the spring of 1858, as chairman of the "Mercantile Line of the Free Colored People of North America"—a paper organization which included Delany and Dudley as nominal officers—Myers requested information about West Africa from Thomas Clegg, the Manchester, England, cotton merchant who had been promoting the cultivation of cotton in West Africa since almost the beginning of the decade; the Royal Geographical Society of England; and, more surprisingly, Stephen A. Benson, the president of Liberia. Myers also informed Clegg that the black company planned to send an exploring party to Africa's Niger Valley to establish an "industrial colony." To be capitalized at $100,000, the firm would be "owned and governed by the free colored people of North America," the company's vessels would be manned entirely by blacks, and "the first vessel intends carrying an efficient corps of scientific men of color in North America, numbering 150 to 200, to locate and establish the colony." The colony itself would include some men "thoroughly acquainted with the cultivation of cotton, sugar, rice, and tobacco, and any others adapted to that climate" while other settlers would introduce "the mechanical arts" into the area and trade with the natives. To complete the commercial ties between the colony and North America, a trading center and an emigration agency would be established at Kingston, Canada West.[8]

People; Held at Cleveland, Ohio, on Thursday, Friday and Saturday, the 24th, 25th and 26th of August, 1854 (Pittsburgh: A. A. Anderson, 1854), pp. 9, 18. On Myers's wealth in 1860, see manuscript schedule, Eighth Census of the United States: 1860—Milwaukee County, First Ward.

8. On Clegg, see Eugene Stock, *The History of the Church Missionary Society, its Environment, its Men, and its Work* (London: Church Missionary Society, 1899), II, 110–111; Jean Herskovitz Kopytoff, *A Preface to Modern Nigeria: The "Sierra Leonians" in Yoruba, 1830–1890* (Madison: University of Wisconsin Press, 1965), p. 36. For the letter to Clegg and Clegg's reply, see *Manchester (England) Weekly Advertiser*, July 17, 1858, p. 7. Clegg urged Myers's committee to "depute a dozen of your number to visit and settle on the Niger, at...some...of the stations where cotton already bonds; open a brisk trade with the natives for cot-

The Search for a Place: Africa 177

While Myers was communicating with England and Africa, Delany simultaneously moved to secure other financial support for his exploring party. He turned for help to the American Missionary Association, a nonsectarian antislavery missionary organization which Lewis Tappan, Amos Phelps, and others in the American and

---

ton ... teach them the American method of cleaning, packing and shipping the cotton, and generally try to benefit your countrymen whilest you make a profitable trade...." He also warned the group against going to the Niger Valley as a large body intent upon establishing a colony: "The fear I should have a body of Africans going there from America would be that the chiefs and others in the interior, who are so fond of war ... would not let you settle peaceably in the interior if you went in a body." The communication to the Royal Geographical Society was originally sent to Professor Joseph Hobbins, a British-born physician at the University of Wisconsin and president of the state St. George's Society, a British-American charitable organization. Hobbins forwarded Myers's letter to the Geographical Society with a note of his own testifying to the character and financial condition of the black association and describing how the militantly self-sufficient aims of the mercantile company would not be inconsistent with the interests of British commerce. "The intention of the Company," Hobbins stated, "[is] to own, equip and to arm its own ships, to man them exclusively with coloured sailors—not to be dependent for protection upon any government or people, unless such protection should become absolutely necessary and then at once to seek the protection of the English government." The Society then forwarded Myers's own letter—simply five questions about the suitability of various areas in Africa for settlement—to Dr. Thomas Hodgkin, a British physician long associated with the Pennsylvania Colonization Society. Hodgkin suggested that although emigration-minded blacks would likely avoid any overt ties with either the American Colonization Society or Liberia, those blacks wishing to settle in West Africa should "go to Liberia in the first instance ... to prepare themselves for their ultimate destination." See "Questions Regarding the interests of the Colony in accessions to the interior of Africa," signed by J. J. Myers, Chairman, Martin R. Delany, Secretary, and Ambrose Dudley, Treasurer, Madison, Wisconsin, May 31, 1858; Dr. Joseph Hobbins to Royal Geographical Society, Madison, Wisconsin, June 7, 1858, Royal Geographical Society Papers, London. The questions and Hodgkin's replies were printed in *The Colonization Herald*, March, 1859, p. 416. On Hobbins, see *Dictionary of Wisconsin Biography* (Madison: State Historical Society of Wisconsin, 1960), pp. 173–174. For Hodgkin, see E[dward] H. Kass, "Thomas Hodgkin, Physician and Social Scientist," *Guy's Hospital Reports*, CXV (1966), 269–280. Mention of the letter to Benson is in *New York Colonization Journal*, October, 1858, p. 2.

Delany later claimed the letters were sent without his knowledge, but they evidently did not disturb his relationship with Myers, for several months later when the Niger Valley Exploring Party was first publicly announced, Delany and his fellow explorers were said to represent a Wisconsin emigration organization as well as Delany's Chatham-based group. Delany, *Official Report*, pp. 10, 16n; *Chatham Tri-Weekly Planet*, September 8, 1858, p. 2.

Foreign Anti-Slavery Society had formed in 1846 and which was presently sponsoring the Mendi mission in West Africa. Delany asked the A.M.A. whether he could obtain assistance from the trustees of the $150,000 left to the organization by the philanthropist and antislavery minister Charles Avery for the propagation of the Gospel and the dispersal of the fruits of Western civilization in Africa. Delany explained that during his long residence in Pittsburgh he had known Avery well, and that he was also acquainted with the executors of Avery's estate and two members of the faculty of the college Avery had founded to educate local blacks. Delany then put his own plans in the most favorable light for the American Missionary Association: his exploring party expected to leave the following year for the Niger Valley, where they would search for a suitable location for the future emigration of educated and highly trained blacks. Once this was found, he and his companions would "negociate [sic] with the natives for Territory or Land" and there establish "an Enlightened and Christian Nationality in the midst of these tractable and docile people which shall not cease till its influence shall have reached the remotest parts of that intensive and interesting country."[9]

For Delany, who believed Christianity was undermining the ability of blacks to cast off the shackles of servitude and docility, assuming the Christian Nationalist position James Theodore Holly was propounding must have been awkward and uncomfortable. Still, the existence of Avery's trust and the establishment by the American Missionary Association of a black communal experiment in Jamaica may have induced Delany to lay aside his antipathy to spiritual endeavours. When George Whipple, the secretary of the Association, replied indicating interest, Delany expressed his willingness to subscribe to the A.M.A.'s evangelical principles. Delany

---

9. Delany to Rev. H. W. Beecher, Chatham, C.W., June 17, 1858, "Canada File," American Missionary Association Papers, Amistad Research Center and Race Relations Department, Dillard University; hereafter cited as A.M.A. Papers. When Avery founded his Institute, Delany lavished praise upon the school's benefactor and claimed that Avery had erected "a monument to his memory that shall last as long as mind exists in the being of the colored people of Alleghany county." Delany was especially pleased by the provision in the Institute's charter requiring that two-thirds of the college's trustees always be black. *The North Star*, July 6, 1849, p. 3.

even assured Whipple that he would not participate in bringing civilization to Africa "if the most elevated idea of the Virtues of Civilisation, and Christian Graces by a *Righteous* Evangelisation, were not implied to their fullest extent." Very likely conscious of the gap between the principles he was professing to Whipple and the reality of the positions he had held to for many years, Delany added that he was not a " 'religious brawler,' having generally very little to say about religion ... never having considered myself a fit nor worthy instrument for the propagation of religious truths." However, he was still a member, in absentia, of the Wylie Street Methodist Church in Pittsburgh. Most telling, he claimed to have "once professed to have tested the regenerating influence of the love of God, by Redemption through Christ, which love and faith I have ever held as my guideposts to the Kingdom of never ending bliss." Delany concluded by stressing the religious connections of Robert Douglass, Jr., and Robert Campbell, the two men he considered committed to the exploring party.[10]

Despite Delany's evocation of religious faith, the A.M.A. did not agree to contribute funds for the Niger Valley Exploring Party. Finances remained a problem. Equally troublesome for the Chatham emigrationist was the necessity of legitimizing the project in the eyes of the black community. In an attempt to give the venture both the semblance of collective support and the appearance of having developed naturally from his emigration movement of the mid-1850's, Delany called a third meeting of the almost moribund National Emigration Convention. The convention two years earlier had revamped the structure of future meetings; as a result, the Chatham convention was limited to members of the National Board of Commissioners, the Board of Trade, and the Board of Publication. Acting upon Delany's request, Holly, as the corresponding secretary of the National Board, in late June notified the members of the boards of the upcoming convention.[11]

When the emigrationists convened at Chatham in early August of 1858, only a shadow of the organization Delany had constructed earlier remained. The presiding officer of the two previous emi-

10. Delany to George Whipple, Chatham, July 3[?], 1858, "Canada File," A.M.A. Papers.
11. *Frederick Douglass' Paper*, July 23, 1858, p. 4.

gration meetings, the Reverend William C. Monroe, was absent—perhaps because he was concentrating his energies upon securing a missionary post in Haiti after a brief flirtation with Elihu Burritt's ill-fated National Compensated Emancipation Society. James M. Whitfield also failed to attend, as did H. Ford Douglass. Not all of the old emigrationists avoided the Chatham meeting; Holly came from New Haven, even though he was of course primarily interested in propagating the cause of Haitian emigration.[12] Of the others in attendance, William Howard Day was by far the most prominent. In early 1858 Day had moved to Canada following a brief experience editing *The People's Record*, a Cleveland monthly which publicized Day's continued opposition to Frederick Douglass. After purchasing a farm in Dresden, near Chatham, Day devoted his time to the wood trade. But he became increasingly involved with the economic and social problems of the black community in Canada, and in June, 1858, he asked the philanthropist Gerrit Smith to help him establish a newspaper to replace the *Provincial Freeman*, at the time suspended.[13] Preoccupation with these concerns, not with emigration, motivated Day to sit with Delany and the other emigrationists.

If Day's presence at the convention was anomalous—as he himself implied during the proceedings—his election to the presidency of the Board of Commissioners was on the surface even more surprising, for he never adopted the positions of the nationalist-emigrationists. On the contrary, the convention itself moved to embrace Day's sentiments without overtly opposing Delany. Asserting its opposition to general emigration, the convention simply declared itself in favor of all efforts to acquire information concerning suitable sites for those individuals wishing to emigrate. No particular location was recommended. Moreover, the Chatham convention also broadened its platform; to attract individuals with diverse viewpoints, it changed its name from the National Emigration Convention to the "Association for the Promotion of the Interests

12. *Chatham Tri-Weekly Planet*, August 23, 1858, p. 2. On Monroe and Burritt's organization, see *New York Tribune*, August 31, 1857, p. 6.

13. *Provincial Freeman*, June 9, 1855, p. 54; September 29, 1855, p. 90; January 19, 1856, p. 142; William Howard Day to Gerrit Smith, Detroit, March 27, 1856; Day to Smith, St. Catherines, C.W., June 21, 1858, Gerrit Smith Papers, Syracuse University.

of the Colored People of Canada and the United States." Summarizing the Convention's general orientation, Day testified to how thoroughly Delany's emigration movement of the mid-1850's had been disemboweled. "I am in favor of just such nationalities as that of Hayti," Day told the gathering, "and would do what I could to sustain them; but feel bound in Canada to use every effort to unite the colored people's interest to that of our British brother here; to know no separate interest...."[14]

Although Delany and Holly both spoke to the convention (the latter giving another report on his 1855 trip to Haiti), and letters from Haiti, Central America, and the Yoruba country in West Africa were read to the delegates, the convention's direction as a whole must have troubled the two veteran emigrationists. Delany was obviously disappointed by its failure to endorse African emigration or to assist his Niger Valley Exploring Party. Still, the Chatham emigrationist could at least take some consolation from the fact that the convention's very eclecticism allowed him ample room to maneuver on his own, and thus he accepted the position of special foreign secretary on the organization's governing body—now the General Board of Commissioners. Holly, far less conciliatory, removed himself from the organization entirely. With an unyielding attachment to Haitian missionary-emigration encouraged by his own black Episcopalian supporters, Holly had little reason to accept Day's leadership and his diffuse and all-enveloping orientation. Moreover, Day's platitudinous reference to the Haitian nationality could not overcome the reality that Holly had received little, if any, concrete support for his own commitment to Haitian emigration. From Holly's point of view, then, the gathering was an unhappy denouement to the movement for hemispheric emigration. As he later wrote to Delany, the Chatham convention saw "a quiet conservatism inaugurated under the presidency of Prof. Wm. Howard Day, and this...offset in yourself at the head of the Central African exploring expedition."[15]

If Delany concurred with Holly's observation that the convention had balanced his own interests with those of Day, he was deluding himself. Yet he still believed an organizational stamp of

14. *Chatham Tri-Weekly Planet*, August 23, 1858, p. 2.
15. *Ibid.*, August 23, 1858, p. 2; February 15, 1861, p. 3.

approval was vital to the success of his exploring expedition, now numbering five members—Delany himself as chief commissioner; Robert Douglass, Jr., and Robert Campbell, artist and naturalist, respectively, as assistant commissioners; Amos Aray, a Chatham doctor, as surgeon; and James W. Purnell, 25, a Pennsylvania-born clerk who was a nephew of the Pennsylvania abolitionist and moral reformer William Whipper, as secretary and commercial reporter. Some three weeks after the Chatham convention had concluded its proceedings Delany received from the General Board of Commissioners selected at the Chatham meeting an endorsement so tepid as to be of negligible value. The Board awarded Delany an "African Commission" authorizing him and his four companions to serve as "The Niger Valley Exploring Party" to undertake a "Topographical, Geological and Geographical Examination of the Valley, and other parts of Africa... for the purposes of science and general emigration." The venture should not be considered the precursor to any black emigration scheme, for the commissioners emphasized that they were "entirely opposed to any Emigration there as such." Of course, what Delany and his fellow explorers wished to do while in Africa was of no direct concern to Day's organization, and the board added "that nothing in this Instrument be so construed as to interfere with the right of the Commissioners to negotiate in their own behalf, or that of any other parties, or organization for territory." In a final statement of disinterest, the board also announced its exemption "from the pecuniary responsibility of sending out this Expedition."[16]

While the "African Commission" provided no substantial support for Delany's expedition, it served to publicize his scheme and to give the appearance of collective approval for what was still entirely a personal undertaking. Both the *Chatham Tri-Weekly Planet*, a white paper noted for its unsympathetic treatment of Canadian blacks, and the *Provincial Freeman* reported that the "Association for the Promotion of the Interests of the Colored People of Canada and the United States" and a Wisconsin emigration group (obviously Myers's) had jointly "commissioned" the Niger Valley

---

16. Delany, *Official Report*, pp. 12–13. Purnell is listed in the manuscript schedule, Eighth Census of the United States: 1860—Columbia Borough, Lancaster County, Pennsylvania.

The Search for a Place: Africa

Exploring Party to investigate "what can be done in and for Africa." Further organized support soon came from New York. " 'The African Civilization Committee,' " wrote the Reverend Theodore Bourne, a white minister, to the *New York Tribune* in September, "... will co-operate with the 'Niger Valley Exploring Party,' and they recommend their project to the favorable notice and aid of all sincere opponents of Slavery and the slave-trade in all parts of our land, as well as of all who desire the elevation of the colored race here and abroad."[17] Whether Delany welcomed this new source of support is not clear, but, as we shall see, given his unalterable conviction that blacks should control their own affairs independent of white influence, he should not have.

BLACK EMIGRATION AND WHITE COLONIZATION

Delany and his followers were not the only blacks to read the works of Thomas J. Bowen and David Livingstone or to become intrigued by reports about the fertile soil and healthy climate of the Yoruba region of West Africa. In the urban areas of the North —principally in New York City, where the energetic and well-traveled Henry Highland Garnet was influential—blacks not directly touched by Delany's emigration movement of the mid-1850's began during the spring and summer of 1858 to consider African emigration as an alternative to continued degradation and futile political agitation. Yet these blacks required material assistance, and the likelihood of the black community providing any significant aid was remote. Consequently, when white colonizationists sought to capitalize upon this interest in Africa by providing blacks with support, it is not surprising that Garnet and other black leaders were able to overcome their previous feelings of hostility toward the colonizationists and accept the new offers of support. Later, and with much more caution, Delany also sought aid from the white colonizationists.

Significant numbers of New York City blacks began to demonstrate a vague yet discernable interest in Yoruba during the spring

17. *Chatham Tri-Weekly Planet*, September 8, 1858, p. 2; *Provincial Freeman*, n.d., quoted in *The Colonization Herald*, October, 1858, p. 395; *New York Daily Tribune*, October 26, 1858, p. 6.

of 1858. By the end of May this had attracted the notice of Benjamin Coates, a Philadelphia wool merchant and self-styled abolitionist-colonizationist who had long followed the English attempts to grow substantial quantities of cotton in West Africa. "Some few northern colored men are disposed to emigrate to Africa, on their acct. independent of the Am. Colon. Soc.," he commented, adding that he believed the travels of Bowen and Livingstone had been instrumental in awakening this new enthusiasm. The Reverend John B. Pinney of the Colonization Society's New York auxiliary agreed with Coates's observations: "There is a large movement among the colored people which tends toward a nucleus near Lagos for African settlement.... They are afraid that if the Col. Soc. moves[,] the old abolition hostility will be reawakened."[18]

Yet the Colonization Society did move, if covertly, for Pinney had already contacted "a promising young man ... now anxious to move among the colored men"—Theodore Bourne. A Dutch Reformed minister with a contentious and egotistical personality, Bourne was the son of the early abolitionist and anti-colonizationist George Bourne, and he was not one to avoid trading upon his father's name and reputation. But, as one observer somewhat sympathetic to African emigration would note, "... men are not measured by their fathers, but by themselves.... Mr. Bourne will [not] die a martyr to the anti-slavery cause if his present status [in the African Civilization Society] is all that he has to sustain his profession...." Eclectic in his reform interests, Bourne was publicly associated with Burritt's National Compensated Emancipation Society when the Yoruba movement among New York City blacks began to reach noticeable proportions in May, 1858.[19] By the end of the

18. Benjamin Coates to Ralph R. Gurley, Philadelphia, May 28, 1858; J. B. Pinney to Gurley, New York, May 31, 1858, Domestic Letters, American Colonization Society Papers, Manuscript Division, Library of Congress; hereafter cited as ACS Papers. On Coates, see *Friends' Intelligencer and Journal*, XLIV (May 7, 1887), 300; and Coates's *Cotton Cultivation in Africa* (Philadelphia: C. Sherman & Son, 1858).

19. Pinney to Gurley, New York, May 31, 1858, Domestic Letters, ACS Papers; Theodore Bourne to William Lloyd Garrison, New York, November 8, 1858, William Lloyd Garrison Papers, Boston Public Library (hereafter cited as Garrison Papers); *Frederick Douglass' Paper*, July 8, 1859, p. 1; Bourne to Lewis Tappan, New York, July 25, 1858, A.M.A. Papers; Peter Tolis, *Elihu Burritt: Crusader*

month Bourne had seen both Pinney and Coates in his search for a position with a state colonization society. Pinney, intrigued by the current interest in Yoruba, decided to employ the young minister as an agent of the New York Society to move among the blacks.[20]

Although Bourne was not placed on the payroll of the New York auxiliary until early fall, he immediately familiarized himself with the issues involved in promoting Yoruba emigration among free blacks and, in the summer, demonstrated his command of the subject in a series of articles published in the *Christian Intelligencer*, the organ of the Dutch Reformed Church. Derivative in nature and evangelical in spirit, Bourne's articles touched on the major emigrationist arguments of the period; more significantly, they showed a keen awareness of the concerns of free blacks and the motivations of those earnestly involved in the growing Yoruba movement. Like Delany and other black emigrationists, Bourne argued that the black man was being oppressed in the North— especially with newly arriving European immigrants pushing black workers out of jobs. A few blacks may rise, Bourne acknowledged, but "it will be centuries before the entire population will be elevated. . . ." Consequently, the majority, stunted by existing prejudice, should emigrate to Yoruba; there "they could establish an Anglo-African Nationality." In Bourne's eyes Yoruba was an especially blessed region and highly suitable for Afro-American settlement. The land there, he explained with great certitude but little knowledge, "is open to *purchase* from the chiefs who have nominal possession. Thus in responsible hands, a *valid title* may be immediately obtained, and, with our present facilities for settlement, a flourishing nationality might spring into vigorous existence in the space of a few years."[21]

---

for Brotherhood (Hamden, Conn.: Archon Books, 1968), p. 257. Theodore Bourne paid homage to his father in "George Bourne, the Pioneer of American Anti-Slavery," *Methodist Quarterly Review*, LXIV (January, 1882), 68–91.

20. Coates to Gurley, Philadelphia, May 28, 1858; Pinney to Gurley, May 31, 1858; Pinney to William McLain, New York, December 22, 1858, Domestic Letters, ACS Papers.

21. Pinney to McLain, December 22, 1858, Domestic Letters, ACS Papers; *Christian Intelligencer*, July 1, 1858, p. 4; July 8, 1858, p. 8; July 15, 1858, p. 12;

Even as Bourne was formulating his philosophical underpinning for Yoruba emigration, elements within New York's black community were beginning to discuss the emigration issue openly. At a meeting at the Spring Street Hall in July, supporters of both Haitian and Liberian emigration appeared. James Theodore Holly proposed that "a large emigration of intelligent colored people... take place... to Hayti... and [aid] the Haytiens in establishing a nationality to compete with any people in all the elements of national strength and glory." Five thousand blacks in Indiana were prepared to emigrate, Holly further announced. T. Morris Chester, a Pennsylvania-born Liberian lawyer and educator later prominent in Louisiana after the Civil War, spoke for Liberia. Well aware of the persistent hostility of Afro-Americans to his country, Chester stoutly defended Liberia as an independent Christian nation serving as an example of black capabilities of self-governance and also as "the harbinger of a community of civilized and Christian African States." Henry M. Wilson, pastor of the Seventh Avenue Presbyterian Church and soon to help channel existing emigration sentiment into the formation of the African Civilization Society, supported Holly's Haitian emigration proposals while also admitting that Liberia might be an attractive alternative for some blacks. Another prominent Presbyterian minister who would likewise take an important role in the organization of the Civilization Society, Henry Highland Garnet, though present, did not speak, and Bourne was unable to attend. However, Bourne endorsed the purposes of the meeting in a letter which was read to the gathering and which centered upon two points: "that a nation of Anglo-Africans would develop energies and resources now obscured..." and "That it was glorious work to found a Christian nation, as a model for all people...."[22]

July 22, 1858, p. 13; August 12, 1858, p. 25; September 9, 1858, p. 41. Bourne's arguments and much of his rhetoric from these articles are summarized in his small pamphlet, *African Evangelization and Civilization* (n.p.: n.d.).

22. *New York Colonization Journal*, August, 1858, p. 2; *Maryland Colonization Journal*, July, 1859, p. 27; *New York Evening Express*, July 17, 1858, p. 1. On Chester, see William J. Simmons, *Men of Mark: Eminent, Progressive and Rising* (Cleveland: Geo. M. Rewell & Co., 1887), pp. 671–676; William Ivy Hair, *Bourbon-*

A month later, blacks met again at the Spring Street Hall in what was ostensibly a British West Indies emancipation celebration but was in reality another opportunity to discuss the emigration issue. The Reverend Moore Walker, a black minister, declared himself to favor both African emigration and "the great convention to be held in Canada... as a movement which has for its objects the sending of the Gospel to Africa...." Bourne, too, was aware of the upcoming Chatham meeting, and although probably holding few illusions about the depth of Delany's concern with the Christian regeneration of Africa, he recognized the black emigrationist's interest in exploring Yoruba. Bourne specifically mentioned Yoruba to the Spring Street Hall audience as a suitable location for "a settlement, which should be the nucleus of an Anglo-African Christian Nation."[23] Evidently more and more blacks in New York City agreed, for activity on behalf of Yoruba emigration proceeded unabated. In fact, the movement gained impetus during the late summer, with Garnet emerging as its leading spokesman.

Born into slavery in Kent County, Maryland, in 1815, Garnet and his family fled to Delaware in 1824 and then on to New York, where he was educated at the African Free School. After a tour of duty as a cabin boy on a vessel traveling between the United States and Cuba, Garnet returned home to find that his family had scattered when visited by professional slave-catchers. Alone but still anxious for an education, he entered a high school for blacks on Canal Street; he also attended the Sunday School at Reverend Theodore S. Wright's First Colored Presbyterian Church. In the mid-1830's Garnet enrolled in Noyes Academy at Canaan, New Hampshire, but an angry mob destroyed the school shortly after he arrived. He then journeyed to Whitesboro, New York, to study at the Oneida Institute, an interracial manual labor school. Finally, in the early 1840's, Garnet settled at Troy in upstate New York and studied theology. Licensed to preach in 1842, he became pastor

---

ism and Agrarian Protest: Louisiana Politics, 1877–1900 (Baton Rouge: LSU Press, 1969), p. 89.

23. *New York Evening Express*, August 3, 1858, pp. 1, 4. Bourne's and Walker's speeches have been transcribed from past to present tense and have been made into direct quotations.

of Troy's Liberty Street Presbyterian Church. At this time he began issuing his own antislavery newspaper, *The Clarion*, having previously assisted William G. Allen in publishing *The National Watchman* in Troy.[24]

For most of the 1840's the young Presbyterian minister held firmly to the view that blacks should not leave the United States, but should remain to agitate against both servitude in the South and oppression in the North. For example, speaking at the annual meeting of the American Anti-Slavery Society in New York in 1840, Garnet tied the plight of the "nominally free" northern black to that of the slave. "Nothing but emancipating my brethren can set me at liberty," he asserted, adding that he refused to "[listen] to the harp-like strains that whisper freedom among the groves of Africa . . . while three millions of my country are wailing in the dark prison-house of oppression." Eight years later Garnet lashed out specifically at African colonization: "We are now colonized. We are planted here, and we cannot as a whole people, be recolonized back to our fatherland." He also added more than a tinge of patriotism to these anti-colonization sentiments: "America is my home, my country, and I have no other. I love whatever of good there may be in her institutions. I hate her sins."[25]

Committed to remaining in the United States to fight for the abolition of slavery, Garnet was equally convinced that the institution could be overthrown only through political involvement. Of course, blacks would first have to secure the vote, and from the late 1830's well into the following decade he participated in an unsuccessful campaign to convince the state legislature in New York to abolish voting restrictions against blacks. Moreover, as the first black man of stature to participate in Liberty party affairs, Garnet

24. Andrew E. Murray, *Presbyterians and the Negro—A History* (Philadelphia: Presbyterian Historical Society, 1966), pp. 135–136; Jane H. Pease and William H. Pease, *Bound with Them in Chains: A Biographical History of the Antislavery Movement* (Westport, Conn.: Greenwood Press, 1972), p. 164; Earl Ofari, "*Let Your Motto Be Resistance*": *The Life and Thought of Henry Highland Garnet* (Boston: Beacon Press, 1972), pp. 3–5; I. Garland Penn, *The Afro-American Press and Its Editors* (Springfield, Mass.: Willey & Co., 1891), pp. 52, 54.

25. American Anti-Slavery Society, *Seventh Annual Report* (1840), p. 7; Henry Highland Garnet, *The Past and the Present Condition, and the Destiny of the Colored Race* (Troy, N.Y.: J. C. Kneeland and Co., 1848), pp. 25, 29.

delivered a major address to a convention of the Massachusetts branch of the party at Boston in February, 1842. He also argued the merits of the Liberty party before black audiences, and at the National Convention of Colored Citizens in Buffalo in August, 1843, he successfully overcame the opposition of Frederick Douglass in convincing the convention to endorse the party. Two weeks later Garnet spoke at the Liberty Party convention in Buffalo and in the fall of the following year, when campaigning on behalf of the party, he defended his political activities at a New York State black convention at Schenectady. There Dr. James McCune Smith of New York City attacked the black minister for linking the suffrage issue to the fortunes of the Liberty party. When the Garrisonian *National Anti-Slavery Standard* later supported Smith's position, Garnet took the opportunity to castigate whites for meddling in the affairs of blacks and to ridicule those blacks (such as Smith and his allies) who were satisfied only when "fawning around the feet of their oppressors."[26]

If Garnet believed that political activity represented a viable alternative to the moral suasionist appeals of the Garrisonians, the Presbyterian minister still doubted whether there would be immediate benefits from political action, for at least twice during the 1840's he called for slave rebellion. At the 1843 National Convention of Colored Citizens in Buffalo and again at the 1847 Troy convention, Garnet delivered his "Address to the Slaves," arguing that slaves should no longer submit to the degradation and oppression heaped upon them by their masters. They were duty bound to strike the first blows against thralldom, shedding their own blood if necessary: "Brethren, arise, arise! Strike for your lives and liberties. Now is the day and the hour. Let every slave throughout the land do this, and the days of slavery are numbered. You cannot be more oppressed than you have been—you cannot suffer greater cruel-

---

26. *Colored American*, August 19, 1837, p. 3; September 2, 1837, p. 1; Quarles, *Black Abolitionists*, pp. 184–185; *Minutes of the National Convention of Colored Citizens; Held at Buffalo, on the 15th, 16th, 17th, 18th and 19th of August, 1843...* (New York: Piercy and Reed, Printers, 1843), pp. 15–16, 21–22; Jane H. Pease and William H. Pease, "Negro Conventions and the Problem of Black Leadership," *Journal of Black Studies*, II (September, 1971), 33. See also Pease and Pease, *Bound with Them*, pp. 170–176.

ties than you have already. *Rather die freemen than live to be slaves.*"[27]

Advocating both slave resistance and political action, still hostile to colonization, Henry Highland Garnet was a man whose diverse opinions could not coexist indefinitely. On the one hand, he believed blacks should remain in the United States to secure through political action the emancipation of the slave and the achievement of full political and civil rights for all blacks. Yet by calling for those in bondage to liberate themselves with force if necessary, Garnet was admitting that political agitation was unlikely to be successful in the near future. Torn by two conflicting views of the future, Garnet could only have been disturbed by the apparent inadequacy of both positions, for by the late 1840's the slaves had not heeded his call, and political antislavery was making only slow progress in turning public opinion against the South's peculiar institution. Perhaps he began to regard colonization as a way out of the intellectual dilemma posed by the confrontation of his two other beliefs. Whatever the motivation, in early 1849 he broke with his previous sentiments to champion both African colonization and the Republic of Liberia: "... my mind of late, has greatly changed in regard to the American Colonization scheme.... I would rather see a man free in Liberia, than a slave in the United States." Nevertheless, Garnet himself was not prepared to leave the United States, for although he urged that "every colored man who sincerely believes he can never grow to the stature of a man in this country, ought to go there immediately, if he desire," he personally believed that "there is work enough for me here...."[28]

Although disillusioned with what the future promised blacks in the United States, Garnet had not yet emerged as a forceful advocate of emigration when he left New York for England in the summer of 1850. After lecturing before antislavery groups for several months, he applied to the United Presbyterian Church of Scotland for a missionary post in either the West Indies or Africa. In the fall of 1852 the church appointed Garnet as a missionary to Stirling, Jamaica. Garnet spent three years there. Whether his decision to labor on the island can be considered an integral part of

27. Pease and Pease, *Bound with Them*, pp. 180–181.
28. *North Star*, January 26, 1849, p. 3; March 2, 1849, p. 1.

The Search for a Place: Africa

a developing commitment to emigration is doubtful, for he never justified his decision to go there in other than purely missionary terms, and once in Jamaica he devoted his energies mainly to missionary work. He built up his congregation over time despite confrontations with fever, inclement weather, and licentious church members; he also taught a class of recaptured Africans. Because of illness Garnet left Jamaica for the United States in early 1856, and although he originally hoped to return to the island, he decided to remain in the United States. In the spring he succeeded Samuel Cornish as pastor of the Shiloh Presbyterian Church in New York. Garnet also began meeting with other black Congregational and Presbyterian clergymen—several of whom were connected with the American Missionary Association—in what was seemingly a continuation of an organization of black Congregational and Presbyterian pastors formed in the 1840's by many of the ministers then active participants in the A.M.A.'s predecessor, the Union Missionary Society.[29]

Exactly why Garnet turned to emigration in the summer of 1858 is unclear. Perhaps the frustrations and isolation which he had experienced in Jamaica convinced him that solitary missionary work was only marginally beneficial to blacks in the West Indies and Africa and of no value at all to black Americans. Afro-American emigration, however, could be combined with missionary work to the benefit of both the black bearers of Christianity and civilization and the heathen recipients. Whatever his motivations, in August, 1858,

---

29. *The Non-Slaveholder*, V (June, 1850), 127; *Anti-Slavery Reporter*, n.s. VI (June 2, 1851), 87; *Missionary Record of the United Presbyterian Church of Scotland*, VII (November, 1852), 187, and VIII (February, 1853), 231; Henry Highland Garnet to Gerrit Smith, Boston, March 25, 1856; Garnet to Smith, New York, October 3, 1856, Smith Papers; *American Missionary*, 2nd ser., I (April, 1857), 77; II (December, 1858), 298; *The Minutes and Sermon of the Second Presbyterian and Congregational Convention, Held in the Central Presbyterian Church, Lombard Street, Philadelphia, on the 28th Day of October, 1857* (New York: Daly, Printer, 1858). See also *The Weekly Anglo-African*, September 24, 1859, p. 2; *Union Missionary*, I (August, 1844), 22. The best record of Garnet's experiences in Jamaica can be found in the *Missionary Record of the United Presbyterian Church of Scotland*, esp. IX (May, 1854), 85–86; X (August, 1855), 138–139. Consult also his extremely interesting letter to the secretary of the British and Foreign Anti-Slavery Society, L. A. Chamerovzow, Stirling, Grange Hill, Jamaica, October 2, 1854, Anti-Slavery Papers, Rhodes House, Oxford, and reprinted in Ofari, "Let Your Motto Be Resistance," pp. 155–160.

Garnet spoke at an emigration gathering at which two other black ministers, Walker and J. V. Givens, were also prominent. Although Garnet did not specifically mention the Yoruba region of West Africa—as Givens did—he was the most effective of the three in answering the charges of several opponents of a separate nationality. "[I]t is time," Garnet declared, "for the colored people to look at things for themselves through their own spectacles. While we *hate* Slavery with intense abhorrence, and intend to fight it to the last, no man should deprive me of my love for Africa, the land of my ancestors." Glorifying Africa's past, Garnet said he was proud of his African heritage and he hoped that some day he would be able to show his children "a land where they could gratify every longing desire for elevation and progress, with a national flag which shall call out all the patriotism of the colored man's heart." Finally, he assured his listeners that this African nationality would be both commercially and spiritually viable: "A few thousand intelligent and enterprising men would be enough to plant a Christian nation which should be a centre for moral and religious as well as commercial and social influence for Africa."[30]

After almost a decade of personal wandering and ideological uncertainty, Garnet had emerged as a committed emigrationist. Moreover, with his rhetorical skills and reputation, he was the obvious leader to channel and develop the interest in African emigration which, supported by such whites as Theodore Bourne, had been growing during the summer. In September—when Bourne publicly announced the intention of "The African Civilization Committee" to cooperate with Delany's Niger Valley exploring party—the African Civilization Society was formed, with Garnet the president and Bourne the corresponding secretary; by mid-October the organization had adopted and printed its constitution. Soon thereafter Garnet issued a statement giving the organization's aims: to promote "the civilization and evangelization of Africa, and the descendants of African ancestors in any portion of the earth, wherever dispersed" by laying "the foundation of a future commonwealth, of the Repub-

---

30. *New York Evening Express*, August 11, 1858, p. 1; *New York Daily Tribune*, August 11, 1858, p. 7. Garnet's speech has been changed from past to present tense and has been made into direct quotation.

lican form, on the Coast of Africa."[31] Garnet, then, was proposing a Christian alternative to Delany's basically secular Black Nationality. Delany did not comment on the emergence of a rival organization, for he undoubtedly wished to maintain the independence of his exploring party. Certainly, he wished to keep it together.

For Delany, maintaining control over his small party became almost as troublesome as raising funds. Robert Campbell was the prime source of his difficulties. Born in Kingston, Jamaica, to a mother of African and English parentage and a Scottish father, Campbell had served as an apprentice printer before entering a teacher-training college for two years. He subsequently left Jamaica for the United States, where he obtained a teaching position at the Institute for Colored Youth in Philadelphia. Having given Delany the impression that he would accompany the Niger Valley Exploring Party, Campbell in October demonstrated the free-wheeling independence characteristic of his relationship with Delany over the next two years by publicly withdrawing from the expedition in a letter to *Frederick Douglass' Paper*. While critical of Delany's operations, Campbell was still very much in favor of African emigration itself. He believed, with Bourne, Benjamin Coates, and several others, "that by free labor [,] cotton can be procured cheaper from Africa, than slave labor cotton from America, and that that country, ultimately, can be made to furnish even a larger supply than America. . . . in the development of these [facts], slavery will be struck her death blow." However, he was dubious that Delany could locate adequate financial support, and thus he considered the black physician's plans as premature. Claiming that his name was being used "not only without my sanction, but contrary to my expressed injunction," Campbell completely severed his ties with the Niger Valley Exploring Party. "[I]t would affect me very immaterially," he said, "whether the expedition should set out or not, and if the whole affair should end in smoke."[32]

---

31. *New York Daily Tribune*, October 26, 1858, p. 6. The constitution is enclosed with T. J. Bowen to Gurley, New York, October 14, 1858, Domestic Letters, ACS Papers. See also *The American Missionary*, 2nd ser., III (January, 1859), 17.

32. *Frederick Douglass' Paper*, October 29, 1858, p. 3. Biographical information

While Campbell's action changed the composition of Delany's party, William Howard Day—ostensibly still the president of the Chatham-based organization which had "commissioned" Delany's party—provided a blow of a different sort by tearing down the illusion of public support for Delany's scheme. At the Ohio State Colored Men's Convention in Cincinnati in late November, Day broke sharply with the diffuse but ultimately tolerant position he had taken at the Chatham convention in August. Now speaking in favor of a resolution opposed to emigration, Day recalled that "years before, standing on the same spot, [I] opposed the scheme of emigration, and after becoming an emigrant myself, I return to still resist it." Despite the opposition of E. P. Walker—the Toledo barber who had attended both the 1854 and 1856 National Emigration Conventions and who now unsuccessfully proposed a resolution praising Haiti—the anti-emigration resolution which Day had supported was adopted by the Ohio meeting.[33]

Whatever the motivation behind Day's decision to abandon Delany, the Chatham emigrationist himself should not have been surprised. He was conscious of the twists and turns which had marked Day's public career and was probably forewarned of Day's apostasy. Simultaneously, Campbell's resignation from the Niger Valley Exploring Party and the efforts of Bourne and others in New York to attach themselves to Delany's venture forced him to turn inward and place his faith in those closest to him—the Chatham black community. Just as Day was denouncing emigration before the Ohio convention, Delany founded a new organization, the African Civilization Society of Canada. Simply another shadowy organization with an indefinite membership, this new society was able to command only the attention of the debt-ridden and faltering *Provincial Freeman* whose editor, Isaac D. Shadd, was a member of the Society. Outside of the Chatham black community, however, the African Civilization Society of Canada was unknown, and it

---

on Campbell is in Fred I. A. Omu, "The Anglo-African, 1863–65," *Nigeria Magazine*, no. 90 (September, 1966), 206–212.

33. *Proceedings of a Convention of the Colored Men of Ohio, Held in the City of Cincinnati, on the 23rd, 24th, 25th and 26th of November, 1858* (Cincinnati: Moore, Wilstach, Keys & Co., Printers, 1858), pp. 7, 11–13. Day's speech has been transcribed from past to present tense and has been made into direct quotation.

must have dissolved as soon as Delany left Chatham for New York sometime in late 1858 or early 1859.³⁴

But Delany was not as isolated as he may have thought—or may have desired, if he could have counted entirely on black sources for financial assistance. Campbell soon rejoined the Niger Valley Exploring Party; by early December he was cooperating with Bourne and, presumably, Garnet in attempting to co-opt Delany's expedition for the African Civilization Society in New York, now formally organized. Bourne, in fact, acting on behalf of the Society in early December, announced that Delany, Campbell, and Robert Douglass, Jr., composed the Niger Valley Exploring Party which would explore Yoruba "under the auspices" of his group, and he asked for contributions to aid "this voluntary movement on the part of colored Americans for the welfare of Africa." Campbell himself sought financial assistance in a circular printed at this time in the *North American and U.S. Gazette* in Philadelphia. Endorsed by Coates, William Coppinger, the secretary of the Pennsylvania Colonization Society, and other Philadelphia whites, the circular appeared below a statement by the newspaper lauding both Campbell and the interest in Yoruba in general and also claiming that the explorers were trying to raise $6,000 "to proceed to Africa and select a suitable location for the establishment of an industrial colony." Campbell also directly associated Delany's venture with Garnet's organization by announcing that once an African location was discovered, "the party will report to the 'African Civilization Society' of New York, which will then be prepared to aid emigrants at once to begin the great work."³⁵

The members of the Niger Valley Exploring Party also turned directly to the American Colonization Society for financial assistance. Perhaps spurred on by the action of the Society's Pennsylvania chapter, which in late 1858 voted Campbell $60, the

---

34. Entry for November 23, 1858, I. D. Shadd Diary, located in front and back of Abraham W. Shadd Ledger, North Buxton Museum, Canada; *Provincial Freeman and Weekly Advertiser*, January 28, 1859, p. 66; Delany, *Official Report*, p. 13. The *Freeman* appeared intermittently during this period. Only two issues—January 28 and June 18, 1859—are known to be extant, and both are housed in the Slavery Collection, Cornell University Library.

35. *Frederick Douglass' Paper*, December 3, 1858, p. 3; *North American and U.S. Gazette*, December 3, 1858, p. 1.

Philadelphia teacher and James W. Purnell visited Ralph R. Gurley in Washington in mid-February, 1859. Intent on preserving Liberia's hegemony in African colonization, Gurley encouraged the two blacks to visit Liberia before traveling to Yoruba; Campbell and Purnell agreed to this. As they wrote to the chairman of the Society's Executive Committee, "in making a selection [the exploring party's] choice would be of that place which under every circumstance possesses the greatest advantages; and hence they have concluded to avail themselves of the advice and experiences of the authorities of Liberia before they enter upon their work."[36]

Despite expressions of interest, the American Colonization Society refused to assume financial responsibility for the black exploring party. The A.C.S. Executive Committee, however, agreed in April to Pinney's suggestion that the Colonization Society grant the Niger Valley Exploring Party free passage on a colonization ship. Not surprisingly, neither Delany, Campbell, nor Purnell—now the entire Niger Valley group—was impressed with the offer, and Campbell sailed immediately to England, where he hoped to raise some $300. Delany, on the other hand, was still committed to beginning his African journey on Liberian soil, and he remained in New York to look for funds.[37]

For Delany, the preceding months had been difficult ones. Although in January *The Anglo-African Magazine* started serial publication of his novel *Blake; or, the Huts of America*, he hoped to publish the work in book form partially for financial reasons. As he wrote to William Lloyd Garrison in February from his New York boarding house, "I am anxious to get a good publishing house to take it, as I know I could make a penny by it, and the chances for a Negro in this department are so small, that unless some disinterested competent persons would indirectly aid in such a step, I almost de-

36. Minutes of the Board of Managers of the Pennsylvania Colonization Society, December 14, 1858, Library, Lincoln University, Pennsylvania; Pinney to Gurley, New York, February 8, 1859; Robert Campbell and J. W. Purnell to Dr. Harvey Lindsly, Washington, February 17, 1859, Domestic Letters, ACS Papers; Gurley to Dr. James Hall, Washington, February 15, 1859, Maryland State Colonization Society Papers, Maryland Historical Society.

37. Journal of the Executive Committee of the American Colonization Society, 1855–68, p. 179 (April 22, 1859); Pinney to Gurley, New York, April 11, 1859; William Coppinger to Gurley, Philadelphia, April 22, 1859; Pinney to Gurley, New York, April 28, 1859, Domestic Letters, ACS Papers.

The Search for a Place: Africa 197

spair of any chance." Conceivably, Garrison was offended by the tone of the story about a pure black West Indian slave who advocates a general rebellion in the southern United States and later becomes the leader of a black insurrectionary force in Cuba. If Garrison made any efforts on Delany's behalf, they were clearly unsuccessful, for the novel was never printed in book form. Delany was forced to continue his fund-raising efforts in other directions.[38]

Although the African Civilization Society had few resources of its own, the Society did have the support of Pinney and other white colonizationists in New York. Gambling on his ability to tap these resources, Delany sought to maintain a connection with the Civilization Society. Several weeks before Gurley declined to support the expedition, Campbell inexplicably refused to show Bourne the financial books of the Niger Valley exploring party; consequently, Delany agreed to cooperate with the young minister. In turn, Bourne informed the Colonization Society that his own organization recommended Delany's group "and their cause to your favorable regard." In April, Delany traveled to Boston with Purnell; there he spoke at a fund-raising meeting at the Old South Chapel. While in the city, the two men assured local colonizationists that they would definitely explore Liberia as well as Yoruba, and that they would report back impartially. Despite these calming words, Delany and Purnell raised only a small amount of money in Boston before returning to New York.[39]

Delany seems to have been more successful in New York, since Yoruba interest among the local white colonizationists made them more natural donors; not only was Pinney the corresponding secretary of the New York State Colonization Society, but one of the organization's Managers (Isaac T. Smith, a banker) was also treasurer of the African Civilization Society. Delany continued to give

38. Delany, *Official Report*, p. 13; Delany to Garrison, New York, February 19, 1859, Garrison Papers. The twenty-six chapters published in the magazine plus an additional forty-eight which only appeared later in *The Weekly Anglo-African* have been put together into the first book publication of *Blake; or, the Huts of America* (Boston: Beacon Press, 1970). Unfortunately, the final chapters—numbering perhaps six in all—have not yet been located. For an analysis of the novel, see my introduction to the Beacon edition.

39. Bourne to Gurley, New York, March 14, 1859; Tracy to Gurley, Boston, April 5, 1859, Domestic Letters, ACS Papers; Massachusetts Colonization Society, *18th Report* (1859), pp. 6, 8.

colonizationists in New York and Philadelphia assurances that he would sail directly to Liberia from the United States, even though Campbell had already left for Liverpool on April 23. By early May, Delany and Purnell had committed themselves to sailing as cabin passengers on the *Mendi*, a bark recently chartered by three blacks—one of whom, John D. Johnson, had been speaking on the commercial advantages of Liberia before meetings of the African Civilization Society in New York.[40] When Purnell decided not to go, Delany prepared to return to the land of his ancestors alone. Now totally isolated from the emigration movement he had sustained during most of the decade, and aided by the very colonizationists he had earlier ridiculed and assailed, Delany set off for the west coast of Africa in search of a hospitable home for the Black Nationality he wished to create.

Exploring West Africa

Delany spent nine months in Africa—first in Liberia and then in Yoruba, where he joined up with Robert Campbell and negotiated a treaty with the Egba people for the right to establish a colony of black Americans on Egba land. Although his expedition to Yoruba was consistent with the aims he had been propounding during the year before his departure to Africa, Delany's visit to Liberia was surprising, for he had long considered the black republic a captive nation unnecessarily subordinating its independence and potential vitality to the demands of white colonizationists—in brief, the antithesis of a Black Nationality. Nevertheless, on the morning of May 24, 1859, Delany stood on board the *Mendi*, then anchored at the Sandy Hook outside of New York harbor, and watched the Liberian flag—a single white star on a blue background—rise to the top of the ship's mast.[41]

Few, if any, of the other forty-four passengers had demonstrated

40. Tracy to Gurley, Boston, April 30, 1859; Pinney to McLain, New York, May 3, 1859, Domestic Letters, ACS Papers; *The Colonization Herald*, April, 1859, p. 419; *New York Colonization Journal*, May, 1859, p. 4. For Smith's organizational pedigree, see *New York Colonization Journal*, December, 1850, through December, 1863; circular enclosed with Bourne to Gerrit Smith, New York, February 16, 1859, Smith Papers.
41. *New York Colonization Journal*, June, 1859, p. 3.

similar ideological contradictions. For example, the Reverend William C. Monroe was traveling to Liberia as a missionary. Monroe had resigned his pastorate at St. Matthew's Church in Detroit the preceding fall to secure an Episcopal missionary position in Haiti, but the Foreign Committee of the Protestant Episcopal Church had failed to endorse him. The Committee evidently acted in response to two white Episcopal laymen in Detroit, whose less than enthusiastic letters testified to the soundness of Monroe's character and intentions but found him unsuited to missionary work. One commentator referred to his "lack of energy"; the other to "a want of force of character," adding in his letter to the Church's Foreign Secretary: "You have seen hundreds of such men—good, well disposed, nay, anxious to serve in the Lord's vineyard, but not knowing exactly how to do it effectually." Rebuffed, Monroe decided to try for a position in Liberia. After receiving a promise of partial assistance from the New York State Colonization Society, he turned again to the Foreign Committee in May, 1859. Deferring for the moment the question of an actual missionary appointment, the committee voted the black minister $200 "to emigrate to Liberia & to give himself to missionary work in that country." Poor and feeble in health at age 60, the Reverend Monroe was bringing to Liberia his second wife, Mary, their two children, Rhinard, 11, and Blandford, 8, and an undaunted Christian spirit.[42]

Of the remaining passengers, thirty-three were emigrants sent out by the American Colonization Society; they included three

42. *The Spirit of Missions*, XXIII (October, 1858), 472; S. D. Denison to H. P. Baldwin, New York, November 10, 1858; Baldwin to Denison, Detroit, November 13, 1858; C. C. Trowbridge to Denison, Detroit, November 15, 1858, Domestic and Foreign Missionary Society Papers: Haiti Papers; Minutes of the Foreign Committee of the Domestic and Foreign Missionary Society, May 3, 1859, Church Historical Society, Austin, Texas. After reaching Monrovia, Monroe remained in the city for at least a week, but then soon left with a large number of immigrants from the *Mendi* for Careysburg, some forty miles inland. In the next few weeks he caught a fever, and he died on November 9, 1859. His wife and two children later returned to the United States; Monroe himself reportedly was planning to return when he died. Holly delivered a eulogy for Monroe at Masonic funeral rites in New Haven in April, 1860. *New York Colonization Journal*, October, 1859, p. 2; *The Weekly Anglo-African*, September 24, 1859, p. 3; October 1, 1859, p. 1; March 17, 1860, p. 3; April 14, 1860, p. 3; William C. Monroe to Denison, Careysburg, Liberia, October 8, 1859, Domestic and Foreign Missionary Society Papers: Liberia Papers.

farmers, two laborers, a coachmaker, milliner, cooper, tinner, accountant, and apothecary. Also on board was B. E. Castendyke, a German traveler, and the three blacks who had chartered the *Mendi*. Of the three, only John D. Johnson, 35, was a Liberian. New York–born, Johnson had emigrated to Liberia in 1852 from Williamsburg, New York, where he had been a barber. In Liberia he first resided at the settlement of the New York–based Liberian Emigration and Agricultural Society; he soon moved to Monrovia, where he entered into business and concluded that "any man may get rich here if he will work half as much as he would in the United States." The other two men—Joseph Turpin, 30, a tailor and landowner, and Charles B. Dunbar, 28, a physician—were New York City residents who planned to remain in Liberia. Johnson was bringing his family; Dunbar was accompanied by a fifteen-year-old nephew. The three entrepreneurs also carried some $20,000 worth of goods to trade in Liberia for agricultural produce and cash. They later advanced Delany some of this merchandise so the black explorer could earn part of his expenses by trading with native Africans.[43]

The voyage itself was uneventful. On July 10, the forty-third day out from New York, the *Mendi* landed at Cape Palmas, Liberia. Delany and a few others left the ship and were greeted on shore by several native Africans and a number of Liberians, including a former Johnstown, Pennsylvania, resident, the Reverend Samuel Williams, who had defended Liberia from Delany's attacks in the

---

43. The passenger list is in the *New York Colonization Journal*, June, 1859, p. 3. Only forty-four are listed, although the accompanying story mentions forty-five on board; Castendyke was omitted from the list. Discussion of the Colonization Society's emigrants is in Pinney to McLain, New York, May 27, 1859, Domestic Letters, ACS Papers. For information on Johnson, Turpin, and Dunbar, see the *New York Colonization Journal*, August, 1859, p. 3; *The Colonization Herald*, June, 1859, p. 426; Delany, *Official Report*, p. 25. Also for Johnson, consult the *New York Colonization Journal*, October, 1852, p. 2; March, 1853, p. 2; April, 1852, p. 3; *Williamsburg, New York, Directories*, 1850–51, 1852; manuscript schedule, Seventh Census of the United States: 1850—Kings County, Village of Williamsburg. Turpin and Dunbar are listed in the *New York City Directories*, 1854–1859; manuscript schedule, New York State Census: 1855—New York City, 5th Ward, 3rd Electoral District. Ages for all three individuals have been drawn from the ship's passenger list. Although Delany claimed the *Mendi* carried $40,000 worth of cargo (*The Weekly Anglo-African*, September 24, 1859, p. 1), I have used the colonization press's estimate.

mid-1850's. The *Mendi* passengers visited the city briefly; after nightfall they returned to the ship. Less than two days later Delany was in Monrovia.[44]

Delany's immediate problem upon arriving in the capital city was to mollify those who remembered the virulence and persistency with which he denounced the Republic, and who might well have reacted with suspicion to the visit of their nation's new-found friend. An opportunity presented itself during Delany's second day in Monrovia, when a group of nine prominent Liberians—including the educator and author Edward W. Blyden, who had answered Delany's *Condition, Elevation, Emigration, and Destiny of the Colored People* several years before in a Liberian newspaper—wrote to Delany, inviting him to present a public lecture. Although alluding to Delany's earlier attempts to discredit Liberia, the group nevertheless extended the community's welcome to the Afro-American traveler "recognizing, as [we] do in you an ardent and devoted lover of the African race." Delany replied favorably to the invitation, although he claimed his previous remarks had been misconstrued: "You are mistaken, gentlemen, in supposing that I have ever spoken directly 'against Liberia,' as wherever I have been I have always acknowledged a unity of interest in our race wherever located; and any seeming opposition to Liberia could only be constructively [*sic*], for which I am not responsible." Although his comments were obviously specious, Liberians had little interest in prolonging a needless quarrel. They recognized that Delany's inconsistency was far less important to their own interests than his current attitude toward Liberia, and they accepted his denials of any previous lack of love for their nation. At a meeting several days after Delany's arrival, the chairman testified that he had never considered "Dr. Delany and his class of Abolitionists as ... opposed to Liberia ... from such I have never heard a word uttered in disparagement of Liberia or of Liberians."[45]

Nevertheless, to Liberians, the visit of an old enemy was an important event. Daniel Laing, a Liberian doctor who had studied

---

44. *The Weekly Anglo-African*, September 24, 1859, p. 1; Delany, *Official Report*, p. 16.

45. Delany, *Official Report*, pp. 17–18; *The Weekly Anglo-African*, October 1, 1859, p. 1.

briefly with Delany at Harvard Medical School in the winter of 1850–51, described the Afro-American's stay in Liberia as "quite an epoch in the history of this country: he was greeted enthusiastically and received with open arms; he has 'thundered' to delighted audiences." Another American-educated doctor, H. J. Roberts, also noted that Delany "has been flatteringly received . . . [and has] been warmly invited to Regard us as brothers, friends, a part of themselves, making mighty efforts to accomplish *One* great end: viz., a *Colored Nationality*. . . ."[46]

Delany accepted this invitation by strongly identifying himself with the interests of his black brethren who were attempting to govern a small and impoverished nation. "*Your country shall be my country*," he told a cheering throng during one of his public appearances. Privately, he informed the Reverend John B. Pinney that "I am highly interested in, and pleased with, Liberia and her people— a noble, struggling people, who only require help from the intelligent of their race, to make them what they desire and should be." He repeated this message to the *Provincial Freeman* in Chatham, while to a Liberian audience he explained that, since Afro-Americans would never achieve significant political power in the United States, they must emigrate to Africa. There "they may join the one hundred and sixty millions of their degraded brethren, assist to elevate them, and from this point—from such a nationality the reflex influence upon America must be felt and must be powerful, in behalf of the slaves." Liberians as "men who hold political intercourse with the nations of the world and *the reins of Government in their own hands*" could begin creating a more powerful nation by absorbing into their country the surrounding African peoples.[47]

These sentiments led Liberians to believe that Delany might advocate emigration to their country. Blyden even reported to Pinney that Delany was so pleased with Liberia that he now claimed the country had been misrepresented in the United States. Perhaps,

46. Dr. H. J. Roberts to [McLain?], Monrovia, July 28, 1859; Daniel Laing to McLain, Monrovia, August 25, 1859, African Letters, ACS Papers.

47. *The Weekly Anglo-African*, October 1, 1859, pp. 1–2. The quotation from Delany's speech has been changed from past to present tense. The letter to Pinney was printed in the *New York Colonization Journal*, October, 1859, p. 3; the communication to the *Freeman* was reprinted in *The Colonization Herald*, November, 1859, p. 448.

Blyden surmised, Delany would be "the Moses to lead in the exodus of his people from the house of bondage to a land flowing with milk and honey. He seems to have many qualifications for the task. Let him be encouraged and supported." Dr. Roberts also observed that Delany "is much gratified with the Liberian territory—highly pleased with the Republic & all that he has seen in her of her operations, both political & Religious." Roberts, too, believed that Delany might recommend Liberia to Afro-Americans "as the fairest hope for themselves & posterity." Delany's favorable reaction to Liberia was a good omen in the eyes of the country's president, Stephen A. Benson. Benson believed that Delany, while not necessarily advocating Liberian emigration, would agree to the wishes of the Colonization Society and thus allow Liberia to undertake any Yoruba settlement scheme. The Liberian president had met with Delany only briefly before departing Monrovia on a mission up the coast, but he wrote to Gurley of the Colonization Society: "From all I have learned unofficially, as yet he favors the view you express, of not operating in the formation of a new settlement, if prosecuted at all, otherwise than under the auspices of this government."[48]

Despite Benson's impressions, Delany was still committed to moving on to Yoruba to carry out his projected explorations free from Liberian influence. Although he had been deeply affected by what he had witnessed in Liberia, he realized that by linking his nationalist-emigrationist plans to the black republic, he could only join an existing nationality with obvious infirmities, rather than build one anew. Delany boarded the *Mendi* and left Monrovia for Cape Palmas on August 5; he arrived two weeks later, partially disabled by malaria. Convinced that he could cure his fever through activity, Delany traveled fifty miles along the Cavalla River into the Liberian interior with the Reverend Alexander Crummell, the American-born black missionary then serving as principal of an Episcopal school near Cape Palmas.[49]

---

48. *New York Colonization Journal*, October, 1859, p. 3; Dr. Roberts to [McLain?], Monrovia, July 28, 1859; Stephen A. Benson to Gurley, Schooner Quail Off Bereby, August 1, 1859, African Letters, ACS Papers.

49. Delany, *Official Report*, p. 18; *Chatham Tri-Weekly Planet*, November 29, 1859, p. 2.

The son of Boston Crummell—reportedly a Temne prince stolen from Africa when he was thirteen, and later active in New York City's black community—Alexander Crummell was born in 1819 in New York. With Henry Highland Garnet, he was educated at the African School #2 and later at the high school for blacks on Canal Street. Like Garnet, he was forced to leave Noyes Academy in New Hampshire after the school was sacked by an angry mob; he subsequently entered Oneida Institute. As a young man, Crummell was active in the antislavery crusade and in campaigns for black suffrage in both New York and Rhode Island. He simultaneously worked to become an Episcopal minister. In 1837 he applied for admission to the General Theological Seminary in New York; although rejected because of his race, he studied under the Reverend Peter Williams, Jr., and became a candidate for Holy Orders in the church in 1840. From this time until his ordination as a minister in 1844, Crummell was a lay reader at a struggling black Episcopal church in Providence, Rhode Island. In 1847 he left the United States for England, where he studied at Queens College, Cambridge. By 1851 he had become interested in the redemption of Africa; two years later—after receiving his degree from Queens College—Crummell accepted an Episcopal missionary appointment to Liberia. His somewhat turbulent relations with his Episcopal superiors led him to resign his appointment in 1857, and he accepted the post of principal at Mt. Vaughan School at Cape Palmas, where Delany found him. Like Delany, Crummell was committed to the creation of a commercially viable black nation. Still, the missionary felt Delany's efforts on behalf of Yoruba were misdirected. Intelligent and skilled New World blacks, Crummell contended, should assist the Christian and commercial elevation of Liberia—the center of an emerging black nationality. Of course, Crummell disagreed with Delany most strikingly over the role of Christianity in Africa: in Crummell's eyes, Providence assured the regeneration of Africa by working through black missionaries.[50]

50. Kathleen O'Mara Wahle, "Alexander Crummell: Black Evangelist and Pan-Negro Nationalist," *Phylon*, XXIX (Winter, 1968), 388-389; Simmons, *Men of Mark*, pp. 530-532; Quarles, *Black Abolitionists*, pp. 69, 171-172; Julian Rammelkamp, "The Providence Negro Community, 1820-1842," reprinted in John H. Bracey, Jr., et al., eds., *Free Blacks in America, 1800-1860* (Belmont, Calif.: Wadsworth Publishing Company, 1971), p. 92; Robert Glenn Sherer, Jr., "Negro

Despite these sharp differences, Crummell and Delany complemented each other during their expedition on the Cavalla River, as Crummell preached and Delany presented a "dissertation on *political economy*" to the Africans who welcomed them. The river itself impressed Delany with both its beauty and its navigability. The latter was of special interest to him, since he had been concerned with the commercial possibilities of the interior from the very beginning of his Liberian visit. In fact, while still at Monrovia, he had traveled up the St. Paul's River with the American Consul John Seys and Castendyke. At the time he had noted that "A suitable little steamer is now much needed on the St. Paul river, and I know of nothing that would pay better just now and for a time to come." The Cavalla appeared even more promising; he concluded that it could be navigated by "the largest class of steamers from the bar mouth to the falls, a distance of 90 miles." But dreaming of the commercial exploitation of the interior failed to cure Delany's fever. When he returned to Cape Palmas, he was incapacitated for a week.[51]

In mid-September Delany left on the British steamer *Armenian* for Lagos, where he spent five weeks. He was particularly attracted by the city's bustling commercial life and by the presence of large numbers of black traders and merchants, most of whom were originally from Sierra Leone. "This city," Delany observed, "from location, is destined to be the great black metropolis of the world." At the end of October he left for the interior. Traveling inland along the Ogun River, Delany arrived early the following month at

---

Churches in Rhode Island before 1860," *Rhode Island History*, XXV (January, 1966), 23; *The Spirit of Missions*, XVIII (April, 1853), 126; XXII (November and December, 1857), 576; XXIII (October, 1858), 503; A. C. Coxe to S. D. Denison, Baltimore, May 6, 1857 (with an extract from Rev. Dr. Carswall to Coxe, April 15, 1857), Domestic and Foreign Missionary Society Papers: Liberia. Summaries of Crummell's thinking can be found in Wahle, "Crummell," pp. 390–392; Robert W. July, *The Origins of Modern African Thought: Its Development in West Africa during the Nineteenth and Twentieth Centuries* (New York: Frederick A. Praeger, 1967), pp. 105–106. See also Alexander Crummell, *The Duty of a Rising Christian State to the World's Well-Being and Civilization* ([Boston?]: Massachusetts Colonization Society, 1857), pp. 13, 21, 23–24; Crummell, *The Relations and Duties of the Free Colored Men in America to Africa...* (Hartford: Press of Case, Lockwood and Company, 1861), pp. 25, 26, 31 and, for brief mention of Crummell's encounter with Delany, pp. 6, 45.

51. *Chatham Tri-Weekly Planet*, November 29, 1859, p. 2; *The Weekly Anglo-African*, September 24, 1859, p. 1.

Abeokuta, the home of the Egba and the center of Yoruba. Here he found "a singular, romantic, antiquated city in appearance, the houses all being of unburnt clay, and ruled by a combination of powerful chiefs and elders." But more significant for Delany was the city's commercial role. "It is the great centre of the cotton trade, there being many gins and cotton presses at work, as well as many merchants who simply purchase the raw material...."[52] At Abeokuta, Delany also found the other half of the Niger Valley Exploring Party—Robert Campbell, already in the city for two months preparing for the party's mission and waiting for Delany.

Campbell, spurning the American Colonization Society's offer of a free steerage passage to Liberia, had sailed from New York to Liverpool on April 23. Arriving in England, he contacted Gerard Ralston, a former member of the Pennsylvania Colonization Society then serving as the Liberian consul in London, who asked Campbell to visit Liberia. Ralston hoped, of course, that the black explorer would then advise Afro-Americans to emigrate there rather than to Yoruba. Reasonably confident that Campbell would favor the new African republic, the consul introduced the explorer to Henry Christy, an English ethnologist and philanthropist who had met Delany several years earlier while in Canada. Although Christy became Campbell's major benefactor, the former Philadelphia schoolteacher won the support of other English abolitionists as well. Wisely calling attention to his own status as a British citizen, Campbell also emphasized that Canadian blacks would comprise a significant number of the New World emigrants who would settle in Yoruba. In mid-May he issued from Manchester a circular in which he identified himself as a member of Delany's Niger Valley Exploring Party. The expedition, Campbell announced, would explore Yoruba "to study the Agricultural and Commercial facilities of the country, and the disposition of the Natives towards strangers as settlers; also to negotiate for the grant or purchase of land" for an industrial settlement which would supply free-labor cotton to compete with that grown in the slave states of the United States. Beyond the sum previously raised in the United States, 250 pounds was needed to provide Campbell with his passage from England to

52. Delany, *Official Report*, pp. 29–30; *The Colonization Herald*, June, 1860, p. 476.

Africa, outfitting for the expedition and, finally, goods for trading with the indigenous Africans.[53]

Campbell's stress upon the proposed colony's role as a supplier of free-labor cotton appealed to Thomas Clegg, the Manchester cotton merchant. In turn, Clegg provided Campbell with a letter of introduction recommending his project as "the most feasible plan of helping on my scheme of superseding Slavery, by letting the African grow in his own country what every one wants him to grow elsewhere." L. A. Chamerovzow, secretary of the British and Foreign Anti-Slavery Society, also endorsed Campbell's work and aided him in collecting funds. In addition, the Society's journal, the *Anti-Slavery Reporter*, echoed Clegg's views that the Niger Valley Exploring Party's mission could expedite the abolition of slavery in the United States by encouraging cotton production in Africa.[54]

Thus supported publicly by influential Englishmen, Campbell was able to raise between $500 and $600 before leaving Liverpool in June. The British government, responding to the request of English cotton interests, provided Campbell with free passage aboard the mail steamer *Ethiope*, which was also transporting three Africans and an American white man, John Bennett. Formerly of Hornellsville, New York, Bennett was traveling to Lagos with two cotton gins purchased at Manchester and with ten bushels of cotton seed.[55] The *Ethiope* anchored at Freetown, Sierra Leone, on July 12. Here Campbell met Augustus Washington, a Liberian cotton and sugar trader originally from Hartford, Connecticut, who presumably touted Liberia's prospects to Campbell. Five days later Campbell reached Cape Palmas, where he first learned that Delany had already arrived in Monrovia. Although ashore for only a few hours, Campbell was greeted by Crummell, who took him to a church

---

53. Gerard Ralston to Gurley, London, June 24, 1859, Domestic Letters, ACS Papers; *The Colonization Herald*, February, 1860, p. 460; Cyril Edgar Griffith, "Martin R. Delany and the African Dream, 1812-1885" (Ph.D. dissertation, Michigan State University, 1973), pp. 91-92; Delany, *Official Report*, pp. 14-15.

54. *Anti-Slavery Reporter*, June 1, 1859, pp. 137-138.

55. William Coppinger to Gurley, Philadelphia, September 16, 1859, Domestic Letters, ACS Papers; *The Colonization Herald*, February, 1860, p. 460; *The Weekly Anglo-African*, September 3, 1859, p. 2; Griffith, "Delany and the African Dream," p. 93.

where, to Campbell's gratification, more than a hundred Africans, "including an old chief, listen[ed] with deep attention to the word of God." Finally, on July 22, Campbell arrived in Lagos.[56]

With Delany still in Liberia, there was little for Campbell to do in Lagos but wait for his colleague. He did, however, begin to make contacts with the local authorities, and shortly after arriving in the city he presented the acting British Consul with a letter of introduction from Lord Malmesbury, recently the British minister for foreign affairs, who asked the consul to provide the explorer and other members of his party with "your advice and assistance in the selection of such a situation as shall by its fertility be calculated to meet their wishes...." Malmesbury claimed Campbell's mission involved only free blacks from British North America; there was no mention that Afro-American emigrants might also emigrate to whatever colony was established. While in Lagos, Campbell also conferred with the African-born Anglican missionary, the Reverend Samuel Ajayi Crowther, who was then visiting the city. Crowther informed him that the Egba at Abeokuta in Yoruba would welcome a settlement of Afro-Americans in the region between Abeokuta and Lagos on the Ogun River.[57]

Since no territorial negotiations could be undertaken until Delany's arrival, Campbell decided to use the time available to explain his mission to King Docemo of Lagos. Accompanied by the British consul and a small party, the black explorer spent an hour with the king. Docemo was pleased with the plans of the Niger Valley exploring party; according to Campbell's report of the interview, the king informed him that "... so far as his dominions extended ... emigrants might select land suitable for their purpose, and he would gladly give it." While undoubtedly flattered by the king's offer, Campbell himself had little interest in settling in Lagos. As he wrote to a Philadelphia friend, "Of Lagos or any other place on the coast

---

56. *The Colonization Herald*, February, 1860, p. 460. For a statement by Washington defending Liberia's cotton potentiality, see *The Cotton Supply Reporter*, August 1, 1859, pp. 185–187. Washington first came to Liberia in 1853 with William Nesbit and the Rev. Samuel Williams; see note 1 above. Also see the *African Repository*, XXVII (September, 1851), 259–265.

57. Foreign Office 2/28, June 11, 1859, Public Records Office, London; *The Colonization Herald*, February, 1860, p. 460; *The Weekly Anglo-African*, October 8, 1859, p. 2.

The Search for a Place: Africa

I think very poorly.... All these [coastal] places are unhealthy, and I myself would never live in one of them, much less with my family." Campbell's reaction was understandable, for during his stay in Lagos he was taken with malaria for a few days, and his fear of another attack was one factor which prompted him to leave the city.[58]

After waiting for Delany for six weeks, Campbell departed Lagos for Abeokuta in the more healthful interior. He was accompanied by two sons of the Reverend Crowther, Josiah and Samuel, Jr. Both younger Crowthers had been born in Sierra Leone, where they had been educated at the Anglican Church Missionary Society schools before being sent to England for practical training—Josiah in cotton packing and processing at Thomas Clegg's factory in Manchester, and Samuel in medicine at King's College, London. They then returned to Yoruba and settled at Abeokuta, where one ran and the other advised the Church Missionary Society's cotton projects during the 1850's. Considered immigrants or "saros" by the Egba at Abeokuta, the Crowthers were natural companions for Campbell. Together the three traveled ninety miles up the Ogun River to Aro, the landing place for Abeokuta in the rainy season and only four miles from the city's business center.[59]

The trip lasted five days; at night they stopped in small villages and camped under a tent which Henry Christy had given to Campbell. Acting on the Reverend Crowther's recommendation, the black explorer surveyed the surrounding countryside and looked for possible locations for an industrial settlement. Although he did not decide upon a particular site, Campbell concluded that the general area was well suited for a colony of Afro-Americans. His reasons were partly aesthetic and partly practical: "I never saw a more beautiful country than can be seen on both banks of the river Ogun ... abounding with game, well watered and the scenery unsurpassed.

---

58. Robert Campbell, *A Pilgrimmage to My Motherland; An Account of a Journey among the Egbas and Yorubas of Central Africa, in 1859–60* (New York: Thomas Hamilton, 1861), pp. 19–21; *The Weekly Anglo-African*, January 14, 1860, p. 2.

59. Campbell, *A Pilgrimmage*, pp. 22–27; Kopytoff, *Preface to Modern Nigeria*, pp. 285–286. For a further discussion of the role of the saros in Abeokuta affairs, see Earl Phillips, "The Egba at Abeokuta: Acculturation and Political Change, 1830–1870," *Journal of African History*, X: 1 (1969), 122–124.

The Ogun for seven or eight months of the year is deep enough to be navigated by steamers of light draft, within three miles of Aro...." Campbell also noted that there was already a good road between Abeokuta and Lagos, although it was in need of straightening and widening. Finally, in evaluating the advantages of the area, Campbell observed that "Good timber abounds along the entire way; and, with a small saw-mill and shingle-mill, all the materials for building could easily be procured." Having concluded his investigations at Aro, Campbell left the Ogun River with the two Crowthers and proceeded for an hour's ride on horseback to Abeokuta.[60]

For the next two months Campbell waited in Abeokuta for Delany. It was impossible for him to remain in the Egba city without revealing his mission, and in fact he had little reason to conceal his intentions. Consequently, shortly after Campbell's arrival, Samuel Crowther, Jr., asked the Reverend Henry Townsend, an English missionary for the Church Missionary Society who also served as one of the Society's agents for collecting cotton, to help procure lodgings for Campbell. Ever since Townsend's instrumental role at the Battle of Aro in 1851, when the Egba defeated the Dahomey, the missionary had been a highly influential figure at Abeokuta, serving as honorary secretary to the Alake of Abeokuta—the king of the Egba. It was also rumored that, although a European, Townsend sat on the Ogboni—a closed judicial and administrative body composed of leading chiefs. For Campbell, then, Townsend's willingness to search for housing was less important in itself than the fact that Townsend's action would provide Campbell and his mission with legitimacy in the eyes of the Egba. But to Campbell's surprise and consternation, Townsend refused to aid the black explorer; instead, he informed Crowther that he would oppose any colonization or emigration scheme with all the resources he could command. The explorer instantly recognized the possible effects of the missionary's attitude: "This threat, of course, I would care nothing about, were I not assured that he had power, more than any in Africa, of executing it.... he had to be brought over by all means...."

To win Townsend's allegiance, Campbell sent him a letter ex-

60. *New York Colonization Journal*, November, 1859, p. 4; Campbell, *A Pilgrimmage*, pp. 26-27.

plaining the purposes of the exploring expedition and listing various American and English supporters. In response, Townsend appeared to reverse his position by inviting Campbell to his house, where they conversed for some time. Yet the Anglican missionary remained unconvinced; as he immediately wrote his superior in London, Henry Venn, the secretary of the Church Missionary Society, "I have a doubt about American projects—I don't know what to say or do in [*sic*] it. [H]e asked my help & influence—." Troubled by Campbell's presence and uncertain of what action to take, Townsend nevertheless decided to accompany Campbell a few days later to a meeting with the Alake. Most likely, Townsend felt he could more effectively influence the progress of the Niger Valley Exploring Party if he did not oppose the venture overtly.[61]

When Campbell appeared before the Alake, the monarch was bare to the waist, wearing a shocoto (a pair of loosely fitting half-trousers). He sat on a mat fondling an infant on his knees; one of his several wives sat nearby, fanning him. The elders of the Ogboni council sat next to the Alake, and Townsend was on the end of the mat. Only Campbell sat on a chair. After presenting a letter of introduction from the British consul at Lagos, Campbell explained the exploring party's plans. According to Campbell's account of the meeting, the Alake "observed that for people coming with such purposes, and for missionaries, he had great 'sympathy'...." However, it is doubtful whether the Alake fully understood that Campbell and Delany wished to obtain land for a separate colony operating largely outside his jurisdiction. In fact, Campbell himself reported that the Alake was disturbed by the immigrants from Brazil, Cuba, and Sierra Leone who were then living or trading in Abeokuta, and it is unclear exactly how Campbell distinguished the future Afro-American settlers from other black foreigners.

---

61. For this and the preceding paragraph, see *New York Colonization Journal*, February, 1860, p. 1; Saburi O. Biobaku, *The Egba and Their Neighbours, 1842–1872* (Oxford: At the Clarendon Press, 1957), p. 45; Fred I. A. Omu, "The 'Iwe Irohin,' 1859–1867," *Journal of the Historical Society of Nigeria*, IV (December, 1967), 38; *Anti-Slavery Reporter*, 3rd ser., VI (March 1, 1858), 64; Henry Townsend to Henry Venn, Abeokuta, September 6, 1859, Church Missionary Society Papers, CA 2/085, Church Missionary Society Archives, London (microfilm available at the University of Wisconsin Library); hereafter cited as CMS Papers. For a description of the Ogboni, see Biobaku, *Egba and Their Neighbours*, pp. 5–6, 21–22.

Whatever Campbell said, however, the Alake was pleased, for he presented his visitor with cowries (shells used for local exchange). During the next few days Campbell attempted to solidify the good will he believed he had created. Visiting the leading chiefs, he explained his scheme to them and gave each a small gift. The chiefs, in turn, presented Campbell with presents of cola nuts and cowries. Atambala, one of the few chiefs involved in the cotton trade, was reported to have given Campbell around 500 acres of land, but in reality, Atambala lacked the power to alienate land.[62]

Despite these initial activities, for the most part Campbell simply waited for Delany to arrive in Abeokuta. He passed idle moments playing the African game of wari with the Alake, whom he described as "a good-natured old gentleman." His mission was not far from his mind, however. He decided upon a plot of land for the colony—"immediately without the eastern gate of the city (the Ijaye gate), an indefinite extent of beautiful farming country, almost entirely unoccupied, on which we will be at liberty to settle. . . ." Finally, in early November, Delany arrived in Abeokuta still not fully recovered from the fever he had caught after leaving Monrovia for Cape Palmas.[63] The two explorers attempted to negotiate for land with the Egba at Abeokuta, thus plunging themselves into a network of rivalries and hostilities which, during the next two years, would affect their own plans. In turn, their efforts at Abeokuta would have a profound (if at times indirect) impact upon those struggling for power and influence among the Egba.

Well before Delany and Campbell arrived at Abeokuta, two outside elements were competing for hegemony in the city—Townsend on the one hand, and the saros or immigrants from Sierra Leone on the other. Like Delany and Campbell, the saros were interested in the expansion of Abeokuta as a commercial center which would bring "civilization" to the Egba and profit to themselves. For the Crowthers and other saros, the prospect of a number of Afro-

62. Campbell, *A Pilgrimmage*, pp. 28-29; Omu, "The 'Iwe Irohin,' " 38; *New York Colonization Journal*, February, 1860, p. 1; J. F. Ade Ajayi, *Christian Missions in Nigeria, 1841-1891: The Making of a New Elite* (London: Longmans, Green, 1965), p. 164; G. F. Bühler to Venn, Württemberg, Germany, February 24, 1860, CMS Papers, CA 2/024.

63. *The Weekly Anglo-African*, January 14, 1860, p. 2; *The Colonization Herald*, February, 1860, p. 460.

Americans coming into the area was appealing from a mercantile viewpoint. Samuel Crowther, Jr., who was just beginning to challenge Townsend's political authority, may also have considered Delany and Campbell as likely to side with the saros in any extended conflict with the missionary. For the explorers, too, the Sierra Leonians as "Westernized" blacks were natural allies. Delany and Campbell thus started to ignore the Europeans at Abeokuta and to seek advice only from Sierra Leonians such as Crowther and the Wesleyan missionary Edward Bickesterth.[64]

Delany and Campbell's most important contacts, then, were the non-Western commercial elements at Abeokuta. Eventually they were compelled to deal directly with the Egba to accomplish their mission, however. Wishing to steer clear of Townsend's influence, they turned to the Crowthers for help. On December 27, accompanied by the African missionary and his son Samuel, and without Townsend present, the two explorers met with the Alake and his chiefs to negotiate a treaty. With the Crowthers as witnesses, Delany, Campbell, and the Egba authorities signed a four-article treaty that proved to be a source of controversy altering the balance of power in the city and deferring the plans of Delany and his followers.

The very ambiguity of the treaty, which was probably intentional on Delany's part, resulted in confusion and conflict over its provisions. The first article granted "on behalf of the African race in America, the right and privilege of settling in common with the Egba people, on any part of the territory belonging to Abeokuta, not otherwise occupied"; the final article acknowledged "That the laws of the Egba people shall be strictly respected by the settlers." If this could be read to signify that Delany and Campbell had agreed to settle among the Egba rather than to group their followers together into an independent colony, other parts of the treaty implied otherwise. In fact, the second article provided "That all matters requiring legal investigation among the settlers, be left to be disposed of according to their customs." The final part of the last

---

64. Ajayi, *Christian Missions*, pp. 189–191; Bühler to Venn, Württemberg, Germany, February 24, 1860, CMS Papers, CA 2/024; Delany, *Official Report*, p. 34; Kopytoff, *Preface to Modern Nigeria*, pp. 113, 328n; *The Cotton Supply Reporter*, July 2, 1860, p. 173.

article even presumed equality between the settlers and the Egba, for it held that in "all matters in which both parties are concerned, an equal number of commissioners, mutually agreed upon, shall be appointed, who shall have power to settle such matters."[65] In sum, the Alake and his chiefs had endorsed a document which gave the prospective immigrants far greater latitude than the Egba could possibly have desired, since they had no intention of allowing the establishment of a separate colony on their lands.

In addition to its lack of clarity, the document conflicted sharply with Egba tradition. In fact, the idea of a "colony" settling on "unoccupied land" had no standing under Yoruba land law. Campbell and Delany both misunderstood this—largely because they had been misled by the Reverend Thomas J. Bowen, who had claimed that there was no landed property in Yoruba and that land was merely "common property." In Campbell's eyes, this interpretation took on an additional meaning: "... land ... is deemed common property; [thus] every individual enjoys the right of taking unoccupied land, as much as he can use, wherever and whenever he pleases." Delany's view was somewhat more accurate: "... landed tenure is free, the occupant selecting as much as he can cultivate, holding it so long as he uses it, but cannot convey it to another...." In actuality, land in Yoruba was not owned by communities or states such as the Egba, but by kinship groups. Normally, only full members of the kinship group could work and inhabit the land, although sometimes strangers were accepted into the group. Moreover, since the kinship group owned the land on behalf of themselves and their future descendants, neither the king, chief, nor any other individual could alienate the land.[66] According to Yoruba law and tradition,

---

65. The treaty is printed in full in Delany, *Official Report*, p. 35, and Campbell, *A Pilgrimmage*, pp. 143–145.

66. T[homas] J. Bowen, *Central Africa; Adventures and Missionary Labors in Several Countries in the Interior of Africa, from 1849 to 1856* (Charleston: Southern Baptist Publication Society, 1857), p. 307; Campbell, *A Pilgrimmage*, p. 35; Delany, *Official Report*, p. 59; P. C. Lloyd, *Yoruba Land Law* (London: Oxford University Press, 1962), pp. 87, 92, 245; Taslim Olawale Elias, *Nigerian Land Law*, 4th ed. (London: Sweet & Maxwell, 1971), pp. 73–74, 147, 152; G. B. A. Coker, *Family Property among the Yorubas*, 2nd ed. (London: Sweet & Maxwell, 1966), pp. 29–33. The British explorer Sir Richard F. Burton understood Yoruba land law; his criticism of Campbell's view of "common property" is, despite its racist overtones, basically correct. Burton is also critical of Bowen. See his *Abeokuta*

then, it was impossible for the Alake to "grant" land to Afro-American settlers for an independent colony. Rather, the Alake could at best only assign American blacks the right to use the land.

In the light of both Yoruba land law and practical realities, the Crowthers acted foolishly in endorsing the treaty. To some extent, they were simply careless. But they also had reason to believe that Delany and Campbell had completely modified their plans and were willing to have their followers settle among the Egba at Abeokuta rather than in a distinct colony. As recently as four weeks prior to the signing of the treaty, Delany and Campbell had indicated to the Reverend T. A. Reid, a Southern Baptist missionary working among the Yoruba, that their settlers would intermingle among the people. Reid agreed with this decision; he felt that "This is the only safe and successful course for them to pursue, because a separate government would not be allowed by the rulers and people." Later, when the treaty was being drawn, the two explorers concurred with a similar argument by the senior Crowther, who added his view that the country was not densely settled enough to profit from the presence of a colony in its midst. Delany and Campbell also agreed with the black missionary's prediction that their settlers concentrated together would not be as influential as if they were widely dispersed. In fact, even after the treaty had been signed, others in the Yoruba area were convinced that Delany and Campbell had abandoned their original plans to establish an independent colony. The Reverend R. H. Stone, the Baptist missionary at Ijaye, reported that although the explorers had investigated Yoruba "with a view of settling with a colony," they were now willing to have "The colonists ... settle in common with the natives."[67]

---

and the Cameroons Mountains: An Exploration (London: Tinsley Brothers, 1863), I, pp. 96–97.

67. Rev. Samuel Crowther to Venn, postscript of April 9, 1860, to letter of April 4, 1860, Lagos; Crowther to Venn, Abeokuta, April 6, 1861—CMS Papers, CA 3/04a; Samuel Crowther, Jr., to Lord A. Churchill, London, April 18, 1861, Slave Trade Correspondence (Consular), *Parliamentary Papers*, LXI (1862), pp. 6–7; *The Commission*, March, 1860, pp. 275–276; April, 1860, p. 309. Samuel Crowther, Jr.'s statement—in his April, 1861 letter—that the first article of the treaty had been changed at the time of signing to read "That the King and Chiefs ... grant ... the right and privilege of farming in common with the Egba people, and of building their houses and residing in the town of Abbeokuta, and intermingling with the population" was a contrivance to cover up his own and his

With the treaty signed, Delany and Campbell anticipated spending the next several months traveling further into the interior. But illnesses first to Campbell and then Delany delayed their departure from Abeokuta until January 16. Although recurrent fever continued to hamper them, their exploration was hindered more seriously by the outbreak of the Ijaye War then spreading throughout Yoruba. The war had been brewing for some time, but the catalyst was the issue of Oyo succession. Formerly the most prominent of the many politically independent and often warring states which were all considered as Yoruba because they shared a common language and a common culture, Oyo had collapsed in the early nineteenth century. Although another Oyo state soon emerged, Yoruba was now dominated by the newer states such as the Ijaye and the Ibadan, as well as by the Egba, an older kingdom. When the Alafin or king of Oyo died in April, 1859, the Ijaye refused to recognize the claim of the Alafin's son to the throne. Soon small incidents broke out between the Oyo, who were supported by Ibadan, and the Ijaye. As the Egba moved closer to intervening on the side of the Ijaye during early 1860, Delany and Campbell traveled as far into the interior as Ilorin. But Delany was stranded at Oyo while returning to Abeokuta, and Campbell was captured by Ibadan soldiers.

Eventually both explorers reached the Egba capital, where they remained only a few days before leaving for Lagos and the ship which would carry them to England. Campbell had spent seven months in the interior, and Delany five. On the morning of April 10 they left Lagos on board a British mail steamer. That evening the Ijaye and the Ibadan fought the first major encounter in a war which would last five years. But Delany and Campbell were already heading up the West African coast, satisfied in their own minds that they had accomplished their mission in Africa. In mid-May the two travelers arrived in England.[68] They had located a site for their colony; all they needed now were benefactors.

---

father's carelessness. The Reverend Crowther, in his letter to Venn on April 6, 1861, argued that Delany and Campbell had agreed not to settle in a colony, but he quoted the first article of the treaty as it was printed in the United States.

68. For this and the preceding paragraph, see Campbell, *A Pilgrimmage*, pp. 82–133, 145; J.F. Ade Ajayi and Robert Smith, *Yoruba Warfare in the Nineteenth*

Among the British

Having left an unhealthy climate and internecine war behind them, Delany and Campbell arrived in England to continue a struggle which differed in kind, although not necessarily in intensity, from what they had experienced in West Africa. With their funds nearly exhausted, Delany and Campbell's first priority was to maintain themselves in England long enough to gain financial support for the colony they planned to establish in Yoruba. But beyond problems of sustenance, there were other concerns which would shape their entire stay in Great Britain. This was especially true for Delany, whose desire to be considered the representative of a black constituency rather than of a white-controlled organization dominated his actions while in Great Britain. During his seven months in England and Scotland he successfully warded off threats to his independence from the Reverend Theodore Bourne, who was now the African Civilization Society's agent in England. With the help of William Howard Day and the Reverend William King of Canada, he established himself as the leading spokesman for a Yoruba movement increasingly allied with English commercial and humanitarian interests.

However, when Delany arrived in England with Campbell, he found that many of the Englishmen interested in his plans believed that he and Campbell had been sent out by the white-influenced African Civilization Society. Of course, the Niger Valley Exploring Party and the African Civilization Society had similar aims; both groups sought to establish in Yoruba an Afro-American settlement which would spread civilization, commerce, and Christianity—the last an aim of far greater importance to Garnet and his followers than it was to Delany—among the indigenous peoples. Moreover, Campbell's cooperation with the Civilization Society and its sup-

---

Century (Cambridge: Cambridge University Press, 1964), pp. 76–81, 83–84, 87; Robert Campbell, *A Few Facts Relating to Lagos, Abbeokuta, and Other Sections of Central Africa* (Philadelphia: King & Baird, Printers, 1860), p. 18. On the nature of the various Yoruba states, see Robert Smith, *Kingdoms of the Yoruba* (London: Methuen, 1969), pp. 10–11, 15, 17, 151–161; Ajayi and Smith, *Yoruba Warfare*, pp. 1–5; S. A. Akintoye, *Revolution and Power Politics in Yorubaland, 1840–1893: Ibadan Expansion and the Rise of Ekitiparapo* (New York: Humanities Press, 1971), p. 34.

porters in the winter of 1858–59 had made it even more difficult for the English to unravel the complicated strands which comprised the Yoruba movement. The Jamaica-born explorer himself compounded this confusion by corresponding on the subject with Garnet, who on at least one occasion referred to "our commissioners in Yoruba...." The appearance in England of Jonathan J. Myers also contributed to the confusion over who ran the Yoruba movement, because the English believed that Myers's mission to Port Natal and Cape Colony was "a branch" of the African Civilization Society. Myers actually came to England for friendship and advice rather than money, and he represented only himself and his sole companion, his teen-age son.[69]

Theodore Bourne's presence in England as the African Civilization Society's "foreign secretary" was also incompatible with Delany's desire for independence; while in Africa, Delany had railed against Bourne and maintained that his own expedition had no relationship at all to Bourne's activities. Although Bourne came to England in the summer of 1859 ostensibly to combat the influence of American "ultra-abolitionist" opposition to the Yoruba movement in general and to the African Civilization Society in particular, his real motives lay elsewhere. Since assistance from New York colonizationists had not provided the Civilization Society with sufficient funds to send a contingent of emigrants to Yoruba, Bourne hoped "to awaken a proper interest in behalf of our objects among the English people, and [to] solicit funds from them to aid the work...." He thus wished to ingratiate himself to English abolition-

---

69. *The Weekly Anglo-African*, February 11, 1860, p. 3; March 17, 1860, p. 3; Thomas Hodgkin to J. J. Myers, London, August 18, 1859; Hodgkin to ?, London, August 22, 1859; Hodgkin to Sir George Grey, London, October 3, 1859; Hodgkin to Myers, London, June 30, 1860; Hodgkin to Lord Alfred Churchill, London, July 30, 1860, Thomas Hodgkin Papers, microfilm in the possession of Dr. Edward H. Kass, Channing Laboratory, Boston. Myers had originally sailed to England in late July from Quebec. Before leaving Canada, he wrote the *Milwaukee Daily Sentinel and Gazette* that he hoped "the time will soon come when American rulers will find that the African nation will yet flourish with other nations of the earth, although now downtrodden and oppressed." In his letter he also claimed to be self-supporting. After a short stay in England, Myers spent several months in South Africa—principally in Port Natal and Cape Colony—before returning to the United States in May, 1860. *Milwaukee Sentinel*, August 2, 1859; *New York Daily Tribune*, May 19, 1860, p. 10.

ists, many of whom thought highly of his English-born father, George Bourne. Soon after his arrival in England, Bourne met with leaders of the British and Foreign Anti-Slavery Society, which had originally opposed his visit. He then reported to Garnet that the most loyal and steadfast of the English abolitionists supported the Civilization Society because they too believed that Yoruba emigration would contribute to the downfall of American slavery. Bourne also cultivated Dr. Thomas Hodgkin, a physician and philanthropist long active in both colonization and antislavery work, who introduced Bourne to a wider circle of Englishmen interested in Africa.[70]

Bourne must have believed that Delany and Campbell, if allowed to roam England unchecked, could damage the interests of the African Civilization Society and perhaps even dilute his own influence within the organization. Consequently, he convinced English abolitionists that he and the African Civilization Society were the prime movers in an emigration movement which included Delany's Niger Valley Exploring Party. Following one meeting between Bourne and a group of philanthropists, the *Anti-Slavery Reporter* announced that funds previously raised for Campbell and Delany's exploring expedition would now "be regarded as the commencement of the subscription-list to be hereafter devoted to carrying out the [African Civilization] Society's objects."[71]

Although Bourne was now recognized as the chief fund-raiser for the Yoruba movement, his mission in England was still not complete; he was aware that the successful prosecution of a Yoruba colonization scheme required the cooperation and active support of English commercial elements committed to developing a "legitimate trade" with Africa. Bourne thus turned to Englishmen who were interested in the potential cotton production of Yoruba; such men feared that England's almost total dependence upon American cotton would present economic problems for everyone engaged in cotton production should the American supply be cut off.

70. Bühler to Venn, Württemberg, Germany, February 24, 1860, CMS Papers, CA 2/024; Bourne to Gurley, New York, April 22, 1859, Domestic Letters, ACS Papers; *The Weekly Anglo-African*, September 3, 1859, p. 2; Hodgkin to Dr. Norton Shaw, London, August 10, 1859; "To the friends of the African Negro race," undated note, signed "T.H.," Hodgkin Papers.

71. *Anti-Slavery Reporter*, October 1, 1859, p. 224; *The Christian Intelligencer*, September 15, 1859, p. 45.

Bourne's action represented merely the latest and most self-interested manifestation of the free-produce movement which had been a minor yet persistent part of antislavery activity since the eighteenth century. Although Quakers had dominated the free-produce movement in the United States, a few blacks had also embraced the argument that goods produced by free labor would drive slave-grown or -manufactured products from the marketplace. In 1831 James Cornish and other Philadelphia blacks formed the Colored Free Produce Society, and Frederick Douglass, Garnet, and Crummell all supported the cause during their respective visits to England. In fact, in 1851 Garnet had anticipated parts of Bourne's position when he told a London meeting of the British and Foreign Anti-Slavery Society that England should "invest some of her capital in producing... [cotton] by free labour in Australia and in Africa; their American friends would then find it did not pay to keep slaves...."[72]

In March, 1860, Bourne presented the claims of the Civilization Society to an audience concerned about the impending cotton crisis. The meeting appointed Bourne, Hodgkin, Sir Culling E. Eardley, and Lord Alfred S. Churchill to a committee charged with promoting the "Yoruba movement." Churchill, a member of Parliament, had been active in the Cotton Supply Association, an organization founded at Manchester in 1858 to search out new areas of cotton production. The new Yoruba committee decided to broaden the campaign Bourne had been waging for the New York organization. Not only would an English society ancillary to the African Civilization Society be formed "conjointly... [to] carry out the objects of promoting the Christian civilization of Africa...," but an English commercial company would also be created "to employ the services of [Christian] coloured agents... in Yoruba and other districts of Central Africa... to purchase, collect, and forward articles of African commerce, especially cotton, sugar, rice, palm-

---

72. Early Quaker involvement in the free produce movement is discussed in Thomas Drake, *Quakers and Slavery in America* (New Haven: Yale University Press, 1952), pp. 115–119, 171. On black participation, see *Genius of Universal Emancipation*, XII (May, 1831), 6; Howard Temperly, *British Antislavery, 1833–1870* (Columbia: University of South Carolina Press, 1972), p. 166; *Anti-Slavery Reporter*, n.s. IV (June 1, 1849), 91–93; n.s. VI (June 2, 1851), 87–88.

oil, &c.; and in return to sell to the natives of Africa the various articles of British manufacture." A large English benefactor of the Civilization Society had indicated he would buy stock in the proposed commercial company. Ecstatic over these developments, Bourne wrote Garnet in the United States: "Let colored men arouse [*sic*]; England is ready to back them, as Sir Culling Eardley says, 'with a million pounds sterling, all in good time.' "[73]

While Bourne was pushing the claims of the African Civilization Society, Delany and Campbell arrived in England in mid-May, 1860. On their second day in London they met with Lord Churchill and others intent upon making humanitarianism profitable. The two explorers described their travels and stressed the riches of the territory they had visited. According to his version of the affair, Delany told the group of the expedition's "true position as independent of all other societies and organizations then in existence...." If so, his remarks failed to convince the *Anti-Slavery Reporter*,

---

73. *The Times* (London), September 22, 1859, p. 7; *Anti-Slavery Reporter*, April 2, 1860, p. 74; May 1, 1860, p. 98; *New York Colonization Journal*, May, 1860, p. 4. Almost nothing is known of Lord Churchill's background or other activities. However, at the close of the Civil War he succeeded Thomas Fowell Buxton as president of the London Freedmen's Aid Society, an organization aiding the newly emancipated blacks in the American South. Christine Bolt, *The Anti-Slavery Movement and Reconstruction: A Study in Anglo-American Co-operation, 1833–1877* (London: Oxford University Press, 1969), p. 49. By early 1860 the Cotton Supply Association was so convinced that a crisis in the United States would soon force England to find an alternative source of cotton that the organization joined other groups—such as the Liverpool Chamber of Commerce—in abandoning the tenets of laissez faire to urge the government to help the search for cotton areas. However, the Association's concern proved unnecessary; at the beginning of the Civil War, England was oversupplied with raw cotton, and the War prevented glutted markets. After mid-1862, when England's initial supply was exhausted, she turned to India—not Africa. *The Cotton Supply Reporter*, November 1, 1858, p. 33; January 2, 1860, p. 2; February 1, 1860, pp. 17–18; Liverpool Chamber of Commerce, *Report of Council*, 1858; Peter Harnetty, "The Imperialism of Free Trade: Lancashire, India, and the Cotton Supply Question, 1861–1865," *Journal of British Studies*, VI (November, 1966), 96; Robert Hugh Jones, "Anglo-American Relations, 1861–1865, Reconsidered," *Mid-America*, XLV (January, 1963), 44–45; Frenise A. Logan, "India—Britain's Substitute for American Cotton, 1861–1865," *Journal of Southern History*, XXIV (November, 1958), 476; Eugene A. Brady, "A Reconsideration of the Lancashire 'Cotton Famine,'" *Agricultural History*, XXXVII (July, 1963), 156–162. On the Cotton Supply Association's efforts in Africa, see A. J. Anjorin, "European Attempts to Develop Cotton Cultivation in West Africa, 1850–1910," *Odu*, n.s. III (July, 1966), 6.

which described the travelers as representatives of the Civilization Society. This impression could only have been strengthened two weeks later, when Delany, Campbell, and Bourne all spoke in London before a meeting called "in behalf of the objects of the African Civilization Society of New York." In his opening remarks Lord Alfred Churchill suggested that England support the Civilization Society to free herself "from complicity with American slavery" and from dependence upon slave-grown cotton. Black American cotton cultivators in Africa would solve England's economic and moral difficulties. Bourne also spoke for free-labor cotton, and the Anti-Slavery Society's secretary, L. A. Chamerovzow, offered a resolution calling for the promotion of cotton production in Africa. Chamerovzow's resolution, which specifically endorsed the African Civilization Society, was seconded by Campbell in a brief speech. Whatever Delany may have thought about his colleague's remarks, he confined his own comments to supporting a general resolution commending "the determination of a portion of the Christian and intelligent free colored people of America to engage in evangelizing and civilizing the inhabitants of Africa...." During his remarks he announced his intention to settle in Africa and denounced those American abolitionists critical of Yoruba emigration. "Any one who opposes Africa," he concluded, "opposes liberty, as well as the negro race."[74]

Why Delany was unable at this time to separate himself from Bourne's activities is unclear. Perhaps he was willing to suffer temporarily the indignity of being regarded as a representative of Bourne's society in order to receive the exposure Churchill, Hodgkin, and others could provide him. In June, Delany read a paper, "Geographical Observations on Western Africa," before a session of the Royal Geographical Society. Although the paper itself was a highly detailed description of the terrain he and Campbell had traversed, in his closing remarks Delany announced that the expedition had "originated from a large portion of the intelligent and educated descendants of the Africans in the United States and the Canadas, who are anxiously desirous by their own efforts and self-

74. Delany, *Official Report*, p. 62; *Anti-Slavery Reporter*, June 1, 1860, p. 121; *The Weekly Anglo-African*, June 30, 1860, p. 2. All quotations—except for the resolution—have been changed from past to present tense.

reliance to regenerate their father-land." Nevertheless, Lord Churchill, who followed Delany to the podium, reiterated the general misconception that the two explorers had been sponsored by the African Civilization Society.[75]

While it was difficult for Delany to move outside the orbit of the Civilization Society, the presence in England of two other Canadians willing to ally themselves with the emigration cause helped the explorer eventually to emerge as the acknowledged leader of the Yoruba movement. William Howard Day and the Reverend William King had first arrived in the British Isles in the summer of 1859 to raise funds for King's Elgin Association, a community of black emigrants from the United States who had settled near Chatham. A Presbyterian minister born in Ireland and educated in Scotland, King had started the Elgin community in 1849 shortly after he had freed and brought to Canada the fifteen Louisiana slaves he had inherited from his wife. Elgin, a quasi-self-sufficient agricultural community, soon became the most successful of the all-black communities operating in Canada West. By 1859, however, the community was feeling the effects of a widespread economic depression; in response, King contemplated developing a large-scale lumber industry in Elgin. He came to Great Britain in 1859 in search of potential investors for a joint-stock company. He was also attempting to raise money for another school in Elgin specifically for the fugitive slaves coming into the community.[76]

Yoruba emigration appealed to King for a variety of reasons. First, the primacy of evangelization and Christianization in the rhetoric of much of the Yoruba movement tapped his missionary temperament. By vocation a missionary to the fugitive blacks in Canada, the Scotch-Irish minister had originally hoped that Ca-

75. *Proceedings of the Royal Geographical Society of London*, IV (1859–60), 218–222.

76. *The Weekly Anglo-African*, July 23, 1859, p. 3; *Chatham Tri-Weekly Planet*, October 20, 1859, p. 2; *Daily Scotsman* (Edinburgh), November 17, 1859, reprinted in pamphlet material in the William King Papers (microfilm), Public Archives of Canada, Ottawa. On King and Elgin, see William H. Pease and Jane H. Pease, *Black Utopia: Negro Communal Experiments in America* (Madison: State Historical Society of Wisconsin, 1963), pp. 84–108, esp. 94–95; Robin W. Winks, *The Blacks in Canada: A History* (New Haven: Yale University Press, 1971), pp. 208–218; Victor Ullman, *Look to the North Star: A Life of William King* (Boston: Beacon Press, 1969).

nadian blacks Christianized at Elgin would carry the gospel back to the land of their ancestors. As he wrote in 1849 while organizing his community, "We take but a narrow view of this mission if we confine its effect to the colored population in the Province. It will extend to Africa...."[77] For King, then, a colony in Yoruba would be a Christian colony continuing the work he had begun at Elgin. However, the minister's motives were undoubtedly more complex and less disinterested than what was implied by his desire to see Christian blacks from Canada proselytize among the heathen in Africa. With Elgin still laboring under financial difficulties, King may well have felt that the community would reap part of the profits if it could train blacks for a commercially profitable African colony. In the meantime, of course, contacts with such commercial-humanitarians as Lord Churchill and Thomas Clegg could not harm his fund-raising efforts.

William Howard Day's purposes in coming to England were somewhat more modest than King's. Day had accompanied King to England to aid the fund-raising for the projected school for fugitive slaves at Elgin. When King returned to Canada at the end of 1859, Day stayed to advocate Elgin's cause and to search for funds for the newspaper he was still hoping to publish in Canada West as a replacement for the more or less moribund *Provincial Freeman*. Day advertised his presence in Glasgow in March, 1860, by distributing a circular which announced that he was devoted "to establishing in Canada, a PRESS for the Religious, Moral, and Social Improvement of the People, and 'to advocate the cause of the Fugitive in the land of his adoption.' "[78] But Day's campaign was moving slowly because British philanthropists were looking for a more attractive cause. Consequently, when King returned to England in May—at approximately the same time Delany and Campbell arrived from Africa—Day may have wished to broaden his appeal and ingratiate himself more fully into the English humanitarian

---

77. *Chatham Tri-Weekly Planet*, October 20, 1859, p. 2; William King to Rev. J[ohn] Bonnar, Toronto, July 15, 1849, King Papers.

78. *Daily Scotsman* (Edinburgh), November 17, 1859, reprinted in pamphlet material; Circular, "The Bible, The School, and The Press, for the Fugitive Slave," both in King Papers.

community. If so, the two black explorers with their tales of African adventure could help him.

From Delany's point of view, the presence of King and especially of Day helped further his own aims. The minister was in a position to endorse Delany's claims that there were New World blacks willing to emigrate to Yoruba. Although Day had denounced emigration at the Ohio State Colored Convention in 1858, he was ostensibly still the president of the "Chatham Convention" which had "commissioned" Delany's Niger Valley Exploring Party. With the leader of this rather shadowy organization by his side, Delany was able to argue more effectively that he was totally independent of other Yoruba societies and movements. Happily for Delany, Day's willingness to resume publicly the presidency of the "Chatham Convention" coincided with the creation in England of a new organization, the African Aid Society.

An outgrowth of the committee which Churchill and Bourne had established in March, 1860, to assist the latter's efforts on behalf of the African Civilization Society of New York, the African Aid Society was not formally organized until early July. Later that month Day and Delany, both representing the interests of the future black immigrants to Yoruba, attended a large meeting of the new organization in London; the Manchester cotton manufacturer Thomas Clegg was also present. By this time England's new Yoruba organization was in the process of rejecting Bourne. Ever since Delany and Campbell arrived in England, Bourne had been competing for attention with the two articulate blacks who had only recently visited the very country Englishmen were being asked to help Christianize and civilize. Moreover, the disadvantages of being a white man proselytizing on behalf of black men began to tell. Delany, who disliked Bourne intensely, began to use color to his advantage. Or so Hodgkin claimed when he wrote to Garnet, saying that "Delany is courted for his colour, & I fear that flattered by this [he] may stay to the injury of the cause."[79]

79. Delany, *Official Report*, pp. 62–63; *Morning Chronicle* (London), July 18, 20, 23, 1860; Hodgkin to William Coppinger, London, June 30, 1860; Hodgkin to Churchill, London, July 30, 1860; Hodgkin to Pinney, London, August 29, 1860; Hodgkin to H. Highland Garnet, London, August 29, 1860, Hodgkin Papers.

For Delany, personal and racial pride had merged inextricably; whatever attention may have been paid to him because he was black must have appeared natural. Quite reasonably, he saw himself and not Bourne as the natural representative of the Africa both he and the English philanthropists were dedicated to "uplifting." Since Delany's emphasis upon self-reliance and independence assumed that only blacks should speak for other blacks, he could easily view any personal flattery as simply an acknowledgment of the ideological position he had been pronouncing for years. Regardless of how he interpreted his acceptance by Churchill and the African Aid Society, Delany's presence as an advocate for the Yoruba movement diminished Bourne's effectiveness, and his agency for the Civilization Society was discontinued in the fall of 1860. Bourne lingered on in England until the following March, when he returned to the United States to advocate first Liberian and then Jamaican emigration.[80]

Meanwhile, during the latter part of 1860, the African Aid Society, assisted by various abolitionists, provided support for both Delany and Campbell to tour England. The Society also gave the two men sufficient funds to return to North America. Campbell, no longer closely allied with Delany, went home alone sometime in the fall. In late November he appeared in an African robe to lecture in Brooklyn on Central Africa; shortly thereafter he spoke to the American Geographical and Statistical Society, with historian George Bancroft in the audience.[81] Delany remained in England, apparently enjoying his role as the interpreter of the Yoruba movement to the British.

Delany stressed two themes during these final months in Great Britain: the importance of an alternate cotton supply for the British economy, and the necessity for blacks to be treated as self-reliant individuals who, when the Yoruba industrial settlement proved com-

80. *Anti-Slavery Reporter*, October 1, 1860, p. 247; Open letter from Bourne, London, December, 1860, with printed list of English contributors to African Civilization Society, A.M.A. Papers; *Twenty-ninth Annual Report of the Board of Managers of the New York State Colonization Society* (New York: John A. Gray, Printer, 1861), pp. 22–24; *The Weekly Anglo-African*, August 17, 1861, p. 2.

81. Hodgkin to Churchill, London, July 30, 1860, Hodgkin Papers; Delany, *Official Report*, p. 65; *Brooklyn Daily Eagle*, November 20, 1860, p. 2; *The Weekly Anglo-African*, December 15, 1860, p. 2.

mercially successful, would pay back whatever assistance the Englishmen had tendered them. Delany even went so far as to tell members of the African Aid Society that they should only aid those blacks willing to act for themselves. Criticizing the American Colonization Society for "sending out promiscuously...all the people who could be got together, without any self-help on their own parts," Delany advised the African Aid Society to be more stringent. "Make [blacks]...find a part of the money themselves, and afterwards repay what was advanced, so that they might retain their self-respect, and feel themselves responsible." At Leeds, where he spoke with Day in December, Delany portrayed the development of his nationalist-emigrationist movement of the mid-1850's as primarily an exercise in self-help; he again emphasized that "self-reliance is the best dependence." Delany also argued that commercially minded Western blacks could provide England with enough cotton to avert a crisis should the American supply be curtailed. "Supposing a war breaks out between this country and America...or supposing a movement like that of John Brown's is successful, what is to become of three-fourths of the British people depending on cotton manufactures? There is no other people who can raise cotton like the black, for both his nature and country are adapted for it." Of course, Africa herself would serve Great Britain's needs, for in Africa "There is every facility...for producing a sufficient supply of cotton."[82]

Cotton, then, would be Africa's contribution to Great Britain's salvation. For Delany this was not merely rhetoric; while in Scotland, he contacted Henry Dunlop of the African Aid Society and other Scottish cotton dealers, and he arranged for them to handle the cotton he intended to produce once he returned to Abeokuta.[83] But this was still months off—even in the most optimistic estimates. First, Delany had to return to Canada to raise the party of selected, well-trained blacks who would cultivate Yoruba cotton and generate in West Africa a new Black Nationality—a goal he had mini-

---

82. Undated clipping from the *New York Independent*, enclosed in Coppinger to McLain, Philadelphia, September 10, 1860, Domestic Letters, ACS Papers; Delany, *Official Report*, pp. 70–71; *The Cotton Supply Reporter*, November 2, 1860, p. 297. Quotations have been changed from past to present tense.

83. Delany, *Official Report*, pp. 69, 72.

mized during his seven months in Great Britain. In mid-December he left Liverpool for Chatham to begin collecting a colony. There would be difficulties ahead for Delany, as well as for those who had not only caught the nationalist-emigrationist fever but were also interested in planting Christian industrial settlements in Yoruba.

THE AFRICAN CIVILIZATION SOCIETY'S MISSION IN AFRICA

Although the African Civilization Society had discontinued Theodore Bourne's agency in England, the New York organization did not abandon its interest in Yoruba emigration. In fact, while accepting Delany and Campbell as its own representatives, the Civilization Society also began the work of establishing its own colony in Africa, asking Lord Churchill for assistance with its plans to send a company of emigrants to Yoruba. Garnet was still the president at this time; he and J. Sella Martin of Boston were the Society's leading spokesmen, and since October, 1859, the Reverend A. A. Constantine, a white Baptist minister and former missionary to Liberia, had been serving as corresponding secretary.[84]

Since its inception in the fall of 1858 the African Civilization Society had found it easier to win verbal endorsements than to secure financial support. Successfully warding off the attacks of such anti-emigrationists as George T. Downing, William Wells Brown, and William C. Nell during the late summer of 1859 and the spring of 1860, the Society had built a substantial following—principally in New York City, where interest in Yoruba emigration had first developed to visible proportions. At a March, 1860, meeting at the Cooper Institute in New York, Garnet unveiled his organization's intention to purchase land in Yoruba. There they would build a settlement and teach the local residents to cultivate cotton and other crops: "We believe that Africa is to be redeemed by Christian civilization, and that the great work is to be chiefly achieved by the free and voluntary emigration of enterprising

---

84. *The Cotton Supply Reporter*, November 16, 1860, p. 314; *Chatham Tri-Weekly Planet*, April 8, 1861, p. 2; *The Weekly Anglo-African*, September 3, 1859, p. 2; *The Missionary Jubilee: An Account of the Fiftieth Anniversary of the American Baptist Missionary Union*..., rev. ed. (New York: Sheldon and Co., 1871), p. 243.

The Search for a Place: Africa

colored people." Although not naming Delany and Campbell, the black minister mentioned having heard from "our commissioners in Yoruba" who had signed a treaty with local chieftains for "a large and sufficient tract of land, and . . . are permitted to form their own municipal laws, subject only to the common law of that country." Garnet also announced that the African Civilization Society was trying to raise $6,000 to send out its first company to Africa. Apparently this was an impossible task. In the fall of 1860, when Garnet began corresponding with Lord Churchill's organization in England, the African Civilization Society was still weak and financially unstable, despite the numerous prominent white colonizationists and religious figures who publicly expressed support. One observer commented that the Civilization Society possessed "just enough of life to move in the newspapers."[85]

Nevertheless, when an opportunity developed to send a small party to Yoruba, the Society responded affirmatively. The Civilization Society's agent in this undertaking was the Reverend Elymas P. Rogers. His background and attitudes resembled, in many ways, those of the other black leaders active in the Society. A Presbyterian minister like Garnet, Rogers had even as a child expressed a desire to visit Africa. Born in 1815 in Madison, Connecticut, Rogers decided to become a minister in 1835, when he entered a school established by Gerrit Smith in Peterboro, New York. Subsequently he taught at a public school for blacks in Rochester, and he graduated from the Oneida Institute in 1841—only two years after Garnet had completed his training there. He then moved to Trenton, New Jersey, where he continued to teach school and undertook his theological education. Licensed by the New Brunswick Presbytery in 1844 and ordained the following year, Rogers accepted a call to the Plane Street Presbyterian Church in Newark in 1846; there he remained until he left for Africa in 1860. Meanwhile he wrote two volumes of satiric verse—*The Repeal of the Missouri Compromise Considered* and *A Poem on the Fugitive Slave Law*. A member of the Evangelical Association of Colored Ministers of Congregational

---

85. Howard Holman Bell, *A Survey of the Negro Convention Movement, 1830–1861* (New York: Arno Press, 1969), pp. 229–235; *New York Herald*, March 8, 1860, p. 10; Coppinger to Gurley, Philadelphia, November 17, 1860, Domestic Letters, ACS Papers.

and Presbyterian Churches, Rogers, like several of the association's members, became an active member of the African Civilization Society. For Rogers, the organization's emphasis upon the Christian regeneration of the continent was compatible with his own religious and racial beliefs. By September, 1860, Rogers was planning to visit Africa. Like Holly's trip to Haiti five years earlier, Rogers's journey was to serve two distinct purposes: he would make arrangements for the colony the Civilization Society planned to send to Yoruba, and he would investigate opportunities for establishing a mission at Abeokuta for the American Missionary Association. With $200 from the Missionary Association and some additional money from his own savings, Rogers was ready to carry Christianity and the genesis of a Black Nationality to Yoruba.[86]

Accompanied by two assistants, S. V. Douglass and J. B. Simpson, both of whom acted as agents for the Civilization Society, Rogers left New York in early November. The group brought with them a large supply of Bibles and an assortment of agricultural tools; as Garnet observed when they departed, "Our object is not only to point the children of Africa to the Savior of mankind but likewise to illustrate to them the advantages of agricultural and other sciences." After arriving in Sierra Leone in December, Rogers observed that "the most effectual way to redeem Africa is, to plant Christian colonies under soil, and set the natives an example in industry and piety worthy of imitation. . . ." Of course, in his letters to the American Missionary Association, Rogers discussed the missionary opportunities that Africa presented: "God is about to visit and redeem his people . . . [and] those very portions of Africa which have been plundered of her children, shall [soon] become vocal with the praises of the Saviour's name. . . ." Later, from Liberia, Rogers reasserted his commitment to both African missionary work and Yoruba colonization. Portentously, he added that although missionaries "may fall at their post . . . they may derive consolation

---

86. Joseph M. Wilson, *The Presbyterian Historical Almanac, and Historical Remembrancer, of the Church, for 1862* (Philadelphia: Joseph M. Wilson, 1862), pp. 191–194; Joan R. Sherman, "Connecticut's Nineteenth-Century Black Poets," *Connecticut Review*, V (April, 1972), 19–20; *New York Colonization Journal*, December, 1860, p. 3. On the Evangelical Association of Colored Ministers, see *Minutes and Sermon of the Second Presbyterian and Congregational Convention*; *The Weekly Anglo-African*, September 24, 1859, p. 2.

from the thought that if they lose their lives they shall find them again." Ten days later, with the Reverend Alexander Crummell by his side, Rogers died from malaria at Cape Palmas, Liberia.[87]

With the death of Rogers in early 1861 the black exploratory missions to West Africa came to an end. By this time Martin R. Delany and Robert Campbell had returned home to tell of their travels. Jonathan J. Myers had concluded his expedition to South Africa even earlier. Although Myers announced that he would sell his property in Wisconsin and move to Africa, the black grocer quickly settled in Milwaukee, where he opened a "museum" of African "curiosities" and later went into the fruit business.[88]

Nevertheless, the African emigration movement was far from over. Both Delany and Henry Highland Garnet would continue to agitate for an Afro-American settlement in Yoruba through 1861 and into 1862. However, Yoruba emigration found itself competing for support with another emigration movement—one which could, in part, trace its roots back to Delany's conventions of the mid-1850's. James Theodore Holly and his black Episcopal followers had not foresworn their desire to establish a Christian Black Nationality in Haiti. For a time in the early 1860's, they must have believed their dreams would soon be fulfilled.

87. *New York Colonization Journal*, December, 1860, p. 3; April, 1861, p. 1; *The American Missionary*, March, 1861, pp. 49-50; April, 1861, pp. 73-74; May, 1861, p. 112; *The Weekly Anglo-African*, March 30, 1861, p. 3; Wilson, *Presbyterian Historical Almanac*, p. 193.

88. *New York Daily Tribune*, May 19, 1860, p. 10; *Milwaukee Sentinel*, June 11, 1859; July 25, 1861. Myers eventually left Milwaukee and may have emigrated to Haiti. Apparently he never returned to Africa. Vollmar, "Negro in Milwaukee," p. 72; *The Pine and Palm*, March 27, 1862, p. 4.

CHAPTER 7

The Search for a Place: Haiti

For James Theodore Holly and his small band of missionary-nationalists, the failure of the August, 1858, Chatham convention to endorse Haitian emigration was not an insurmountable problem. Nor did Delany's advocacy of African emigration or the emergence of Yoruba emigration fever in New York City dissuade Holly from continuing along the path he had marked out earlier. His belief in the future of Haiti, in the viability of emigration to the independent black nation, and in the necessity for the Episcopal Church to expand into Haiti far outweighed any allegiance he could have felt to Delany. Fortunately for Holly and his supporters, sentiment favoring Haitian emigration increased markedly among blacks in the North and in Canada for a brief period beginning in 1859. As in 1824, the Haitian government provided liberal inducements to prospective emigrants and established an emigration agency in the United States. These actions combined to spur emigration of a magnitude far greater than Delany or other African emigrationists had seriously anticipated. Ultimately, however, the Haitian emigration movement floundered as disillusioned emigrants returned to the United States with tales of death and despair. Although Holly stayed, even for him the dream of creating a Black Christian Nationality in the Caribbean had been swept away by harsh realities.

Since the mid-1850's Holly had consistently advocated a missionary-emigration to Haiti. He veered away from this commitment only briefly when in early 1858 he assured Missouri Congressman Frank P. Blair that North American blacks would indeed emigrate to

Central America, where Blair had been urging the federal government to establish a black republic. By July, however, Holly was again championing Haitian emigration; as indicated earlier, he presented the claims of the Caribbean country to a New York audience which also heard spokesmen advocating emigration to both Yoruba and Liberia. Holly maintained that a large emigration to Haiti would "aid the Haytians in establishing a nationality to compete with any people in all the elements of national strength and glory." In Indiana alone, he announced, some 5,000 blacks were reported willing to emigrate to Haiti under the auspices of Delany's emigration movement.[1]

At this point Holly was not the leader of a movement with a broad base of support. Delany's organization did not back Holly at Chatham any more than it backed Delany himself. Lack of support from an emigration movement now totally in disarray had little effect upon Holly, for his support within Delany's emigration organization had essentially been drawn from black Episcopalians committed only to emigration to Haiti; their faith had not diminished over the years. In late August, 1859, Holly brought his missionary-nationalists together at his home church in New Haven for the fourth annual convention of the Protestant Episcopal Society for Promoting the Extension of the Church among Colored People. Representatives of only three black Episcopal churches—Holly's St. Luke's, William C. Monroe's former parish of St. Matthew's in Detroit (now served by the Reverend Samuel V. Berry), and Berry's former church, St. Phillip's in New York City—were present at the gathering. The New Haven meeting selected Berry, William Lambert (a prominent layman in St. Matthew's who had been active in Delany's emigration movement), and John P. Anthony and Henry S. Merriman (both members of the skeletal Board of Trade chosen at the 1856 Cleveland Emigration Convention) as officers. Indicative of the major thrust of the convention, the delegates adopted Holly's resolutions which held "That the people of Hayti, from contiguity of position, historical coincidents, and simi-

---

1. *The Pine and Palm*, September 24, 1862, p. 11; Frank P. Blair, Jr., *The Destiny of the Races of this Continent...* (Washington, D.C.: Buell & Blanchard, Printers, 1859), pp. 34-37; *New York Evening Express*, July 17, 1858, p. 3.

larity of destiny, have peculiar claims upon American Christians for their sympathy and support," and that the Episcopal Church should establish a mission on the island.²

Attempting to further his missionary plans, Holly once again turned to the Episcopal Church hierarchy for assistance in establishing a Haitian mission. In the fall of 1859 he persuaded Gregory T. Bedell, assistant bishop of Ohio, to remind the annual meeting of the Board of Missions that Haiti desperately needed Christian laborers; early the following year Holly requested that he be appointed a missionary to the Caribbean nation. However, in March the Board's Foreign Committee repeated its action of five years earlier and denied Holly's request. Undaunted by the Committee's decision, Holly in April asked the Episcopal Bishop of Louisiana, Leonidas Polk, to make an annual supervisory visitation to Haiti should an Episcopal church be established in the black republic. But the Louisiana churchman did not take any positive steps to help the missionary-emigrationists.³

Meanwhile, Holly was also hoping to stimulate a large if "select" emigration by reaching a black audience wider and more diverse than that represented by his own Episcopal followers. During the latter half of 1859 and into the following year, the New Haven minister employed the pages of the new black literary periodical, *The Anglo-African Magazine*, to develop a lengthy argument favoring Haitian emigration. Published in seven installments, Holly's "Thoughts on Hayti" revealed again how closely he conceived the relationship between what black emigrants could do for the material prosperity of Haiti and what black missionaries could contribute to the spiritual health of the Haitians. Reiterating the stand he had taken upon his return from Haiti in 1855, he argued that the Roman Catholic Church—"at best covered with the superstitions of the dark ages"—represented an inadequate remedy for

2. *The Weekly Anglo-African*, October 22, 1859, p. 2.
3. David McEwen Dean, "James Theodore Holly, 1829–1911, Black Nationalist and Bishop" (Ph.D. dissertation, University of Texas, 1972), p. 62; S. D. Denison to Rev. Horatio Southgate, New York, March 14, 1860; Denison to Holly, New York, March 29, 1860, S. D. Denison Letterbook, Domestic and Foreign Missionary Society Papers: Haiti Papers, Church Historical Society, Austin, Texas; James Theodore Holly to Rt. Rev. Leonidas Polk, New Haven, Ct., April 26, 1860, Leonidas Polk Papers, Historical Manuscripts, Yale University.

Haiti's spiritual and cultural deficiencies. Only through "a select, judicious and discreet" emigration of deeply religious Afro-American Protestants could Haiti lift herself from spiritual and economic stagnation. In Holly's view, an emigration movement to Haiti "should assume the shape of well-organized religious communities, headed by an educated ministry, and backed and sustained by learned laymen" who would be the skilled tradesmen and agricultural workers capable of bringing industrial civilization to the black republic. All the emigrants should eschew the two habits of mind which had led to the failure of the 1824 Haitian emigration—excessive docility on the one hand, and political ambition on the other.[4]

While the settlers would have to recognize that "the political destiny of Hayti is already committed to other hands that must always be preferred before them," Holly remained convinced that, if black American emigrants were willing to function as the civilizing force, they would help create the force that was indispensable for stopping the slave trade and emancipating those already in chains—*"a strong, powerful, enlightened and progressive negro nationality, equal to the demands of the nineteenth century, and capable of commanding the respect of all the nations of the earth. . . ."* The time had never been more propitious for an Afro-American emigration. Not only was Haiti's new ruler, President Fabre Geffrard, encouraging emigration, but since replacing the deposed tyrant, Emperor Faustin I, Geffrard had avoided the dangers of both anarchy and despotism. "[T]he present crisis in her affairs," Holly observed in concluding his articles, "is the auspicious era when an intelligent emigration of colored Americans may set toward those shores, with every prospect of ultimate success in the regeneration of that people, and the promotion of the cause of the descendants of Africa throughout the world."[5]

As Holly developed his case for emigration in *The Anglo-African Magazine*, a Haitian emigration was already underway. Beginning in 1859, this new thrust resembled the 1824 movement in two ways. First, the Haitian government itself again decided to encourage a

4. *The Anglo-African Magazine*, I (June, 1859), 185–187; (July, 1859), 220–221; (August, 1859), 241–243; (September, 1859), 300.
5. *Ibid.*, (October, 1859), 328–329; (November, 1859), 365–366; II (January, 1860), 17–18.

sizable immigration of black Americans to augment the native laboring force. Haiti started promoting an immigration policy soon after Geffrard took office, and several hundred Louisiana blacks left New Orleans for Port-au-Prince sometime during 1859 and early 1860. By the spring of 1859 a former participant in Delany's emigration movement—H. Ford Douglass—and other blacks in Chicago had held several meetings to consider Geffrard's invitation to black Americans.[6] Geffrard and other Haitian officials also realized that only through a well-organized network of agents in the United States could Haiti hope to convince significant numbers of blacks to emigrate, and that only through an American agency could the government handle the transportation arrangements. Fortunately for Geffrard, James Redpath, a Scottish-born American journalist and abolitionist, was willing to serve functions similar to those which the young white minister, Loring D. Dewey, had performed in the 1820's. Whatever Redpath's motivation, he publicly advocated emigration to Haiti as "an agency of strengthening a colored Nation" and as a free-labor economic "lever" for destroying southern slavery.[7]

Although the Haitian government waited until the summer of 1860 before completing the arrangements with Redpath for the establishment of an agency in the United States and Canada, Geffrard and his aides formulated the specific inducements to be offered prospective emigrants as early as August, 1859. To encourage agricultural development, Haiti agreed to pay the passage for all emigrants willing to engage in farming in Haiti, and to provide board and lodging for eight days. Although Afro-American farmers would first work on shares, eventually land would become available for purchase. The government also agreed to allow the emigrants to settle together, subject to Haitian law and authority; equal protection of the law would be provided immediately, and citizenship would come after a year's residence. In an attempt to ease fears that Protestant emigrants would not be allowed to practice their religion

---

6. Willis D. Boyd, "James Redpath and American Negro Colonization in Haiti, 1860–1862," *The Americas*, XII (October, 1955), 170; *Chatham Tri-Weekly Planet*, May 4, 1859, p. 2; March 22, 1860, p. 3.

7. James Redpath, ed., *A Guide to Hayti* (Boston: Thayer & Eldridge, 1860), pp. 9–10.

freely, the government proclaimed that "The religious belief of the emigrants, to whatever Christian sect they belong, shall always be respected." Moreover, Haiti agreed to exempt the emigrants themselves (although not their children) from military service. Finally, emigrants were free to leave the country whenever they wished, although those transported at government expense were required to remain in the country for three years.[8]

As the Haitian government committed itself to sponsoring and financing a mass immigration of black Americans, two black visitors to the Caribbean aided the embryonic movement by boosting the advantages of the area. William P. Newman, a former slave and long-time resident of Canada West, visited Haiti in the fall of 1859. In letters to the *Chatham Tri-Weekly Planet*, Newman claimed that since "we may live here on one-half of the labor of the Northern States and Canada, and get rich," blacks from Canada should emigrate to Haiti. Another boon to Haitian emigration was the publication of J. Dennis Harris's *Summer on the Borders of the Caribbean Sea* in the latter part of 1860. A black plasterer from Cleveland, Harris had argued unsuccessfully against William Howard Day's anti-emigration resolution at the 1858 Ohio black convention. Shortly thereafter Harris wrote to Frank P. Blair, congratulating the congressman for favoring the establishment of a black settlement outside the boundaries of the United States. "[W]e want to be identified with the ruling power of a nation," Harris told Blair, adding that he was willing to serve as an agent "whether it be to spread such information as will awaken... [blacks] to their true interests, or to carry out some plan or expedition that may be devised...."

Although in early 1859 Harris accepted an appointment as a general lecturer for the largely black Ohio State Anti-Slavery Society, emigration was not far from his mind. In June, he formed a Central American Land Company in Cleveland. The organization proposed "to send out as early as the first day of December, 1859, a delegation of colored men as Commissioners to select a permanent location, purchase the land, and upon their return sell the same in suitable quantities to such persons as wish to establish themselves

---

8. Boyd, "Redpath and Colonization," p. 172; Redpath, *Guide*, pp. 10, 94–96.

in a free and independent country." Harris was the company's general agent, and H. Ford Douglass served as one of several field agents. Although this land scheme fizzled, the young Cleveland emigrationist appeared in early October, 1859, before a hostile audience in Chatham, Canada West, to advocate emigration to Jamaica. The following summer Harris traveled to the island of Hispaniola. While he visited only the Spanish part of the island, his letters (later collected for his book) included an extensive account of the Haitian Revolution, as well as first-hand impressions of Santo Domingo. In the Caribbean, Harris stated, Afro-Americans would find both visual beauty and commercial opportunity.[9]

As Harris was touting the Caribbean, the Haitian government was completing arrangements with Redpath to run a Haytian Emigration Bureau from Boston. Geffrard hoped the Bureau would stimulate large numbers of blacks to come to the fertile Artibonite Valley, which ran some sixty miles east of the port of St. Marc. The Louisiana emigrants of 1859 had homesteaded there, and two surveyors had already been selected to divide the land into plots of varying size for the new emigrants. Of course, Redpath first had to recruit agents for his Emigration Bureau; by the end of 1860 he had several men in the field. These included Harris, traveling in Ohio; Holly, touring New Jersey and Pennsylvania while maintaining his position as rector of St. Luke's in New Haven; Samuel V. Berry, in Michigan; and Henry Highland Garnet—still active in the Yoruba movement—the resident agent for New York. Some of the agents were able to tap the latent interest in Haiti almost immediately. Not surprisingly, Holly was one of the most effective. William Coppinger of the Pennsylvania Colonization Society observed in December, 1860, from Philadelphia, "The Haytian Move-

9. On Newman, see *Chatham Tri-Weekly Planet*, December 20, 1859, p. 2; January 5, 1860, p. 2; William H. Pease and Jane H. Pease, *Black Utopia: Negro Communal Experiments in America* (Madison: State Historical Society of Wisconsin, 1963), pp. 71–72. For Harris, see *Cleveland City Directories*, 1859–60 and 1861; *Proceedings of a Convention of the Colored Men of Ohio, Held in the City of Cincinnati, on the 23d, 24th, 25th and 26th of November, 1858* (Cincinnati: Moore, Wilstach, Keys & Co., Printers, 1858), p. 7; Blair, *Destiny of the Races*, p. 34; *Cleveland Morning Leader*, February 2, 1859, p. 1; February 9, 1859, p. 3; June 2, 1859, p. 2; *Chatham Tri-Weekly Planet*, October 8, 1859, p. 3; J. Dennis Harris, *A Summer on The Borders of The Caribbean Sea* (New York: A. B. Burdick, 1860), pp. 159–160.

ment appears to have made considerable headway in this City. About forty are reported to have engaged to start next month, and a larger number in the spring." It is very likely that some of these were among the first group which left New York in early January. Forty-one additional emigrants left Boston in February, ten more in March, and James Theodore Holly and some 160 other emigrants prepared to leave Boston and New Haven near the end of April.[10]

The greatest boon to the movement was the announcement in the spring of 1861 that Frederick Douglass, the most persistent critic of emigration during the previous decade, would sail with Holly's party on an exploratory mission. Douglass had opposed all forms of emigration for most of the 1850's. Yet in a speech to the American and Foreign Anti-Slavery Society in New York in 1853, Douglass reiterated his opposition to African colonization but argued that blacks someday might have to emigrate to points within the hemisphere where "we may still keep within hearing of the wails of our enslaved people in the United States." Douglass even went so far as to predict that all North American blacks might "mould them[selves] into one body, and into a powerful nation." Whatever motivated him on this occasion, his remarks were clearly an anomaly, since he denounced all emigration schemes during the rest of the decade. In fact, he specifically opposed the first murmurs of interest in Haitian emigration in Chicago in the spring of 1859.[11]

Nevertheless, the domestic developments during the 1850's—"Bloody Kansas," the *Dred Scott* decision, the execution of John Brown—and especially Lincoln's obvious desire to compromise following the election of 1860 had all pushed Douglass to the point where he would demonstrate increasing tolerance toward those blacks wishing to leave the United States. As he admitted in January, 1861—undoubtedly with reluctance—"Whatever the future may have in store for us, it seems plain that inducements offered to the colored man to remain here are few, feeble and very uncertain...." Then he added a statement most welcome to Holly, Redpath, and

10. Boyd, "Redpath and Colonization," pp. 172, 176; *Cleveland Morning Leader*, November 22, 1860, p. 2; *Douglass' Monthly*, January, 1861, p. 399; William Coppinger to Ralph R. Gurley, Philadelphia, November 17, 1860, Domestic Letters, American Colonization Society Papers, Manuscript Division, Library of Congress.

11. Philip Foner, *The Life and Writings of Frederick Douglass*, II (New York: International Publishers, 1950), 252–253; *Douglass' Monthly*, May, 1859, p. 70.

the other Haitian emigrationists: "We can raise no objection to the present movement towards Hayti.... We can no longer throw our little influence against a measure which may prove highly advantageous to many families, and of much service to the Haytian Republic." By April, Douglass's support for the Haitian emigration movement had progressed to the extent that he and his daughter accepted Redpath's invitation to sail with Holly from New Haven to Haiti near the end of the month. However, with the outbreak of the Civil War following the firing at Fort Sumter, Douglass canceled his Haitian trip: "The last ten days have made a tremendous revolution in all things pertaining to the possible future of the colored people of the United States. We shall stay here and watch the current of events, and serve the cause of freedom and mankind." Despite Douglass's decision, Holly and his party prepared for the voyage to Haiti.[12]

By then Holly's emigration activity and church labors were finally coming together in a common enterprise. Despite the rebuffs of the Foreign Committee, Holly found some support within the church; the assistant bishop of the Diocese of Connecticut endorsed Holly's plan to establish a missionary parish in Haiti. Holly and the Reverend Samuel V. Berry would head the mission, and they would be accompanied by J. Dennis Harris—a new recruit to Holly's missionary-emigrationism—and six other lay teachers. Explaining that the 1824 emigration made a Haitian mission imperative, Holly assured potential Episcopal benefactors that his church would be self-supporting within five years. Harris was assigned to make personal appeals within the state. Clothing, French hymn books, Bibles, and money eventually totaling $450 slowly began to come in from churches in Glastenbury, Stamford, Hartford, Norwich, and New Haven.[13]

Besides drawing upon the Church to further his missionary-

---

12. *Douglass' Monthly*, January, 1861, pp. 386–387; March, 1861, p. 420; May, 1861, pp. 449–450.

13. *The Calendar*, November 17, 1860, p. 359; December 1, 1860, p. 381; February 9, 1861, p. 44; February 16, 1861, p. 52; February 23, 1861, p. 59; March 9, 1861, p. 75; March 30, 1861, p. 99; May 4, 1861, p. 141; *Journal of the Seventy-Eighth Annual Convention of the Protestant Episcopal Church in the Diocese of Connecticut, Held in Bridgeport, June 10th and 11th, 1862* (Hartford: Press of Case, Lockwood and Company, 1862), p. 52.

emigration plans, Holly traveled in the East as an agent for the Haitian Emigration Bureau during the winter of 1861. Defending the Bureau from its critics, he answered Martin R. Delany's charges that, in appointing Redpath as the general agent of the Bureau, the Haitian government had selected a white man over Holly and other possible black candidates and had thus violated principles Delany had long advocated—"*self-reliance* . . . [and] a Black Nationality." Redpath, Holly assured his former ally, "is not the head of this movement by the black government of Hayti. He is the white servant, Geffrard the black master . . . [and] the appointment . . . does not detract one iota from the idea of negro sovereignty, nationality, and independence." Shortly thereafter he replied to James McCune Smith's denunciations of Haitian emigration by urging his readers to accept the government's invitation to settle there. He also blamed the failure of the 1824 emigration upon "a generation of colored Americans [who] were wholly incapacitated for the duties of independent self-respecting freemen." Although Holly claimed this was no longer true, he engaged in religious exhortation to ensure that it be so. "You are less than men," the Episcopal minister proclaimed, "if you would permit any amount of sufferings and privations to prevent your going forth to build a nationality of your race to do service in the cause of God and humanity."[14]

Evidently a significant number of blacks were willing to sacrifice themselves for their convictions, for Holly's 150-member "New Haven Pioneer Company of Haytian Emigrants" prepared to leave for Haiti at the end of April. Redpath's Bureau in Boston had completed the embarkation arrangements, and Holly's party would settle as a group some three miles from Port-au-Prince on an estate belonging to President Geffrard. In late April the *Madeira*, a British ship from Barbados, left Boston with fifty-two emigrants; after a stop in New Haven on May 2, 111 blacks in all—far fewer than the 150 anticipated—departed for Haiti. Only a small portion of the party was from New Haven; this included Holly and John P. Anthony, their families, and the widow and two children of the late William C. Monroe. Most of the other emigrants were from

14. *The Weekly Anglo-African*, March 16, 1861, p. 2; *Douglass' Monthly*, May, 1859, p. 70; *Chatham Tri-Weekly Planet*, January 21, 1861, p. 3; February 15, 1861, p. 3.

Canada West. Shortly before the *Madeira*'s departure Holly described his party as a "*Mayflower* expedition of sable pioneers in the cause of civil and religious liberty, which it falls to your lot to Hayti in the name of New England." Fittingly, while on board the emigrants pledged in a "Madeira Compact" to "seek less to advance our temporal interest than to labor for the establishment of the Kingdom of God in Hayti."[15]

As Holly and his colonists sailed toward the Caribbean, the Haitian emigration movement was just beginning to operate effectively. In mid-March the new resident agent for the Bureau in New York, George Lawrence, assumed the editorship of *The Weekly Anglo-African*, which in May became the official organ of the movement as *The Pine and Palm*. Moreover, emigrant vessels continued to leave eastern ports. In May and June 140 blacks from four different ships disembarked at Port-au-Prince. Another 757 emigrants were reported to have sailed during the remainder of the year; this number included some 113 blacks from Canada West. Prospective emigrants from as far west as Kansas were applying to Redpath's agency in Boston for berths. At the center of the movement were the traveling agents, who were paid an average of twenty dollars a week plus an additional two dollars for each emigrant recruited. Throughout 1861 the agents sent back encouraging news to Redpath. From Canada, John Brown, Jr., reported that forty to fifty emigrants were prepared to leave Windsor in June to sail from Boston. H. Ford Douglass, laboring in Illinois, was also enthusiastic about the response he was receiving, and from Pittsburgh the Reverend J. B. Smith wrote in July that both Martin H. Freeman, who had advocated emigration in the mid-1850's, and George B. Vashon, Freeman's onetime antagonist in the emigrationist struggles, were considering moving to Haiti.[16]

---

15. *The Weekly Anglo-African*, March 23, 1861, p. 4; April 27, 1861, pp. 2, 3; *The Calendar*, May 11, 1861, p. 149; Dean, "Holly, Nationalist and Bishop," pp. 76, 79; Robin W. Winks, *The Blacks in Canada: A History* (New Haven: Yale University Press, 1971), p. 164.

16. *The Weekly Anglo-African*, March 16, 1861, p. 2; Boyd, "Redpath and Colonization," pp. 175–176; Winks, *Blacks in Canada*, p. 165; James Redpath to Victorien Plésance, Boston, May 27, 1861, Letters and Reports of James Redpath, General Agent of Emigration to Hayti, to M. Plésance, Secretary of State of Exterior Relations of the Republic of Hayti, and others, dated Mar. 31-Dec. 27, 1861,

During the summer of 1861 another strident anti-emigrationist of the previous decade became an agent for the Haitian movement. As the associate editor of *Frederick Douglass' Paper*, William J. Watkins had written some of the strongest denunciations of Delany's emigration plans. Now he was convinced that Haitian emigration was "a movement emanating from the branch of our own people who cannot but have the welfare of the whole race at heart. It does not fatten upon prejudice against color, nor does it sympathize with the absurd and accursed dogmas of our inherent inferiority." The new emigrationist also argued that the Haitian movement would hasten the success of the abolitionist crusade. Considered "an effective speaker" by Redpath, Watkins worked first in Ohio; in mid-October he replaced the black author and lecturer William Wells Brown as the traveling agent for Canada.[17]

Despite these development, certainly not all blacks acclaimed the Haitian emigration movement. Although probably closer to a mass movement than any other emigration development since the Haitian emigration of the mid-1820's, this new movement was also stimulating opposition on a scale surpassing all similar outbursts since Garrison had orchestrated the spate of anti-African colonization meetings in 1831. Long-time antagonists to emigration such as George Downing, James McCune Smith, and J. W. C. Pennington led the attack upon the emigration movement in the North. For example, in late July, Smith evidently helped finance the birth of another *Weekly Anglo-African* as an anti-emigration organ to fill the void created by the acquisition and re-christening of the paper by Redpath's Bureau. At this time Downing accused the promoters of the Haitian movement of trying "to create in the minds of the colored people the impression that they cannot be anything in this country." Frederick Douglass also joined the anti-emigrationists after his brief flirtation with Haitian emigration. By mid-summer he was denouncing what he now considered to be a perversion of the original humanitarian spirit into "a national movement . . . [with] a national creed. . . ." As a result of this develop-

---

Manuscript Division, Library of Congress; hereafter cited as Redpath Letters and Reports; *The Pine and Palm*, August 3, 1861, p. 4.

17. *Ibid.*, August 3, 1861, p. 4; *Cleveland Leader*, October 1, 1861, p. 2; Redpath to Plésance, Boston, October 13, 1861, Redpath Letters and Reports.

ment, he asserted, the Haitian movement resembled both the African Civilization Society and the American Colonization Society in championing "the old exploded ideas of prejudice and caste...."[18]

These traditional views were augmented by reports from Haiti telling of dissatisfied emigrants, poor conditions, governmental negligence, and the like. At two meetings in Boston in late October a returned emigrant described intolerable conditions in Haiti; those attending the second meeting adopted two anti-emigration resolutions. One advised blacks not to listen to "certain intelligent, but misguided colored men and white men" promoting Haitian emigration; the other opposed all black emigration until the slaves were emancipated. The revived *Weekly Anglo-African* issued its own condemnation in early November. Criticizing a concordat between Geffrard and the Pope which established an archbishopric and four bishoprics in Haiti, the newspaper argued that blacks should not migrate to a nation which had succumbed to white religious influence and thus was in the process of losing control over its own affairs. The concordat, *The Weekly Anglo-African* explained, signified that "the *controlling* religious *influence must be white*, which requires nothing more but *time*, to make the entire *political* influence also *white*, when the liberty of the black race must be at an end...."[19]

In Canada—where Redpath's Bureau had anticipated a large emigration—the opposition was persistent and extensive. Mary Ann Shadd Cary hurled the most abuse. From September, 1861, into the spring of 1862, she vilified Redpath in particular and the Haitian movement in general. Although engaging in highly personal and sometimes arcane denunciations, Cary also developed a rationale for her position: Haitian emigration was simply reviving the discredited ideas of African colonization; emigration agents consistently stifled public disagreement with their views; and Haiti herself had proved to be a death trap for blacks from Canada and the

---

18. Redpath to Plésance, Boston, June 8, 1861, August 11, 1861, Redpath Letters and Reports; William Edward Farrison, *William Wells Brown: Author & Reformer* (Chicago: University of Chicago Press, 1969), p. 337; *Douglass' Monthly*, July, 1861, p. 484.

19. Farrison, *Brown*, pp. 351-352; *The Weekly Anglo-African*, November 2, 1861, p. 2.

United States.[20] Others were also alarmed by the high rate of death and disease decimating the first group of emigrants to the island. A New Haven meeting in January, 1862, condemned the Haitian emigration movement itself, leveling particular blame at James Theodore Holly for his apparent indifference to the sufferings of those dying in Haiti. Everyone associated with Haitian emigration, the gathering proclaimed, would be considered "the real enemies of the colored people in this country...."[21]

Reports of sickness and death, broken dreams and intolerable living conditions were not the fabrications of the anti-emigrationists. By late 1861 it was obvious that conditions in Haiti were far less idyllic than either the emigrants or the emigrant agents had anticipated. Mary O. Monroe, the widow of the African missionary, returned from Haiti with her two sons in the fall of 1861 and reported the death of the Reverend John W. Lewis, the leader of the Lawrence Colony. Another emigrant, Joseph W. Williams, arrived back in the United States to tell of unsanitary water, inadequate shelter, and poor farming conditions; Williams's wife and children had died from exposure and fever, and he himself was suffering from dysentery and rheumatism. Even some emigrants generally pleased with Haiti complained. J. W. Duffin of Geneva, New York, observed, "The Haytien Government however is a slow 'coach' and do not facilitate things fast enough to suit the emigrants and many become dissatisfied and impatient before they get their lands."[22] Not all the emigrants who suffered complained about conditions in their adopted country. Three months after Holly's New Haven Colony arrived in Haiti, Holly's mother and infant

---

20. Cary's letters are in *The Weekly Anglo-African*, September 28, 1861, p. 2; October 19, 1861, p. 2; October 26, 1861, p. 2; November 9, 1861, p. 1; December 28, 1861, p. 2; February 15, 1862, p. 2; April 5, 1862, p. 2. See also Redpath to Auguste Elie, n.p., March 12, 1862, Correspondence of James Redpath, Commercial agent of Hayti for Philadelphia, Joint commissioner plenipotentiary of Hayti to the government of the U.S. & General agent of emigration to Hayti for the U.S. and Canada, December 31, 1861 to May 12, 1862, Schomburg Branch, New York Public Library; hereafter cited as Redpath Correspondence.

21. *The Weekly Anglo-African*, January 25, 1862, p. 2.

22. *Ibid.*, October 5, 1861, p. 3; Boyd, "Redpath and Colonization," p. 178; J. W. Duffin to Gerrit Smith, St. Mark, Hayti, November 15, 1861, Gerrit Smith Papers, Syracuse University.

daughter were dead, as were John P. Anthony, Anthony's parents, and nine other members of the Colony. Although Holly believed the deaths resulted from the doctors' inability to control typhus fever, his religious convictions would not tolerate total despair. As he observed of those who had passed away, "Their very deaths were a triumphant witness in behalf of the noble cause of Haytian emigration." *The Weekly Anglo-African* found this outrageous: "It does seem a queer way to build up 'colored nationalities' by enriching a soil already the richest in the world."[23]

Troubled by reports emanating from Haiti, Redpath immediately disowned Holly's statement and criticized the minister for not following the prescribed regulations in Haiti. However, in November, 1861, he complained to Victorien Plésance, then secretary of state for foreign relations, that the government was neglecting the emigrants and that charges made by those who had returned to the United States were destroying the movement. The following February, Redpath noted to Henry Melrose, the corresponding secretary of the Bureau in New York, that "The indications are that, if the Directors of the Bureau [*sic*] in Hayti give the Emigrants their lands promptly, (which has been the greatest obstacle hitherto & has caused much complaint) there will be a very large influx of intelligent industrious, moral & religious people of your race to Hayti. . . ." At the end of March, confronted by growing hostility to the movement, Redpath guaranteed to at least one party of emigrants free passage back to the United States for any member who decided within two months in Haiti that Redpath has misrepresented conditions in the black republic.[24]

Despite Redpath's actions, descriptions of Haiti brought to the United States by returning emigrants slowly destroyed the emigration movement. In the spring of 1862 E. P. Walker of Ohio, a former ally of Delany, lost forty-five of his colony of sixty because of the statements of an earlier emigrant who had returned to Ohio. Several other colonies—including one which William J. Watkins

23. *The Weekly Anglo-African*, August 31, 1861, p. 2; October 5, 1861, p. 3; *The Pine and Palm*, September 28, 1861, p. 4 (page dated September 21).

24. *The Pine and Palm*, September 28, 1861, p. 4 (page dated September 21); Winks, *Blacks in Canada*, p. 165; Redpath to Henry Melrose, n.p., February 8, 1862; copy of a guarantee, March 25, 1862, Redpath Correspondence. See also Redpath to Elie, n.p., February 13, February 17, 1862, Redpath Correspondence.

had raised, and another called "Bustill's Regiment"—were destroyed by similar developments. As Redpath explained to Auguste Elie, Haiti's director-general of emigration, "Thus, the Spring Emigration has been a total failure in consequence of these things." By summer the Haitian emigration movement was more or less moribund. Sometime in the fall Redpath abandoned the cause entirely.[25]

Of those who had already emigrated to Haiti, evidently most either died, returned to the United States (if they could under the stringent terms the government had established), or were absorbed by the native population. Few of the emigrant colonies remained as identifiable groups. In fact, D. C. Donohue, who visited Haiti in the first few months of 1864, could locate only about 200 of the original immigrants. Edward L. Hartz, also in the country at this time, reported at the end of February that there were at Aux Cayes "about forty or fifty emigrants who had settled there under the guidance of James Redpath about 2 years previously who in consequence of their impoverished and suffering condition were desirous of returning to the U.S." Hartz helped them return.[26]

Yet not all of those who survived the emigration to Haiti in the early 1860's left the country or were absorbed by the native population. James Theodore Holly, if not others, stayed to labor among those he considered ignorant and heathen. Previously Holly had preached that those blacks who emigrated should be prepared to make sacrifices, and he himself fulfilled that expectation. Not only had he lost his mother and infant daughter soon after reaching Haiti, but by the end of 1861 his wife, two additional members of his family, and thirty-eight other members of his New Haven Colony had also perished. In January, 1862, Holly and other survivors of the party finally began clearing their land on Geffrard's estate at Drouillard, three miles from Port-au-Prince; by spring, thirty acres had been cleared and planted with cotton and vegetables. Holly also distributed food to the sick, taught Sunday School, and held

25. Redpath to Elie, n.p., May 3, 1862; Redpath to Elie, Boston, May 21, 1862, Redpath Correspondence; Boyd, "Redpath and Colonization," p. 181.
26. Boyd, "Redpath and Colonization," p. 181; Edward L. Hartz Journal, entry for February 29, 1864, Edward L. Hartz Papers, Manuscript Division, Library of Congress.

weekly services in a building on the estate. Now, after years of preparation, he was ready to regenerate Haitians by introducing the Protestant faith to the country. "I have passed from the misty world of *thought* to the field of ACTION," he observed in late August, 1862, adding in familiar tones: "My fundamental idea is that it is necessary to engraft the staid morality and stern principles of the Anglo-Saxon upon the polished yet unstable element of French civilization, now existing in Hayti, before this Republic can rise to her destined greatness."[27]

Holly's optimism notwithstanding, in the fall of 1862 the Foreign Committee again refused to sponsor his mission. However, the American Church Missionary Society—an Episcopal-based rival to the Protestant Episcopal Church's Foreign Committee—almost immediately assumed responsibility for Holly's Trinity Mission in 1862. In 1864 the Society officially adopted Haiti as a missionary field and gave Holly a regular missionary appointment. Years later Holly became the Episcopal bishop of the independent Orthodox Apostolic Church in Haiti, which depended heavily on the support of the Church in the United States. Long before this, however, he had become convinced that—as he wrote Alexander Crummell in 1864, when the latter was involved in a black separatist Episcopal movement in Liberia—"Black men must hold up one another's hands ... for we have not much to expect from white men."[28]

His Episcopal mission was the only legacy of Holly's emigration activities, for the Haitian movement of the early 1860's had failed to spark a large-scale migration of black Christians to the Caribbean

---

27. Clipping from *American Church Almanac and Yearbook for 1912*, n.p., in Holly files, General Theological Seminary, New York; *The Pine and Palm*, July 3, 1862, pp. 4-6; September 24, 1862, p. 11; *Journal of Connecticut Diocese Convention of Protestant Episcopal Church, 1862*, p. 52.

28. Dean, "Holly, Nationalist and Bishop," pp. 91-92; Julia Emery, *A Century of Endeavor, 1821-1921: A Record of the First Hundred Years of the Domestic and Foreign Missionary Society of the Protestant Episcopal Church in the United States of America* (New York: Department of Missions, 1921), pp. 151-152; Minutes of the Executive Council of the American Church Missionary Society, entries for November 3, 1862, May ?, 1863, November 7, 1864, Church Historical Society, Austin, Texas; Holly to Alexander Crummell, Port-au-Prince, Haiti, April 22, 1864, Alexander Crummell Papers (microfilm), Schomburg Branch, New York Public Library. For Holly's career in Haiti—where he remained until his death in 1911—see Dean, "Holly, Nationalist and Bishop," pp. 89-215.

nation. Whether unable or unwilling, the Haitian government did not provide sufficient land, supplies, and medical care for those emigrants who had descended upon the country. In addition, the outbreak of the American Civil War diverted the attention of blacks in the United States and Canada to other fields. If the supporters of Haitian emigration were despondent, then they were not alone. Dreams were also deferred for those black emigrationists who had turned not to Haiti, but to West Africa.

CHAPTER 8

African Dreams Deferred

Although neither Martin R. Delany nor any other black emigrationist would explore West Africa again during the 1860's, the African emigration movement did not simply disappear once Delany returned to North America and the African Civilization Society's E. P. Rogers died in Liberia. Rather, both Delany and the Civilization Society's Henry Highland Garnet still hoped that British and American philanthropy might underwrite the costs of emigration of American and Canadian blacks to West Africa. Although unsuccessful in their efforts, both men labored throughout 1861 and into early 1862 to fulfill the dreams they had been nurturing for several years. However, developments both in West Africa and in the United States forced them to abandon their plans to establish a colony in Yoruba. Instead, they turned their attention to their enslaved brethren in the American South.

Delany continued to pursue his Yoruba emigration plan after he arrived in Portland, Maine, from England on Christmas, 1860. While there were no demonstrations to greet the black adventurer and entrepreneur when he disembarked from the steamship *Anglo-Saxon*, and Portland's minuscule black community did not show any unusual interest in Delany's brief presence in its city, Delany could still congratulate himself upon his accomplishments. He had concluded a treaty with the Egba of Yoruba which, he believed, would allow him to return to Abeokuta with a quasi-independent colony—the nucleus for the Black Nationality he envisioned as spreading throughout Africa. He had also made important contacts with Englishmen of wealth and humanity and, in the process, had established his independence from the white-dominated African

Civilization Society of New York. England's African Aid Society had already provided him with funds to return to Africa and had promised to assist the settlers Delany brought with him. All this, however, was behind him.[1] Now, as he made his way unheralded from Portland back to Chatham in Canada West, he could contemplate the problems he faced in raising a party to accompany him to Abeokuta.

The Chatham black community was Delany's obvious constituency. He had not lived in Pittsburgh for almost five years, and that city now offered no obvious support for his colonization schemes. Moreover, in New York, where there was considerable emigration sentiment, Garnet and his African Civilization Society were well established. Only in Chatham, his home since he had left Pittsburgh, could Delany expect to find an enthusiastic response to his nationalist-emigrationist plans. His contacts in Chatham were still extensive, and the Reverend William King's Elgin Association in nearby Buxton could serve as a training center to help provide Delany with the black emigrants he desired. Nevertheless, raising a colony in Chatham would be difficult. The problems were rooted mainly in the criteria Delany had established for members of his party, for Delany's desire to bring only economically self-sufficient individuals—"select and intelligent" settlers—was, if laudable, also self-defeating. Few blacks were likely to have the material resources to pay for any significant portion of a trip to Yoruba, and even fewer possessed the experience in cotton cultivation which Delany believed necessary for his industrial colony.[2]

Delany's immediate task upon arriving in Chatham on December 29 was to promote his emigration scheme, while simultaneously mollifying those blacks who were convinced that he favored mass emigration. In mid-January he appeared at Chatham Town Hall with King and the mayor to discuss his plans. After referring briefly

1. *Daily Eastern Argus* (Portland, Maine), December 27, 1860, p. 2; manuscript appeal and enclosures of Lord Alfred Churchill for the African Aid Society, February 25, 1861, Anti-Slavery Papers, Rhodes House Library, Oxford; copy of letter from Churchill to William McCoskry, London, n.d. [but probably between September 1-7, 1861], William King Papers (microfilm), Public Archives of Canada, Ottawa.

2. Delany's description of the ideal emigrants is in the *Chatham Tri-Weekly Planet*, January 21, 1861, p. 3.

to the general lack of knowledge about Africa—an ignorance "formerly heightened by improbable stories in School geographies"—Delany described his trip and the commercial resources of the areas he had traversed. Emphasizing the cotton prospects of West Africa, he warned his fellow British citizens of the consequences should an American crisis curtail England's cotton supply. Speaking particularly to his black listeners, he emphasized his opposition to a general emigration: "A few men of the right stamp are wanted to aid in the cotton supply, and self-government, and the work will go on." Delany reiterated this commitment to a "select" emigration in a public letter to James Theodore Holly and through the pages of *The Weekly Anglo-African*.[3]

During the first few months of 1861 Delany moved well beyond mere rhetoric by convincing several Chatham blacks to emigrate; he then informed the African Aid Society that he would leave Canada for Abeokuta in June. Working along parallel lines, King told the Society that he would send out "experienced, intelligent, practical Christian men" from his Elgin community. Evidently King's settlers were to be members of Delany's party. By late February at least nine Chatham blacks were planning to emigrate under the auspices of the African Aid Society. These included Osborn P. Anderson, the only black man from Chatham with John Brown at Harpers Ferry; Anderson's friend Minerva Caldwell; Isaac D. Shadd and his sister Amelia; J. H. Harris and his wife; and Dr. Amos Aray. Both Shadd and Harris had attended the Chatham convention in August, 1858. Aray, it will be recalled, had briefly considered accompanying Delany to Africa and for a time was listed as a member of the Niger Valley Exploring Party. In addition to the nine already pledged to emigrate, Mary Ann Shadd Cary contemplated at least a temporary residence in Africa, regardless of her feelings toward African emigration at this time. In February, 1861, she wrote the American Missionary Association to inquire about a missionary appointment there. "I would delight," she stated, "to instruct the heathen and preach to them ... to teach them of a

3. *Ibid.*, January 4, 1861, p. 2; January 18, 1861, p. 3; January 21, 1861, p. 3; *The Weekly Anglo-African*, January 26, 1861, p. 2. Delany's remarks have been changed from past to present tense.

more acceptable way than bowing to idols or traffickering [*sic*] in their fellow men...."[4]

Although by April another twenty to thirty Chatham blacks had expressed their desire to leave for Africa, the black community itself was ambivalent in regard to Delany's and King's emigration plans. Even those intending to emigrate acknowledged the sensibilities of those wishing to remain in Chatham. For example, at the close of a lecture by Delany on Africa and the African Aid Society in late March, Cary offered a resolution—seconded by Anderson—which, while lauding Delany personally for his accomplishments in both Africa and England, pointedly avoided endorsing emigration itself. While Delany and King had located potential emigrants, they had not achieved a community consensus supporting their efforts.[5]

In the face of such doubt and hesitation, Delany and King labored through the spring and summer of 1861. Perhaps they were not fully aware of what impact the hostilities then beginning in the United States would have upon their efforts. Delany continued to inform the African Aid Society that he would soon be ready to return to Abeokuta with a party of settlers, and in April he asked Lord Russell, the British Foreign Secretary, for free passage to Africa in June. "The last four years of my life," Delany explained plaintively, "having been spent entirely in this undertaking, may be given to your Lordship as a reason for asking this favor."[6] While waiting for Russell's reply, Delany devoted himself to other concerns—chiefly to completing the report of his exploring venture

---

4. Churchill to King, London, March 9, 1861; two lists of names, dated February 26 and April 27, 1861, written on both sides of the same sheet of paper, King Papers. Also see the February 27, 1861, entry in the manuscript diary of John Brown, Jr., January 1–July 29, 1861, John Brown, Jr., Papers, Ohio Historical Society. For Cary's query, see her letter to George Whipple, Chatham, February 26, 1861, "Canada File," American Missionary Association Papers, Amistad Research Center and Race Relations Department, Dillard University. As was indicated in Chapter 7, Cary in the fall of 1861 was denouncing African colonization as part of her campaign against the Haitian emigration movement.

5. See note 4; *Chatham Tri-Weekly Planet*, March 29, 1861, p. 3.

6. F. Fitzgerald, Secretary of the African Aid Society, to Thomas Hodgkin, London, August 21, 1861, Thomas Hodgkin Papers, microfilm in possession of Dr. Edward Kass, Channing Laboratory, Boston; Delany to Lord John Russell, Chatham, C.W., April 2, 1861, FO 84/1159, Public Records Office, London.

and preparing it for publication. Yet as he worked in Chatham, efforts were already underway to prevent any colony of North American blacks from gaining a foothold at Abeokuta.

Since Delany and Campbell signed their treaty with the Alake of Abeokuta and his chiefs in December, 1859, the uneasy balance of power in the Egba city made conflict over the document almost inevitable. By early 1861 there were those who were attempting to repudiate the entire agreement. Henry Townsend, who, as indicated above, had been suspicious of Delany's and Campbell's activities from the very beginning, was the major force working to undermine the treaty. When Townsend learned of the treaty with the Alake, he feared that it signified threats to his authority from both the Crowthers and the black settlers who would arrive in the Abeokuta area. By early February, 1861, Townsend had convinced the Alake and the chiefs to issue a statement denying that they had ever signed a treaty with Delany and Campbell. In fact, the Alake insisted that he had simply assigned the two explorers land for farming.[7]

Even after the uproar in Abeokuta over the treaty resulted in the expulsion of Samuel Crowther, Jr., Townsend did not rest. In the spring he used his bilingual newspaper, *Iwe Irohin*—reorganized with Campbell's help when the former apprentice printer was in Abeokuta in 1859 and 1860—to attack the proposed Afro-American immigration.[8] Townsend first claimed that Delany and Campbell had operated through stealth: "this treaty ... is made

---

7. J. F. Ade Ajayi and Robert Smith, *Yoruba Warfare in the Nineteenth Century* (Cambridge: Cambridge University Press, 1964), pp. 101, 103; J. F. Ade Ajayi, *Christian Missions in Nigeria, 1841–1891: The Making of a New Elite* (London: Longmans, Green, 1965), p. 192; Slave Trade Correspondence (Consular), *Parliamentary Papers*, LXI (1862), 4–5.

8. Ajayi, *Christian Missions*, p. 192; Fred I. A. Omu, "The Anglo-African, 1863–65," *Nigeria Magazine*, no. 90 (September, 1966), 208. Townsend considered his newspaper a potential weapon against Delany and Campbell long before he attacked the treaty in the *Iwe Irohin*. As he wrote Henry Venn while Delany and Campbell were still in Africa: "In connection with the Printing Press I must bring to your notice the need of using it to influence the public mind. This is the more necessary as ere long we shall have another class of men to deal with. Free Blacks from America full of bitterness against all white men." Townsend to Venn, Abeokuta, February 5, 1860, Church Missionary Society Papers, CA 2/085A, microfilm of original papers at the Church Missionary Society Archives, London, available at the University of Wisconsin Library; hereafter cited as CMS Papers.

in secret, no one knows of it, the Alake has no copy of it and denies all knowledge of it, and his statement is confirmed by the Ogboni Chiefs who by laws are the great rulers of the country with the King." Moreover, the provision allowing the immigrants to settle on unoccupied land violated Egba land law. "[T]here is no land," Townsend explained, "without an owner to it in the whole country." But the Anglican missionary saw other reasons for objecting to the proposed colony. With the Liberian experience obviously on his mind, he complained that Afro-Americans would disrupt the local community by introducing Western racial prejudice to Abeokuta: "The introduction of a large number of free blacks filled with certain notions of freedom, republicanism, and contempt for their uncivilized fellowmen ... cannot but be attended with the greatest danger to the native governments and people." He added that black emigrants should settle in Liberia, which was, in a sense, already their country.[9]

Both Townsend's charges and the Alake's denial of having signed the treaty were quickly answered—although not by Delany and Campbell, neither of whom at this time could have known of the developments at Abeokuta. Rather, the Reverend Crowther immediately wrote to Henry Venn in England, saying that while Delany and Campbell had agreed with his suggestion not to settle in a separate colony, still "the Alake and his seven leading war chiefs did sign the treaty and perfectly knew what they were about...." Crowther pointed directly to Townsend as the culprit in stirring up the Alake, and he also sharply denounced the European missionary for portraying himself and his son as "false witnesses to what was never done, or done ignorantly."[10]

Despite Crowther's statement, Henry Grant Foote, the consul at Lagos, was generally sympathetic to Townsend. The consul's report to England implicitly supported their position that no treaty had been signed. The African Aid Society now felt it obligatory to substantiate the treaty's validity. Fortunately for the Society's pur-

---

9. *Iwe Irohin*, March 25, April 5, 1861. See also Rev. Samuel Crowther to Venn, Abeokuta, April 6, 1861, CMS Papers, CA 3/04A; Fred I. A. Omu, "The 'Iwe Irohin', 1859-1867," *Journal of the Historical Society of Nigeria*, IV (December, 1967), 41-42.

10. Crowther to Venn, Abeokuta, April 6, 1861, CMS Papers, CA 3/04A.

poses, Samuel Crowther, Jr., had come to London after his expulsion from Abeokuta. Apparently at the behest of the African Aid Society, he wrote a lengthy defense of the legitimacy of the treaty and asserted that Delany and Campbell had agreed to settle in common with the Egba. Crowther later charged that Townsend had engineered the Alake's repudiation of the treaty.[11]

With Crowther no longer at Abeokuta, Townsend reigned supreme among the Egba. But his triumph proved to be short lived, for his attack on the Crowther family aroused many of the Sierra Leonian merchant class to outright opposition, and eventually the Church Missionary Society recalled Townsend to England to review his policies. Still, he had succeeded in calling into question the validity of the Delany-Campbell treaty. As a consequence, the British Foreign Office, which had decided in late April not to assist Delany or other New World blacks until they reached Africa, began to reconsider whether the government should co-operate in any way with the African Aid Society's efforts to establish a Yoruba colony. The Foreign Office was still undecided when Foote died at Lagos in May. His successor, William McCoskry, was a trader whose long-standing antagonisms toward the Egba motivated him to support the Crowthers and the treaty. "The meaning of each clause of the Treaty," McCoskry stated, "was explained to the Alake and Chiefs by the Rev. S. Crowther before they signed... [and] there was no secresy [sic] in the matter; and... it was not until a powerful opposition influence had been brought to bear upon the Alake and the Chiefs that the Treaty was denied."[12]

If McCoskry's defense of the treaty helped further confuse the British Foreign Office, it also provided some backing for the efforts of Lord Churchill and the African Aid Society. Both King and Delany had already sent lists of emigrants to the Society, and plans were moving ahead in Canada West for a party to be sent out in the near future. Churchill forwarded the names of prospective Canadian emigrants to the Foreign Office, which, in turn, passed the lists

---

11. Slave Trade Correspondence (Consular), *Parliamentary Papers*, LXI (1862), 6–9.

12. Ajayi, *Christian Missions*, p. 193; Ajayi and Smith, *Yoruba Warfare*, pp. 101, 103, 105; Cyril Edgar Griffith, "Martin R. Delany and the African Dream, 1812–1885" (Ph.D. dissertation, Michigan State University, 1973), p. 132; Slave Trade Correspondence (Consular), *Parliamentary Papers*, LXI (1862), 12.

along to McCoskry at Lagos. Although the Foreign Office asked the consul "to afford these emigrants the benefit of your advice and assistance in the event of their proceeding to Lagos," Lord Russell hoped no sizable party of settlers would travel there. As his aid explained to Churchill, Russell believed "it would be unwise to attempt to procure for the American emigrants territorial rights or privileges which might hereafter lead to disputes, and rouse the jealousy of the Chiefs and people of Abbeokuta...." Russell further maintained that "before any considerable number of emigrant negroes are sent to Lagos, precise information should be procured as to the terms on which such emigrants will be received in Abbeokuta."[13]

Although the Foreign Office was obviously equivocating, the African Aid Society decided to continue with its plans, apparently believing that, regardless of the government's position, McCoskry would cooperate with any group of black colonists arriving in Lagos. It was early September when Churchill informed the consul that the Society would advance money only to those settlers who could provide their passage to Lagos (which Delany, ironically, could not do), and that McCoskry should loan each settler a small sum primarily to pay for the costs of landing at Lagos and proceeding to Abeokuta. Any excess sums could be used by the emigrants to help them upon their arrival at Abeokuta. Soon after Churchill sent McCoskry instructions, the African Aid Society's secretary, Ferdinand Fitzgerald, informed King of the organization's procedures and assured the Canadian minister that McCoskry would provide assistance and protection at Lagos.[14]

Throughout this maneuvering in London, Lagos, and Abeokuta, little was heard from Canada—other than assurances that Delany would lead a party to Abeokuta. As of August, however, only two or three families were willing to accompany Delany, who was obviously finding it difficult to locate pioneers for his industrial colo-

13. Slave Trade Correspondence (Consular), *Parliamentary Papers*, LXI (1862), 13–14. Copies of the Foreign Office's letter to Churchill and of McCoskry's (see preceding paragraph) were forwarded to King by the African Aid Society. Fitzgerald to King, London, August 8, 1861, King Papers.

14. Copy of a letter from Churchill to McCoskry, London, n.d. [but probably between September 1–7, 1861]; Fitzgerald to King, London, September 7, 1861, King Papers.

ny.[15] His lack of success is not surprising. With the onset of the Civil War in the United States, Canadian blacks must have thought it more profitable to consider the plight of their brethren still enslaved in the southern states than to contemplate uplifting backward heathens in a strange land across the Atlantic. And by then the repudiation of the treaty by the Alake of Abeokuta, along with Townsend's opposition, must have discouraged would-be emigrants by raising the possibility of a hostile reception at Abeokuta. Moreover, the Ijaye War was continuing in the interior, and few Canadian blacks could have welcomed the thought of entering war-torn Yoruba. Finally, the blacks' lack of personal resources must have loomed as an insurmountable obstacle, for the African Aid Society was willing to advance only meagre amounts of money. Delany's emphasis on self-reliance had ultimately become meaningless, because it was impossible for most North American blacks to raise enough money to carry them to Lagos. Only a relatively wealthy man such as Jonathan J. Myers or an individual with white religious affiliations could obtain the resources for a trans-Atlantic trip. In fact, even Henry Highland Garnet's white-backed African Civilization Society was struggling.

In the spring of 1861 the Civilization Society had many more prospective emigrants than their financial resources could support. In March, Garnet claimed that more than a hundred blacks were willing to carry on the late E. P. Rogers's mission to establish a settlement in Yoruba. Garnet himself would lead the party, which the African Aid Society's Lord Churchill described as including "all skillful, carefully selected Christian men and women, cotton and sugar cane growers, and mechanics." Yet aware that Churchill's rhetoric would not carry his party across the Atlantic, Garnet began to search for financial assistance. At a March meeting on behalf of the Society, a resolution was passed recommending "the raising of at least ten thousand dollars, for the purpose of sending out the proposed company. . . ." Garnet, Corresponding Secretary A. A. Constantine, and Delany's exploring companion Robert Campbell all appeared at another fund-raising meeting a few weeks later in Brooklyn. Besides disavowing a general emigration, Garnet announced that he was ready to lead a company of twenty-five al-

15. Fitzgerald to Hodgkin, London, August 21, 1861, Hodgkin Papers.

ready selected emigrants, and that $10,000 would be necessary to transport the settlers and begin the colony.[16]

Despite the magnitude of Garnet's projection, the white leaders of the Civilization Society insisted that the Yoruba party should be supported by American and not British donors. At the Society's anniversary meeting in May, the Reverend Joseph P. Thompson forewarned his listeners of the British threat and assured them that "the Anglo-Africans who go from America, though offered British aid and British protection, prefer to keep up the name and associations of their native land, though she has turned them out of doors, and trampled them as children of the bond-woman." American philanthropy would preserve the integrity of the colony—or so Thompson argued. Of course, Thompson was proclaiming a patriotism that many of the emigrants did not share—especially Garnet, who only six weeks earlier had admitted that he loved the United States only as much as the Gospel required and no more. At the end of August, Garnet renounced the anglophobia stressed by the white leaders of the Civilization Society and sailed for England and another attempt to tap the pockets of British philanthropy.[17]

Convinced of the impossibility of obtaining funds in the United States for a Yoruba colony, Garnet devoted almost three months in England to the advocacy of his cause. In mid-October he appeared at a meeting of the African Aid Society in Birmingham, with Lord Churchill and Robert Campbell—then en route to Africa—on the platform. Garnet introduced a resolution supporting the emigration

16. *Chatham Tri-Weekly Planet*, April 8, 1861, p. 2; *The Weekly Anglo-African*, March 23, 1861, p. 3; April 13, 1861, p. 2; *Constitution of the African Civilization Society together with the Testimony of Forty Distinguished Citizens of New York and Brooklyn to the Importance of the Objects Contemplated by Its Friends* . . . (New Haven: T. J. Stafford, 1861), pp. 7-8. At the African Civilization Society's March meeting, the resolution adopted also provided that all money raised would be held by the organization's treasurer, Robert Lindley Murray, to be expended with the consent of an advisory committee consisting of several leading white ministers, including Henry Ward Beecher and Stephen H. Tyng, and Isaac T. Smith, the banker active in the New York Colonization Society.

17. *Constitution of the African Civilization Society*, p. 37; *The Weekly Anglo-African*, April 13, 1861, p. 2; September 7, 1861, p. 3. The Civilization Society did not even come close to the goal of $10,000; in the fall of 1861 an observer reported the Society's yearly receipts as $862.44. Willis Boyd, "Negro Colonization in the National Crisis, 1860–1870" (Ph.D. dissertation, University of California at Los Angeles, 1954), p. 211.

of blacks from Canada (not the United States) to Africa to advance Christianity and civilization; he also praised England's recent acquisition of Lagos. In seconding the black clergyman's resolution, Campbell said that he had just shipped from London to Africa 250 pounds of cotton machinery for use at Abeokuta to process cotton before shipment to England. Garnet spoke to at least one other African Aid Society meeting (with William Howard Day beside him) before leaving England for the United States in late December.[18] Evidently his mission had accomplished little.

By the time Garnet returned to New York, Delany had made his peace with the African Civilization Society. His motives for merging with the organization are obscure; probably the disadvantages of remaining a man with a reputation but without followers prompted him to seek an alliance with the New York organization. In early November, after moving to New York, he attended a special conference designed "to effect and complete a oneness and harmony of sentiment and action, that their white friends, as aiders and assistants, may have a true and definite point as a datum before them." A committee which included Delany, Robert Hamilton of *The Weekly Anglo-African*, and several others was appointed "to draw up a basis as a fundamental principle by which the African Civilization Society shall be governed, and its objects and designs defined." Three days later, the merger was completed at another meeting of the Society at which Delany presented a supplement to the African Civilization Society's Constitution. The supplement consisted of three articles, two of which embodied Delany's major concerns. First, the Society disavowed mass emigration and stated that it "will aid only such persons as may be practically qualified and suited to promote the development of Christianity, morality, education, mechanical arts, agriculture, commerce, and general improvement...." Second, the Society announced that its advocacy of emigration rested upon a belief in "Self Reliance and Self Government [and] ... the principle of an African Nationality, the African race being the ruling element of the nation, controlling and directing their own affairs."[19]

18. *The Weekly Anglo-African*, November 16, 1861, p. 4; *Anti-Slavery Reporter*, n.s. X (January 1, 1862), 1.
19. *Constitution of the African Civilization Society*, pp. 3–5.

In actuality, the Civilization Society had altered few of its basic objectives. Admittedly, Delany's supplementary articles placed his personal stamp upon the Society, for he was much more interested in the development of an African Nationality than in the Christian regeneration of Africa. In addition, his emphasis upon self-reliance undoubtedly represented an attempt to purge the organization of white influence. Nevertheless, until at least 1864 the Civilization Society retained the Philadelphia merchant Benjamin Coates and several other whites as vice-presidents, and a substantial number of whites were listed as references, should potential donors have doubts about the integrity of the organization.[20] Moreover, in rejecting general emigration, the Civilization Society was simply reiterating a previous position.

Whatever advantages each side gained from the merger, Delany and the missionary-nationalists of the African Civilization Society continued to advocate African emigration to a black community increasingly concerned with issues developing from the war with the Confederacy. Delany maintained he would soon return to Africa, and in January, 1862, he explicitly denied that he had abandoned the African movement. Not only was he still planning to emigrate, but "all those who originally intended to go to Africa, are making vigorous preparations for the consummation of our designs...." Two months later, in speaking on "The Commercial Advantages of Africa" to a largely white audience in Providence, Rhode Island, he again said he and his family would soon move to Africa to cultivate cotton on a 700-acre farm which he had already selected. Even as late as March of the following year he appeared in Chicago in an African chief's wedding dress for two lectures on Africa. Of course, Delany was not the only member of the African Civilization Society to continue his efforts on behalf of African emigration. In the fall of 1863 Garnet and several other black members of the Society asked James Mitchell, the federal government's com-

20. *An Appeal in Behalf of the Education of the Freedmen and their Children* ([New York?]: n.p., [1864?]), p. 4. Sterling Stuckey, in *The Ideological Origins of Black Nationalism* (Boston: Beacon Press, 1972), p. 23, claims that in joining the Civilization Society, Delany "proceeded to lead a movement to purge that organization of its white officers...." However, the *Constitution of the African Civilization Society*, which included the supplementary articles, was published in late 1861, and the list of officers on p. 6 included a significant number of whites.

missioner of emigration, for $5,000 to carry out the Civilization Society's objectives, but the government was unwilling or unable to comply with this request.[21]

As the war progressed, emigration became less important. To some extent, the nationalist-emigrationists turned to such collective racial efforts within the United States as conventions to determine, in Delany's words, "a general policy" on major political and social issues. Delany and Garnet also devoted their energies to the plight of the southern slave during the conflict. Before a New York war rally, Delany argued that "if Great Britain or other power undertakes to raise the blockade to assist the South, at the expense of the liberty of the blacks, then let our war be 'insurrection' and let the government not interfere." Emancipation was also Garnet's concern. Speaking in May, 1862, alongside his former arch-enemies James McCune Smith and George T. Downing, the Presbyterian minister maintained that the most important goal for blacks was the abolition of slavery. With the Lincoln administration proposing colonization in Central America, Garnet announced that "all the negro asks is freedom, and then we will go to Hayti, Africa, or Central America, without the aid of the Government." Totally committed to victory for the Union and to the emancipation of all southern slaves, both Delany and Garnet were recruiting black soldiers for the Army by 1864, if not before.[22]

As both Delany and Garnet devoted themselves to military recruiting and to the larger issues engendered by the war itself, the

21. *The Weekly Anglo-African*, January 25, 1862, p. 2; *The Pine and Palm*, April 3, 1862, p. 3; *Chicago Daily Tribune*, March 20, 1863, p. 3; African Civilization Society to James Mitchell, New York, September 12, 1863, Documents Relating to the Suppression of the Slave Trade (microfilm, reel 8), National Archives.

22. *The Weekly Anglo-African*, January 11, 1862, p. 2 (page incorrectly dated January 4); January 25, 1862, p. 2; *The Pine and Palm*, May 22, 1862, p. 2. Delany's and Garnet's speeches have been changed from past to present tense. Garnet was active at the black National Convention of 1864 at Syracuse; see Howard H. Bell, "Negro Emancipation in Historical Retrospect: The Nation—The Condition and Prospects of the Negro as Reflected in the National Convention of 1864," *Journal of Human Relations*, XI (Winter, 1963), 221–231. On Garnet's military recruiting, see Richard K. MacMaster, "Henry Highland Garnet and the African Civilization Society," *Journal of Presbyterian History*, XLVIII (Summer, 1970), 111. On Delany's activities in this regard, see *Chicago Daily Tribune*, March 20, 1863, p. 3; April 15, 1863, p. 4. Also see Dudley Taylor Cornish, *The Sable Arm: Negro Troops in the Union Army, 1861–1865* (New York: Longmans, Green, 1956), pp. 105–111.

African Civilization Society as a whole followed suit by shifting the focus of its concern from Africa to the South. At the Society's fourth anniversary meeting in New York in May, 1863, the Reverend George W. Levere spoke to this point: "We have, indeed, been hindered from planting our standard on African soil, but happily our constitution is universal in its language and spirit; therefore, when the African door was shut, we turned our attention toward the Contrabands or Freedom of the South." Shortly thereafter the Reverend Ennals J. Adams, a black Congregational minister active in the Civilization Society but at the time a missionary in Africa for the American Missionary Association, also saw a new missionary field opening up. "[W]hen I read some of your reports of visits to the 'contrabands' in Virginia," Adams wrote from Good Hope station on Sherbro Island, Sierra Leone, "and consider what a great work is to be done in America, the result of the war, my heart bounds back across the broad, deep, blue ocean to my native land, and mingles with my oppressed brethren." From 1863 through at least 1867 the Civilization Society established schools for freedmen in Washington, D.C., and elsewhere; fittingly, E. P. Rogers's widow taught at one of the Society's schools.[23] Clearly, then, many of those who had combined nationalism and emigrationism into a coherent ideology were having second thoughts as war raged in both Yoruba and the United States, and as the anticipated emancipation of the southern slave gave rise to new hopes and new dreams.

23. *The Anglo-African* (formerly *The Weekly Anglo-African*), January 3, 1863, p. 4; May 30, 1863, p. 4; February 13, 1864, p. 2; February 20, 1864, p. 3; September 3, 1864, p. 3; *The American Missionary*, VIII (February, 1864), 26. For information on the later activities of the African Civilization Society, see *The Anglo-African* for 1864–65; the *Annual Reports* of the Society, 1866–68; *The People's Journal* (Brooklyn, N.Y.), [1867–68].

Epilogue

The almost simultaneous demise of both Yoruban and Haitian emigration movements marked the end of organized antebellum black emigration and colonization. With the Lincoln administration's decision to recruit black soldiers in late 1862, some of the nationalist-emigrationists of the 1850's and early 1860's immediately joined the Union cause. H. Ford Douglass became one of the earliest blacks to join the Army when he enlisted in the 95th Illinois Regiment shortly after the war broke out; later he was commissioned a captain of the Independent Colored Kansas Battery and in November, 1865, he died in Leavenworth, Kansas. As will be recalled, both Delany and Garnet recruited black soldiers for the army; so did Mary Ann Shadd Cary, who raised a black regiment after receiving a commission from the governor of Indiana. Delany committed himself to a more active role on February 26, 1865, when he was commissioned the first black major in the United States Army. Garnet, for his part, moved to Washington, D.C., in 1864; there he served as minister of the Fifteenth Street Presbyterian Church, participated in various efforts to aid the freedmen and, in February, 1865, became the first black to preach in the House of Representatives. Although he eventually returned to his pulpit in New York City, Africa could not have been far from his mind. In 1881 he became the minister resident to Liberia, where he died soon after his arrival.[1]

1. On Douglass, see *South Carolina Leader*, December 16, 1865, pp. 1-2; *Report of the Adjutant General of ... Kansas, 1861–1865; The Daily Times* (Leavenworth, Kansas), November 12, 1865. For Shadd, see Elsie M. Lewis, "Mary Ann Shadd Cary," in Edward T. James, ed., *Notable American Women, 1607–1950: A Bio-*

Epilogue

Other ante-bellum advocates of emigration demonstrated that their earlier commitment had left an indelible imprint. For example, Martin H. Freeman, the Pittsburgh schoolteacher, found the cause of Africa more compelling than that of civil strife; in 1863 he migrated to Liberia, where he served the College of Liberia as a teacher and later as president. In 1889 Freeman died in Monrovia. Robert Campbell also settled in Africa. He arrived in Lagos in 1862 and the following year established a newspaper, *The Anglo-African*, which won the plaudits of Campbell's old antagonist, the missionary Henry Townsend. Another of Delany's allies, the Buffalo poet James M. Whitfield, may never have left the United States. After virtually disappearing from public view at the end of the 1850's, Whitfield surfaced in California in 1862 as one of the almost 240 blacks who petitioned Congress for financial assistance "to promote the emigration of free colored resident natives of the United States to Africa or the tropical regions of America...." Whitfield remained in the West, however, writing poetry and working as a barber in California, Oregon, Idaho, and Nevada before his death in San Francisco in 1871.[2]

Of the leading nationalist-emigrationists of the late ante-bellum period, Delany and James Theodore Holly were the most vocal champions of emigration and black solidarity in the years after the Civil War, undoubtedly influencing late nineteenth-century and

---

graphical Dictionary (Cambridge: Belknap Press of Harvard University Press, 1971), I, 301. Delany's military appointment is told in Frank A. Rollin, pseud. [Frances E. Rollin Whipper], *Life and Public Services of Martin R. Delany*... (Boston: Lee and Shepard, 1868), pp. 162–174; see also *The Anglo-African*, March 4, 1865, p. 2. Garnet's later years are summarized in Earl Ofari, *"Let Your Motto Be Resistance": The Life and Thought of Henry Highland Garnet* (Boston: Beacon Press, 1972), pp. 114–123.

2. For Freeman, see Middlebury College, *General Catalogue: Sesquicentennial Edition* (Middlebury, Vt.: Middlebury College, 1950), p. 130. Campbell's editorial career is treated in Fred I. A. Omu, "The Anglo-African, 1863–65," *Nigeria Magazine*, no. 90 (September, 1966), 208–212; *Iwe Irohin*, June 22, 1863. On Whitfield, see "Colonization of Free Blacks; Memorial of Leonard Dugged, George A. Baily, and 240 Other Free Colored Persons of California...," in *House of Representatives Miscellaneous Documents No. 31, 37th Cong., 2d Sess.* (Washington: Government Printing Office, 1862); Joan R. Sherman, "James Monroe Whitfield, Poet and Emigrationist: A Voice of Protest and Despair," *Journal of Negro History*, LVII (April, 1972), 175–176; Joan R. Sherman to the author, New Brunswick, N.J., July 18, 1973.

twentieth-century black emigration and Pan-African movements. True to form, Delany maintained his interest in Africa until his death in 1885. Although a sub-assistant commissioner in the Freedmen's Bureau in South Carolina until August, 1868, he had already become convinced that the future was bleak for southern freedmen. In January, 1868, he urged blacks to join the American Colonization Society's *Golconda* expedition to Liberia; the next year he unsuccessfully sought an appointment as the American minister resident to Liberia. In the late 1870's, after a turbulent political career in South Carolina during Reconstruction and then brief service as a Charleston trial justice, Delany participated in the ill-fated attempt of the Liberian Exodus Joint Stock Steamship Company to carry large numbers of disenchanted South Carolina and Georgia blacks to Liberia. Along with Henry M. Turner, later a bishop of the African Methodist Church and the leading black emigrationist of the late nineteenth and early twentieth centuries, Delany spoke at the March, 1878, dedication of the *Azor*, the Liberian Exodus company's recently purchased ship whose maiden voyage to Africa that spring was a disaster for both the emigrants and their sponsors. While Delany did not accompany the *Azor* across the Atlantic, he never abandoned his desire to return to Africa. In 1880 he wrote to William Coppinger of the Colonization Society that Africa was still "the field of my destined labor," and a year later he again tried to secure a position as minister to Liberia. But despite the Society's support, the government by-passed Delany to select Garnet.[3]

To an even greater degree than Delany, Holly, who resided in

---

3. "Two Thousand Freedmen"—an appeal of the American Colonization Society —enclosed in William Coppinger to John Hodgkin, February 25, 1868, Thomas Hodgkin Papers, microfilm in the possession of Dr. Edward Kass, Channing Laboratory, Boston; Delany's application to President Grant, Washington, D.C., October 18, 1869, and the three accompanying petitions of recommendation, Record Group 59, National Archives, Washington, D.C.; George Brown Tindall, *South Carolina Negroes, 1877–1900* (Columbia: University of South Carolina Press, 1952), pp. 153–168; *Charleston News and Courier*, April 5, 1878, pp. 1, 4; M. R. Delany to Coppinger, Charleston, S.C., August 18, 1880, Domestic Letters; and Coppinger to Delany, Washington, D.C., March 23, 1882; Coppinger to John H. B. Latrobe, Washington, D.C., March 23, 1882, Letterbooks, American Colonization Society Papers, Manuscript Division, Library of Congress. On Turner, see Edwin S. Redkey, *Black Exodus: Black Nationalist and Back-to-Africa Movements, 1890–1910* (New Haven: Yale University Press, 1969).

Haiti until his death in 1911, can be considered a bridge between the ante-bellum nationalist-emigrationist movement and later black nationalist developments. In 1899 he was invited to the London organizing conference of what a year later became the Pan-African Association—an ephemeral yet historically seminal organization which the Trinidad-born, London-based lawyer Sylvester Williams had inspired partly as a reaction to the intensification of British imperialism in Africa. At the 1900 meeting in London, the young W. E. B. Du Bois emerged as an articulate spokesman of this new Pan-Africanism when he wrote his widely known appeal, "To the Nations of the World." Although unable to attend the 1899 preliminary gathering, Holly was, like Du Bois, appointed a regional representative of the Pan-African Association in 1900. This revived his interest in emigration, and that same year—now almost a half-century after he had first championed emigration and pan-black unity—he called for the U.S. government to purchase European-held islands in the Caribbean as a precursor to Afro-American emigration to the area and the establishment of a black-governed West Indies Confederacy.[4]

Like turn-of-the-century Pan-Africanism, ante-bellum black emigration most frequently involved minuscule organizations of committed leaders who rarely acquired what even resembled a mass following. It thus differed markedly from such emigration and nationalist movements as those of Bishop Turner in the 1890's and early 1900's or Marcus Garvey later in the twentieth century. Although neither Turner nor Garvey was able to induce large numbers of blacks to return to Africa, both men consciously and effectively directed their rhetoric toward those blacks on the bottom levels of the social and economic order. For Turner, these were the poor black sharecroppers and itinerant laborers submerged in a South which was hardening its class and caste lines as the slight gains of Reconstruction withered away. Garvey, on the other hand, drew to his United Negro Improvement Association large numbers of lower-class blacks flocking into the increasingly crowded and rigidly

4. David McEwen Dean, "James Theodore Holly, 1829–1911, Black Nationalist and Bishop" (Ph.D. dissertation, University of Texas, 1972), pp. 136, 202–205; Imanuel Geiss, "Notes on the Development of Pan-Africanism," *Journal of the Historical Society of Nigeria*, III (June, 1967), 725–726.

separated black ghettoes of the northern cities during and after World War I. The ante-bellum black emigrationists, however, failed to reach working-class blacks in either the urban centers or the rural countryside of the North. In the end, probably less than ten thousand free blacks found the inducements of the Haitian government attractive during the two waves of emigration to the black Caribbean nation, and fewer still heeded black emigrationist exhortations to migrate elsewhere.

Several factors contributed to the ante-bellum black emigrationists' inability to attract a larger following to their cause. For one thing, only a few Afro-Americans possessed the material resources necessary to emigrate, let alone succeed in another country. Second —as those who have downplayed the importance of ante-bellum emigration have argued—large numbers of blacks simply regarded themselves as more American than African. To many of these individuals, the United States possessed material advantages which far overshadowed the nation's harsh and oppressive treatment of its black inhabitants. Africa—or Haiti, for that matter—promised little but unrelenting toil and perhaps illness or death. Africa, too, for some of these people, was the physical presence of a degraded and barbarian past they wished to extirpate through neglect. Although other Afro-Americans were less critical of Africa and other locales in which blacks congregated, they believed that large-scale free black emigration from North America was, in effect, an abandoning of their brethren still enslaved as well a symbolic endorsement of white colonizationists who viewed deportation as a means of ridding the nation of people they considered inherently inferior.

Part of the explanation for the small number of free blacks who left North America—small even when one includes those blacks carried to Liberia under the auspices of the American Colonization Society—also rests with the sentiments of the black emigrationists themselves. As implied earlier, the emigrationists were unable to reach beyond the thin layer of middle-class blacks in the professions, small businesses, and skilled trades. In this respect they hardly differed from their opponents, for during the ante-bellum period few black laborers and domestic workers publicly embraced *any* political or social position. Many of the emigrationists, by renouncing general or mass emigration in favor of a more limited, "select" movement, actively excluded the participation of all but the educated, skilled, and propertied. In part, these emigrationists were attempting to answer those opponents who claimed that large-scale free black emigration would help preserve the institution of slavery in the southern states. Essentially, however, this rejection of mass emigration was integrally related to the moral reform and self-help ideology which permeated the thinking of most emigrationists.

Although the adoption of moral reform and self-help rhetoric certainly did not distinguish the emigrationists from other black activists of the ante-bellum period, in the context of emigrationism, the emphasis upon moral reform insured that the call for a limited emigration would indeed be heeded. Moral reformers in general held that blacks failing to achieve material success and respectability should be held personally accountable for their social and economic situation, but the exhortations of Delany, Lewis Woodson, and some of the other emigrationists contained especially harsh notes of paternalism and rebuke which could only have offended whatever black workers they may have reached. In addition, the writings of Cuffe, Holly, and other missionary-emigrationists were imbued with a sense of Christian righteousness which showed disdain for those whose lack of external accomplishments mirrored, so these emigrationists believed, an impure inner life. Finally, moral reform ideology sharply contradicted the basic assumptions of emigrationism, since self-help implied that moral conversion would inevitably enable blacks to overcome the larger social and economic problems they confronted. Of course, if this were the case, emigration from North America would be unnecessary.

However, despite the small number of free blacks who left the United States and Canada during the seventy-five years between the Constitutional Convention of 1787 and the unveiling of the Emancipation Proclamation, emigration was a strikingly resilient and pervasive element in the social and intellectual history of ante-bellum free blacks. From Prince Hall in the 1780's to Frederick Douglass immediately prior to the Civil War, almost all the major black leaders at least for a time in their lives adopted the position that emigration was a viable solution to the plight of free blacks in the United States and Canada and, furthermore, that emigration could expedite the abolition of slavery. Since the pioneering work of Howard H. Bell, it has generally been accepted that many black leaders in the late 1850's and early 1860's embraced emigrationism, but what is less well known is that individuals such as Richard Allen, James Forten, and Samuel Cornish—all repeatedly singled out by historians for the potency of their opposition to emigration—were at particular times active proponents of emigration. Whatever the attractions of American citizenship to blacks in the decades following the Civil War, the pervasiveness and persistence of emigration as an element in black thought during the ante-bellum period, when many blacks were enslaved, when few could vote or hold office and when citizenship had not yet been conferred, suggests the depth of alienation experienced by a sizeable number of articulate and prestigious black spokesmen in the United States and Canada.

A further indication of the depth of this alienation is the fact that at one time or another, almost all black leaders regardless of the nature of their reaction to emigration were compelled to acknowledge what both Delany and Douglass independently announced in the 1850's—that blacks in the United States were "a nation within a nation."[5] From the earliest efforts of the African Union Society of Newport throughout the entire ante-bellum period, Afro-American leaders called for blacks to admit that, because of their isolation from the political liberties and economic abundance enjoyed by other Americans, they should join together to protect themselves from the intrusions of outsiders as well as to promote their own clearly identifiable interests. Both emigrationists and anti-emigrationists urged blacks to run their own churches, newspapers, and protests, and both groups increasingly recognized that even white abolitionists and philanthropists were uncertain allies. Only a few extremely optimistic blacks during this period insisted that the color line in American life should not be acknowledged and that

5. Delany's statement is in Martin Robison Delany, *The Condition, Elevation, Emigration, and Destiny of the Colored People of the United States, Politically Considered* (Philadelphia: By the Author, 1852), p. 209. Douglass's comment—that blacks were "becoming a nation, in the midst of a nation which disowns them"—can be found in the *Thirteenth Annual Report of the American and Foreign Anti-Slavery Society, Presented at New York, May 11, 1853* (New York: John A. Gray, Printer, 1853), p. 184.

Epilogue

independent racial organizations could only create hitherto non-existent divisions and barriers.

Pointing to the common "nationalist" tendency within the thinking of both emigrationists and anti-emigrationists is not to suggest that either ideological proclivity fathered the other, for the drive toward separate institutions which recognized that blacks were indeed a distinct caste within the larger society was deeply rooted in the conditions of black life in the North during the three-quarters of a century before the Civil War. That emigrationism and anti-emigrationism often intersected and overlapped (as their adherents moved nimbly from one position to another or combined elements of each ideological strain) points to the basic instability of black ideologies at this time. Most likely, this instability reflected the short-run political and economic limitations of almost any position free blacks might propose. It also resulted from the ever-present duality inherent in the status of blacks in America: they were both Africans and Americans, feeling the tug of ancestral loyalties and social distinctiveness as well as being shaped, perhaps scarred, by the realities of life in the United States. Nevertheless, the attachment to racial solidarity and unity demonstrated by almost all black leaders of the period independent of their stand on the emigration issues suggests that even those blacks committed to the proposition that Afro-Americans were fundamentally American, and thus should remain on American soil, seriously doubted whether blacks would soon be integrated fully into the larger society.

If ante-bellum black emigrationism quite often contained large doses of what can be called black nationalism, it also was imbued with another important strain in black thought—a proto-Pan-Africanism anticipating the more full-blown Pan-Africanism which Sylvester Williams and then Du Bois stimulated in the twentieth century. Essentially a belief in the interconnectedness of all black peoples—historically, culturally, and politically—this early Pan-Africanism also held that Africa and her peoples possessed a grand, heroic past which must be rescued from the darkness to which European and American prejudice had consigned it. Uncovering this past was no mere exercise in historical excavation, for there was the belief that the recognition of the rich, complex civilizations which had existed in Africa before the arrival of the European slavers would instill in the minds and hearts of Africans and their New World brethren a sense of pride in their past and thus in themselves. It would also serve the political function of attacking the racist notions of white superiority. These notions, resting partly on the belief that Africa itself had no history other than the history of barbarism, had become an ideological justification for slavery and, in the nineteenth century, for the beginning of the physical conquest of Africa herself.

Although not all ante-bellum black emigrationists propounded even a nascent Pan-Africanism, implicit in even the most non-ideological expressions of emigrationism was a recognition of the oneness of all black peoples. By mid-century, moreover, the Pan-African strain in black emigrationism was overt as Delany and Holly, among others, grafted a sense of a new Black Nationality arising outside the confines of the United States on to the plans for a commercial connection between blacks in America and blacks in Africa which Cuffe, Peter Williams, Jr., and Hezekiah Grice had earlier proposed. Throughout the 1850's and into the 1860's, then, embryonic Pan-Africanism was a vital element in the thinking of the black emigrationists. The ultimate objectives now were not only to flee American degradation and oppression, but also to establish a black nationality whose political and commercial strength would soon lead to the destruction of American slavery while simultaneously putting to rest European and American notions of black inferiority. In this sense, then, the ante-bellum black emigrationists were the ideological forerunners, if not forefathers as well, of twentieth-century Pan-Africanism.

While acknowledging the unity of all black peoples, the ante-bellum black emigrationists were convinced that they themselves were destined to lead their less fortunate brethren along the path of spiritual and material redemption. Whatever the state of Africa's past glories, her inglorious present bore all the visible signs of the cultural and economic scars imposed by the Europeans since the advent of the slave trade. Healing those scars, the emigrationists believed, would be the task of those blacks in the Diaspora who, whatever the impact of slavery upon their ancestors, had felt the uplifting embrace of Western civilization. Consequently, many of the black emigrationists were condescending at best, and almost implicitly exploitive at times when they proposed their remedies for the assorted spiritual and economic problems ravaging Africa and other areas of black concentration. Whether it be the African Union Society of Newport speaking of the conversion and education of their African brethren in the late eighteenth century, Holly wishing to rescue Haiti from the depths of ignorance and savagery which he felt slavery and Catholicism had foisted upon the black nation, or, finally, Delany's emphasis upon the economic and political salvation of Africa, black emigrationists in North America saw their relationship to blacks elsewhere as that of an elder brother whose inherent superiority had conferred upon him extraordinary responsibilities. Delany best expressed this attitude in 1861 after returning from Africa, when he demanded *"Africa for the African race, and black men to rule them"*—adding that "By black men I mean, men of African descent who claim an identity with the race."[6]

If Delany's oft-quoted but usually only half-understood comment epitomizes one aspect of the duality now generally considered to be the central thread of black intellectual and cultural history, the dilemma of the anti-emigrationists illuminates still another aspect. They were confronted with the paradox of wishing to be fully accepted by a society dedicated to their subjugation. Although the anti-emigrationists believed they would eventually break down those barriers which prevented them from becoming incontestably *American*, the impenetrability of white racism inevitably reinforced those tendencies which united blacks and made a virtue of their isolation. Many, of course, believed this distinctiveness was

---

6. See M. R. Delany, *Official Report of the Niger Valley Exploring Party* (New York: Thomas Hamilton, 1861), p. 61. This statement has been used by Hollis R. Lynch, George Shepperson, and, most recently, Imanuel Geiss to support their very apt descriptions of Delany as an early Pan-Africanist or, in Lynch's terms, a Pan-Negro Nationalist. None of the three, however, has recognized the ambiguity of Delany's remarks. See Lynch's "Pan-Negro Nationalism in the New World," *Boston University Papers on Africa*, II (1966), 171; Shepperson's "Pan-Africanism and 'Pan-africanism': Some Historical Notes," *Phylon*, XXIII (Winter, 1962), 350; and his "Notes on Negro American Influences on the Emergence of African Nationalism," *Journal of African History*, I: 2 (1960), 301; and Geiss's "Notes on Pan-Africanism," 724. Interestingly enough, approximately two years before Delany published his *Official Report*, Thomas Clegg, the Manchester cotton merchant, was quoted as urging "*Africa for the Africans—Europe for the white man.*" *Douglass' Monthly*, August, 1859, p. 120.

not incompatible with the drive for political and economic liberty and equality. Yet as this campaign faltered, those blacks committed to living out their days in the United States were confronted with the unhappy fact that their separation was increasingly viewed as a necessity by a white society convinced of black inferiority. Sadly, then, the emigrationists—whatever their other limitations—proved to be the more perceptive social prophets.

Essay on Sources

Perhaps to a greater extent than many works in black history, the present study has exploited a multitude of disparate and often obscure materials. Given the variety of movements and individuals discussed in the preceding pages, much of the material consulted is relatively narrow in focus and has served to document only a small portion of the entire narrative. As a result, a full-fledged bibliographical essay would represent an ungainly monument to the rigors of historical scholarship while also taxing the stamina of even the most committed specialist. With these considerations in mind, I have elected simply to discuss the most pertinent materials.

Much to my surprise, manuscripts were an unexpectedly valuable source for this work. Without the manuscript record book of the African Union Society of Newport, Rhode Island (in binder labeled "Union Congregational Church, 1790–1796") at the Newport Historical Society, Chapter 1 could not have been written. Unfortunately, however, manuscript collections of substance exist for only a few black figures of the ante-bellum period. The ample collection of Paul Cuffe Papers at the New Bedford, Massachusetts, Free Public Library is the exception rather than the rule. (Cuffe letters can also be found in the Philanthropists, Simon Gratz, and Dreer Collections at the Historical Society of Pennsylvania, the Morse Family Papers at Yale University, Friends House Library, London, and the New York Historical Society.) Other useful manuscript sources for this early period in the history of black emigration and colonization include Daniel Coker's Diary, April 21-September 21, 1821, and the Christian Wiltberger, Jr., Diary, February 2-December 31, 1821. Both items are in the Manuscript Division of the Library of Congress. The Wiltberger diary is of particular value since it includes, besides Wiltberger's own entries, extracts from the original journals of Jonathan B. Winn and Samuel Crozer and Elijah Johnson, a colonist who came to Africa with Coker on the *Elizabeth*.

I was able to locate only a few Martin R. Delany manuscripts for the period under investigation. The American Missionary Association Papers at the Amistad Research Center, Dillard University, contain two Delany letters written in 1858, when he was attempting to raise funds for his African exploring expedition. Delany's letter to William Lloyd Garrison asking his assistance in securing a publisher for *Blake*, Delany's novel, is in the Garrison Papers at the Boston Public Library. Surprisingly, the Gerrit Smith Papers at Syracuse University are devoid of letters from or even about Delany, although the collection holds a few items of interest—principally communications from Henry Highland Garnet, William Howard Day, and Theodore Bourne.

Material pertaining to Delany and many other individuals considered in this work can be gleaned from various manuscript collections of white institutions. For example, the voluminous American Colonization Society Papers in the Manuscript Division of the Library of Congress reveal the relationship between John B. Russwurm and the Society, and, more significantly, provide valuable insights into the activities of Delany and Robert Campbell during the late 1850's and early 1860's. Personal information on Russwurm can be found in the papers of his cousin, John Sumner Russwurm, at the Tennessee State Library and Archives. In addition, several collections pertaining to the Protestant Episcopal Church enabled me to understand the dual commitments of such Christian nationalists as James Theodore Holly and William Charles Monroe. Of greatest assistance in this regard were the Papers of the Domestic and Foreign Missionary Society of the Protestant Episcopal Church housed at the Church Historical Society in Austin, Texas. The Haiti Papers of the Domestic and Foreign Missionary Society's collections demonstrated the extent of Holly's and Monroe's interest in establishing an Episcopal mission in Haiti. The Domestic and Foreign Missionary Society's Liberia Papers provided fresh, if limited material concerning Monroe's trip to Liberia in 1859, as well as some very significant information on the relationship of Alexander

Crummell to the Protestant Episcopal Church in the United States. Given my purposes, I could not do justice to the available sources on Crummell. Additional Holly material is in the American Church Missionary Society Papers (also housed at the Church Historical Society), the General Theological Seminary in New York City, and the Episcopal Diocese of Connecticut Archives, the latter located in the library of Trinity College, Hartford. There are also references to Holly's role in the Haitian emigration movement in the James Redpath letterbooks. Redpath's correspondence with the Haitian government from March 31 through December 27, 1861, is in the Manuscript Division, Library of Congress, while material between December 31, 1861, and May 12, 1862, is in the Schomburg Branch of the New York Public Library.

Two collections enabled me to untangle some of the complexities of the story of the Niger Valley Exploring Party's trip to Africa and England. The Church Missionary Society Papers, located the Church Missionary Society Archives in London, but also available on microfilm from the University of Wisconsin Library and the Center for Research Libraries, Chicago, assisted me in completing and straightening out an intricate narrative and in understanding the attitudes of Henry Townsend and the Reverend Samuel Ajayi Crowther toward the Yoruba colonization plans of Delany and Campbell. The Thomas Hodgkin Papers explained, in general terms, the nature of the Bourne-Delany conflict and provided insights into the activities of the British commercial-philanthropists in Africa in the late 1850's and early 1860's. I was fortunate to use photocopied prints of the microfilm made by Dr. Edward H. Kass, director of the Channing Laboratory of the Harvard University Medical School and Boston City Hospital, of the original papers in the possession of the Hodgkin family in England.

Also useful were the William King Papers, on microfilm at both the Public Archives of Canada in Ottawa and the Chatham Public Library, Chatham, Ontario. King's papers provided information on the African Aid Society and the abortive plan to send Canadian blacks to Abeokuta in 1861. The Public Archives of Canada also hold a small collection of Mary Ann Shadd Cary Papers which helped to clarify the nature of black factionalism in Canada in the early 1850's. I also used the I. D. Shadd Diary, which is in the front and back of the Abraham W. Shadd Ledger held by the North Buxton Museum near Chatham.

Newspapers and contemporary periodicals were also an essential source for this study. For the period from 1827 on, black newspapers were extremely valuable, even though they presented certain problems for the historian attempting to understand the full range of ideological alternatives discussed by blacks before the Civil War. After *Freedom's Journal* (New York, 1827–29) appeared in March, 1827, as the first black newspaper in the United States, there were several lengthy periods when no black papers were published. Only occasionally did more than a single black newspaper appear at any one time. Moreover, complete runs of ante-bellum black papers are rare. For example, only two copies of Delany's *The Mystery* (Pittsburgh, 1843–48) are extant. (Both are held by the Carnegie Library of Pittsburgh.) Issues of *Frederick Douglass' Paper* (Rochester, 1851–59) between 1855 and 1859 are few and widely scattered, with copies at the American Antiquarian Society, Connecticut State Library, New York Historical Society, New York State Library, and the Library of Congress; a few issues are on the American Council of Learned Societies' microfilm of Negro newspapers, and a single issue is on a microfilm reel of miscellaneous newspapers in the King Papers at the Public Archives of Canada. Only two issues of *The Provincial Freeman* (Windsor, Toronto, Chatham, 1853–60?) could be located between 1858 and 1860—the years when Delany was most involved in organizing and then implementing his African designs. Both of these are in the Slavery Collection, Cornell University Library; issues prior to September, 1857, are on microfilm available from the University of Pennsylvania Library.

Despite these limitations, many black papers were read with profit. As is true of *Freedom's Journal* mentioned above, a number of these papers have been microfilmed. Although all important papers used are included in the discussion that follows, only the locations of papers (or issues) either not on microfilm or on microfilms not generally available, will be given: *The Rights of All* (New York, 1829); *The Colored American* (originally *The Weekly Advocate*; New York, 1837–42)—an important issue not microfilmed is in the Boston Public Library's collection at the New England Depository Library; *Palladium of Liberty* (Columbus,

Essay on Sources

Ohio, 1843-44)—at the Ohio Historical Society; *The Impartial Citizen* (Syracuse, Boston, 1849-51)—American Antiquarian Society, Cornell University Library (Slavery Collection), Library of Congress, and Harvard University Library; single issue of William Howard Day's *Aliened American* (Cleveland, 1853-55?); Henry Bibb's *Voice of the Fugitive* (Windsor and Sandwich, Canada West, 1851-53); *The North Star* (Rochester, 1847-51); *Frederick Douglass' Paper* (Rochester, 1851-59)—for information on extant issues between 1855 and 1859, see preceding paragraph—*Douglass' Monthly* (1859-63); and *The Weekly Anglo-African* (New York, 1859-65; published as *The Anglo-African* beginning in 1863)—short run on microfilm, other issues at the American Antiquarian Society, Library of Congress, and Harvard University (Houghton Library). For the chapter on the Haitian emigration movement of the early 1860's, I relied heavily on *The Pine and Palm* (Boston, 1861-62). Although not strictly a "black newspaper," it was directed toward an almost exclusively black audience; various runs of the paper are at the American Antiquarian Society, Library of Congress, Boston Public Library, and the Massachusetts Historical Society.

A broad range of white newspapers was also consulted. I found the colonization press unusually fruitful for much of this study. In addition to the American Colonization Society's *African Repository* (Washington, D.C., 1825-92), I read the more obscure organs of the state societies: *The Colonization Herald* (organ of the Pennsylvania Colonization Society; Philadelphia, 1835-68)—located at the Boston Public Library, State Historical Society of Wisconsin, Maryland Historical Society (included with the newspaper section of the Maryland State Colonization Society Papers), and American Antiquarian Society; *New York Colonization Journal* (New York, 1850-63)—New York Public Library and State Historical Society of Wisconsin; and the *Maryland Colonization Journal* (Baltimore, 1841-61)—Maryland Historical Society and Enoch Pratt Free Library, Baltimore. White antislavery newspapers were less directly helpful, but still important information was gleaned from the following: Benjamin Lundy's *Genius of Universal Emancipation* (Mount Pleasant, Ohio; Philadelphia; Baltimore; etc., 1821-39)—University of Missouri Library; Lundy's *Genius of Universal Emancipation and Baltimore Courier* (Baltimore, 1825-27)—also at the University of Missouri; *The Non-Slaveholder* (Philadelphia, 1846–50, 1853–54)—Western Reserve Historical Society and Library of Congress; *Anti-Slavery Bugle* (Salem, Ohio, 1845–61)—Ohio Historical Society; *The Pennsylvania Freeman* (originally *National Enquirer and Constitutional Advocate of Universal Liberty*, Philadelphia, 1836–54)—Columbia University; *The Liberator* (Boston, 1831–65); and, very sparingly, *The National Anti-Slavery Standard* (New York, 1840–70). I also used the British and Foreign Anti-Slavery Society's *The Anti-Slavery Reporter* (London, 1840+)—located at the Library of Congress and Yale University—to track down Bourne, Delany, and Campbell while all three were in Great Britain.

Church newspapers provided significant insights into the activities of Henry Highland Garnet, James Theodore Holly, and others. I read selectively in the *Missionary Record of the United Presbyterian Church of Scotland* (Edinburgh, 1846–65)—at the Yale Divinity School Library—for material on Garnet's work in Jamaica. For Holly, I used the organ of the Episcopal Diocese of Connecticut, *The Calendar* (Hartford, 1845+)—at the Episcopal Diocese of Connecticut Archives, Trinity College Library—and two other Episcopal organs published in New York: *The Churchman*—located at the General Theological Seminary—and *The Church Journal*—in the Yale Divinity School Library.

Several general audience white newspapers were used at various points in this study. For the period before 1830 I consulted *Poulson's Daily American Advertiser* (Philadelphia); *Boston Recorder; American and Commercial Daily Advertiser* (Baltimore); and the *Commercial Advertiser* (New York). Odd issues of the following papers proved useful for the later period: *New York Daily Tribune, New York Times, New York Evening Express, Chicago Daily Tribune*, and the English *Manchester Weekly Advertiser*. More helpful was *The Chatham Tri-Weekly Planet*, which provided important reports on Delany's African exploration and on his activities after he returned to Chatham. In addition, *The Cotton Supply Reporter* (Manchester, England, 1858–72)—housed at the Baker Library of the Harvard Business School—was essential for my understanding of the English commercial-philanthropists.

A large and diversified body of printed materials was read for this study. The primary materials, which include biographical sketches, travel accounts, minutes and proceedings of black conventions, essays and addresses, are much too numerous for detailed scrutiny here. Special mention, however, should be made of the Arno Press reprint series—The American Negro: His History and Literature—which has made available to a wide audience specialized works long difficult to locate. Of direct relevance to this study is Arno's reprinting of Martin R. Delany's *Condition, Elevation, Emigration, and Destiny of the Colored People of the United States, Politically Considered*, originally published in 1852, and Howard H. Bell's edited *Minutes of the Proceedings of the National Negro Conventions, 1830–1864* which gathers together in a single volume the proceedings of the twelve national black conventions between 1830 and 1864. Not included in this volume is the *Proceedings of the National Emigration Convention of Colored People; held at Cleveland, Ohio...the 24th, 25th and 26th of August, 1854* (1854), which was essential for my purposes.

Several secondary sources are worthy of comment because of their inclusiveness. Although there has been no previous book-length study of either ante-bellum black emigration or ante-bellum black nationalism, closest to such a work is Howard Holman Bell's pioneering 1953 dissertation, *A Survey of the Negro Convention Movement, 1830–1861* (reprint ed., 1969). Long before contemporary events led scholars to examine the historical manifestations of black nationalism, Bell noted both the extensive interest in emigration among many ante-bellum black leaders and the nationalistic coloration of much of this sentiment. Also helpful is Sterling Stuckey's introduction to *The Ideological Origins of Black Nationalism* (1972), a collection of documents exemplifying various tendencies in ante-bellum black nationalism; and Hollis R. Lynch's "Pan-Negro Nationalism in the New World, before 1862," *Boston University Papers on Africa*, II (1966), 147–179, which focuses upon the Liberian educator and statesman Edward W. Blyden, Alexander Crummell, James Theodore Holly, and Delany. Several other writers have treated ante-bellum black nationalism in broad, provocative terms. See especially August Meier, "The Emergence of Negro Nationalism," *Midwest Journal*, IV (Winter, 1951–52), 96–104, and IV (Summer, 1952), 95–111; Bill McAdoo, "Pre-Civil War Black

Nationalism," *Progressive Labor*, V (June–July, 1966), 31–56, 65–68; Imanuel Geiss, "Notes on the Development of Pan-Africanism," *Journal of the Historical Society of Nigeria*, III (June, 1967), 719–740; and two articles by George Shepperson—"Notes on Negro American Influences on the Emergence of African Nationalism," *Journal of African History*, I (1960), 299–312; and "Pan-Africanism and 'Pan-africanism': Some Historical Notes," *Phylon*, XXIII (Winter, 1962), 346–358.

Index

Abeokuta, 205–215, 230, 250, 254, 255, 256, 257
Abolitionism, 89–90, 188–189
Abolitionists, 128, 129
Adams, Ennals J., 263
Adams, Jonathan, 64
"Address to the Slaves" (Garnet), 189–190
Afric-American Printing Company, 168
Afric-American Quarterly Repository, 166, 167
African Aid Society: formation, 225; and African Civilization Society, 225, 229, 258, 259, 260; and Campbell, 226; and Delany, 226, 227; and controversy over treaty, 255–256; and Chatham emigrants, 256–257, 258; mentioned, 251, 252, 253
African Benevolent Society, Newport, 8
"African Civilization Committee, The," 183, 192. *See also* African Civilization Society
African Civilization Society: formation and objectives, 192–193; and Niger Valley Exploring Party, 195, 197, 217–218, 223, 228, 229; and white colonizationists, 197; and Bourne, 217, 218, 220–221, 225, 226, 228; and British abolitionists, 219, 222; and Churchill, 228, 229; and Rogers's expedition to Africa, 229, 230–231; and Yoruba emigation after Rogers, 258–259; accommodation with Delany, 260–261; seeks government aid, 261–262; turns to war effort, 263; mentioned, 184, 186, 197, 198, 244, 250–251
African Civilization Society of Canada, 194–195
African colonization: and Cuffe, 45–52; opposed by blacks, 48–49, 50, 55, 74, 78, 82–90, 112, 126–127, 141, 155, 156, 171, 188, 239; and founding of Liberia, 54–74; and Russwurm, 85–88; and Delany, 171, 270; and Garnet, 188, 190
African Educational Society, Pittsburgh, 95
African Education and Benevolent Society, Chillicothe, Ohio, 95
African Education Society, 45
African Free School, New York, 187
"Africania," 99
African identity: of Afro-Americans, 170. *See also* Pan-Africanism
African Institution of London, 26, 27, 29, 30–31, 36, 39, 40, 43
African Institution of New York, 34, 35, 43, 48, 77
African Institution of Philadelphia, 34, 35, 43, 48, 49
African Lodge No. 1, 4
African Methodist Episcopal Bethel Society, Baltimore (Bethel Church), 58
African Methodist Episcopal (A.M.E.) Church: and Coker, 58–59; mentioned, 14, 78, 95, 146
African Repository, 86
African School No. 2, New York, 204

African School of Boston, 35
African School, Philadelphia, 82
African Sierra Leone Benevolent Society, 35
African Society of Boston, 34–35
African Society of Providence, 15, 16–17, 18, 19
African Union Society of Newport: organization and tenets, 8–9; relationship with Thornton, 9–10, 11; and Sierra Leone, 10, 11; attitudes toward indigenous Africans, 10, 12, 273; and Boston blacks, 11; and Philadelphia blacks, 12–13, 14; and Providence blacks, 12–13, 17; and black unity, 12–13, 14, 101, 271
Alafin of Oyo, 216
Alake of Abeokuta, 210–215, 254, 255, 256, 258
Aliened American, 141
Allen, Richard: and Free African Society, 14; opposes African colonization, 48–49, 74, 82; and African Institution of Philadelphia, 49; and Finley, 49–50; favors African emigration, 50; criticized, 57; selected bishop of A.M.E. Church, 59; and Haitian emigration, 78, 80; mentioned, 93, 270
Allen, William, 27, 29, 30, 31, 36, 39, 43
Allen, William G., 188
A.M.E. Church: and Coker, 58–59; mentioned, 14, 78, 95, 146
America and Other Poems (Whitfield), 138
American African Union Society, 70–71
American and Foreign Anti-Slavery Society, 103, 177–178, 239
American Anti-Slavery Society, 188
American Church Missionary Society, 248
American Colonization Society: early formation of, 45; opposition to, 48–49, 55, 82, 83–84, 89, 104, 119, 125, 129, 130, 136, 156; black support for, 54; and founding of African colony, 55–73; opposes Haitian emigration, 77; and Holly, 108–109; and Delany, 119, 125, 129, 130, 196, 197, 227; and Yoruba emigration, 184, 195–196; mentioned, 51, 52, 54, 100, 110, 141, 172, 199, 203, 206, 244, 266, 268
American Continental and West India League 113, 167
American Geographical and Statistical Society, 226
American League of Colored Laborers, 104
American Missionary Association: formation of, 103; and Delany, 177–179; and black ministers, 191; and Rogers, 230; mentioned, 106, 108, 171, 252, 263
American Moral Reform Society, 95–96, 102, 116
Amherstburg Association, 147
Amherstburg convention (1853), 114–115, 162
Amistad captives, 103
Anderson, Osborn P., 252, 253
Anderson, William Wemyss, 111
Andrus, Joseph R., 68, 70
Anglo-African, The (Lagos), 265
Anglo-African, The Weekly, 170, 242, 243, 244, 246, 252, 260
Anglo-African Magazine, The, 170, 196, 234, 235
Anthony, John P., 166, 167, 168, 233, 241, 246
Anti-Slavery Reporter, 207, 219, 221
Aray, Amos, 182, 252
Arguments, Pro and Con, on the Call for a National Emigration Convention, 142, 148
Arnold, Thomas, 33
Aro, Battle of, 210
Asbury, Francis, 58
Ashmun, Jehudi, 72, 73
"Association for the Promotion of the Interests of the Colored People of Canada and the United States," 180–181, 182
Atambala (Egba chief), 212
"Augustine." *See* Woodson, Lewis
Avery, Charles, 178
Avery Institute, 153, 173, 178
Ayres, Eli, 71, 72–73

Index

Bacon, Ephraim, 68, 70
Bacon, Samuel, 58–64, 68
Ballette, Emil de, 163
Baltimore blacks: and Haitian emigration, 78; favor colonization, 83
Baltimore Emigration Society, 77, 79
Bancroft, George, 226
Bankson, John, 58, 61, 62, 64
Baptist Board of Foreign Missions, 68, 69
Baptist General Convention of the United States, 147
Bathurst, Lord, 40, 41
Bedell, Gregory T., 234
Bell, Howard H., 270
Beman, Amos G., 107
Bennett, John, 207
Benson, George, 15. See also Brown, Benson and Ives
Benson, Martin, 18–19
Benson, Stephen A., 176, 203
Berry, Samuel V., 165, 167, 233, 238, 240
Bethel Church, Baltimore, 58, 78
Bethel Church, Philadelphia, 48, 49, 78
Bibb, Henry: and nationalist-emigrationism, 94, 105, 107; background, 107; and continental black unity, 111, 112–113, 114–115; and controversy over Refugee Home Society, 113; and National Emigration Convention, 142–143; eulogy for, 149; mentioned, 110, 125, 130, 136, 145, 146, 151, 157
Bibb, Mary, 113, 145, 166
Birney, James, 90
Black nationality: Delany for, 128, 150, 171–172, 260; and H. F. Douglass, 152; and Bourne, 185
Black unity: movements and calls for, 12, 13, 34, 95, 101–102, 104, 111–112, 114–115, 128, 134, 135, 136–137, 139, 140, 152, 262
Blair, Frank P., 169, 232–233, 237
Blake; or, the Huts of America (Delany), 196–197
Blyden, Edward W., 130, 201, 202–203
Board of Publications: established at 1856 emigration convention, 166, 167, 168, 179
Board of Trade: established at 1856 emigration convention, 166–167, 179, 233
Boston blacks: and emigration, 3, 4–6, 11, 12, 34–35, 42, 141
Bourne, George, 184, 219
Bourne, Theodore: and Niger Valley Exploring Party, 183, 197; background, 184; and Yoruba emigration movement, 185, 186, 187, 192; as African Civilization Society representative in England, 217, 218–221, 222, 226; and Delany and Campbell, 219, 225, 226; mentioned, 193, 194, 195, 228
Bowen, Thomas J., 173, 183, 214
Boyer, Jean Pierre, 76, 77, 78, 81
Brander, Nathaniel, 61
British and Foreign Anti-Slavery Society, 207, 219, 220, 222
British Foreign Office, 256–257
British West Indies emigration: supported, 101, 114
Brown, Benson and Ives, 15, 17, 18
Brown, John, Jr., 242
Brown, Moses, 7, 33
Brown, Nicholas, 15. See also Brown, Benson and Ives
Brown, William Wells, 228, 243
Bullom people, Sierra Leone, 28
Burgess, Ebenezer, 56, 62
Burritt, Elihu, 180, 184
"Bustill's Regiment," 247

Caldwell, Minerva, 252
Calumbine, Charles, 41
Camaraw, Thomas, 61
Camp, Abraham, 57
Campbell, Robert: and Niger Valley Exploring Party, 182, 193, 195; background, 193; relationship with Delany, 193; and white colonizationists, 195–196, 197; and African Civilization Society, 195, 228, 229; travels to England en route to Africa, 196, 198, 206–207; in Africa, 206–216; and treaty with Egba, 213–215, 254, 255, 256; in En-

gland with Delany, 217, 221, 222; and African Aid Society, 226; returns to U.S., 226; with Garnet in England, 259, 260; settles in Africa, 265; mentioned, 174, 179, 194, 198, 217–218, 219, 224, 225, 231, 258
Campelar, 62, 63, 65
Canadian blacks: and 1854 emigration convention, 142–144
Canadian emigration: supported, 101, 106, 107, 110, 111, 114, 143–144, 146, 150, 157–158, 161; and Delany, 127, 130, 150, 160–161; denounced in Cincinnati, 157–158
Cary, Lott: compared with Coker, 56; background and views, 68; on *Nautilus*, 69–70; organizes black colonists, 70–71; at Cape Mesurado, 71–72; as vice-agent of Liberia, 73
Cary, Mary Ann Shadd: attacks Haitian emigration movement, 244–245; on African emigration, 253; recruiting soldiers, 264. See also Shadd, Mary Ann
Castendyke, B. E., 200, 205
Central Africa: Adventures and Missionary Labors (Bowen), 173
Central American emigration, 148, 150, 169
Central American Land Company, 237–238
Chamerovzow, L. A., 207, 222
Chatham black community: and Delany, 166, 172–173, 194, 251; plans to migrate to Yoruba, 252–253
"Chatham Convention," 225. See also "Association for the Promotion of the Interests of the Colored People of Canada and the United States"
Chatham Tri-Weekly Planet, 182, 237
Chesapeake and Liberian Trading Company, 119–120
Chester, T. Morris, 186
Christian Herald, The, 146
Christian Intelligencer, 185
Christophe, Henri, 75
Christy, Henry, 206, 209
Churchill, Alfred S.: and Yoruba emigration, 220; and African Civilization Society, 222, 223, 228, 229, 258; and African Aid Society, 226; and Delany's emigrant party, 256–257; and Garnet, 259; mentioned, 221, 224, 225
Church Missionary Society, 209, 210–211, 256
Cincinnati blacks: on emigration and colonization, 79, 156, 157–158
Cincinnati Haytien Union, 79
Clarion, The, 188
Clark, Molliston M., 137, 172
Clark, Peter H., 158
Clarkson, Thomas, 30, 31, 36, 75
Clay, Henry, 45, 83, 109
Clegg, Thomas, 176, 207, 209, 224, 225
Cleveland Morning Leader, The, 149
Coates, Benjamin, 184, 185, 193, 195, 261
Coker, Daniel: and Cuffe, 34, 59; as middle man between Colonization Society and colonists, 55–56, 58, 59, 60–61; compared with Cary, 56; background, 58–59; and A.M.E. Church, 58–59; and difficulties with *Elizabeth*'s colonists, 62–70; as acting agent for government and Colonization Society, 64–65, 66–67; relations with new colonists, 70, 71; remains in Sierra Leone, 71; mentioned, 68, 69, 89
Coker, Susan, 58
Collins, George, 34
Colonization. See African colonization
Colonization Herald, The, 129–130
Colonization within the United States, 47, 48, 138
Colored American, The, 96
Colored Free Produce Society, Philadelphia, 112, 220
Colored National Convention: *1848*, 118, 122, 135, 145; *1853*, 134–144, 156; *1855*, 137
Colored Union Congregational Church, Newport, 8
Columbine, Edward H., 27–28, 29, 46
Commercial organization and ventures: black support for, 29, 31–32, 34, 43, 87, 166–167, 172, 176, 272
Condition, Elevation, Emigration, and Destiny of the Colored People of the United States, Politically Considered,

The (Delany), 125-131, 135, 141, 172, 201
Constantine, A. A., 228, 258
Conventions: Pennsylvania, *1841*, 103, 110; Toronto, *1851*, 111-112, 113, 114, 125, 167; Amherstburg, *1853*, 114-115, 162; Pennsylvania, *1848*, 118; Cleveland, *1848*, 118, 122, 135, 145; Rochester, *1853*, 134-144, 156; Cleveland, *1854*, 134, 137-157, 160-161, 166, 175, 194; Philadelphia, *1855*, 137; Ohio, *1849*, 141, 151; Ohio, *1853*, 141; Ohio, *1852*, 150, 151; Cleveland, *1856*, 159, 160, 165-166, 179, 194, 233; Chatham, *1858*, 179-181, 232; Buffalo, *1843*, 189; Troy, *1847*, 189; Ohio, *1858*, 194, 225
Coppinger, William, 195, 238, 266
Cornish, James, 220
Cornish, Samuel E.: favors Haitian emigration, 77; background, 82-83; opposes emigration and colonization, 82, 83-84, 88-89, 102; and *Freedom's Journal*, 83, 84; edits *The Rights of All*, 88-89; opposes separatism, 89; and Union Missionary Society, 103; as an emigrationist, 270; mentioned, 93, 128, 191
Cotton: and English support of African emigration, 219-220; Delany on, 226, 227, 252
Cotton Supply Association, 220
Crane, William, 68
Creecy, Francis, 62-63
Crowther, Josiah, 209, 210, 212-213, 215, 254, 256
Crowther, Samuel Ajayi, 208, 209, 212-213, 215, 254, 255, 256
Crowther, Samuel, Jr., 209, 210, 212-213, 215, 254, 256
Crozer, Samuel, 58-63
Crummell, Alexander, 203-205, 207-208, 220, 231, 248
Crummell, Boston, 204
Cuffe, David, 23
Cuffe, John, 23, 24
Cuffe, Paul: change in emigration emphasis, 21-22, 44, 52; childhood and youth, 22; as shipowner and trader, 23; champions black suffrage, 24; member of Society of Friends, 25; views on Africa, 25, 26; travels to Africa and England (1811-12), 27-33; and black African Institutions, 33-35, 43, 48; and emigrant party, 34-35, 37, 40-42, 56-57; opposes War of 1812, 36; seeks American government permission to trade with England, 37-39; attempts to get English trading license, 39-40, 42-43; and white colonizationists, 44-47, 48, 52; and interest in Sherbro Island, 46; and black colony in U.S., 47, 51; and Forten, 47, 50, 51; nationalistic tendencies of, 53; and Coker, 59; Christian influence upon, 269; mentioned, 20, 54, 55, 74, 75, 77, 93, 94, 119, 130, 167, 272

Dahomey, 210
Daily Cleveland Herald, The, 149
Daily Morning Post (Pittsburgh), 153-154
Day, William Howard: background, 141-142; on emigration, 141-142, 194, 237; at 1854 emigration convention, 149; and 1858 emigration convention, 180, 181, 194; and Delany, 194, 225, 227; in England, 223-225, 227, 260; mentioned, 144, 150, 152, 217
Dean, William, 37
Delany, Catherine, 145
Delany, Martin R.: and nationalist-emigrationism, 93, 94, 104, 115, 125, 132-133, 134; and Woodson, 94; and Frederick Douglass, 104, 132; at Toronto convention, 111, 125; as abolitionist, 115, 117-119; childhood and youth, 116; in Pittsburgh, 116-118; and American Moral Reform Society, 116; and *The Mystery*, 117-118, 119; and *The North Star*, 118-119; denounces American Colonization Society and African colonization, 119, 125, 129, 171; self-help views of, 119-122, 123-124, 126, 128, 132, 226-227, 241, 258, 260, 261, 269; on Liberia, 120, 129, 130, 172, 198, 201-203; and racial solidarity, 122; on religion, 122-123, 128-129, 171,

178–179; contradiction in thought of, 123–124; advocates emigration, 124, 126, 127–128, 129, 132, 150, 158; suffers personal abuse, 124–125; and *Condition*, 125–132, 135, 172, 201; on Canadian emigration, 127, 150, 158, 160–161; attacks abolitionists, 128, 129; and 1853 national convention, 135–136; and 1854 emigration convention, 137–153; and division within emigration movement, 157, 168–169, 171, 172–173; moves to Canada, 158–159; and Chatham blacks, 159, 160, 172–173, 194, 251–252, 253; and 1856 emigration convention, 160, 166; and African emigration, 169, 171–172; plans African exploration, 172–183; and Niger Valley Exploring Party, 174–175, 192–197; and Myers, 175–176; and American Missionary Association, 177–179; and 1858 emigration convention, 179, 180, 181, 182; and Campbell, 193; and white colonizationists, 196, 197–198; and *Blake*, 196–197; and African Civilization Society, 197; in Liberia, 201–205; in Yoruba, 205–206, 212–216; and treaty with Egba, 213–215, 254, 255, 256; in England, 217, 221–223, 225–228; and Bourne, 218, 225–226; and African Aid Society, 226; and African Civilization Society, 228, 229, 260–261; attacks Haiti, 241; raising emigration party in Chatham, 251–252, 253, 256, 257; and select emigration, 260; recruits soldiers for Civil War, 262, 264; post-Civil War career in South Carolina, 266; and Pan-Africanism, 272; imperialistic views toward Africa, 273; mentioned, 53, 59, 101, 103, 105, 107, 154, 155, 156, 165, 167, 170, 187, 200, 208, 209, 210, 211, 219, 224, 231, 232, 233, 246, 250, 258, 270
Delany, Pati, 116
Delany, Samuel, 116
Dewey, Loring D., 76–77, 79, 81, 236
Dillwyn, William, 26
Docemo, King of Lagos, 208
Douglass, Frederick: establishes newspaper, 104, 118–119; and Delany, 104, 117, 118–119, 122, 130, 159; and establishment of black organizations, 104; and racial solidarity, 122; self-help views of, 122; nationalistic tendencies of, 134, 270; on Whitfield, 138; attacks emigration, 138–139, 140, 142, 154, 239, 243–244; favors hemispheric emigration, 239; flirtation with Haitian emigration, 239–240; mentioned, 141, 142, 144, 155, 156, 158, 180, 189, 220, 269
Douglass, H. Ford: background, 150; at 1854 emigration convention, 150–151, 152, 161; in Canada, 159, 160; on Haitian emigration, 161, 236, 242; death, 264; mentioned, 166, 180, 238
Douglass, Robert, Jr., 174, 175, 179, 182, 195
Douglass, S. V., 230
Downing, George T., 228, 243, 247, 262
Du Bois, W. E. B., 267, 271
Dudley, Ambrose, 175, 176
Duffin, J. W., 245
Dunbar, Charles B., 200
Dunlop, Henry, 227

Eardley, Culling E., 220, 221
Egba peoples, 206–216, 254, 255
Elgin community (Elgin Association), 223, 224, 251, 252
Elie, Auguste, 247
Elizabeth: expedition, 57–70
Emancipation: and colonization, emigration, 52, 81, 87, 93, 114
Evangelical Association of the Colored Ministers of Congregational and Presbyterian Churches, 229–230

Faustin I, Emperor, 235
Finley, Robert, 45, 46, 47, 50
First Baptist Church, Richmond, 68
First Colored Presbyterian Church, New York, 82, 187
Fisher, Charles, 80
Fisher, J. T., 110, 111, 125
Fitzgerald, Ferdinand, 257
Fleet, John H., 108
Foote, Henry Grant, 255, 256

Index

Forten, James: and Cuffe, 47; favors emigration, 49, 50, 78, 270; and Finley, 49–50; opposes colonization, emigration, 51, 74, 82, 83
Foster, Joseph H., 151, 161
Fourah Bay, 69
Fowler, Joseph, 156
Franklin, Benjamin, 25
Frederick Douglass' Paper, 136, 138, 154, 193, 242
Free African Society of Philadelphia, 13–15
Freedom's Journal, 83, 84, 85–87, 88
Free labor argument: supported, 112, 220; and cotton supply, 193, 206, 220, 222; and Haitian emigration, 236; mentioned, 47
Freeman, Martin H., 153, 155, 166, 173–174, 242, 265
Friendly Society of Sierra Leone, 31–32, 34, 41, 42, 43, 56
Fugitive Slave Act of 1850, 104, 106, 107, 113, 124

Gage, Thomas, 47
Gaines, John I., 158
Gallatin, Albert, 33
Gardner, Caleb, 8
Gardner, Cato, 22
Gardner, Newport, 7–8, 9, 17, 18, 20, 21, 52, 93, 94
Garnet, Henry Highland: and Union Missionary Society, 103; free labor views, 112, 220; and African Civilization Society, 170, 192–193, 228, 258–259; background, 187–191; and Yoruba emigration movement, 187, 191–192; opposes emigration, 188; and political action, 188–189; advocates slave resistance, 189–190; favors colonization, 190; missionary in Jamaica, 190–191; and Niger Valley Exploring Party, 218; and African Aid Society, 229, 258, 259–260; agent for Haytian Emigration Bureau, 238; seeks government emigration aid, 261–262; recruiting soldiers, 262, 264; later years and death, 264, 266; mentioned, 99, 131, 183, 186, 195, 217, 219, 221, 225, 230, 231, 250, 251
Garrison, William Lloyd: and black opposition to colonization, 55, 89; supports colonization in 1820's, 90; opposes establishment of black paper, 104; and Delany, 117, 130, 131, 132; mentioned, 84, 95, 196, 197, 243
Garvey, Marcus, 267
Geffrard, Fabre, 235, 236, 237, 238, 241, 244, 247
General Board of Commissioners (of "Association for the Promotion of the Interests of the Colored People of Canada and the United States"), 181, 182
General Convention for the Improvement of the Colored Inhabitants of Canada (1853), 114–115, 162
General Theological Seminary, 204
George (king of the Bullom people), 28
Georgetown, District of Columbia, blacks: oppose colonization, 48
Givens, J. V., 192
Gloucester, Duke of, 30
Gloucester, John, 82
Gore, Christopher, 37
Granville, Jonathan, 77–78
Green, Augustus R., 136, 146, 149, 150, 156, 158, 161, 166
Grice, Hezekiah, 87, 119, 272
Grummetta people (Sierra Leone), 36
Guin, William, 41
Gurley, Ralph R., 73, 86, 87, 196, 197

Haitian emigration: in 1820's, 54–55, 74–81, 147, 162, 163, 235, 241; supported at Amherstburg convention, 114, 162; supported at 1854 emigration convention, 161; and missionary role, 162, 163–164, 167–168, 169, 171; supported at 1858 Ohio convention, 194; early 1860's, 232–249; mentioned, 186
Hall, James, 119
Hall, Prince, 4, 13, 16, 269
Hall, Zerah, 61, 66
Hamilton, Robert, 260
Harris, J. Dennis, 237–238, 240

Harris, J. H., 252
Hartz, Edward L., 247
Harvard Medical School, 124, 202
Haytian Emigration Bureau, 238, 243, 244
Haytian Emigration Society of Coloured People, New York, 77, 78, 79, 80
Haytien Emigration Society, Philadelphia, 78, 80–81
Henson, Josiah, 113
Hodgkin, Thomas, 219, 220, 222, 225
Holly, James Theodore: and nationalist-emigrationism, 94, 105, 107–108, 157, 235; background, 108–109, 161; and Colonization Society, 108–109; debates brother, 109; and North American black unity, 110, 111, 113, 114–115; and Canadian emigration, 110; and controversy over Refugee Home Society, 113–114; and 1854 emigration convention, 142–143, 144, 145, 146, 149, 161; and emigration following, 157, 165, 167, 169, 171, 181, 232, 233–234; and Haitian emigration, 161, 162, 165, 167, 186, 232–249; religious orientation of, 161, 162, 163–164, 167–168, 169, 171, 269; trip to Haiti (1855), 162–163; and Protestant Episcopal missionary authorities, 162–164, 234, 248; as rector of St. Luke's Episcopal Church, 165; at 1856 emigration convention, 166; and *Vindication*, 168; and 1858 emigration convention, 179, 180, 181; leaves Delany's emigration movement, 181; and Haitian emigration movement of 1860's, 232–249; agent for Haytian Emigration Bureau, 238, 240–241; and Protestant Episcopal Church, 240; leaves for Haiti, 241–242; in Haiti, 246, 247–248; Bishop of Orthodox Apostolic Church in Haiti, 248; later career in Haiti, 266–267; and Pan-Africanism, 267, 272; mentioned, 125, 135, 136, 137, 148, 152, 178, 230, 231, 252
Holly, Joseph, 108, 109, 110

Hopkins, Samuel, 6–7, 15, 19, 21
Hopkinson, Joseph, 49

Ibadan, 216
Ijaye, 216
Ijaye War, 216, 258
Illinois blacks: oppose emigration, 140–141
Inginac, Joseph Balthazar, 75, 80, 81
Institute for Colored Youth, Philadelphia, 193
Ives, Thomas, 15. See also Brown, Benson and Ives
Iwe Irohin, 254

James, Frederick, 61
James, John, 26, 27
Jarvis, Thomas, 35, 40, 41
Jenkins, David, 140
Johnson, Elijah, 72
Johnson, "Fiddler," 118
Johnson, John D., 198, 200
Johnson, Oliver, 130–131
Jones, Absalom, 14
Jones, John, 107

Kemp, James, 77
Kennedy, John H., 86
King, William: background, 223–224; in England, 223, 225; and Yoruba emigration, 223, 252, 253, 256, 257; and Elgin Association, 251; mentioned, 217
King's College, London, 209
Kizell, John: background, 31; and Friendly Society, 31, 32, 43; and Cuffe, 44; and Sherbro Island, 46; Mills's reaction to, 56; and *Elizabeth*'s colonists, 62–63, 64, 65; attacks Coker, 67, 70
Koya Temne people, 28

Laing, Daniel, 124, 201–202
Lambert, William, 161, 166, 167, 233
Land law: among the Egba, 214–215, 255
Langston, Charles H., 151
Langston, John M., 151–152, 154
Lawrence, George, 242

Index

Levere, George W., 263
Lewis, John W., 245
Liberator, The, 131
Liberia: origins of, 54–74; black opposition to, 112, 126–127; and Delany, 120, 126–127, 171n, 172, 200–205, 266; and Yoruba emigration, 196, 197, 203, 206; mentioned, 55–56, 74, 85, 119, 124, 154, 159, 186, 198, 199, 264, 265, 268
Liberian Emigration and Agricultural Society, 200
Liberian Exodus Joint Stock Steamship Company, 266
Liberty party, 117, 147, 188–189
Liberty Street Presbyterian Church, Troy, N.Y., 188
Little, Hannah, 37
Livingstone, David, 173, 183
Lockes, Perry, 35, 37, 40, 41, 56
Lundy, Benjamin, 81, 87, 90

Macaulay, Zachary, 19, 26–27, 30
McCarthy, Charles, 40, 41, 42, 61–62, 71
McCoskry, William, 256, 257
McCrosky, Samuel A., 161
McKenzie, James, 15–21
McLain, William, 109
Macon's Bill No. 2, 33
Madison, Dolley, 37
Madison, James, 33, 37, 108
Malmesbury, Lord, 208
Malvin, John, 148
Martin, J. Sella, 228
Maryland State Colonization Society, 119
Masonry, 4, 16, 168
Massachusetts Colonization Society, 124
Maxwell, Charles, 32
Melrose, Henry, 246
Mendi: trip of, 198–201, 203
Mendi mission, 178
"Mercantile Line of the Free Colored People of North America," 176
Merriman, Henry S., 167, 233
Mesurado, Cape, 71
Michigan Anti-Slavery Society, 147
Mills, Samuel J., 45–46, 48, 56, 62

Missionary Travels and Researches in South Africa (Livingstone), 173
Mitchell, James, 261
Monroe, Blandford, 199
Monroe, James, 57
Monroe, Mary O., 199, 245
Monroe, Rhinard, 199
Monroe, William C.: at 1853 national convention, 136; background, 146–148; at 1854 emigration convention, 146, 148, 149; and 1856 emigration convention, 159, 165–166; interest in Haitian missionary post, 162, 164; and Holly, 165, 167, 168; leaves for Africa, 199; mentioned, 107, 161, 180, 233, 241
Moses, Ruth, 22
Mt. Vaughan School, Cape Palmas, Liberia, 204
Myers, Jonathan J., 171, 175–176, 177, 182, 218, 231, 258
Mystery, The, 117–118, 119, 146, 158

National Anti-Slavery Standard, 189
National Board of Commissioners, 153, 155, 158, 160, 162, 163, 166, 179, 180
National Compensated Emancipation Society, 180, 184
National Convention of Colored Citizens (1843), 189
National Council, 134, 136–137, 140, 142, 144, 148, 156
National Emigration Convention: *1854*, 134, 137–157, 160–161, 166, 175, 194; *1856*, 159, 160, 165–166, 179, 194, 233; *1858*, 179–181, 232
National Watchman, The, 188
Nationalist-emigrationism, 93–94, 105, 107, 115, 133, 134–135, 157, 267, 271
Nautilus, 68, 69
Nell, William C., 108, 228
New Bedford, Mass., blacks, 141
Newman, William P., 237
Newport, R.I.: emigration activity in, 3, 6–18
New York blacks: and Haitian emigration of 1820's, 77, 78; favor Yoruba emigration, 186, 187, 228

New York Evangelical Missionary Society, 82–83
New York State Colonization Society, 184, 185, 197, 199
New York Tribune, 183
Niger Valley Exploring Party: planning for and formation of, 173–183, 195–196; and white colonizationists, 195–196; in Africa, 198–216; and African Civilization Society, 217–218; in England, 217–228; mentioned, 171, 192, 193, 194, 197, 206, 207, 219, 225, 252
Nonintercourse Act of 1809, 26, 27
North American and U.S. Gazette (Philadelphia), 195
North American and West India Trading Association, 166–167
North American Convention, 125. *See also* Toronto convention (1851)
North American League, 111, 112
North Star, The, 118–119, 121
Nott, Henry, 167
Noyes Academy, 187, 204
Nubia, Salmar, 7, 20, 21

Ogboni: of the Egba, 210, 211, 255
"Ohio in Africa," 166
Ohio State Anti-Slavery Society, 237
Ohio State Colored Convention: *1849*, 141, 151; *1853*, 141; *1852*, 150, 151; *1858*, 194, 225
Olney, William, 17, 18
Oneida Institute, 187, 204, 229
Orthodox Apostolic Church, Haiti, 248
Oyo, 216

Palladium of Liberty, 140
Pan-African Association, 267
Pan-Africanism: and Blyden, 130; turn-of-the-century movement, 267, 271; and pre–Civil War emigrationists, 271–272
Patterson, Louis, 160
Parrott, Russell, 49, 84
Paul, Thomas, 76
Peck, Nathaniel, 61
Pemberton, James, 25
Pennington, J. W. C., 243

Pennsylvania Colonization Society, 195, 206, 238
Pennsylvania Freeman, The, 130–131, 132
Pennsylvania Society for Promoting the Abolition of Slavery, 25
Pennsylvania State Colored Convention: *1841*, 103, 116; *1848*, 118
People's Record, The, 180
Perservance Island, 71
Phelps, Amos, 177
Philadelphia blacks: organizations of, 3, 14; oppose colonization, 48–49; favor Haitian emigration in 1820's, 78; and Haitian emigration movement of 1860's, 238–239
Pickering, Timothy, 37
Pine and Palm, The, 242
Pinney, John B., 184, 185, 196, 197, 202
Pittsburgh African Educational Society, 95
Plane Street Presbyterian Church, Newark, 229
Plésance, Victorien, 246
Poem on the Fugitive Slave Law, A (Rogers), 229
Polk, Leonidas, 234
Prime, Thomas, 167
Protestant Episcopal Foreign Committee, 162, 163–164, 199, 240, 248
Protestant Episcopal Society for Promoting the Extension of the Church among Colored People, 167–168, 233–234
Providence blacks: and emigration, 3, 13, 15–17, 20, 42
Provincial Freeman, 143–144, 157, 158, 159, 160, 166, 180, 182, 194, 202, 224
Provincial Union, 144
Purnell, James W., 182, 196, 197, 198

Quaumino, John, 7
Queens College, Cambridge, 204
Quok Walker case, 4
Quonn, William W., 167

Raisin Institute, 107
Ralston, Gerard, 206
Randolph, John, 45

Index

Rathbone, William, 43
Redpath, James, 236–247
Refugee Home Society, 113–114, 143, 144, 157
Reid, T. A., 215
Repeal of the Missouri Compromise Considered, The (Rogers), 229
Report on the Political Destiny of the Race on this Continent, 149–150, 151
Richards, Aaron, 29, 30
Richmond African Baptist Missionary Society, 68
Richmond blacks: oppose colonization, 48
Rights of All, The, 88–89
Robbins, Asher, 33
Roberts, H. J., 202, 203
Roberts, Joseph J., 120
Rogers, Elymas P., 229–231, 250, 258
Rotch, William, Jr., 37
Royal Geographical Society of England, 176, 222
Ruggles, David, 102
Russell, John, 253, 256
Russwurm, John Brown, 84–89

St. Luke's Chapel, Brooklyn, 164, 168
St. Luke's Church, New Haven, 166, 233
St. Matthew's Episcopal Church, Detroit, 147, 161, 199, 233
St. Phillip's Church, New York, 233
Sampson, R. H., 72
Sanders, Prince, 35, 75, 163
San Francisco blacks: and emigration, 141
Saros, 209, 212–213, 256
Saunders, Prince. *See* Sanders, Prince
Select emigration, 251, 252, 260, 269
Self-help views: of Cuffe, 47; of Delany, 120–122, 123–124, 126, 128, 132, 260; and emigrationism, 269
Separate black institutions: support for, 93, 103–104, 110, 114–115, 132–133; opposed, 89
Separate black settlements: in U.S., 47, 48, 138; in Canada, 113–114
Seys, John, 205

Shadd, Abraham, 105
Shadd, Amelia, 252
Shadd, Isaac D., 160, 166, 194, 252
Shadd, Mary Ann: and nationalist-emigrationism, 94, 105; background, 105–106; calls for Canadian emigration, 106, 157–158; attacks Refugee Home Society, 113; and *Provincial Freeman*, 143–144; and Delany's emigration movement, 157, 158, 160; criticized, 157–158; defended by Delany, 159; mentioned, 115, 166. *See also* Cary, Mary Ann Shadd
Sharp, Granville, 10–11, 12
Sherbro Island, 46, 56, 62, 63, 263
Shiloh Presbyterian Church, New York, 191. *See also* First Colored Presbyterian Church
Sierra Leone Company, 26
Simpson, J. B., 230
Slave Trade Act of 1819, 57
Slocum, Cuffe, 22
Slocum, John, 22
Smith, Gerrit, 90, 180, 229
Smith, Isaac T., 197
Smith, James McCune, 136, 189, 241, 243, 262
Smith, J. B., 242
Snowden, Isaac, 124
Société Philanthropique d'Haiti, 79–80
Society for Promoting the Emigration of Free Persons of Colour to Hayti, 77
Society of Friends, 25, 27, 40, 52
Society of Sierra Leone, 28, 29
South America: emigration to, 150, 169
Spear, London, 12
Stanton, Lucy, 141
State Convention of Colored Citizens of Pennsylvania (1848), 118
State Convention of the Colored Freeman of Pennsylvania (1841), 103, 116
Stewart, Henry, 13, 14
Stiles, Ezra, 7
Still, John N., 166
Stockton, Robert Field, 71
Stokes, Eli Worthington, 165
Stone, R. H., 215

Summer on the Borders of the Caribbean Sea, A (Harris), 237, 238
Survance, Antony, 41

Tappan, Arthur, 90
Tappan, Lewis, 90, 108, 177
Taylor, Anthony, 10
Taylor, James L., 107, 111
Teague, Colin, 68, 69–71
Temperance Society of the People of Color of the City of Pittsburgh, 116
Thomas (king of the Koya Temne), 28
Thompson, Joseph P., 258
Thornton, William, 9–10, 11, 15, 21
"Thoughts on Hayti" (Holly), 234–235
Toliver, Philip, 156
Toronto convention (1851), 111–112, 113, 114, 125, 167
Townsend, Henry: background, 210; and Campbell, 210; opposes treaty, 254–255, 256, 258; mentioned, 212, 213, 265
Tracy, Joseph, 109
Treaty: between Delany, Campbell, and the Egba, 213–215, 229, 254–256, 258
Trinity Church, New Haven, 165
Troy, N.Y., national convention (1847), 189
Turner, Henry M., 266, 267

Union Missionary Society, 103, 191
Union Moral and Mental Improvement Society, 147
United Negro Improvement Association, 267
United Presbyterian Church of Scotland, 190

Vashon, George B., 154–155, 242
Vashon, John B., 95, 96, 154, 155
Venn, Henry, 211, 255
Vindication of the Capacity of the Negro Race (Holly), 168
Voice of the Fugitive, The, 107, 110, 112, 113, 130, 143, 151

Wadsworth, Alexander, 67
Wagoner, H. O., 107
Walker, E. P., 166, 194, 246
Walker, Moore, 187, 192
Ward, Samuel R., 113, 143
Washington, Augustus, 207
Watkins, William J.: attacks colonization, emigration, 84, 139–140, 142; and Haitian emigration of 1860's, 243, 246–247; mentioned, 141, 144
Watson, Joseph, 99
Watt, James, 19
Weekly Anglo-African, The, 170, 242, 243, 244, 246, 252, 260
Western hemispheric emigration: and Delany, 127–128, 129, 130, 132, 172; attacked by Blyden, 130
West Indies: emigration to, 146
Wheaton, Laban, 37
Whipper, William, 95, 96, 97, 102, 182
Whipple, George, 178–179
Whitfield, James M.: at 1853 national convention, 136, 138; and 1854 emigration convention, 137–140, 142, 145, 146; background, 138; advocates separate settlements within U.S., 138; as poet, 138, 265; at 1856 emigration convention, 166; later life and death, 265; mentioned, 148, 180
Wigfall, Edward T., 61, 65, 66
Wilberforce, William, 30
Williams, Joseph W., 245
Williams, Peter, Jr., 43, 77, 79, 80, 167, 204, 272
Williams, Samuel, 171n, 200, 208n
Williams, Sylvester, 267, 271
Wilson, Alexander, 26
Wilson, Henry M., 186
Wilson, James H., 174, 175
Wilson, Samuel, 41, 56–57
Wiltberger, Christian, 68, 70, 71
Winn, Jonathan, 68, 70
Wisconsin blacks: emigration interest of, 175
Wise, James, 31
Woodson, Lewis: early nationalist-emigrationist, 94; and Delany, 94, 97n, 115–116; background, 94–95; and American Moral Reform Society, 95–96; as "Augustine," 96–102, 103; and black churches, 97–98; and separ-

ate black settlements, 99–100; favors emigration, 100–101; calls for black unity, 101–102, 103–104; criticized, 102; attacks suffrage restrictions, 103; rejects emigration, 103; contradictions in thought of, 123–124; at 1853 national convention, 136; and self-help views, 269; mentioned, 105, 110, 134
Woodson, Thomas, 99
Wright, Isaac. *See* Coker, Daniel
Wright, Theodore S., 187
Wylie Street Methodist Church, Pittsburgh, 179

Yamma, Bristol, 7, 15
Yonie, 65, 66, 67
Yoruba: acquisition of land in, 185, 208, 212, 214–215, 255
Yoruba emigration: black interest in, 170, 183–184, 185, 186, 187; and Delany, 171; and white colonizationists, 184, 195–196; and Liberia, 196, 197, 203, 206; and King, 223, 252, 253, 256, 257
Young Men's Union Society of Cleveland, 138